UTTARANCHAL
VISION AND ACTION PROGRAMME

About the Editors

Madan Lal Dewan (Ph.D., Cornell), a Soil Scientist, started work on soil conservation in the Damodar Valley Corporation during 1949-52. He had a distinguished career as an International Civil Servant with Food and Agriculture Organization for over three decades (1953-83). He worked as Chief of the FAO Regional Bureau for Asia and the Pacific. He had FAO assignments in Iran and Bulgaria and was at FAO Headquarters in Rome for 14 years.

Dr. Dewan was Visiting Professor and Coordinator of Himalayan Eco System Programme with Centre for Policy Research, New Delhi. He was a Member of the National Land Use and Conservation Board of Government of India during 1984-87. He is founder Chairman and Trustee of HIMCON (Himalaya Consortium for Himalayas Conservation) and has established a Centre "Himalaya Sanrakahsan Ashram" at Ranichauri, Distt. Tehri Garhwal, Uttaranchal. Soil of Iran, Soil Conservation of Iran Agriculture and Rural Development in India, People's Participation and Rejuvenation of Himalayan Environment and ten other books are amongst his published works in addition to more than 100 papers on various aspects of soils, soil conservation, land and water development.

Dr. Jagdish Bahadur is M.Sc. (Physics), Lucknow, 1958 and Ph.D (Physics), Pune, 1969. After teaching Physics to B.Sc. students for one year at Lucknow, he joined Oil and Natural Gas Commission, Dehradun, in 1959. In 1964, he was selected by UPSC to the post of Research Officer at Central Water and Power Research Institute, Pune.

Immediately after his Ph.D. he was sponsored by Government of India for the award of a global post-doctoral fellowship from Norwegian Agency for International Development, Oslo. At Oslo, he worked on Snow and Glacier Hydrology with Professor Dr. Gunnar Ostrem, a world famous glaciologist and successfully completed a project on evaluation of annual accumulation on a cold and highest Norwegian Glacier in collaboration with Swedish and Danish scientists. During 1970-72 he actively participated in organizing Inter-Departmental Expeditions to Indian Glaciers. During 1972-82 he worked on efficient utilization of water and fertilizer for crop production at Indian Agricultural Research Institute, New Delhi. In 1978, he was deputed to work as a Consultant Hydrologist in Libya for agricultural reclamation and development. During 1982-96, he worked at the Department of Science and Technology and piloted the programme on National Testing and Calibration Facilities; Integrated Arid Zone Research and Development; Himalayan Glaciology; Mountain Research and Technology Development and Establishment of Agro-Advisory Services Based on Medium Range Weather Forecasting in the country to enhance agricultural production. Besides, a large number of papers and technical reports to his credit, he has published three books, viz., 'The Himalayan Environment (1999)'; 'Indian Himalayas – An Integrated View (2003)' and 'Himalayan Snow and Glaciers – Associated Environmental Problems, Progress and Prospects (2004)'

Concept's Discovering Himalayas Series – 9

UTTARANCHAL
Vision and Action Programme

Editors
M.L. Dewan
Jagdish Bahadur

CONCEPT PUBLISHING COMPANY, NEW DELHI-110059

ISBN 81-8069-196-9

First Published 2005

Published and Printed by
Ashok Kumar Mittal
Concept Publishing Company
A/15-16, Commercial Block, Mohan Garden
New Delhi-110059 (INDIA)

Phones: 25351460, 25351794
Fax: 091-11-25357103
E-mail: publishing@conceptpub.com.

Foreword

The book "*Uttaranchal: Vision and Action Programme*" is a timely one. There are great expectations from the young state of Uttaranchal since it is rich in natural, cultural and spiritual heritage and could therefore become the flagship of the movement for bio-happiness and sustainable human security. The publication covers various areas of the physical, biological and agricultural endowments of the state.

The book not only provides a vision for the future but also a road map for converting the vision into action. Very important areas like snow and glacier fields and revitalizing the Ganga have been covered. Ganga was described as the river of India by Jawaharlal Nehru in his last will and testament. The ecological security of Uttaranchal is therefore not only essential for the happiness of the people of the state but also for the well being of the children, women and men living in the Indo-Gangetic plains.

I hope the book will stimulate action at all levels. Fusion of political will, professional skill and people's participation can help us to achieve seemingly impossible tasks. This book will serve as the catalyst in bringing about such a fusion. We owe a deep sense of gratitude to Dr.M.L. Dewan and his colleagues for this labour of love.

Dr. M.S. Swaminathan

Glory to Uttaranchal

Where the Himalayas Peaks are Snow clad
And Shining in Glory
Where the Mother Ganga Originates from Glaciers
And has Hundreds of Tributaries

Where Our Rishis and Munis
Meditated, Thought and Chartered
Love for God, A Path of Progress
A Way to Success through Human Values
Like Love, Peace, Non-violence, Karma the Right Action
And the Words come out from the Depth of Truth
Thus Vedas and Upanishads
Are Born From This Sacred Land

Where The Clear streams of Reason
Have Not lost their way into the Caves
And Dreary Wasteland of Dead Habits
Where The lovely Forests
And Fruits, Flowers, And Medicinal Plants
Grow in Their Majesty

Where The mind is Led Forward by
Thee into ever Widening Thought and Action
Where the Youth and Old Work for
Greening The Himalayas Rejuvenating The Region
In Unison For A Glorious State
Of a Glorious Motherland India

Into that Heaven of Freedom and Divine Bliss
My Father and Mother, Let My Uttaranchal and Awake progress

M.L. Dewan
Inspired by Poet Rabindra Nath Tagore, Gitanjali,
(Song No. 35, March 1913)

December 25, 2003

Preface

The present publication "Uttaranchal — Vision and Action Programme " edited by Dr. M.L. Dewan and Dr. Jagdish Bahadur is a tremendous effort. At the outset, let me express that I know both the editors for over four decades. Dr. Dewan is an internationally known Soil Scientist and Watershed Management Expert and Dr. Bahadur is an Agricultural Physicist with specialization in Isotope and Glacier Hydrology. Both these persons have devoted themselves for the exploration and development of the Himalayan region.

In the prologue, a number of steps are outlined for the action to be taken for human and economic development for Uttaranchal . The introduction includes the highlights of different contributors to the text. I am particularly happy that the publication is coming out following the UN — International Year of Mountains-2002 for the new state of Uttaranchal.

In this context, I recall my address on "Ecological Security of the Himalaya" delivered on 14th September 1991 at G.B. Pant Institute for Himalayan Environment and Development, Almora. The ecological security o f Himalayas is not only vital for the welfare of hill people but also for the food security of the country. In this mega-biodiversity region, we must tackle the problems of poverty, population growth and environmental degradation. It is a complex job and calls for a multidisciplinary and participative approach integrating the principles of ecological sustainability, economic efficiency and social equity. This demands a land and water use strategy for each compact agro-ecological zone, promoting conservation areas, restoration areas and sustained intensification of agriculture. Need is felt for anticipatory research in areas of renewable energy sources, consumer preferences, packaging, marketing, and adoption of bio-technology and computer simulations techniques with a back-up consortium of various government departments, technical institutions and universities to provide technical guidance and oversight the programme. These concept provides an unique opportunity for the new state of Uttaranchal.

I was delighted to note the recent remarks made by Shri. N. D. Tiwari, Chief Minister of Uttaranchal as the independence day greetings. He has outlined his vision for the state for two decades emphasizing on hydro power generation, tourism development, industrial development and turning Uttaranchal as IT-hub and the steps taken towards promoting e-governance involving public and private institutions. I am sure that these efforts will prove very effective in transforming the state of Uttaranchal to me of the leading states in the country in the field of power generation, tourism I.T and Sustainable horticulture. An Organic state with emphasis on medicinal and aromatic plants, more prosperous farms and farming communities as well as Sustainable forestry on principles of Soil and Water Conservation and land and water care is in offing. This is the Vision and Action Program for the young and vigorous State.

Acknowledgements

Uttaranchal Vision and Action Programme is a book result of over 12 years extensive work in the field of Soil and Water Conservation and Watershed Management in Uttaranchal. Several colleagues and experts have joined in this effort which has been edited by the both the Editors. This work is mainly with the help, co-operation, inspiration and contribution of a large number of people. Grateful acknowledgement is made to all the authors of different chapters. It would be a Himalayan Task to acknowledge directly their contribution and of other partners, NGOs, Government Departments and above all farmers and people of Uttaranchal. However, we are indebted to the following:

1. Hon'ble N.D. Tewari ji, Chief Minister of Uttaranchal who has encouraged and inspired us for this task.
   Also grateful thanks to Dr. Tolia, Ms. Vibha Puri Das, and Mr. Sanjeev Chopra for encouragement in our work and also for allocating Kanatal Farm to HIMCON.
2. Dr. M.S. Swaminathan, who as Chairman of the Himalayan Task Force was responsible for bringing out the Report of the Task Force for the study of Eco-Development in the Himalayan Region (Planning Commission, March 1982). Also as chairman, Land and Water Care Movement of M.S. Swaminathan Research Foundation and Soil Conservation Society of India. Also for kindly writing the Preface for this book.
3. Special thanks to all the authors of the chapters specially
   - Dr. Sunil Agarwal, DST
   - Dr. Anil Joshi
   - Mr. R.P. Agrawal
   - Dr. Aabha Chowdhry
   - Dr. C.S. Raghav
   - Dr. L.M.S. Palni
   - Mr. S.P. Malhotra
   - Mr. R. Sreedhar
   - Mr. Yogeshwar Kumar

- Dr. S.D. Garg
- Dr. P.L. Gautam, Vice Chancellor, Dr. M.C. Nautiyal, Dean Hill Campus, Dr. V.K. Kediyal, and Dr. and Mrs. Datta of the Hill Campus of the Pant Nagar Univ.
- Shri. Ashok Dilwali, for taking and giving us the wonderful photos of Himalayas which form a part of this book.
- Shri. Manoj Pande, Dr. Piyoosh Rautela, Rakesh Bahuguna, Naresh Kumar, Shiv, Gopal Bahuguna and all members of HIMCON and sister NGO's in the Uttaranchal who are devoting their life to the betterment of the Himalayan Watersheds and Himalayan Communities.
- Last but not the least to my wife Smt. Sudershna Dewan who is founder of HIMCON and who bears with me for all the travels and work in Uttaranchal region and in preparing this book. Thanks are also due to Dr. Indu Patnaik of Planning Commission for helping in the edition of this book.

Madan Lal Dewan
Jagdish Bahadur

Contents

Part 3: Natural Resource Development, Monitoring and Evaluation

Part 4: Vision and Action Programme

Annexures

Appendices

List of Coloured Plates

Prologue

A new State took birth on 9th November, 2000. The people of Uttaranchal look forward to a better economic and social order. The expectations are large, the challenges of being a hill state are many and concerted efforts are required both from the Government and the people to lay the foundation of a strong and vibrant economy.

The vision for the state would include both human and economic development. To meet these goals, the following actions are envisioned:

I. The conservation and rejuvenation of the Himalayan environment. Hence economic development should ensure that the environment is disturbed in the least possible manner and every effort is made to preserve the rich bio-diversity and unique topography of the state.

II. Improvement in the quality of life of the people, specially women, youth and children. This requires Poverty Eradication through income generating schemes both self-employment and wage employment as well as facilities such as health, sanitation and education.

III. A Land and Water Care movement with emphasis on bio-industrial watershed management. The on-going watershed development programmes need to be strengthened and converted into bio-industrial watershed projects by making bio-mass processing industries an integral part of Watershed management. Bio industrial projects hold the promise of transforming the rural areas. Such projects would not only increase rural employment, they could also reduce out-migration from the region. Real income would increase and regional imbalances would decrease. Each Watershed/micro watershed should be developed with local participation through

(i) Water harvesting including run off harvesting, through contour bunding or ridges; flood water harvesting through level flooded terraces, check dams for aquifer recharge, surface dams and sub-surfaced dams.

(ii) Regeneration of water sources, particularly spring and seepages by employing the concept of "Spring sanctuary" using physical and *biological measures.*

(iii) Increased agricultural productivity through the use of appropriate technologies that are profitable, labour intensive and dependable should be the major means of increasing purchasing power of the people. Proper land capability classification and its mapping on macro and micro scale is necessary for the region. Based on land classification, sustainable agriculture can be promoted which should form the basis of commercial agriculture. Promotion of organic farming and organic food through appropriate policy interventions and, transition from food-grain based subsistence agriculture to commercial cultivation of high value-low volume crops is called for making use of comparative advantage and niche.

(iv) Encouraging land based activities which are in consonance with the environment such as Sericulture, Horticulture and Pasture development based on biofertilizers and bio pesticides.

(v) Processing, marketing and quality control facilities for medicinal and aromatic plants, nuts, fruits and vegetables and milk and milk products.

IV. Renewable energy which can be used to serve the lighting, cooking and heating needs of people of the area and the small and medium industries. This includes introduction of bio-gas and high efficiency fuel wood stoves so that the pressure on forest is reduced. Further briquettes from biomass and bio-gas, ethanol, methanol can be used to meet the energy needs of the farm family, solar technology, *i.e* solar water heaters, solar cookers, solar crop drying and solar photo volataic cells for lighting and pumping, wind mill technology; mini and micro hydel technologies.

V. Building up the communication system in remote areas and the use of information technology to convey the information regarding development plans and programmes to the people. Industrial development based on software development and information technology could provide an important source of livelihood to the educated youth without adverse impact on the ecology of the region. As distance and topography do not pose barriers for the latest tools in the development of information technology, the state could see itself as a high profile technology destination.

VI. The tourism potential of the State should be exploited in full particularly in view of its scenic beauty. Various pilgrim centres should also be further developed to market the state as a destination for religious tourism. Himalayas are an inspiration and this aspect should be promoted for Eco and Religious Tourism on a large scale, sustained with efficiency and sound management principle.

VII. Awareness and organization building through Self-Help Groups, Mahilla Mangal Dals, Seed and Health Banks, Van Panchayats and Grain Banks.

VIII. Involvement of the people starting from the students to the elderly through mass movement, training programmes and building of local organizations including the Panchayati Raj Systems.

PART 1
INTRODUCTION

1.1

Introduction

The invited papers from the individual authors or organisations have been included with a minimum of editorial alteration or modification in the publication. In this introduction, the important points made by the authors have been included so as to enable the reader to get a feel of the coverage in respective articles. There are some unavoidable overlapping while discussing various issues connected with the vision and action programme as expressed by the contributors. For completeness of information, some annexes are included as listed. Paper-wise highlights are:

Vision ad People's Participation Programme for Development of the New State, M.L. Dewan (4.1)

The author has given a personal note of love and affection to Uttaranchal as his family migrated to Dehradun at the partition time (1947) and had a home in Hardwar and established a cottage at Ranichauri. Being a Soil Conservationist in Food and Agriculture Organisation (FAO) for 31 years, and having been associated with land and water conservation and development—a regional programme for Himalayan region, International Centre for Integrated Mountain Development, Indian Council of Agricultural Research (ICAR), Centre for Policy Research (CPR), he has decided to develop a cottage and ashram at Ranichauri, near the hill campus of GB Pant University of Agriculture and Technology, Pantnagar. His life mission is to serve the people of Ranichauri through Himalaya Consortium for Himalayan Conservation (HIMCON) and Tree for Life (TFL). He is doing anything and everything to green and rejuvenate Himalayas, improve awareness of local inhabitants by education, training and demonstration. Local, state, and central financial assistance are mobilized along with assistance from NRIs, foreign NGOs and other corporate agencies and organisations to improve the quality of life of Uttaranchalis.

Bio-Industrial Watershed Development, J.S. Bali, Human Environment Action League, Delhi-92 (4.2)

Under the Bio-Industrial Watershed Development Programme—a poverty eradication project, the basic foundation is the care and conservation of land and water through cooperative movement. It is envisaged that the medicinal plants be grown in upper elevations; vegetables, fruits, nuts and agro-forestry in middle elevations and milk, milk products could be introduced with advantage as the main responsibility of the project management and to ensure proper returns to the farmers of the watershed. Government should provide infrastructure for health care, education for better awareness, roads/ropeways for carrying the produce to market places. Communication facilities and energy availability must be improved. Non-conventional sources of energy, e.g. fuel bricks from organic wastes, solar, wind, mini and micro-hydro power and biogas etc. should be developed for overall regeneration and greening of the environment. Rural tourism, i.e. travel into the villages by foreign visitors offers great opportunities for cultural tourism. This could be availed of clean and comfortable places of stay could be developed at the community centres or at Panchayat Ghars as the rural scenes with scenic beauty, are having greater attraction than the Five-Star cities.

Economic Strength of Traditional Economy, HIMCON, Ranichpuri (2.1)

Over the centuries, through trial and error and also through the accumulated knowledge of generations, the people of the region have evolved strategies of management suited to its physiographic resource and climatic conditions. Due to several reasons, these traditional systems suffered a jolt in the pre- and post-independence period and the disintegration of socio-cultural practices of resource management and the alienation of the masses and the disintegration of socio-cultural practices of resource management. Besides being eco-friendly, these traditional techniques are cost effective and there is a need to study these scientifically for seeking acceptable alternatives.

Towards Tradition by A.P. Joshi, HESCO, Dehradun (2.2)

India's traditional wisdom being simple, location specific and eco-friendly, was one of the richest in the world. This time tested wisdom was used by people in planning the development strategies. These centuries old technologies have not been updated but aggressively eliminated by introducing alien systems which have resulted in indifferent attitude in the rural community due to inaccessibility and other physical constraints. A serious view has to be taken to revamp local wisdom to the satisfaction of local community.

Traditional agricultural crops of great diversity are being replaced by wheat and rice creating new environmental stresses affecting ecosystems and the well-being of the people. Fruits and vegetables grown in the mountains have their own specification and rating for the quality. Horticultural crops have not found due importance and there is need to introduce more scientific horticultural practices to check slope instability, soil erosion and degradation of the environment.

Water, being the basic resource for development, its use in drinking, irrigation, storage and other uses needs perennial supply and is a real challenge, yet to be adequately met by modern methods in preference to local traditional approaches which varied depending on the local environmental setting.

Forests have been of key importance to villagers to satisfy their needs of fuel, fodder and fertilizer. Traditional forest practices have given the sole responsibility to village folks for their collective management. Despite state intervention, the changes to introduce fast growing trees and other modern practices have resulted in poor upkeep of these vital resources and the active participation of the people is being increasingly sought for their regeneration.

Herbal wealth in the region finds traditional knowledge in folk medical remedies and needs proper documentation to take advantage from recent advances in plant therapy and medical practices.

Apex Snow and Glacier Fields, Jagdish Bahadur, New Delhi (2.3)

Apex snow and glacier fields of Himalayan mountains form the world's largest natural reservoir of renewable freshwater resources having a substantial influence on the purity and productivity of the land resources. These cold reservoirs form tall water towers, having unique engineering and technological problems, needing multi-disciplinary coordination and integration of information on soils, snow and ice for their satisfactory solution. The information on Himalayan soils, snow and ice are fragmentary and needs systematisation. Uttaranchal occupies roughly 10 per cent of the Indian mountain region. The region lies in between the cold arid western region and warm pre-humid eastern region and is equally affected by westerly disturbances and easterly air circulations. Characteristics (e.g. location, length, area, elevation range etc.) of some prominent glaciers has been included along with their drainage characteristics. It is suggested that the snow and glacier fields feeding reservoirs of Tehri Hydroelectric Project (THP)—a major venture in Uttaranchal, needs to be monitored for efficient and economic functioning of the mega national project.

Potentials and Problems of Soil and Water Conservation. V.N. Sharda and V. Singh, Central Soil and Water Conservation or Research and Training Institute (CSWCR&TI), Dehradun (2.4)

The soil and water conservation form the essential ingredients of a watershed management for optimum and sustained production with minimum occurrence of damages from natural hazards. The state of Uttaranchal has major part of its area as hilly terrain (93%) having primarily rain-fed subsistence agriculture. Its undulating topography, varied climate, scanty cultivated land, overwhelming percentage of small and marginal holdings, difficult working conditions, high input costs and low returns on food grain crops, sparse settlement, soil erosion and land degradation, inadequate infrastructure and lack of industrialisation and entrepreneurship greatly affect the development of the region.

National Watershed Development Project for Rain-fed Areas (NWDPRA) of Central Ministry of Agriculture is being implemented in 73 out of 95 development blocks of the State. 30 development blocks are earmarked for watershed development through District Rural Development Agency (DRDA) under the centrally sponsored Scheme of Soil Conservation for enhancing productivity of degraded lands in the catchments of River Valley Projects and Flood Prone Rivers.

CSWCR&TI has been engaged for last three decades on evolving strategies for soil and water conservation on watershed basis, tackling mass erosion problems such as, landslides, mine-spoils and torrents, demonstration of technology for popularisation of imparting training. The Institute has successfully demonstrated the reclamation technologies of gravelly/boulders soils, bio-remediation, runoff harvesting, management of common property resources (CPR) and community participation. More recently, a concept of Agro-ecosystem research has been evolved to tackle various issues of networking with different organisations and cross-cutting administrative or political boundaries in order to optimize the indicators of the agricultural system, viz. productivity, stability, sustainability and environmental security under the National Agricultural Technology Project (NATP), supported by the World Bank. The agro-vision should clearly identify the problems, analyze the gaps and plan short and long term measures for development of hill agriculture and other developments in the mountain region.

Opportunities, Challenges and Prospects in Agriculture and Forestry, S.P. Malhotra, FAO, New Delhi (2.5)

District-wise land utilisation of Uttaranchal has been included. Out of about 75 per cent of gross cropped area, 73 per cent is covered by cereal crops and 2 per cent by pulses. Among cereal crops, wheat accounts for 30 per cent while rice covers about 21 per cent of the gross cropped area. District-wise statistics about the area, production, yield by various grain crops demonstrates that the crop yields are generally lower than the average for the country.

With the limited land and water resources availability, it is essential to introduce improved integrated farming systems, adopting eco-friendly organic farming practices such as application of farm yard manure, compost, crop rotation using legumes, vermi-culture, bio-fertilizers, bio-pesticides etc. Improved farming techniques such as appropriate farm machinery and implements, greenhouse technology, integrated nutrient supply systems, integrated pest management systems, improved irrigation systems, improved extension and agricultural marketing systems, as appropriate to the mountain terrain are to be adopted to develop integrated intensive farming systems to improve the economic conditions of the farmers. Depending on the availability of resources, both farming systems (grain, dairy, poultry, vegetable, fruit based) and non-farm sub-systems (enterprises of various kinds) are to be developed to enhance the income of the farmers. To achieve this adequate steps are necessary to resurrect forest and agricultural lands in the mountain state.

A Framework for Sustainable Food Security, P.L. Gautam and V. Singh GB Pant University of Agriculture and Technology, Pantnagar (2.6)

Natural biodiversity of Himalayan region is exceptionally rich and is one of the most important common property resources (CPRs) and a valuable foundation for food security. In the remote and marginal mountain areas, characterized by an overwhelming feature of CPRs—mainly the forests and grasslands, the sustainability cannot be operationalised without an efficient management of biodiversity. The biodiversity could be the greatest resource for socio-economic and cultural renaissance of the highland dwellers. It may be noted that the functional diversity, achievable through combining plant and animal species in synergetic interactions injects sustainability into agro-ecosystems. Traditionally four cropping systems are maintained in the lesser Himalayan areas. These are: (i) homestead-based cropping system in which seasonal vegetables and some fruits are grown essentially for home consumption; (ii) irrigated land cropping system in which rice and wheat are grown; (iii) upland or un-irrigated cropping system, dominantly occupied by a variety of millets and pulses; and (iv) summer camp cropping system, commonly devoted to pseudo cereals (e.g. amaranth and buckwheat) and beans (mainly kidney beans). Besides the above alpine pastures in Greater Himalayas just adjacent to snowline are used for transhument pastoralism and for raising some medicinal and aromatic plants and some rare crops like naked barley.

Agro-systems harbouring enormous biodiversity are extremely resilient. Whereas poor accessibility, fragility, and marginality characteristics of the mountains correlate negatively with resilience, the biodiversity, ecological niches, human adaptation mechanisms are positive attributes to resilience against any type of physical or biotic tribulation to the system.

Rich biodiversity creates barriers against any natural calamity (e.g. drought or pest epidemics). Some living organisms may be host for certain insects or diseases, some may be little more prone to weather extremes or other adverse conditions, but a complex mix of naturally occurring (in natural forest areas) organisms will do away any chances of widespread loss to the farmers. Simple, less complex ecosystems and monocultures are extremely prone to various kinds of damaging agents and hence threaten the security of farmers.

Community-led programmes often translate into succession movements, new philosophies, renaissance and revolutions. We have to work to improve the community based farming systems.

Existing institution system must learn to recognize, encourage, facilitate and promote farmer's traditional strategies, innovations and socio-cultural movements that invariably contribute to biodiversity enhancement, sustainability and food security.

Concerns and Challenges, Sonali Bisht, INHERE, Almora (2.7)

In general, hilly and mountain regions restrain development due to undulating topographic features. The formation of a new state of Uttaranchal has been the culmination of the hopes, dreams, and aspirations of the people living in the hill regions of the parent state of Uttar Pradesh.

The linkages between rural and urban areas are critical in the development of any region. The neglect of the villages and the rural areas in the country have led to a spate of migration to bigger towns and cities in which there is more investment and a spiral of growth in employment opportunities and means. It has also led to mushrooming of slums with appalling conditions of life for those forced to live there.

The valleys have been the granaries providing food security. These granaries are now under threat from the government led urbanisation which sees them only as flat land for more buildings, institutions and amenities. The emergence of small towns are chaotic in nature and bereft of any sewage, sanitation or solid waste disposal and management facility.

Environmental legislations have slowly taken away traditional livelihoods of vast numbers and the rural employment are under great stress. As agriculture is back breaking and does not yield enough for subsistence, the males are forced to migrate making life even more difficult for the families left behind.

The major challenges are promotion of livelihoods to retain people through local employment and income generation to enhance the quality of life of the people living in the villages.

Quality seeds, suited to hill agriculture have to be developed for wider availability. As the soils and topography will not encourage mono-cropping, developed agricultural practices need be adopted. This diversified agriculture could be a healthy mix of animal husbandry, cattle rearing, poultry, fishing, beekeeping etc. We need to reduce our cattle population and improve their productivity. It is also important to introduce organic farming practices to enrich soil and increase soil depth for sustained development in the region.

Evolution of Van Panchayats, Rekha Pai, C/o IG (Forests), New Delhi (2.8)

Van Panchayats have been in operation in these mountain regions for more than seven decades. There are 6,777 Van Panchayats, managing 5241 sq. km. area. District-wise details for forest areas and Van

Panchayats have been incorporated. Several forest areas under these Panchayats have been managed in good condition whereas others have not done as well. Factors which helped the satisfactory functioning Van Panchayats include leadership quality of the Sarpanch, availability of funds, commitment on the part of villagers, proximity of villages to reserved forests, total area and quality of land of Panchayat forest, Single-village Van Panchayats perform better than multistage Panchayats.

More recently, rules for Joint Forest Management (JFM) have been framed to involve village communities and voluntary agencies in efforts to regenerate degraded forest areas. JFM rules, 1997 provides for a three-tier system for village, range and divisional-level committees. Under the programme, the implementation strategy adopts several key elements, e.g. site-specific planning, transparency, decentralisation, funds to be released directly to the village forest committees, creation of the village development fund and involvement of women. The concept of people's participation in the management of natural resources should be completely internalized in the functioning, thinking and policies of the forest department. All development works should be executed adopting the philosophy of JFM. It has to be made very clear to the forest staff, as well as, the local communities that JFM is a process and not a project. Van Panchayats should be strengthened by providing them institutional and technical support.

Micro-Hydropower Potential in Uttaranchal, Yogesh Kumar

Large and medium hydropower potential of Uttaranchal is estimated to be 20,000 megawatts. The state also has substantial hydropower potential for small, mini and micro-hydropower development. Total potential including micro hydropower in the state is of the order of 40,000 megawatts. These power potentials hold enormous promise for socio-economic development and improving the quality of life in the region.

The article discusses the power consumption, benefits of power for agriculture, tourism, household needs and protection of the environment. Difficulties in supplying power in mountain areas could be offset by electrifying marginal areas by mini-micro hydropower units that are not connected to main grid lines and maintained by community efforts. It is beyond doubt that the state government needs to involve people, communities, Panchayats, NGOs etc. in micro-mini hydropower generation and maintenance.

Revitalising Ganga—The Sacred River, S.D. Garg, M.L. Dewan and Piyush Rautela (2.10)

The Ganga is the celestial river of India. It sustains the lives of over three hundred million people along its course of about 2500 km. At its point of origin, i.e. Gaumukh (the snout of Gangotri glacier) in Garhwal Himalayas in Uttaranchal, the river is known as Bhagirathi. Receiving several hill rivers and streams such as the Bhilanagana, the Bhagirathi reaches Devprayag where it receives an important tributary Alaknanda. After the confluence of Bhagirathi with Alaknanda, the river is known as Ganga and it emerges into plains at Rishikesh.

The article describes its route from Himalayas to Bay of Bengal, the special quality of Ganga water and its purity, present scenario in Himalayas, the sources of pollution, Ganga Action Plan and suggesting a clean Ganga movement as people's movement and inputs from modern science and technological developments for the overall revitalisation of the great river system. The activities need primarily land and water care—watershed development and management being the basic requirements.

This is followed by Ode to Ganga by M.L. Dewan written during 14/15th August, 2000 (2.11)

Resource Conservation as a Tool for Economic Development—Problems and Prospects, P.K. Samant and L.M.S. Paini GBPIHED, Almora (3.6)

The authors have dealt with primary resources, resource conservation constraints, impact of resource deficits, resource conservation prospects, tools and measures of resource conservation, indigenous knowledge innovation and practices, adoption of simple technologies, biotechnologies in good details.

For economic development of the state and the very survival of its people, the finite natural resources need to be conserved and developed. The conservation dealing with effective management of resources for sustained use demands maintaining essential ecological processes and life support systems; preserving genetic diversity and utilizing species and ecosystem sustainability. It is indeed a holistic concept encompasses the whole spectrum of activities from *in situ* conservation dealing with population, communities, and ecosystems on one hand, and on the other it deals with *ex situ* conservation involving botanical gardens, arboreta, biological banks etc. *in situ* conservation aims at conserving biodiversity in natural habitats on a holistic basis more as a system than as separate individuals. The first and foremost system under *in situ* category are *the* watersheds which are not only rich in biodiversity but are also intertwined with long-range ecological security.

It is agreed that the technological packages of SALT (Sloping Agricultural Land Technology) and SWEET (Sloping Watershed Environmental Engineering Technology) would be helpful in resolving and sustaining integrity of soil, water and bio-resources and the linkages between them and meeting the needs of the people through efficient and environmentally sensitive production and conservation of natural resources.

Approaches to Plant Biodiversity Utilisation and Conservation, M.P. Shiva, Dehradun (3.2)

Rapid deforestation has aggravated the environment and ecology of Uttaranchal. Unscientific management of natural resources and management of land-used pattern have resulted in low productivity as well as depletion of floral/faunal biodiversity and ecological imbalance. This is illustrated by tabulating the general characteristics of mountains. The role of COMFORPTS (Centre of Minor Forest Products) in documenting and disseminating information and enriching MFP database with various parameters for different user products. Biodiversity Conservation Prioritisation Project (BCCP) report have identified the major threats of human interferences, land fragmentation, over exploitation, loss of habitat, unsustainable harvest, trade etc. Emphasis is made on the utilisation of *in situ* and *ex situ* conservation practices involving local community to ensure NTFP enterprise development to preserve environment as well as socio-economic amelioration of the inhabitants.

Forest Resources: Regeneration and Conservation Impact and Control of Forest Fires, M.L. Dewan and K.D. Singh (3.3)

Uttaranchal's natural forests have been home to hundreds of plant, animal and bird species. Degeneration started with large scale deforestation and introduction of mono-culture of chir-pine for commercial purpose during British regime. Establishment of forest department (FD) has alienated people from the forests as it threatened their livelihood. FD continues to possess about 65 per cent of states geographical area, forest cover merely

42 per cent area, and good forest, with canopy cover exceeding 60 per cent, are confined to less than 5 per cent. Community Concerned Forest Areas (CCFA) are about 20 per cent These areas have maintained high diversity and are in very good condition as established by joint study carried by the authors with PRAKRITI—an NGO under the sponsorship by UNDP and Global Environment Facility Project (GEF). The authors argue that the forests are especially important for using CO_2 and replenishing oxygen and conservation of the environmental quality, the creation of local institutional capacity to manage natural and other resources through collective action, not dependent entirely on the structure and authority of the state, offers a better alternative to bureaucratic approach. People's participation will ensure forest regeneration by harnessing the enormous social energy.

Watershed Development: A Success Story, HIMCON, Ranichauri, Uttaranchal (3.4)

Two village-watersheds (Lawadhar and Ratauri Khala) of Chamba block in Tehri Garhwal district of Uttaranchal were selected by HIMCON/TFL from the region which has been facing severe crisis of essential natural resources, e.g. land, water, fodder and fuel-wood. Mass mobilisation was given the top priority. Two Mahila Mangal Dals (MMD) and two watershed management committees to muster internal resources through self-help groups (SHG) large scale plantation was undertaken in the watersheds. Most of the plantation material was prepared in the nurseries of TFL/ HIMCON. In choosing the species for afforestation, the views of the masses were given due consideration. Plantation of species providing fodder and fuel-wood was taken up in the degraded lands of the villages while fruit bearing varieties were planted in agricultural lands. Health and sanitation and also animal husbandry were accorded priority and a series of meetings and training camps were organized to improve awareness of farmers. A large number of sanitary latrines were constructed and health camps were organized for routine check-ups.

Rainwater harvesting, ground recharge enhancement, spring rejuvenation resulted in increased availability of water. Income generation through vegetable production and dairy products were successfully achieved with better health care and sanitation for the villagers. Continued interaction with the people to monitor their progress and resolve problems for the sustained growth are continuing despite the formal closure of the project work.

Prospects for Walnut Production in Uttaranchal, S.P. Malhotra, FAO, New Delhi (3.5)

District-wise area, production, and yield per hectare in Uttaranchal has been included. Uttaranchal is next to Jammu & Kashmir State in the walnut production but the productivity is less than 50 per cent that of J&K.

Walnut tree flourishes well in temperate belts between altitudes 900-3500 m. It should be grown under climatic conditions that are free from frost during spring and extreme heat during summer. Early frost also injures young shoots causing them to fall to leaf out the ensuing spring. At bloom, temperatures of even 2-3°C below freezing point results in killing of large number of young flowers. Nuts are sensitive to excessive heat in summer when the kernel is being developed: temperatures over 27°C can darken or even shrivel kernels. Extreme low temperatures can also severely affect production. When temperatures are below -10°C, branch injury occurs on fully dormant trees. Adequate chilling is required to leaf out and bloom the tree. Evenly distributed rainfall of 760 mm is considered optimum for good quality crop. Most of the area under walnut is rainfed. The author has discussed walnut utilisation pattern; projections for domestic utilisation; exports from India; competitiveness analyses for the imports; factors affecting world trade and supply projections from India along with the need to render scientific advice to farmers for the increase in yield and the quality of nuts.

Issues Related to Natural Resources Policy, Pankaj Kumar, SPWD, Dehradun (3.1)

The author has given a detailed description of the physiography and farming systems of the State and its natural resources, e.g. forests, including their importance, types, legal distribution and actual forest cover; agriculture including sources of irrigation and the crop yields main grain crops of paddy and wheat. The grain yields get doubled if irrigation is provided as compared to dry-land farming conditions.

Under social economy, average landholding in the region is about 0.89 ha and generally these are scattered to various locations. 92 per cent of total population is engaged in agriculture. Women are overworked as they are not only engaged in agriculture but are required to manage the livestock, fetching fodder, fuel and drinking water besides other chores like cooking, child rearing, sanitation.

For all-round development of the State the financial allocation (Plan-wise) and domestic output sector-wise has been tabulated. Potential for economic growth is discussed emphasizing to recognize the importance of the mountain farming system, conservation and enrichment of forest resources, promotion of small industries, review of current pattern of government and non-government assistance, increase in decentralized energy and the potential and scope of hydro-energy technologies along with the gaps under various schemes. Action required for successful implementation of Micro-Hydro Power Programme (MHP) are to design an integrated system, e.g. treatment of the catchment, road planning, organisation of local agro-industrial cooperation and an organisation for operation and maintenance of plants including training of local population and peoples participation for their success.

To achieve the above, the author has listed various aspects of policy interventions for land, animal husbandry, forestry and water management.

Mountain Tourism for Local Community Development in Uttarakhand R. Sreedhar, Uttaranchal Academy for Mountain Environics, Narendra Nagar (4.3)

Uttrakhand in the state has been long revered as the land of divine— 'Dev Bhumi'. The pilgrim towns of Haridwar and Rishikesh are the gateway to Uttrakhand and draw the largest number of visitors, mostly pilgrims from anywhere in the world.

Sustainable development of mountain communities needs a continuum of policy-programme-project action strategy to utilize the tourist resources of the state. Problems, affecting local community development are lack of basic needs (water, fuel and health services); population growth and expansion of settlement; lack of employment opportunities; improper implementation of development programmes, lack of investment potential, threat of natural hazards and impact of economic reforms. Development of mountain tourism as a significant mechanism for local community development are exploitation of natural resources beyond resilience of ecosystems; lack of linkage of tourism with local or regional production systems; lack of retention of benefits from tourism; high level of seasonably and lack of policy and poor efforts towards building quality institutions.

Mass tourism is a high volume but low value tourism. It does not generate local employment and industry; provides no appreciation of socio-cultural conditions of the state and does not improve the environmental conditions of the destination. On the contrary, the class tourism is better oriented to the range of destinations and is more often trading on a purpose. Among the low-spending class tourists are the pious pilgrims, trekkers, amateur skiers, mountaineers, motorcycle riders, spiritual sanctuary seekers with the numerous ashrams while high spending class tourists are those seeking holiday makers; hygienic space and solitude. At the apex is the value tourism which includes a veteran climber or trekker, researcher, high altitude flora and fauna enthusiast who has traversed his way through the world and is almost romantic about the Himalayas. These are travellers who completely merge with the Himalayan identity and are extremely conscious of the risks to the local ecology and culture.

Mountain tourism needs policy level action as a national policy for mountain region, programme level action to encourage quality tourism and collate data for information for updating policy formulation, planning and monitoring as a regular exercise.

Productive Ageing—A step towards Socio-economic Empowerment of Rural Elderly Women in Himalayan Area, Dr. Aabha Choudhary, Anugraha, New Delhi and Dehradun (4.4)

The population of elderly in India has been rising in the last few decades, The life expectancy of women at 60 (16.8 years) is greater than that of men (15.0 years) and they constitute a larger group than that of men.

In Garhwal Himalayas, the land is not fully able to support the population, adult males in large numbers take to migration to urban industrial centres in search of work, making women to work hard at all fronts. Continuous hard physical work, psychological and socio-economic stresses make women pass a poor quality of life and they age earlier than their counterparts.

The joint family system remains a primary agency of social support to elderly women. Their role and status in the family is largely determined by their contribution in different household chores like rearing of children, washing, cooking, cleaning, milching cattle, fetching fuel-wood, fodder, water, spinning, grinding, as well as engaging in agricultural activities.

The study revealed that the development of programmes of aged women are more or less absent, especially in the remote and inaccessible villages of the hills. The presence of large number of old female destitute women is due to several reasons such as desertion by the husband, out-migration of sons, death of children, having no children and break up of joint family. They constitute a vulnerable group, living in an impoverished state without any source of income or support structure, dependent only on the charity of the village community.

The dependence in agricultural operations by aged women shows an increase with advancing age. It may be noted that 35 per cent of women with 70-79 years age group and 22 per cent women in the age group 80 years and above are involved actively in agricultural operations.

As old age is considered as repository of wisdom, it is considered that there is a need for an intervention plan, aiming at initiating a set of coordinated activities so that disadvantaged conditions which surround older women and which hamper their fuller participation in family and community life are reduced, paving the way for enduring psycho-social fulfilment, economic security and holistic well-being.

Sustainable Environment through Cooperative Action, IFFCO, New Delhi (4.5)

India's forest resources cover about 19 per cent of the country's land area as against 33 per cent recommended under the national forest policy for sustainable environment. For this, the development of cooperative institutions based on the principle of equity and representing the aspirations of the people. The main objectives of cooperatives should be to mobilize community support, assisting in obtaining land, providing finance, training members, creating workable structures, integrating forest production with management, marketing and processing systems and strengthening the economics in the project villages. The cooperative institutions should extend extension activities for improving the rural environment, e.g. upkeep of cleanliness, indiscriminate mining, wastewater discharge in village streets, handling of chemicals, e.g. fertilizers, insecticides etc., increased use of alternate sources of energy and encouraging people to develop social forestry programme and participate in community welfare activities. A culture of mutual respect for each other, joint efforts for a common cause, equity, brotherhood, practice of democratic norms, truthfulness, honesty, caring and sharing the plight of each other are to be developed for cooperation.

The Indian Farm Forestry Development Cooperative Ltd., New Delhi and the National Dairy Development Board (NDDB), Anand and others have successfully demonstrated the importance of cooperatives. National Tree Grower's Cooperative Federation (NTGCF) has been organized at NDDB initiative to reclaim and manage wastelands in Gujarat, Andhra Pradesh and Karnataka. Such an initiative is started in one area for sustainable development in Uttaranchal, and needs extension and strengthening.

Role of Science and Technology in the Integrated Development of Uttaranchal, GBPIHED, Almora (4.6)

Though most of the problems of Himalayan region are of natural origin, yet they are exacerbated by anthropogenic activities. Present rate of exploitation of natural resources are much higher than their regenerative capacity, leading to deterioration in environmental quality in terms of deforestation, poor biological productivity and utility potential, accelerated soil erosion, hydrological imbalances, increasing natural hazards and socio-economic inequalities due to improper planning and execution of developmental projects. What is really needed is a comprehensive strategy based on integrated and area-specific approach.

Historical account is given of various plans and programmes starting from Fifth Five Year Plan (1972-77). Priorities and desired actions for Uttaranchal are itematized for geo-sources (water management, land management), energy resources (hydropower and non-conventional sources of energy), management of natural hazards and disasters, bio-resources (forest, agriculture, animal husbandry, horticulture), infrastructure, communication and connectivity (transport and communication) tourism industry and socio-economic issues (e.g. education, health and sanitation), proper documentation of indigenous knowledge to take fall advantage of modem science and technology for improving the quality of life in the mountains.

Technological Empowerment for Sustainable Livelihood in Mountains: Some Initiatives and Experiences in Participatory Technology Development and Transfer, S.K. Agarwal, Department of Science & Technology, New Delhi. (4.7)

Himalayan mountain ranges epitomize peoples' civilisation that goes back to the dawn of history. The traditional technologies need cost-effective inputs from modern science and technologies to improve the lifestyle of the inhabitants. S&T inputs are also needed for a gender-balanced development. The Department of Science and Technology has recently catalyzed and developed a concept of TIME (Technology Intervention for Mountain Ecosysems). Systems approach for participatory technology development and transfer

(PTDT) is needed. The choice of technology should be such as would upgrade their traditional skills and capabilities; minimize fatigue and reduce drudgery; be innovative and capable of easy assimilation, generate significant and assured added value to existing methods of operation; generate employment and use local resources both men and materials; need low capital investment and should result in low cost production of goods; be capable of replication and adoption and should blend harmoniously with existing ecosystems leading to tangible improvements in the living conditions and self-sustained development of the mountain region. In this endeavour, institutional linkages and active participation amongst voluntary agencies/science and technology based field groups, R&D institutions, financial agencies and above all people who are the primary stakeholders become crucial for improving the quality of life in remote areas to achieve long-term sustainability. Thrust areas for technological intervention are identified and experiences in Uttaranchal for upgradation for fuel/fodder needs in selected villages and establishment of women technology park (WTP) at Dehradun to provide demonstration and training on need-based selected technologies and promoting rural entrepreneurship amongst women in and around the project area. Technological modifications in watermills improved their efficiency and several abandoned watermills have been made operational in the mountain state.

The Best Thing to Give

- to a friend – your ear
- to your child – good example
- to your father – reverence
- to your mother – conduct that will make her proud of you
- to yourself – respect
- to your enemy – forgiveness
- to an opponent – tolerance
- to all – charity

PART 2
WEALTH OF UTTARANCHAL

Bhagwad Gita Teaches

- ❒ Life is Duty – Perform it
- ❒ Life is Love – Enjoy it
- ❒ Life is Tragedy – Face it
- ❒ Life is Struggle – Fight it
- ❒ Life is Promise – Fulfill it
- ❒ Life is Game – Play it
- ❒ Life is Gift – Accept it
- ❒ Life is Journey – Complete it
- ❒ Life is Mystery – Unfold it
- ❒ Life is Goal – Achieve it
- ❒ Life is an Opportunity – Take it
- ❒ Life is Puzzle – Solve it

Summarized by Darshi Dewan-Dusshera Day, Oct. 22, 2004

2.1

Economic Strength of the Traditional Economy

HIMCON, RANICHPURI

It is a harsh fact that the economy of the region as at present is in a bad shape. There exists no gainful employment opportunities and unemployment rates in the region are high. The pace of development has reached an all time low. It is becoming hard for the State to even raise enough revenue to carry out routine developmental work. The scarcity of funds is reflected in the State's over-dependence on liquor revenue. This state of affairs is due to prolonged neglect of the region and its resources and lack of vision that could have revitalised the economic scenario. Though the entire Himalayan belt of the nation was granted separate statehood, despite recommendations of the State Re-organisation Committee the region falling between Nepal and Himachal Pradesh for long remained a part of Uttar Pradesh and was granted statehood only in 2000. The policies were therefore not made specifically for the region. Sharing international frontiers with Nepal and Tibet (China) Uttaranchal is strategically located and encompasses thirteen administrative districts. Before Independence the eastern part of the state (Kumaun) remained under direct British rule while the western part (Tehri Garhwal) was a protectorate state ruled by the native princes.

The state of the economy in this region was however much better than what it is today. The inhabitants of this terrain were living in perfect harmony with nature and they had devised a system of resource management that laid the foundation of a strong and thriving economy in the region. The economic strength of this region is reflected in the magnificent structures of the region that were owned by the common people. The traditional economy of the region was based on pastoralism, trade and agriculture. The nomadic cattle herders of the frontier region played an important role in this economy and supported by their large herds carried out trade with Tibet.

So important was this trade that *Kasdesadhipati* (king of *Kasdes;* land of *Kasas* as the inhabitants are designated in local parlance) Baz Bahadur Chand (1638-78) personally supervised the construction of the Tibet track along the Kali valley (Atkinson, 1882). The border dispute with China and allocation of *terai* lands, over which these people had traditional grazing rights to new settlers, gave a severe jolt to this trade and the economy of the region.

With the closing of free grazing in the forests, mountain agriculture was overcrowded with surplus manpower. It was beyond the limits of hill agriculture to accommodate this manpower and this resulted in low per capita incomes, land fragmentation, and reduced farm inputs and yields. At the same time there were no efforts by the State to set right the situation. Instead of strengthening the economy and providing the masses with gainful employment opportunities the state took recourse to short sighted policies. The beneficiaries of the Tibet trade were declared as being tribals, which cut them from the mainstream of the society of which they were an integral part.

Though with hardship the natural resources of the region were however potent enough to support the hill populations and the self-sufficient inhabitants of this land were living in their own world until the gates of their land were flung open. Armed with the disparity in purchasing powers the new settlers acquired rights over the resources of this virgin land. A welfare state would have interfered at this stage to check the exploitation of the resources, as also the ensuing deterioration in the quality of life of the masses; but the interests of many in power being interwoven with this the state stood testimony to blatant exploitation of the local people.

The natural resources of this terrain were thus plundered at a never before pace and the repercussions are reflected in enhanced frequency of natural disasters and high rates of mass wastage that the terrain experiences at present; apart from a number of impacts that the people face in the plains. With increasing contacts with the world outside the social fabric of the society loosened and this weakened the traditional and time-tested systems of resource management. With no viable alternatives put forth the economy of the region was transformed into one dependent upon outside remittances; and hence began the Era of the Money Order Economy.

With no support and patronage of the state in favour of the indigenous people, the surplus producing economy of the region was transformed as the able-bodied people of the region resorted to out-migration in search of jobs, so as to create surplus to be pumped into the cash starved economy of the region. Though well intentioned, this option further destabilised the economy and the region was to face shortage of farming hands, increasing trend of resource mismanagement, depleting fertility, increasing erosion, depleting water availability, and increasing drudgery of the females.

The present reality is that the region faces severe dearth of working hands, brains, money and youth. Serious and concentrated efforts are needed to revert this trend that seems to have crept deep into the lives of the masses at the grassroots level.

Uttaranchal: Resource Management Heritage

An in depth and unbiased investigation of the socio-religious and cultural heritage of Uttaranchal reveals that, over the centuries, this heritage has provided the rules of sustainable natural resource utilisation that enabled hill communities to survive materially. Every culture grows through a process of accumulated learning and coming together of experience and the pace of cultural growth is dictated by the availability of natural resources. All the cultures thus show harmony with nature. The beliefs and practices of the little traditions therefore reflect an effort towards optimal resource utilisation. A reappraisal and reinvestigation of the relevance of these systems as guides to man's relationship with the environment are important from the point of view of material survival. Destruction of resources and the erosion of life support systems leads to destruction of livelihoods and thus to migration that is rampant in the region.

The indigenous populations of Uttaranchal show a fine tuned balance with nature with deep understanding of the fragile ecological relationship. These people have been for centuries living in perfect harmony with nature. Through experience they learnt to thrive on minimal available resources. Woven around the beliefs of the little traditions of the region are many a sanction that protected the natural environment of the region for centuries.

The intricate relationship between water and the faunal cover was so well understood that a protected forest cover was maintained on the higher reaches (the recharge zones of the natural springs) and local deities *(devatas)* were often installed at such places. These were thus looked upon with reverence and special attention was paid to protect their sanctity. Leave aside lopping; even shoes were forbidden in these sanctuaries to keep them pollution free. This was rather an evolved form of social fencing that was once deep rooted in the hearts of the masses.

The places where water was collected were considered auspicious. Many important rituals were associated with these places *(naulas* and *dharas).* Even today the newly weds are taken to the household *naula* to get the blessings for prosperity. The newly wedded female is thus sought to be as productive as the perennial spring; for in the earlier times it was the fertility of the women that was prized the most for the continuation of the lineage. Under the changed scenario, though the people have not forgotten the age-old practices, the tap is replacing the traditional *naula* and *dhara* and important ritualistic ceremonies are carried out at the location of the tap. This is an example of accommodation, and evolution of the practice through changing times. The cleanliness of the ritualistically important water harvesting structures was also paid due attention and was a social responsibility.

Religious sanctions associated with the traditional practices of resource management ensured that the God fearing people abide by the norms so set. With the changing times these sanctions were however forgotten, and consequently the once thriving SACRED GROVES are degenerating fast. The breakdown of traditional practices has exposed this region to a series of natural calamities. The indigenous people of this land knew how to protect vulnerable locations from landslides by keeping the pore water pressure within threshold limits and traditionally water escape routes *(jungle guls)* were maintained in these regions. The community without any external support maintained these but the practice of over dependence upon the state took toll of the tradition and what happened in August 1998 around Malpa-Okhimath is known to every one.

Practices of water harvesting and recharge zone management are not therefore new to the Himalayas. Excellent examples of rainwater harvesting, recharge pits *(chaals/khals),* and protection of the recharge zone are available in the region. It was through a series of socio-religious sanctions that the recharge zones were maintained and protected and the use of the forest resources at times of need was restricted through a system of sacrifice *(bali).*

Earthquakes are not a new phenomenon in this region and traditional building practices have evolved through centuries of experimentation and are best suited to the physiographic conditions of the region. Four storied houses are common in the region *(goth, chaak, paan, chaj)* and these have survived many earthquakes in the past which suggests that the essentials of earthquake resistance were incorporated into the traditional architecture of the buildings.

Over the centuries through trial and error and also through the accumulated knowledge of generations this region evolved a strategy of resource management that was well suited to its physiographic and climatic conditions.

Many of these practices are imbibed in the culture of the land and should be seen as a form of nature-man-spirit complex or the survival strategy.

However, during the post-independence period the traditional system has suffered considerably due to the alienation of the masses and the disintegration of the socio-cultural practices of resource management.

The traditional practices are more pertinent today as these are cost effective and therefore there is a pressing need to study these scientifically together with evaluating the fall out in the various alternatives put forth so that lessons may be learnt from the past and a comprehensive strategy for rejuvenating the economy of the region could be made.

When people are happy

Be friendly to them
When they are unhappy,
Have compassion for them;
When they do a righteous deed,
Develop an appreciative delight towards them;
If they do a wicked deed,
Develop indifference towards them

—*K.M. Munshi*

2.2

Towards Tradition

Anil P. Joshi*

India has a long and distinguished tradition in science and technology. Going back to the Indus civilisation, the settlements were well-planned with drainage and granaries for the storage of grains. Pioneering mathematical discoveries were associated with the names of Aryabhatta, Varahamihira, Mahavira, Bhaskara and others in algebra, geometry and astronomy. Not only was India vigorous in scientific and technological activity but the beginning of European science and technology also flowed initially from India through the Greek contacts made possible by Alexander and later through the Arabs. Indian manuscripts were translated into Persian and Arabic and thus knowledge traveled onwards from India. India also assimilated technologies and ideas from outside.

India's wisdom and its richness needs to be highlighted. Traditional wisdom is a time-tested approach. Any innovation done by the country in the past was subjected to use and the one found inappropriate was eliminated. This traditional wisdom cannot only be merely considered as incidental as it is the time-tested approach of the community. This has recently been realized and for this reason respect for traditional wisdom has begun to grow. Scientists and planners have been placing traditional wisdom as guidelines in planning the development strategies.

There are ample reasons why traditional wisdom must be respected as it is:

- Time-tested
- Familiar to the villagers

* Himalayan Environmental Studies & Conservation Organisation (Hesco).

- Location specific
- Simple and feasible

Traditional wisdom is now respected worldwide. This is evident from the fact that plants based on this wisdom been widely used in other countries and even patenting dissensions are increasing among different countries. The hitherto neglected traditional wisdom has to be respected because—

- Such wisdom can benefit a large society instead of a few.
- Bringing such knowledge from the informal system to the formal opens avenues for various other need based issues.
- Such knowledge can play an important role in mainstream development of the country.
- Recent patenting of Basmati, Neem and other such items compels us to document our wisdom as a ready reference so that such claims by other countries could be countered in a logical way.
- Old-age knowledge has replaced by newer ideas having no direct bearing on the community. Instead, strengthening of this wisdom with newer inputs would have resulted in sustainable development in rural India.
- Heritage conservation and preservation is our moral responsibility. In order to spearhead the movement for our coming generations, timely preservation of such wisdom and its documentation will be necessary.
- Growing unemployment in rural areas can be ascribed to the neglect of local wisdom.

Our wisdom/knowledge should be immediately documented and upgraded in the light of new wisdom because science and technology has so far had a limited impact on the growth of the country and on industrial production. It has almost no positive impact on the vast rural areas of the country and on the life of the common people. There has been a reason why technology has not reached rural areas. In the last fifty years, science and technology has been largely unrelated to the participatory role of the community in its development. This resulted in various anomalies in the development of appropriate technology for the rural poor. This can be witnessed in the rural areas of the country where centuries old technology has not been updated and new technology has been introduced leading to resentment in the community. Technology is a general term to cover the totality of means and devices with which man tries to adjust himself to or control his material environment. The route of development of technology has been different from community needs. Newer wisdom in technology has not matched local needs. This resulted in on different attitude to newer wisdom in the community. The major features of this indifference were:

- Local technology was never updated.
- Technology for local needs was largely neglected.
- Technologies were introduced.
- Commercial attitude influenced the development of rural technology rather than local needs.

The importance of traditional knowledge should also be conserved as:

- Traditional wisdom is disappearing because of negligence.
- The upgradation of such knowledge in the light of new developments in science and technology will have better returns and will also fit well in the rural context.
- Such wisdom is sometimes limited in use and can be spread to other users after upgradation and documentation.
- Such knowledge also opens new avenues of development.

It is trust that such wisdom developed in areas where inaccessibility and other physical limitations constrained development. This situation was more intense in mountain areas and, therefore, local culture/habitat/habits have developed many local technologies for use. What is required is to seek the entry of new technological developments through available wisdom. As a result constraints like in acceptability and inappropriateness of technologies are ruled out in the initial phase only.

The technologies with no local bearing, but important variously, can also find a place in later phases. There are ample examples where new technologies were denied by the community and at the same time upgraded traditional technologies spread fast.

Unfortunately organized attempts have not been made to review traditional wisdom. This is particularly important when related human resource has also been thrown to disuse. The products made elsewhere from new technologies replaced the traditionally occurring produce. This has totally disrupted the local economic cycle of the region. A serious view has to be taken to revamp local wisdom. A centre of excellence is immediately required to advocate traditional wisdom and scientifically analyze its upgradation. The different imports sector that need to be addressed are given below:

Agriculture Wisdom

Agriculture although often non-remunerative, is a major activity in mountain regions. The age old practices have earned villagers a unique wisdom with deep values rooted in the local ethos. Right from sowing to harvesting and preservations/storage, traditional agriculture practices in mountain areas still have sound basis.

In the course of time new practices particularly in crop types have somehow replaced tradition. However, some of the crops are still sown that suit the region. Majority of land which is unirrigated did not face any change, whereas whenever irrigation was introduced the option for other crop types increased. Wheat and paddy also become almost traditional but were not originally sown here. Owing to the unirrigated land type, environmental stress and non-availability of manure pulses were always an important crop in this area. Mountain pulses have a respected place in the market. But our new cultivation practices and choice of farming does not emphasize pulses. Whereas pulses are economically non-competitive but ecologically suited. Besides, our staple cereals are rapidly losing area of cultivation. This is also because of market forces and changing food habits. These cereals otherwise are age-old crops types here. It is also important to emphasize here that different agro-climatic zone have their specific produce which has a strong bearing on the ecosystem and health of human kind, and change in one, shatters the whole eco-cycle.

The mountain communities have their own specific practices from sowing to storage. These practices have been developed as per need, capacity and local ecology. Any attempt to replace tnem will not be successful. Farmers cannot afford new seeds every time but preserve them through local techniques for the next sowing. There are several other indigenous methods and practices for prevention and cure of diseases.

A great length of debate is necessary on our practices and upto what extent these need to be upgraded. In mountain, past intervention clearly revealed that replacing nature cannot work here. A strategy to upgrade the tradition to match present pace can only work.

Horticulture Practices

Fruits and vegetables grown in mountain do have a specificity. Factors like soil erosion, steep slopes and limited availability of cultivable land makes mountains favourable for horticulture. Unfortunately, except in a few isolated cases, horticulture has not been given due importance.

There are fruit and vegetables which are found solely in the region. Their cultivation methods have emerged out of age-old practices. Storage and preservation technique are traditional and specific. Most of the fruits and vegetables are preserved through drying techniques while others like potato and malta have been preserved by storage in pits dug deep into the soil. Chir pine leaves have often been used for preserving fruits while storing them either directly in sand, earth or amidst sand stored in wooden boxes so that they do not touch each other. Similarly, there are several other methods of preservation and storage which have been devised as per the ecological cycle.

Species of mountain areas have higher rating as local ecology infuse better quality. It has been acknowledged by the experts that horticulture activities in the hills would also help to check soil erosion which is degrading the ecology and is causing in a downslide of the economy. Hence, it can be articulated that the traditional crop pattern of horticulture needs to be encouraged for sound ecology and fiscal gains.

Artisans, Insight

Modern technologies have largely affected the artisan. Their trades are almost at the edge of death. New products made in other parts with newer and faster mechanism have replaced their market. Besides lack of upgradation of their skills has low quality producers.

There are traders like blacksmiths whose products are not popular, as factory-made items. Masons in mountains do not have quality skills to make brick houses and are thus subjugated. Watermills have been replaced by electrical and diesel devices as their pace is slow.

This has significantly affected the local economy besides increased unemployment. If artisanal skills had been enhanced to match diverse needs the scenario would have been different. There are ample examples now where upgradation of artisanal skill has changed the events and has been able to revive the age old traditions. This became possible only after dubbing new wisdom with the old.

Artisans in mountains are large in number. Their occupation is related to local needs. They complete the chain of the ecosystem. Their traditional skills need to be acknowledged and upgraded.

Water Wisdom

The water resources in mountains are abundant but are scarcely available to the residents. In the history of settlement of mountain regions water has been the major factor. Settlements occurred wherever there was a source of water in the form of springs or streams.

Traditionally, there were several techniques for water management which varied with different uses such as drinking, irrigation, storing and bathing. The new knowledge of water supply and irrigation not only disturbed local supply but also has devalued management practices. New practices has not been very useful in this terrain.

Thus, the plight of water scarcity is the major issue of mountain residents. Piped supply has not been very effective. The villagers trust in old water management strategies needs to be served. There used to be *Naulas, Guls* etc. which were locally managed by the community and were in accordance with the local ecology. These traditions have been largely neglected. There are, however, cases where the community has abandoned the Government water supply and has once again stated depending on traditional sources.

Water is the most important resource for the survival of mankind. Local strategies to develop the system will have to be rejuvenated in the wake of the failure of modern methods. Moreover, abundantly occurring water resource have to be made locally useful too. Besides, erecting big dams for the use of the people in the plains, local strategies for provision of water for the people of this hills are equally or more important.

Forest Traditions

This is a largely debated issue. Forests like water have been of key importance to villagers. There are traditional practices which still exist in villages leading to safe forest management.

There are forests placed in Van Panchayats which are solely under the control of the villagers. The management of these forests had been the sole responsibility of the village folk, since these provide immediate need of fodder and fuel to the villagers. This involves restrained grazing, controlled felling for common use, forest fire group and chaukidaar etc. This was all done collectively for common interest. The community had full rights on resource and any calamity was commonly encountered.

There have been several traditions in forest use. A particular tree cannot be fell at a particular point of time. A particular piece of land was donated to God, the idea was to prevent free grazing and saving the piece of forest land. Besides, there is a local provision where the forest cannot be visited in a particular period of time. Similarly harvesting is community based.

Herbal Wealth

An insight into the herbal wisdom of mountains is also imperative when talking about traditional knowledge. The history of folk medicines, which essentially were extracted from plants growing naturally dates back to many centuries. This traditional knowledge of folk remedies survives today among rural people and tribals. Even the modern medicines have their roots in ancient knowledge of the man that used to practise plant therapy.

This is one of the important resources that has not been commercially used by the residents. They have been denied the right to collect and gather herbs growing in the forest by the government polices. Herbal wisdom has largely been used by others. Earlier the wealth was simply collected and sold in the market or remained unutilized. As a result, such vital wisdom has been even lost to other countries.

Documentation such resources and thorough research and meticulous planning have become imperative. Awareness should be spread among hill people for growing herbs for further economic gains. Their age old wisdom should be upgraded with newer inputs.

Health Care

There are several indigenous practices which were earlier ignored but have now proved to be beneficial. For example, massage is an important technique that prevails in tribal areas. This has been practiced for children's health. Massage with the locally available oil has an important effect. Similarly, some of the practices to cure spondylitis are known to have a miraculous impact. For stomach disorders or intestinal displacement local practices of stomach exercises help to regain fitness. All such knowledge is diminishing and needs to be protected. There are several other health-related practices which need to be documented and scientifically proven.

Soil Management

The Mountain community has a very important method of soil management. The land facing any kind of degradation is subjected to plant treatment with specific species. This practice also faded as the land policy changed. Now the land is under the control of either the forest or revenue departments, and the villager's sense of belonging has been lost and therefore this management strategy has also faded away.

Folk Knowledge

Local wisdom in other spheres also needs to be documented and scientifically proven. This wisdom can be classified in two ways. One is in the form of occult and another is folk. There are folk forecasts for many situations in villages, such as cloud bursts, rains and other casual happenings. Their wisdom has a strong foothold but needs to be subjected to wisdom is based on the hypothesis of the priests it still has a value.

Tradition with New Wisdom

There are ample examples now when traditional wisdom has ultimately proved to be more effective than the new interventions. But the pace of traditional activity is certainly slack and therefore the option of associating new wisdom with tradition seems more desirable and important.

Water mills had a slow pace but were deep rooted in local culture. Besides the quality of products of water mills is better, their operation is easier and more cost effective. When water mills are clubbed with newer interventions there succeeded by all means. Beekeeping in mountain areas is done in traditional wall hives. This action diminished with time due to its low productivity. But when coupled with new inputs productivity increased twice and was accepted by the community. On the other hand box hives erased twice and was accepted by the community. On the other hand box hives were not accepted by the community as these were not in accordance with their traditional practices.

Looms in mountains spread more rapidly after the intervention of new knowledge. There are many such examples which show that when tradition was respected by new wisdom acceptability increased manifold. Rudia used to weave baskets for the community through locally available weed. Their business stopped as their products were replaced by other cheaper and durable products. When design inputs were given to traditional art their business revived. It is now an established outfit for pilgrims who buy their products during their Badrinath/Kedarnath Yatra.

IT IS MORE IMPORTANT TO BE KIND

Than to be wise and
Better to help others
Than to judge them
Have patience,
Everything comes out in time.
The gardner daily waters a plant
But it bears fruit only in season.

–Kabir

2.3

Apex Snow and Glacier Fields

JAGDISH BAHADUR*

Introduction

The apex snow and glacier fields of high Himalayan mountains form world's largest natural reservoir of renewable fresh water resource at the highest elevation. These are responsible to make the Himalayan rivers perennial and have a substantial influence on the productivity of Indian subcontinent. It is estimated that the water yield from a Himalayan river catchment is roughly double that of an equivalent catchment area from the snow-free peninsular region in the country.

In a given year, glacier runoff may be greater or less than that year's precipitation because glacier runoff increases if the precipitation is deficient (drought year) and decreases if the precipitation is greater than normal (flood year). Thus, glaciers act as buffers and regulate the runoff from high mountains but needs monitoring to forecast stream flows.

The presence of snow and glacier fields have a great importance to our environment:

- They exert a great cooling or refrigerating effect on the surroundings.
- They constantly interact with weather and climate both in temporal and spatial domains.
- Due to high headwaters, cheap hydropower generation is possible.
- The enormous snow and ice fields not only act as reservoirs for terrestrial and aquatic species but also for snow micro-organisms. The melting of snow and ice covers, the retention of liquid melt-water and the release of soluble nutrients in the high altitude environment, stimulate the growth of complex microbial

* Joint Adviser, DST (Retd.), 10, Shubh Niketan, A-4 Paschim Vihar, New Delhi.

communities influencing the productivity and biodiversity of the region. Associated environmental problems, progress and prospects with the Himalayan snow and glacier fields could be found in some details elsewhere (Bahadur, 2004).

In general, the study of snow and ice (i.e. glaciology) is truly an inter-disciplinary science. Besides environmental and ecological aspects, basic research in the field has been closely integrated with engineering research and technological development in the cold regions of the developed world. We have still a long way to organize such investigations in our region following the international practices evolved by World Data Centres (WDC) supported by ICSI/UNESCO/WMO.

Biogeographically, the Himalaya is a complex region. A sharp and distinct contrast characterizes the eastern region with warm and humid conditions (region of warm glaciers) and the western region with cold and arid environment (region of cold glaciers). The agro-ecosystems in this mountain region have been continuously evolving. The land is not so fertile and is prone to erosion. There are limited irrigation facilities and most of the region is under dry land farming. Traditional farming is largely practiced with crop maturing at different times of the year. Agriculture and animal husbandry are not practiced in isolation but in combination as agri-silvicultural, agri-pastoral and agri-silvi-pastoral systems. The cultivars are individually poor in productivity but collectively the crop mixes are reasonably productive.

The rich biodiversity in plant and animal variety needs inventorisation and conservation. The sustainable development of the region awaits a well coordinated and integrated multi-disciplinary approach, appreciating the interdependence of several aspects of atmosphere, geosphere, hydrosphere and biosphere (Bahadur, 2003).

From engineering research and technological point of view, we need integration of information on soils, snows and ice. For soils, work involves geophysical exploration, geo-technical site investigation, mechanical properties of frozen soils, frost heave, groundwater movement and water supply, excavation and drilling, weapon effect, road and airfield pavements and foundation of structures. For snows, work covers snowdrifts, snow removal from roads and runways, visibility problems, road loads, hydrology, vehicle mobility, avalanches and construction on permanent snow fields. For ice, work involves measurement of ice forces on hydraulic structures in rivers and lakes, construction on and inside glacier. To utilize the hydroelectric potential of the region, it is necessary to study and monitor the Himalayan snows and glaciers in greater details and map the areas with permanent and seasonal snow cover for assessing the volume of water in different parts of the year. We must act coherently and with commitment and support to help ignite the intellectual curiosity of young researchers for the development of the mountain region.

Inventory of Snow and Ice Fields

No consolidated information is available for snow cover in Himalayas. It varies from year to year and it has been pointed out that its inter-annual variability is substantially large affecting the meltwater contributions. A sufficient area of the high mountain system lie higher than the snow line (isotherm 0°C) and in this area snow falls round the year. In these mountains, it is estimated that 10 to 20 per cent of the total surface area is covered by glaciers while an additional area ranging from 30 to 40 per cent is overlain by seasonal snow cover. The maximum extent of Himalayan snow cover could be more than 1.5-2 × 10^6 km^2 while the glacier cover around 100,000 km^2. Variations in estimates of glacier cover as reported by several investigators could be seen from the Table 2.3.1.

Table 2.3.1: Himalayan Glacier Cover

Sl No.	*Area of Glacier Cover*	*Source*
1.	33,200 km^2 of Himalaya (17%) 16,000 km^2 of Karakoram (37%)	Wissman, 1959
2.	94,554 km^2 including Tibet (49.8% in Chinese territory)	Lin Jigun and Xu Shuymg, 1984
3.	38,479 km^2 covering 4795 glaciers	1st generation glacier inventory by GSI, 1983.
4.	25,725 km^2 for principal glacier fed rivers of Indian Himalayas	Bahadur 1985 (Based on data from SOI)
5.	Permanent Snow and Ice Cover 97,020 km^2	Upadhaya, 1985
6.	37,959km^2 covering 5243 glaciers	Glacier Inventory GSI, 1999
7.	About 50,000 km^2 glaciers drain into Indian territory	Bahadur, 2000

Uttaranchal occupies roughly 10 per cent of the Indian Himalayan mountain region. As the State lies in between the cold arid western region and warm per humid eastern region, it is affected equally by western disturbances and easterly air circulations and moderates the two climatic extremes. The State is strikingly rich in natural beauty and has an old distinguished religious and spiritual heritage. The region is mythological land of gods. World's highest pilgrimage centers, e.g. Gangotri, Jamnotri,

Badrinath, Kedarnath, Hemkund Saheb are located here and it is commonly called as 'Devbhoomi.' Towering important high mountain peaks of the State are: Badrinath (7138 m), Bhagirath I (6856 m), II (6454 m), III (6512m), Bhrigupanth (6772m), Chaukhamba (7138m), Dunagiri (7066 m), Gangotri (6590 m), Kedarnath (6940 m), Mana (6795 m), Meru (5831 m), Narayan (5965 m), Nilkanth (6596 m), Satopanth (7075 m), Shivling (6543 m), Sumeru (6350 m), Trisul (7120 m) etc. These high mountain peaks stand in dazzling and enchanting grandeur well over the snow line.

It has been pointed out earlier that we do not know the extent of snow and glacier cover of the Himalayas. In a recent publication, Survey of India (SOI, 2000) has prepared an inventory of major glaciers in Indian Himalayas. The publication shows that the major glaciers cover an area of 2088.6 km^2 in Uttaranchal with an altitude range from 3200 to 7400 m. Characteristics of some prominent glaciers in Uttaranchal are given in Table 2.3.2. It may be pointed out that our landmass receives sufficient meltwater contributions from outside our national boundaries.

Table 2.3.2: Characteristics of some Prominent Glaciers in Uttaranchal

Sl No.	*Glaciers*	*District*	*Length (km)*	*Area (km^2)*	*Elevation range (m)*	*Draining to river*
1.	Arwa	Chamoli	8.0	16.5	5000-6000	Sarswati
2.	Bandar Panch	Uttarkashi	12.0	25.0	3800-5800	Tons
3.	Bhagirath Kharak	Chamoli	18.0	24.0	3800-6000	Alaknanda
4.	Bhrigupanth	Uttarkashi	9.0	14.0	4000-6400	Bhagirathi
5.	Dialing	"	9.0	12.0	4200-5600	"
6.	Chaturangi	"	15.0	14.0	4400-5400	"
7.	Chorabari	Chamoli	7.0	22.5	3800-6000	Mandakini
8.	Dakshni Nandadevi	"	9.0	18.0	4400-5600	Rishi Ganga
9.	Gangotri	Uttarkashi	30.0	75.0	4000-5600	Bhagirathi
10.	Kalbilan	Pithoragarh	20.0	23.0	3800-5800	Gori Ganga
11.	Kedar	Uttarkashi	10.0	38.0	4400-6200	Bhagirathi
12.	Khatling	Tehri	12.0	37.2	3800-6500	"
13.	Mana	Uttarkashi	9.0	30.0	4600-6000	"
14.	Meola	Pithoragarh	8.0	12.0	3200-5800	Dhauli Ganga
15.	Milam	"	12.0	30.0	3500-4800	Gori Ganga
16.	Paschmi Kamet	"	15.0	26.0	4600-6200	Alaknanda
17.	Pindari	Almora	7.0	15.0	3800-5800	Pindar
18.	Raktavam	Uttarkashi	15.0	19.0	4600-6000	Bhagirathi
19.	Sato Panth	Chamoli	15.0	22.0	3800-5300	Alaknanda
20.	Swachand	Uttarkashi	8.0	17.5	4900-5800	Bhagirathi
21.	Trisul	Chamoli	12.0	33.0	4300-5800	Rishi Ganga
22.	Yankchar	Pithoragarh	8.0	14.0	4200-5400	Ramganga

Source: Survey of India, 2000.

Drainage Characteristics of Himalayan Regions

The most critical factors controlling the drainage characteristics of Himalayan region are topography and meteorology. The topographic factors of local relief, slope, angle and aspect influence the timing, volume, and special variability of water and energy. In mountain terrains, from meteorological point of view, there is no regional climate as such, but rather a mosaic of local topo-climates determined by variations in slope angle, aspect and relative altitude (Alford, 1992).

Due to greater precipitation inputs and reduced evaporation in high mountain areas, specific runoff is generally higher than the surrounding plains. In high mountains, some of the precipitation accumulates in snow pack during winter at temperatures below the melting point of 0°C, much of runoff is delayed from the time of precipitation until later in the year. Not only is solid precipitation retained but rain falling over snow cover is absorbed and retarded, discharge flows of streams and rivers in mountains are therefore concentrated in spring and summer months when water is released by melting from snow and ice. By contrast, winter discharges are lower or negligible according to the duration of temperature below freezing, controlled by the frequency of fluctuation of the freezing level. Mountain runoff largely reflects change in heat energy available for melting. Whether the melt is derived from seasonal snow cover alone or from basin also containing perennial snow and glacier ice, runoff is a hydrological response to variation in thermal conditions.

The monitoring of discharge from a glacierized basin is a difficult but important task for the following reasons:

- Discharge is highly variable with strongly marked seasonal variations as well as pronounced diurnal changes during the melt season.
- High kinetic energy of water flow may transport a rather high material load ranging from fine-grained sediments to rocks and boulders, which by their temporary disposition often change the river bed geometry.
- Sediment transport causes heavy abrasion and suffering of the measurement structure, and harsh climatic conditions are other critical factors.
- Long term climatic fluctuation influence glacier behaviour, which in turn is reflected in runoff values.

In addition to storage on snow and ice, liquid water may be stored in glaciers and in marginal lakes against glaciers. An outstanding characteristic of glacier runoff is the occasional outburst floods created by sudden discharge of large quantities of water stored in en-glacial, sub-glacial and ice-marginal sites. Even small water bodies or lakes can produce very large floods because of abrupt release of water. Some of the lakes may dump several times each year, others annually or larger lakes every two to five years.

In a study (NIH, Roorkee, 1994) carried by using data from Landsat (MSS) 1983-87 and IRS (LISS-I) 1988-92, i.e. for a period often years, the following conclusions were drawn:

- on an average, about 9080 km^2 area which is 40.9 per cent of the total drainage area of the Ganga basin up to Deoprayag is covered by snow in the months of March and April and about 3800 km^2, i.e. 19.28 per cent remains covered by perpetual snow and glaciers.
- a ten year average (1983-92), snow and glacier melt contribution in the annual flow volume of Ganga river at Deoprayag is found to be 26.68 per cent and the rest of the flow is from rains.

Integration of remote sensing for snowmelt runoff in Alaknanda river basin upstream of Vishnuprayag (Tangri,1996) and Bhagirathi river basin (Tangri, 2000) have been attempted to develop snowmelt runoff modelling.

Natural Disasters

Natural disasters in the region are associated with the inherent fragility due to immature geology, extreme weather and climatic conditions, intense freeze-thaw cycle and cloud bursts. There are several scales of environmental problems associated with high seismicity, climatic extremes, snow and ice avalanches, debris flow, mud flows, outburst floods. These occur with varying intensity and frequency throughout the region, making it a high risk living zone.

We must remember that there are natural forces working at higher altitudes, i.e. above 3000m (region free of human habitations). Human populations living at lower altitudes are to be protected by constant monitoring of the high altitude phenomena. For the protection of humans and their properties, due regards are to be given for covering of high slopes, tackling slope instabilities, occurrence of freeze-thaw cycle and cloud bursts adopting integrated approaches using eco-friendly and appropriate bio-engineering approaches for managing water flows and sediments as most of the problems are location-specific and not amenable to generalized solutions. In any case, cooperation of all concerned is needed for reduction of natural hazards for regeneration and sustainable development of the region.

Concluding Remarks

In a terrain of great variety and diversity of weather, climate, land, water, plants, animals, human resources, it is impossible to find simplistic and satisfactory solutions of all problems for sustainable development. As most of the problems get related to water, it becomes important to observe the behaviour of perennial snow and ice fields. These apex reservoirs need monitoring not only to learn new technological lessons for resource management but also will help prepare for tackling the adverse or possible catastrophic affects of climate change in the region. What is needed is an all out efforts to develop and utilize a proper mix of traditional and modern approaches for resource management at various locations. The potential for inter-disciplinary cooperation for development of synergies between different subject disciplines or departments is needed. Spatial and temporal coordination of resource data bases has to be harnessed. The need and the challenge of the day is to develop cooperative, participative, and flexible policies for resource management at local, regional, and State levels for the great Himalayan environment.

As Tehri Hydroelectric Project (THP) is a major venture in Uttaranchal, it provides a great opportunity to develop resource data bases. The watersheds in the project area comprise of highly rugged, multi-cycle slopes resulting from glacial, fluvial and neo-tectonic processes. The area lies in a seismically active zone and the glaciers are fast receding. Increasing biotic pressure, deforestation, mining, road construction and over-grazing are creating further instabilities. Both the rivers, i.e. Bhagirathi (originating from Gangotri glacier) and Bhilangana (originating from Kathling glacier) provide challenges and opportunities for a systematic monitoring of the snow and glacier bound area for development of forecast models for melt water contributions to optimize the regulation of water reservoirs and the power production from the project in economic terms. These studies will also be of great value to know the behaviour of high altitude snow and glacier fields for evolving resource management strategies for the changing environment.

References

1. Bahadur, J. (2004), In: *Himalayan Snow and Glaciers—Associated Environmental Problems, Progress and Prospects*, Concept Publishing Company, New Delhi, p. 164.
2. Bahadur, J. (2003), In: *Indian Himalayas—An Integrated View*, Vigyan Prasar, New Delhi, p. 279.
3. Wissman, H. Von *Die Heutige Vergletscherung and Schneegranae in Hoschasien Abh*, Wissenchaft Lit Math-Natura K. 114, pp. 110-40.
4. Jigun, L., Shuying, X. (1984), The contribution of glaciers on the Qinghai—Xizang Plateau & its relationship to atmospheric circulations, International Karakoram Project, Cambridge University Press.
5. GSI (Geological Survey of India), First Generation Glacier Inventory, 1985.
6. Bahadur, J. (1983), *Some Environmental Problems for Development ofHimalayan Water Resources* Proc. Intern. Seminar on 'Environmental Impact Assessment of Water Resources Projects,' University of Roorkee, India 12-14 Dec., 1985 pp. 64-75.
7. Upadhyay, D.S. (1985), In: *Cold Climate Hydrometerology* New Age International Publishers, New Delhi, 1985, p. 345.
8. GSI (Geological Survey of India) (1999), *Inventory of the Himalayan Glaciers—A contribution to the International Hydrological Programme*, GSI Special Publication No. 34.
9. SOI (Survey of India) 2000, *Inventory of Major Glaciers in Indian, Himalayas*, Special Publication, April 2000.
10. Alford, D. (1992), *Hydrological Aspects of the Himalayan Region,* ICIMOD Occasional Paper No. 18, p. 68.
11. Pratap Singh *et. al.* (1994), *Snow and Glacier Contribution in the Ganga river at Devprayag*, Report of National Institute of Hydrology, Roorkee.
12. Tangri, A.K. (1996), *Remote Sensing of Snow melt run off in Alaknanda river basin upstream of Vishnuprayag*, RSAC, Lucknow, April 1996.
13. Tangri, A.K. (2000), *Integration of Remote Sensing Data with Conventional methodology in snowmelt run off modelling in Bhagirathi river basin*, RSAC, Lucknow, January 2000.

2.4

Potentials and Problems of Soil and Water Conservation in the Development of Uttaranchal State

V.N. Sharda and G.P. Tayal*

Soil and water are the basic resources of the country which must be carefully conserved and judiciously utilised to sustain the ever increasing human and livestock population. Watershed management has emerged as a well accepted tool and sound strategy for long term productive agricultural sustainability through efficient management of natural resources, economic viability and social acceptability of production systems and protection of environment. Watershed management essentially relates soil and water conservation to rational utilization of land and water resources for optimum and sustained production with minimum hazard to natural resources. Watershed management is all the more significant in the newly carved Himalayan State of Uttaranchal in order to improve the economy of its marginalized and resources poor farmers and to preserve its environmentally fragile mountain ecosystem. A strong and environmentally sound land care movement supported by a scientific approach is vital for ensuring adequate food supply, enhancing economic development and conserving valuable natural resources through bio-remedial measures with active people's participation.

Uttaranchal State and Problems of Natural Resource Management

The State of Uttaranchal, carved out of Uttar Pradesh and situated in the North Western Himalayas, has about 5.3 million ha. of land mass spread over 13 districts with a human population of about 8.5 million. A major

* Central Soil Conservation Research and Training Institute, Dehradun.

part of its area is hilly terrain (93 per cent); plain area constitutes seven percent of its area only. While the plain area is agriculturally well developed, the hill area is primarily rainfed with subsistence agriculture and has remained largely neglected. Majority of the hill population resides in the elevation range of 600–2000 m and is mostly dependent upon agriculture. Though the forest area is reported to be about 3.5 million ha., constituting 65 per cent of the total land area, a good part of it is in degraded state. The cultivable land constitutes abut 15 per cent of the total area and a major part of it is rainfed and irrigation facilities are available in only 10 per cent of the area. There is quite a variation in climate mostly ranging from subhumid to temperate. Sufficient rainfall is received in most part of the region during monsoon months (June to September), but a major part of it flows down the slopes as runoff. Erratic and uneven distribution of rainfall results in frequent water shortages and droughts.

With ever increasing pressure on natural resources owing to rising population and development activities, the State has been facing grave problems of environmental degradation and food security. The Uttaranchal region, at present, has been adversely affected by problems of degradation of its natural resources due to various development activities. Its undulating topography, varied climate, scanty cultivated land, overwhelming percentage of small and marginal holdings, difficult conditions, high cost and low returns on food grain crops, sparse settlement, soil erosion and land degradation, inadequate infrastructure facilities and lack of industrialization and entrepreneurship greatly affect the development of the region.

The various constraints in agricultural development of Uttaranchal region may be summarized as under:

- Steep slopes and difficult undulating topography.
- Isolated and fragmented holdings and absente landlordism.
- Poor socio-economic conditions of people, hence less risk taking capacity and limited scope for use of inputs.
- Lack of adequate institutional finance.
- Agricultural operations executed by the womenfolk whereas decision making is done by the men, hence limited receptiveness to improved agricultural technology.
- Lack of trained manpower in the field of watershed management and agriculture.
- Migration of able bodied and educated people in search of jobs.

- Variations in microclimate and soils, etc. No generalisation can be made even for a block.
- Subsistence agriculture with limited crop diversification.
- Limited irrigation resources. Most of the water sources located at lower elevation than the fields.
- Limited availability of improved seeds and inputs.
- Inadequate marketing arrangements for the produce and post harvest facilities.
- Non-availability of proper agricultural implements suited to hilly terrain, hence low output and drudgery in agricultural operation.
- Slow returns from orchards due to long gestation period.

Status of Watershed Programmes in Uttaranchal

Realising the vital importance of rainfed farming in the Indian economy, the National Watershed Development Project for Rainfed Areas (NWDPRA) was launched in the year 1990-91 by Ministry of Agriculture, Government of India. It is currently being implemented in 73 out of 95 development blocks of Uttaranchal. Similarly, 30 development blocks are earmarked as DPAP blocks, in which watershed programmes are implemented through District Rural Development Agency. Watersheds falling in the catchments of rivers are being developed under the Centrally Sponsored Scheme of "Soil Conservation for enhancing productivity of degraded lands in the Catchments of River Valley Projects and Flood Prone Rivers."

The State Government of Uttaranchal is implementing watershed projects involving a total outlay of Rs. 3447 lakhs under the Integrated Wastelands Development Programme (IWDP) and Drought Prone Area Programme (DPAP) with the funding support of the Department of Land Resources in the Ministry of Rural Development. In addition, the Department of Land Resources has also sanctioned an outlay of Rs. 327 lakhs for Pilot Projects under financial support of Ministry of Water Resources for the catchment management, eco-restoration of the Himalayas, flood control including river bank and slope stabilisation, etc.

Status of Soil and Water Conservation Research in Uttaranchal

Recognising the importance of soil and water conservation programmes, the Government of India established a chain of Research Centres in the country during the First Five Year Plan. These centres were placed under the Central Soil & Water Conservation Research and Training Institute of the Indian Council of Agricultural Research on 1st April, 1974 with headquarters at Dehradun. R&D activities of the Institute related to Uttaranchal focused on evolving strategies for soil and water conservation on watershed basis, tackling mass erosion problems such as landslides, mine-spoils and torrents, demonstration of technology for popularisation and imparting training. Reclamation technologies of gravelly/bouldery soils, bio-remediation, runoff harvesting, management of common property resources and community participation were amply demonstrated with fairly good degree of success. Over the past four decades, the research efforts at the Institute and its Regional Centres have identified a number of resource conservation techniques which reduce the risk of soil degradation, preserve the productive potential of the soils, decrease the level of inputs required and sustain agricultural productivity in the long run.

Keeping in view the emerging scenarios of competitive biomass production and environmental dictats, the following thrust areas have been identified by the Institute for taking up various research programmes related to Uttaranchal State:

- Development of data base on land degradation, soil and water erosion, vegetation, rainfall, etc. with modern tools and procedures.
- Integrated watershed management for the conservation of soil, water, vegetation and ecosystem diversity.
- Rain water management for *in situ* moisture conservation, ground water recharge, flood moderation, runoff harvesting, storage and its recycling for improving biomass productivity.
- Silvipasture, fuel, fodder, and industrial grasses for degraded lands for realizing their comparative advantages.
- Rehabilitation of minespoil, landslides and torrents for environmental protection.
- Transfer of technology, participatory research, harmonization with indigenous technical knowledge.
- Socio-economic analysis, community participation, institutionalized management of common property resources, equity, income and employment generation for the landless, gender issues and resolution of social conflicts for sustainable resource use.

Watershed Research

This Institute has been a pioneer in developing and popularizing the concept of watershed management in the country since the 1970 based upon the tremendous success of its four pilot Operational Research Project Watersheds including Fakot in Tehri-Garhwal district of Uttaranchal. Fakot watershed is a live model of community-driven, self sustainable and eco-friendly balanced development process in the Himalayas which has proved to be a torch-bearer for the subsequent massive watershed development programme undertaken by the Watershed Directorate of erstwhile Uttar Pradesh and now Uttaranchal State. Fakot watershed project was initiated in 1974 as per farmers' priorities and refinement of indigenous technologies in a resource sharing pattern. The project is being monitored continuously to assess its impact on the production, protection and employment from the point of view of sustainability. Continued increase in the production of food grains, fruits as well as in milk and decline in runoff, soil loss and dependency on forests for fodder even after withdrawal of active intervention has indicated sustainability of the programme as seen from Table 2.4.1.

Table 2.4.1: Production and Protection Impact of Watershed Management Programme during Pre-Project, Active Interventions and After Withdrawal of Interventions (Fakot, Uttaranchal Hills, Area – 327 ha.)

Product	*PPP (1974-75)*	*Average of*	
		IP (1975-86)	*PIP (1987-95)*
Food crops (q)	882	4015	5843
Fruit (q)	Neg.	62	1962
Milk ('000 lit.)	56.6	184.8	237.6
Floriculture ('000 Rs.)	Nil	Nil	120.0**

* PPP: Pre Project Period, IP: Intervention Phase, PIP: Post Intervention Phase.
** Community diversified into Floriculture in 1994.

Further it was found that the increased income from the watershed development programme was relatively more equally distributed in the community.

Time series data recorded in the 370 ha Fakot watershed where net cultivated area ranged from 72 to 80 ha. during 20 years of observations showed that there was remarkable improvement in average yield of all crops ranging from 2.2 to 7.4 times after the watershed interventions (1975-86) (Dhyani *et al.*, 1997). The drought proofing potential of the watershed technology was amply demonstrated in the drought year of 1987, when the per cent yield reduction in the treated watershed was far less than in the untreated one.

Mass Erosion Control

A large area of the hill region of Uttaranchal is afflicted with mass soil erosion and degradation problems caused by landslides, minespoils and torrents. This Institute took up pilot projects for rehabilitation of such highly degraded lands through bioengineering technology. Nalotanala landslide project on Dehradun-Mussoorie highway, Sahastradhara minespoil rehabilitation project and Bainkhala torrent control project are successful examples of this technology. The highly degraded minespoil and landslide slopes were treated with small engineering structures such as loose stone/gabion check dams, contour trenches, wattling, geojute etc. and planted with suitable vegetative species. The bio-engineering technology not only rehabilitated the area but also improved the water and vegetation resource in the area on a sustained basis for use by the local people.

For example, the rehabilitation measures in the landslide affected and mined watershed (64 ha) rejuvenated water springs with sustained water yield even during the dry season (Juyal, *et al.*, 1998). The projects were found economically viable too in the long run, since the rehabilitation efforts saved an amount of about 1.5 lakh being spent annually by the State P.W.D. in removing the debris before the project was undertaken.

The hill torrents and rivers have been causing heavy damage to the adjoining agricultural/forest lands and population by bank cutting and floods due to frequent changing of their course. The Institute has evolved measures for torrent training and utilisation of reclaimed lands along their banks. The laboratory studies carried out in the hydraulic flume helped in safe and economic design of spurs for torrent training.

Agro-Eco-System Research

So far the research activities have been generally carried out in an isolated manner with little or no interaction between different organisations working on similar problems. Recently a concept of Agro-ecosystem research has been evolved to tackle the various issues by networking with different organisations and cross cutting administrative or political boundaries in order to optimise the indicators of the agricultural system, namely, productivity, stability, sustainability and environmental security. Under the National Agricultural Technology Project (NATP), CSWCRTI, Dehradun has already taken up research projects on Watershed Management including their hydrological investigations, erosion appraisal techniques, sustaining dry weather flow, refinement of treatment methodologies etc. at various locations in Uttaranchal.

Conservation Measures

CSWCRTI, Dehradun has evolved conservation for productivity and resource conservation for different agro-climatic regions of the country. Some of the research findings relevant to Uttaranchal are briefly presented below:

Training

Watershed management being a complex activity involving multifarious disciplines, proper training of the personnel is an important aspect. This Institute organises a regular training programme of five-and-a half months duration in soil and water conservation and watershed management. Short courses of duration varying from 3 days to 2 weeks are also organised as per demand of the sponsoring agencies for sensitisation and skill upgradation of field functionaries and managerial staff of different Government organizations, and NGOs including those from foreign countries.

Future Thrust

One of the top most priorities of the State, should be to revive hill agriculture and make it more productive and sustainable. This can be achieved through launching a massive watershed development programme and converging production programme of agriculture/ horiculture/allied sectors into watersheds. The strategy could be to delineate the entire area into macro/sub/micro watersheds prioritize the watersheds and prepare a perspective plan (agro-vision) for 20 to 25 years for development of agriculture in the State. *The agro-vision should clearly identify the problems, analyze the gaps and plan short term, medium term and long-term measures for development of hill agriculture and allied sectors.* A beginning should be made by bringing about convergence between watershed programmes and on-going production programmes in agriculture, horticulture and allied sectors.

Watershed development is a dynamic activity involving new challenges and paradigms.

Keeping this in view R&D efforts on the following issues need to be addressed more vigorously with specific reference to Uttaranchal State:

- Suitable farming systems in which horticulture, floriculture, cash crops and agro-forestry should find a prominent place.
- Appropriate water harvesting systems for different situations, including roof top water harvesting.
- Use of efficient methods of irrigation such as drip and sprinkler to economise water use.
- Appropriate lift irrigation devices such as hydram need to be evolved/refined along with suitable water diversion structures.
- Application of remote sensing and GIS techniques for watershed planning and erosion appraisal.
- Ground water recharge and sub-surface hydrology including the design of recharge structures and their evaluation.
- Alternative sustainable land uses and diversified agriculture for better income generation, food security and environmental protection.
- Policy issues related to community participation, management of common proerty resources and joint management of arable and non-arable lands.
- Convergence and synergy among on-going programmes and initiatives involving different government departments, research organisations, NGOs, financial institutions and Panchayat Raj Institutions and beneficiaries.

References

Dhyani, B.L., J.S. Samra, G.P. Juyal and Ram Babu and V.S. Katiyar, Socio-economic Analysis of a Participatory Integrated Watershed Management in Garhwal Himalayas—Fakot Watershed. Bulletin No. T-25/D-29, CSWCRTI, Dehradun.

Juyal, G.P., V.S. Katiyar, K.S. Dadhwal, P. Joshie, (1998), Reclamation of Mine Spoils in Outer Himalayas. In: *Soil and Water Conservation— Challenges and Opportunities*, Proc. 8th Int. Soil Conservation Conference, Eds. Bhashan, L.S., I.P. Abrol, M.S.R.M. Rao, Vol. 2, IASWC, Dehradun, India, pp. 1345-1354.

Samra, J.S. (1997) Status of Research on Watershed Management. Paper presented at the 173rd meeting of General Body of ICAR, New Delhi.

Sharda, V.N. and Juyal, G.P. 1995. Studies on the Performance of Conservation Bench Terraces *vis-à-vis* Conventional Cultivation Practices in Doon Valley, pp. 24-27, *Annual Report*, CWSCRTI, Dehradun.

ENJOY THE BLESSINGS of this day if
God sends them;
And bear the evils patiently and sweetly;
For only this day is ours;
We are dead to yesterday
And not born tomorrow

When things go wrong
as they sometimes will
when the road you are treading
seems all uphill.
When the funds are low
And the debts are high
And you want to smile
But you have to sigh,
When stress is pressing you
Down a bit
Rest – if you must
But don't you quit
Success is failure
Turned inside out
You can never tell
How close you are
It may be near
When it seems so far
So stick to the flight
When you are hardest hit
ITS WHEN THINGS SEEMS WORST
THAT YOU MUST NOT QUIT.

2.5

Opportunities, Challenges and Prospects in Agriculture and Forestry

S.P. MALHOTRA*

Introduction

The creation of Uttaranchal State, carved out of Uttar Pradesh, in November 2000 has fulfilled the aspiration of the people of this hill region to have a state of their own. Though the demand for the creation of a hill state of Garhwal and Kumaon was raised intermittently from 1949 onwards, the First State Reorganisation Commission turned down the demand on grounds of economic viability. However, years of neglect and lack of development in the region compelled the people of Uttarakhand (as the region was called then) to revive the demand for a separate hill state in the late 1980s. The BJP made the creation of Uttaranchal State a part of its political agenda and with its success in elections in the region, the state was created on November 2000. Uttaranchal State was formed as the 27th State in the Indian Union. It consists of 13 hill districts of Uttar Pradesh. These include Almora, Bageshwar, Champawat, Chamoli, Dehra Dun, Haridwar, Nainital, Pauri Garhwal, Pithoragarh, Tehri Garhwal, Uttarkashi, Rudraprayag and Udham Singh Nagar. The state has an area of 53,000 sq. kilometres, with a total population of 8,479,562 (Census of India, 2001). Tables in Annex 6 give the latest details.

The creation of the new state theoretically should lead to better administration and faster economic development. However, that in itself will not be sufficient. It is not necessary that a smaller state would automatically find the road to development easier. A lot will depend on the leadership and especially a leadership with knowledge, vision and

* FAO (Retd.) New Delhi.

understanding. More importantly they should be allowed to perform effectively. The stability of the elected government in the small state is essential so that the government can get on with the task of administration and development. The administration faces a great challenge to make use of the full economic potential of the State. It is essential to tone up the bureaucracy, which should give correct and proper policy advice and carry out the developmental programmes effectively in the newly formed state.

The new state of Uttaranchal has good potential for development of agriculture, forest resources, tourism and hydel power. This paper deals mainly with the agriculture and forestry sectors.

Problems and Prospects for Agriculture

Agriculture (including forestry) is the mainstay of the economy of Uttaranchal. Around 75 per cent of the state's population depends on agriculture for its livelihood. The main cereal crops grown include rice, wheat, maize and sorghum. Cash crops include apple, citrus, litchi, green peas, onion, potato, some oilseeds and sugarcane.

The land holdings are rather small generally less than one hectare in most districts of the new state, except in two districts, *viz.* Udham Singh Nagar and Pauri Garhwal. The smallest area is found in Almora and Bageshwar Districts. The share of gross cropped area in the recorded area ranges from less than six per cent in Uttarkashi to 48 per cent in the combined Nainital and Udham Singh Nagar Districts. However, gross irrigated area is the lowest in Chamoli (7 per cent) and highest in Dehra Dun (over 43 per cent). In the hill region of the new state farmers devote a large part of their land holdings for raising cereal crops for their subsistence, although some area is also devoted to a few horticultural crops such as apple, citrus and litchi and vegetables such as onion, green peas and potato. In Dehradun, Haridwar and the Udham Singh Nagar Districts sugarcane is also grown.

Food grains account for almost 75 per cent of the gross cropped area, of which cereals are grown on 73 per cent and pulses on the remaining two per cent (Table 2.5.1). Among cereal crops wheat accounts for 30 per cent of the gross cropped area. Rice grown on 21 per cent of the total cropped area, is an important crop in Dehradun, Haridwar, Pauri Garhwal, Nainital and Udham Singh Nagar Districts.

In most hill districts coarse grains are also grown, the major districts in terms of production being Pauri Garhwal, Almora and Tehri-Garhwal.

Table 2.5.1: Uttaranchal: Area, Production and Yield of Principal Crops

	Foodgrains			*Rice*			*Wheat*			*Coarse gains*			*Pulses*		
	Area	*Production*	*Yield*	*Area*	*Production*	*Yield*	*Area*	*Production*	*Yield*	*Area*	*Production*	*Yield*	*Area*	*Production*	*Yield*
1. Almora	135.3	139.5	1,031	23.6	25.7	1,092	46.2	40.7	883	61.9	70.9	1,145	3.6	2.2	609
2. Bageshwar	45.6	59.0	1,294	15.2	21.2	1,393	16.8	18.4	1,094	13.6	19.6	1,441	–	–	–
3. Chamoli	52.0	65.2	1,254	15.2	19.7	1,298	19.1	22.0	1,147	17.1	26.1	1,526	0.6	0.3	404
4. Champawat	29.5	41.2	1,397	8.0	9.4	1,174	12.2	17.8	1,461	9.3	14.0	1,506	–	–	–
5. Dehradun	54.6	83.8	1,536	14.5	29.0	1,999	23.5	34.9	1,482	14.6	18.7	1,281	2.0	1.2	605
6. Haridwar	79.9	178.7	2,237	25.8	56.7	2,199	46.7	114.9	2,458	4.4	5.9	1,341	3.0	1.2	371
7. Nainital	62.4	129.5	2,076	15.6	37.0	2,376	29.0	65.6	2,26	15.6	25.6	1,641	2.2	1.4	664
8. Pauri Garhwal	184.9	210.7	1,140	38.1	43.0	1,130	50.1	50.6	1,010	92.0	115.2	1,252	4.7	1.9	402
9. Pithoragarh	76.2	88.2	1,158	20.7	26.2	1,270	26.1	27.5	1,057	22.3	29.8	1,336	7.1	4.7	657
10. Rudraprayag	25.4	29.5	1,161	7.6	9.4	1,299	9.4	10.1	1,073	8.4	10.7	1,273	–	–	–
11. Tehri Garhwal	108.4	126.0	1,163	19.2	27.8	1,450	38.2	35.0	915	47.5	61.3	1,290	3.5	1.9	533
12. Udham Singh Nagar	191.1	522.2	2,731	99.6	247.8	2,487	83.9	263.2	3,137	3.6	7.8	2,167	4.0	3.4	849
13. Uttarkashi	46.2	62.7	1,357	15.7	25.6	1,628	16.4	17.5	1,067	12.7	18.9	1,488	1.4	0.7	502
14. Uttaranchal	1,091.5	1,736.2	1,591	318.8	578.5	1,815	417.6	718.1	1,067	323.0	424.5	1,314	32.1	18.9	589
15. Uttar Pradesh	20,526.6	40,155.4	1,956	5,932.20	11,615.90	1,958	9,230.7	23,169.5	2,510	2,790	3,172.0	1137	2,573.7	2,198.0	854

* Area 000 hectare; Production 000 tonnes and Yield: kilograms per hectare.

Source: Uttar Pradesh Directorate of Economics and Statistics: Production and Productivity of Crops for the Year 1998-99 (Provis).

The yields per hectare in most districts of Uttaranchal for most food grain crops are generally well below the level achieved in Uttar Pradesh and the all India level. For instance the yield of rice is around 16 per cent lower (*i.e.* 1,815 kgs per hectares compared to 2,148 for UP and 1,990 kgs for India level). Wheat yield for Uttaranchal is less than 50 per cent of the country's average (1,067 kg. against 2,510 kg and 2,485 kgs. respectively for UP and All India). For pulses also yield is 30 per cent lower than that of Uttar Pradesh. *The low yields per hectare reflect the small size and scattered holdings*, difficult terrain, unfavourable climatic conditions for some crops, lack or inadequate availability of improved inputs and technology and lack of credit and marketing facilities. Owing to poor yields of most crops, value of agriculture production per unit of cultivated area and per capita in all the districts, except in Nainital, ranges between 50 to 60 per cent of the level for the whole of Uttar Pradesh (Table 2.5.4). The research studies undertaken in India indicate an inverse relationship between the incidence of poverty and agricultural production per head of rural population. In fact in Uttaranchal agricultural production has almost stagnated with little developmental and infrastructural work

Table 2.5.2: Uttaranchal : Land Utilization in Different Districts: 1998

District	*Av. Holding (Ha.)*	*Per cent Gross area*		*Area sown to*			*Value of agr. Production (Rs.)*	
		Sown	*Irri-gated*	*Wheat*	*Rice*	*C. Grains*	*Per capita*	*Per hectare*
Almora (Incl. Bageshwar)	0.62	23.34	12.47	34.27	–	33.60	948	4,528
Chamoli (incl. Rudraprayag)	0.87	8.43	7.17	32.27	–	26.02	923	6,471
Dehradun	0.97	26.54	43.44	31.52	17.01		685	9,191
Haridwar								
Pauri Garhwal	1.28	17.75	11.73	30.93	38.44		769	3,947
Nainital (incl. Udham Singh Nagar District)	1.67	48.54	12.36	34.97	31.58		2,835	14,401
Pithoragarh (incl. Champawat district)	0.54	19.83	8.28	34.09	27.86		1,593	7,439
Tehri Garhwal	0.84	19.20	17.02	34.84		35.21	831	4,525
Uttarkashi	0.98	5.56	20.09	30.00	23.04		1,213	6,700
Uttar Pradesh	0.89	87.56	66.26	34.95	21.94		1,800	10,690

N.B. share of sown area is in reported area: and of Irrigated area in gross cropped area.

Source: Centre for Monitoring Indian Economy Pvt. Ltd.: Profiles of districts, October, 2000.

undertaken during the last three decades or so. With not much agricultural land available for further expansion, increased productivity of food grains and other crops is essential. This would help not only in raising income and employment in the rural economy of the new state, but would also have a significant effect on poverty alleviation.

Most of the districts are not self-sufficient in staple cereal crops, except perhaps Dehra Dun and Udham Singh Nagar Districts. The low level of productivity per unit of land and labour indicates the vast potential for most crops. However, it also poses enormous challenges to tap this potential.

The area under sugarcane in Uttaranchal State is estimated at over 150 thousand hectares, constituting only 10 per cent of the gross cropped area. The crop is grown in Dehra Dun, Haridwar and Udham Singh Nagar Districts. Sugarcane production is estimated at over 9 million tonnes. Average yield per hectare is estimated at 60 tonnes for Uttaranchal against 62 tonnes for UP and 71 tonnes for India as a whole in 1997/98.

Fruits and vegetables make a valuable contribution to the economy of the state, although these are grown on a limited area. For Uttaranchal the information on area and production is available only for apple, citrus and litchi among fruits and for onion, green peas and potato for fresh vegetables. Total area under fruits is estimated at 187 thousand hectares with output is estimated at 515,000 tonnes. The share of the state comes to 5 per cent in terms of area, but only 1.3 per cent of the total all India output. Area under vegetables in the State is over 65 thousand hectares while production is about 363 thousand tonnes. Vegetables account for one per cent of the total area in the country, but only 0.5 per cent of total production. Table 2.5.3 shows the area, production and productivity of selected horticultural crops in Uttaranchal.

As in the case of food grains, the productivity of the above mentioned horticultural crops in Uttaranchal is generally lower than the average for the country and substantially below that obtained in the more progressive states. For instance for apple the yield per hectare in the state of 3.2 tonnes is almost 50 per cent of the all India level and less than one-third that of Jammu and Kashmir (11 tonnes). For citrus also the productivity compares unfavourably at less than four tonnes against 14 tonnes achieved in Maharashtra. For litchis, the state yield is less than 2 tonnes against 12 tonnes reported in Bihar. For green peas, the state average productivity of less than 5 tonnes compares poorly with 8.5 tonnes achieved in Haryana.

Table 2.5.3: Area, Production and Productivity of Horticultural Crops in Uttaranchal

Crop	*Area (000 hectares)*		*Production (000 tonnes)*		*Yield (tonnes/ha)*	
	Uttaranchal	*All India*	*Uttaranchal*	*All India*	*Uttaranchal*	*All India*
Total Fruits	186.7	3,681.7	515.3	40,050.9	2.8	10.8
Apple	55.6	227.6	176.4	1,320.6	3.2	6.1
Citrus	23.4	482.7	86.2	4,456.2	3.8	8.0
Litchi	8.8	13.3	16.0	454.7	1.8	7.8
Total Vegetables	65.4	5,629.3	362.6	72,831.6	5.5	12.9
Onions	1.35	360.0	16.6	3,200.0	12.3	8.9
Potato	14.4	1,210.0	320.6	17,650.0	22.3	19.3
Greenpeas	13.6	272.5	67.1	2,421.7	4.9	8.9
Total Flowers	161a	73,536a	195b	365,685b	–	–

Note: Data for Uttar Pradesh (Hills) are assumed to pertain to Uttaranchal.
Source: J.P. Negi and Lily Mitra: *Indian Horticulture Database*: National Horticulture Board; September, 1999.

The low yields of most crops indicate the potential which needs to be harnessed. While this offers opportunities for growth in production, income and employment in the rural economy of the state, it also poses an immense challenge that needs to be overcome without losing much time. For meeting the increasing demand for foodgrains and food items like fruits, vegetables and milk, for the new state as well as for the country, it is essential to develop the economy through scientific transformation and modernization of agriculture. Both land and water resources are limited in the State. With declining size of holdings and the scarcity of culturable land, production will have to be augmented mainly through intensification of farming under the integrated intensive holistic farming system in the future. Sustainable production does not seem to be possible through the present method of inorganic or chemical farming with excessive use of chemical fertilizers and pesticides. Their excessive use leads not only to the deterioration of the soil but also to environmental and health problems. This indicates the need to shift to ecological and hi-tech agricultural development for long-run sustainable farming in the state.

With the limited land and water resources in the state, it is essential to introduce an improved integrated intensive holistic farming system. Ecological or organic farming shall bring stability and sustainability to agriculture. It is farming with biological, cultural and natural inputs. Organic farming systems rely on large-scale application of organic or farmyard manure, compost, crop rotation using legumes, vermiculture, mechanical cultivation, biofertilizers, biopesticides and biological control to maintain soil productivity, to supply plant nutrients and to control insects, weeds, other pests and diseases. Under the organic farming system nothing needs to be wasted in agriculture. Farmers should be advised to utilize even the broken twigs, left-over straws and weeds on their farms to increase soil fertility.

Hi-tech agriculture is comprised of significant advances in agriculture in the form of advance packages of practices combining the organic farming system, appropriate farm machinery and implements, green house technology, integrated nutrient supply systems, integrated pest management systems, integrated intensive farming systems, improved irrigation systems coupled with improved extension and agricultural marketing systems. Improved integrated intensive holistic farming system model has been developed and adopted by the farmers in Himachal Pradesh.

Production of food grains and other crops can be increased remarkably by the adoption of an advanced package of practices. As the experience in Himachal Pradesh indicates, the average yield of maize, rice and wheat can be increased by more than 2-3 times compared with the existing average yields of farmers in the state. Similarly, the yields of vegetables and fruits can be raised by 3-4 times compared with the existing average yields. This increase would give a quantum jump to the income of the farmer. The production and income of farmers can be increased further by the adoption of improved cropping systems. For higher production, income and sustainability, foodgrain crops must be intercropped with leguminous pulses and oilseeds. The vegetables and vegetable-based cropping systems would give the highest production and income per hectare. The progressive farmers in Himachal Pradesh have already adopted the improved cropping systems. The intensity of cropping of these progressive farmers having average holdings of 1.33 hectares increased by as much as 230 per cent, which increased their income substantially. Such a high cropping intensity and farm income is sustainable only through organic farming.

The farmers can raise their income further through the adoption of integrated intensive holistic farming system. Farmers should follow a mixed cropping type of farming system. In general, depending on their sources, four farming systems can be recommended, *viz.* Food grain-based, dairy-cum-poultry based, vegetable-based and horticulture-based. Farmers can also adopt various other farm and non-farm sub-systems (enterprises or activities) as a part of the integrated intensive holistic farming systems to further enhance their income substantially. These systems or sub-systems include (i) food grains, oilseeds and other crops (ii) vegetables including potato (iii) fruits, and farm forestry (iv) Dairying (sale of milk, other products and animals) sheep, goats, poultry and sericulture (v) rabbitry, mushrooms, apiculture and fishery (vi) tailoring, photography, carpentry, gold and blacksmithy. Depending on their preferences, resources manpower and availability of training facilities and markets. The farmers can take up all of them on a large scale to increase their production and income.

It should be stressed that a systems approach has to be recommended comprising of the following components:

(i) Integrated intensive holistic farming system with a host of farm and non-farm sub-systems.

(ii) Ecological or organic farming including integrated nutrient management system : farmers should be prepared to use more organic fertilizers in place of inorganic fertilizers and pesticides. In case the nutrient requirement cannot be fully met by organics alone the balanced use of NPK fertilizers should be made available as part of this system instead of using only N or P, keeping in view of the requirement of the crops and sustainable farming on the basis of the soil testing and symptoms of nutrient deficiency in the crops or plants.

(iii) Integrated pest management system.

(iv) Hi-tech packages of practices : The Hill Campus of the State Agricultural University must bring out and distribute Hi-tech packages of practices. Soil testing must be conducted through mobile soil service at the doorstep and fields of the farmers and the results and recommendations given there and then.

(v) It is essential to strengthen the Inter-University cooperative research programmes between the Hill Campus of Pant Agriculture and Technology University and the Himachal Pradesh Agriculture University.

(vi) Provision of irrigation and soil and watershed development are necessary for sustainable agriculture. To promote ecological and sustainable farming provision of cheap water harvesting and storage tanks for irrigation, check dams, earthen-cum-stone field bunds and boundaries, conversion of outward sloping terraces or fields into inward sloping fields, fuel-fodder-grasses-tree plantations, afforestation etc. for soil and water conservation basis have to be taken up on watershed basis and continued on a large scale. Irrigation is also an important factor. Therefore, all sources of irrigation should fully tapped, harvested and developed. Once irrigation becomes available, it is necessary to make changes in cropping patterns, cropping systems and cropping intensity by including more remunerative high value crops. To increase efficiency of irrigation, more efficient methods such as sprinkler and drip irrigation must be used.

(vii) A farmer-oriented marketing system with efficient storage and transportation network is required for this newly formed state.

(viii) Agricultural research, extension and agricultural development work in the State has to be location-specific, need-based, problem solving and production-oriented. For the hilly areas, for instances, it has to be oriented to diversity, niche or comparative advantage like production and marketing of off-season vegetables and temperate fruits. The production patterns, inputs and package of practices have got to be different and specific to such perspectives, specificities and zones.

(ix) Broad-based agricultural extension system is required for effective implementation of all the above mentioned recommendations. The broad-based agricultural extension system consists of initial rapport making with the farm families or villagers to know their problems, knowledge and requirements and to use the same as an entry point. This is to be followed by training, transfer of technology, and human resource development. Development technologies specific to youth farmers and women farmers is especially important.

(x) To fully harness the agricultural potential of the state through the above-mentioned strategy would require higher investment in agriculture, both in the public and private sector, as well as an improved credit system for farmers.

(xi) Currently a large amount of fresh vegetables and horticulture produce go waste owing to the lack of village roads and storage, marketing and agro-processing facilities. These infrastructures must be given due attention. Priority should be given under the recently announced Pradhan Mantri Gram Sadak Yojana not only to build the village roads but also all weather and long lasting pony tracks. Along with village roads and pony tracks, transportation, grading and packing material must be supplied at cheaper rates. Also technical know-how and correct and up-to-date marketing intelligence should be provided to growers. Last but not the least, processing units must be developed in clusters of horticultural crop producing areas. This would help not only to reduce the wastage of produce but also solve the problem of unemployment and ensure better prices to farmers for their produce.

Large Scale Sale of Farm Land

Farmland in the state is limited. However, the farmers in the state are reported to be selling their farm holdings for paltry sums which are being used for commercial gains. This does not bode well for the new state. A large number of farmers along the picturesque Gagar-Mukteshwar highway in Uttaranchal, have sold their holdings to influential builders, businessmen, bureaucrats and politicians. These farmers are now literally on the streets. The farmer's family squanders the money realized from the sale of land on motorcycles, television and other consumer goods. Land sales have been common for years. However, the impact of the lopsided deals is being felt only now. The region's money-order economy is partly to blame. The past decade has seen little commercial production from farmers cultivating fruits, medicinal plants and flowers. Hardly any attempts were made to boost the fruit processing industry in the region on the lines of neighbouring Himachal Pradesh or to profit from medicinal plants which are either smuggled out or sold cheap. Influential builders are using even the forest land for constructing tourist resorts. Compounding the problem are benami holdings. Senior bureaucrats and other influential folk have purchased land in the area and have got it registered in the name of their relatives, spouses and even servants.

These issues are of primary concern to the new state of Uttaranchal. In Himachal Pradesh and Jammu and Kashmir, land use cannot be changed without the permission of the Government. There is also an urgent need to enact such a legislation to help save forest and agriculture land in the state.

Role of Forestry and Agro-forestry

In Uttaranchal the total forest area is estimated at 5.2 million hectares.

This constitutes 49 per cent of the total geographical area. Forests play an important role in the economy of the state. Timber and fuel form the major produce group, while bamboo, drugs, grasses, gum and resins etc., the minor produce group. Forests are the major source of raw material for industries, buildings, railways and other tertiary sectors. However, forest area with a cover of the desired density in the state is getting reduced rapidly. There is an increased pressure on the new state's forests for fuel, fodder, and timber requirements for increasing human and even livestock population. Further, the exploitation of forests for revenue generation and also the increase in agricultural/horticultural activities are putting heavy stress on forests in the state. This has resulted in change in the area under forest, particularly some important commercial species and also the productivity of forest has been affected.

There is a considerable amount of wasteland in the state. This consist of forest degraded area and non-forest degraded land. Culturable wasteland alone is estimated at over 350 thousand hectares (Table 2.5.4). It constitutes over 25 per cent of the currently total cropped area. Destruction and degradation of forests are taking a heavy toll of soil and water resources in the state. A considerable amount of top soil with essential nutrients in the hilly areas is being worked away each year, which seriously affects the economy of the state. The degradation makes land less productive leading to impoverishment of the rural population. It is essential to regenerate degraded forest and wasteland. A programme of generation and restoration of the eco-system will provide productive employment to a large section of rural people. A large area of degraded land in the state can be reclaimed. Apart from wages, little input is required, especially if the local communities themselves organize the work on a cooperative basis. Most of the land needs only basic water and soil conservation measures and some amount of plantation and protective work. These types of work should be organised under the food-for-work programme under which some amount of the huge food grain stock held by the government can be usefully utilized. There is an urgent need to launch a well-planned programme for rural fuelwood plantation schemes and afforestation. These schemes should be based on the local needs and on the capacity of the natural resources and carried out through people's involvement preferably the rural women. Similar schemes for plantation of minor forest produce including medicinal plants should be undertaken. A voluntary Organisation HIMCON–Himalaya Consortium for Himalaya Conservation, based in Ranichauri, Tehri Garhwal district is carrying out programmes for soil and water conservation as well as for regeneration for forests and wasteland, though

Table 2.5.4: Uttaranchal: Land Utilization in 1996-97

(*in Thousand Hectares*)

District			Other Uncultivated Land								
	Total Reporting Area	*Forests*	*Not avail. for cultivation*	*Culturable Waste Land*	*Total*	*Current Fallow*	*Fallow land other than current fallow*	*Net Area Sown*	*Total Cropped Area*	*Net Irrigated Area*	*Gross Irrigated Area*
(1)	(2)	(3)	(4)	(5)	(6)	(7)	(8)	(9)	(10)	(11)	(12)
1. Almora (including Bageshwar Distt.)	726.8	392.1	49.4	59.9	166.6	0.6	7.8	110.3	174.1	10.9	20.4
2. Chamoli (including Rudraprayag Distt.)	883.9	563.5	183.8	33.5	90.9	0.09	1.6	43.9	66.7	2.5	4.75
3. Dehradun	303.2	207.7	19.4	10.8	15.2	2.5	4.6	53.8	85.4	24.0	34.6
4. Haridwar	233.5	70.9	28.4	2.4	3.3	65.4	38.4	123.8	181.9	39.4	45.1
5. Pauri Garhwal	753.3	444.9	52.2	44.8	150.8	0.1	18.0	87.4	135.8	8.0	16.0
6. Nainital	411.7	300.8	11.7	26.4	43.7	1.0	4.3	50.3	85.2	30.3	42.8
7. Udham Singh Nagar	291.7	103.6	26.1	3.5	4.7	1.8	2.8	152.7	257.9	141.83	235.1
8. Pithoragarh (including Champawat Distt.)	637.6	330.7	42.0	55.1	183.4	1.1	12.8	67.5	117.9	6.4	10.9
9. Tehri Garhwal	536.6	359.2	23.9	74.8	77.7	0.06	8.6	67.1	107.4	9.28	18.0
10. Uttarkashi	817.6	726.3	26.7	9.0	30.2	0.04	3.8	30.6	46.6	5.2	9.4
11. Total Uttaranchal	**5,595.9**	**3,499.7**	**463.6**	**320.2**	**736.3**	**72.69**	**102.7**	**787.4**	**1,258.9**	**277.84**	**437.05**
12. Uttar Pradesh	29,794.2	5,150.3	3,516.1	945.1	1,753.6	1,066.6	832.6	17,475.0	26,129.0	11,999.0	17,467.2

Source: Uttar Pradesh Department of Agriculture: Statistical Tables Part I and II.

on a limited scale in the State and many more NGOs and people's organisations like MUD and SHG are joining in these efforts.

Agro-forestry can play an immensely important role in the rural economy of the State. The wasteland can be converted to grow plants, fodder and fuel. This would solve the problem of the women who have to go on long, dangerous and arduous treks to collect fodder and fuel wood. In fact an Ex-serviceman, Jagat Singh Chaudhary, from the tiny village of Kot Malla has successfully converted 1.5 hectares of wasteland in the hills of Rudraprayag district of the state. He had planted 56 species of plants—ranging from trees like Manipuri oak and deodar to evergreeen grasses like teliya and namcha, rare medicinal herbs like Salem panja, Kuth, Sameva or tagar, flowers like roses and lilies and climbers like the Barbati bean. Following the success of this experiment a circular has been issued that it should become the model for agro forestry for the whole of the Uttaranchal area.

These efforts have led to growing ecological awareness in the surrounding villages. Farmers have begun cultivating cash crops and pulses, which has resulted in soil conservation and also enhanced family income. It has also inspired the farmers to grow fruits and flowers on a small scale and engage in apiculture. The villagers seem to have a sense of belonging with the forest. The eco-friendly system of agriculture is based on use of only natural manure and compost. The farmers will be better off if they shift from monoculture farming to a mixed or inter-cropping system. They should adopt alternatives activities like bee-keeping and rabbit farming and also grow new crops and plants such as bamboo and tea to set up forest on community lands. There is an urgent need to undertake tree farming and planting.

Horticultural Crops

Fruits and vegetables make a valuable contribution to the economy of the state, although these are grown on a limited area. For Uttaranchal the information on area and production is available only for apple, citrus and litchi among fruits and for onion, green peas and potato for fresh vegetables. Total area under fruits is estimated at 187 thousand hectares with output estimated at 515, 000 tonnes. The share of the state comes to 5 per cent for area, but only 1.3 per cent of the total all India output. Area under vegetables in the State is over 65 thousand hectares, while production is put at 363 thousand tonnes. The area forms one per cent of the total area in the country, but only 0.5 per cent of total production in India. Table 2.5.3 shows area, production and productivity of selected horticultural crops in Uttaranchal.

2.6

A Framework for Sustainable Food Security

P.L. GAUTAM[1] AND V. SINGH[2]

Himalayan mountains are home to unique farming systems, unique inter- and intra-species diversity in forests, crops, and livestock resources. Local farming cultures are interwoven around this natural diversity. The emerging scenario of dismal state of natural resources, however, threatens food security in the region. Reversal of the current situation and restoration of sustainable livelihood systems and food security, nevertheless, is possible.

Mountains of Uttaranchal, despite ecological degradation, have all the essentials for acquiring a state of sustainability. Natural biodiversity of this region is exceptionally rich and is one of the most important common property resources (CPRs) and a foundation for sustainability and food security. In the remote and marginal mountain areas characterised by an overwhelming feature of CPRs—mainly the forests and grasslands—sustainability cannot be operationalised without an efficient management of biodiversity. Biodiversity in the region still reins both in the farmlands and commons and it could be the greatest source for socio-economic and cultural renaissance of the highland dwellers.

The recently carved out mountainous State of Uttaranchal is the central part of the Himalayan mountains and has everything that could be the best in the entire mountain range. The State now has its own government and needs to evolve a framework based on regional specificities.

1. Vice Chancellor, GBPUA & T, Pant Nagar, Uttaranchal.
2. Professor, Department of Animal Science, College of Agriculture, GBPUA & T, Pant Nagar.

Biodiversity in the Mountains: A Panorama

Mountain areas represent an extreme degree of biodiversity, which is a function of interactions of different factors such as elevation, altitude, geologic and edaphic conditions, steepness and orientation of slope, wind and precipitation, mountain mass and relief of terrain (Troll, 1988). Marginality, inaccessibility, and fragility are the negative attributes associated with the mountain areas. This leads to the impression that this region's contribution to the overall economy would be non-significant. Biodiversity, ecological niches, and human adaptation mechanisms inextricably linked with the mountain agriculture (Jodha, 1990) are the positive attributes indicative of a very high potential the mountain areas offer for the local, national, and global economies.

Performance of the mountain farming systems is influenced enormously by the degree of biodiversity stocked in the forest ecosystems under the domain of CPRs. All the nutrients contained in forest biomass used as fodder flow into farmland via livestock and thus serve to enhance/maintain soil fertility, one of the basic principles of agricultural sustainability.

Mountain farming systems exhibit varying degree of diversity even within short distances. This is because of microclimatic variability in the Himalayan Mountains attributable to altitude, slope orientation, temperature, humidity, rainfall, water sources, and distance from the snowline (or from the plains).

The specific ecological niche vital for specific botanical composition, cropping patterns, and for specific activities and products characterises farming situations. For example, valleys in the Outer Himalayan areas are especially used for growing corn and wheat while these flatlands in the Lesser Himalayas are used for rice and wheat cultivation. Irrigation facilities due to availability of water bodies lead to a change in cropping pattern and genetic diversity in the farms. Irrigated valleys are generally used for cultivating fewer crops of high yielding varieties (HYVs). North direction of a mountain slope receives sunlight for shorter duration as compared to a south-directed slope, making the former direction much colder than the latter. Hence, direction of the slope also becomes important for cropping patterns in the farmland and vegetation type in the forest. Generally sturdy, drought-tolerant crops and their different varieties are cultivated on drier and warmer south-directed slopes. Alpine pastures in the Greater Himalayas just adjacent to snowline are used for transhumant pastoralism and for raising some medicinal and aromatic plants and some rare crops, like naked barley.

Traditionally, four cropping systems are maintained in the Lesser Himalayan areas. These are: (i) homestead-based cropping system in which seasonal vegetables and some fruits are grown exclusively for home consumption; (ii) irrigated land cropping system in which rice and wheat are the main crops; (iii) upland or unirrigated cropping system, dominantly occupied by a variety of millets and pulses; and (iv) summer camp cropping system, commonly devoted to pseudo cereals (e.g., amaranth and buckwheat) and beans (mainly kidney beans).

The diverse cropping systems have been designed and managed by local farmers in tune with varying micro-ecological niches suited to the cultivation of specific crops and crop combinations.

An enormous diversity of plants, both cultivated and wild, offering edible products, is one of the most outstanding features of the mountain flora. Farmers' interactions with plants, animals and their environment and their protection, selection, domestication and cultivation of native plants, introducing and improving exotic plants have all given rise to an enormous genetic diversity in the mountain environments. The crop plant genetic resources of the world can be more or less assigned to the specific centres of diversity identified by Vavilov (1951) on the basis of varietal diversity, homologous variation, endemism, dominant allele frequencies, and disease resistance (Khoshoo (1996). In India, there are eight sub-centres, namely, (i) Western Himalayas, (ii) Eastern Himalayas, (iii) North Eastern Region, (iv) Gangetic Plains, (v) Indus Plains, (vi) Western Ghats, (vii) Eastern Ghats, and (viii) Andaman and Nicobar (Arora and Nayar, 1984). The first three of these fall in the Himalayan belt. There are around 399 species of wild relatives of crop plants belonging to 90 genera in the Western, Eastern, and North-Eastern Himalayas. The Himalayan Region has especially been the source of several cereals, pulses, fruits, oil-yielding plants, spices, tuberous vegetables, and sugar-yielding plants and their close relatives that number 155 (Arora and Nayar, 1984). A list of wild relatives of economic plants in the Himalayan Region is given in Table 2.6.1.

Biodiversity and Sustainability

Agro-ecosystems with many different niches occupied by many different kinds of species—in other words, with a high degree of biodiversity—are likely to be more stable than those with only one species (as in

Table 2.6.1: Wild Relatives of Economic Plants in the Indian Himalayan Region

A. North-West and Northern Himalayas	
Cereals and Millets	*Aegilops tauschii, Avena barbeata, A. fatua var. fatua, A. ludoviciana, Digitaria sanguinalis, Elymus dalutricus, E. dasystachys, E. nutans, E. distans, E. orientale, Hordeum glaucum, H. spontaneum, H. turkestanicum, Penisetum orientale.*
Legumes	*Cicer microphyllum, Lathyrus aphaca, Moghania vestita, mucuna capitata, Trigonella emodi, Vigna capensis, V. radiata var. sublobata, V. umbellata.*
Fruits	*Elaeagnus hortensis, Ficus palmate, fragaria indica, Morus spp., Prunus acuminata, P. cerasoides, P. cornuta, P. napalensis, P. prostrata, P. tomentasa, Pyrus buccata, P. communis, P. kumaoni, P. pashia, Ribes glaciale, R. nigrum, Rubus ellipticus, R.fruticosus, R. lanatus, R. lasiocarpus, R. molluccanus, Zizyphus vulgaris.*
Vegetables	*Abelmoschus manihot (tetraphyllus forms), cucumis hardwickii, C. callous, Luffa echinata, L. graveolens, Solanum incanum, S. indicum, Trichosanthes multiloba, T. himalensis.*
Oilseeds	*Lapidium capitatum, L. latifolium, L. draba, L. ruderale.*
Fibres	*Linum perenne.*
Spices and Condiments	*Allium rubellum, A. schoenoprasum, A. tuberosum and other species, Carum bulbocastinum.*
Miscellaneous	*Saccharum filifolium, Miscanthus nepalensis.*
B. Eastern and North-Eastern Himalayas	
Cereals and Millets	*Digitaria cruciata, Hordeum agricrithon.*
Legumes	*Atylosia barbata, A. scarabaeoides, A. villosa, Canavalia ensiformis, Mucuna bractearata, vigna umbellate, V. radiata var. sublobata, V. pilosa.*
Fruits	*Fragaria indica, Morus spp., Myrica esculenta, Prunus acuminata, P. cornuta, P. jenkinsii, P.nepalensis, Pyrus pashia, Ribes glaciale, Rubus lineatus, R. ellipticus, R. lasiocarpus, R. molluccanus, R. reticulates, Citrus assamensis, C. ichangensis, C. indica, D. hookeriana, Eriobotya angustifolia, Mangifera sylvatica, Musa balbisiana complex, M. manii, M. nagensium, M. sikkimensis, M. supreba, M. velutina.*
Vegetables	*Abelmoschus manihot (pungens forms), Luffa graveolens, Neoluffa sikkimensis, Cucumis hystrix, C. callosus, Momordica dioica, M. cochinchinesis, M. macrophyllata, M. subangulata, Trichosanthes cucumerina, T. dioica, T. dioaelosperma, T. khasiana, T. ovata, T. trumcata, Solanum indicum and tubertypes, Allocasia macrorhiza, Amorphophallus bulbifer, Colocasia esculenta, Dioscorea alata, moghania vestica, Vigna capensis.*
Oilseeds	*Brassica trilocularis types.*
Fibres	*Gossypium aboreum (primitive types).*
Spices and Condiments	*Allium tuberosum, A. sublobatum, Curcuma zedoaria, Alpinia galanga, A. speciosa, Amomum aromaticum, Cucuma amoda, Piper peepuloides.*
Miscellaneous	*Saccharum langisetosum, S. sikkimensis, S. ravennae, Erianchus spp., Miscanthus nudipus, M. nepalensis, M. taylorii, Naranga fallax, Camellia* spp.

Source: Arora and Nayar (1984).

monocropping) and thus give the farmers more security (Reijntjes *et al.*, 1992; Singh, 1998b). Functional diversity, achievable through combining complementary plant and animal species in synergetic interactions, injects sustainability into the agro-ecosystems.

Several scholars (e.g., Partap, 1990; Reijntjes *et al.*, 1992; Senanayake, 1993; Singh, 1995, 1998b) have revealed that diversity causes, enhances, or otherwise contributes to ecological stability of a system. In addition to maintaining the quality of the resource base, the biodiversity contributes to enhance the vitality of the entire agro-ecosystem which is best ensured when the soil is well managed and health of the plants, animals, and people is maintained through biological processes (Reijntjes *et al.*, 1992). Biodiversity provides a base for ecologically sound and environmentally safe agriculture.

Farming systems' management practices involve the use of an ecosystem's produce as a subsidy for the other component (e.g., forest biomass is used as livestock feed and manure for cropland). Biodiversity thus helps strengthen linkages between and within various components of a farming system. This contribution is vital for maintaining ecological integrity of the whole system.

The natural ecosystems endowed with biodiversity are extremely resilient (Quinney, 1984). So are the agro-ecosystems harbouring enormous biodiversity. Whereas poor accessibility, fragility, and marginality characteristics of the mountains correlate negatively with the resilience, the biodiversity, ecological niches, and human adaptation mechanisms are the positive attributes to resilience against any type of physical or biotic turbulences to the system.

Monocultures generally use very high level of costly external inputs and, therefore, their energetic efficiency is very poor. Biodiversity-based systems developed through the application of internally flowing nutrients and renewable energy sources and with only very little or no use of external inputs have uniquely high energy efficiency.

Biodiversity creates barriers against any natural calamity (drought, for example) and pest epidemics. Some living organisms may be host for certain insects or diseases, some may be little more prone to weather extremes or other adverse conditions, but a complex mix of naturally occurring (in natural forest areas) organisms will do away any chances of widespread loss to the farmers. Farmers in Uttaranchal cultivate many-many different varieties for different purposes (productivity, drought resistance, taste, colour, nutritive value, rituals, etc.) and in doing so they enhance the degree of their security. Simple, less complex ecosystems and monocultures are extremely prone to various kinds of damaging agents and hence threaten the security of farmers.

Sustainable Food Security: A Framework

Potential Sources

The Community-based Farming

Agricultural systems in the Uttaranchal mountains are community-based. Only cropland and livestock are the private property resources (PPRs) and the remaining components, e.g., forests, grasslands, water bodies, and biodiversity (including traditional seeds) are the CPRs in terms of community ownership, access, and/or rights provided. This community-based structure in Uttaranchal (also in other States of the Indian Himalayas, and in parts of the plains, like deserts) is a rare feature, which has now vanished from most of the regions of the world. This is the most crucial system evolved by local communities in which all people living in an eco-zone participated with a common wisdom, in complete harmony, and in symbiotic relationship with nature and amongst themselves. A community-based production system promotes cohesion and peace amongst people and avoids any chances of excessive and irrational extraction of resources, thus maintaining the natural resource base in a state of ecological regeneration. This system operates with high ethical and aesthetic values aimed at the primacy of conservation and biodiversity-enhancement.

A well-knit, cohesive, and sensitive farming community, as the one in Uttaranchal mountains, can effectively handle an adverse situation or a crisis that could eclipse the quality of life, by using a common wisdom, building social institutions, applying social sanctions, adopting viable alternatives, and using collective labour. Individual approach is seldom successful and if it ever is, it is hardly sustainable or in the larger interest of the community. Community approach to respond to a crisis, on the other hand, is always foolproof sustainable, and is linked with holistic welfare. Community-led programmes often translate into succession movements, new philosophies, renaissance, and revolutions. *Community-based farming structures as in Uttaranchal must, therefore, be kept intact and further promoted.*

The Common Property Resources (CPR)

Biophysical resource base—land, soil, water sources, forest ecosystems—are basic to the sustainability of the food production in the mountains.

Forest-cropland ratio must be as large enough as possible (forest area, in order to provide a sound ecological balance, must be at least five times larger than the cropland area). Forest ecosystems infuse vitality in the whole food production system by maintaining strong organic linkages amongst livestock, cropland, and human beings. Living soil, one of the bases for sustainable agriculture, is the product of forest ecosystems. Continuous biomass flow from the forest (bedding material in animal sheds, fodder, and mulch material, for example) enriches the soil ecosystem, a process that supports biodiversity and manifests into crop production. Water sources are also a product of the forests. Flow of water within a farming system is vital for the sustenance of all forms of life. Availability of water in the system also ensures higher level of food production.

This diversity of the farming systems that exists in the mountains to this day must be conserved. An adequate forest-cropland ratio exists in Uttaranchal. Any expansion in the area of cropland at the expense of forests would only disturb the balance. Actually, an increase in cropland area becomes necessary when cropland is the only target of food production. Improving the condition of the forests in the area, however, would result in increased productivity of the cropland through increased flow of fodder biomass and water/moisture. Forest areas in the mountains are also a source of high quality food. These uncultivated areas, in fact, have potential to provide more quality food per unit area on sustained basis than the cultivated land. People in the mountains have been extracting food (edible fruits, flowers, buds, seeds, vegetables, mushrooms, honey, etc.) from the forests for centuries. For the management of uncultivated areas for food, CPRs should also be taken into consideration.

CPRs are often appreciated for their contribution to the community of fuel, fodder, and timber. That they can provide the most basic necessity of humans, i.e., a variety of food items, is seldom appreciated. Vital role of uncultivated forest areas for providing different food items to the community is evident from the example of the *Henwal Valley of Garhwal in Uttaranchal Mountains* (see Table 2.6.2). In this Valley as many as 189 different naturally occurring species of plants offer edible products while people cultivate only 92 different food-producing plants on their cultivated land. Comparing this scenario with that of the plains' agriculture in the adjoining areas of the Garhwal mountains, we would find that farmers depend only on 33 plant species for their survival. Thus, from the point of view of plant species *diversity offering food articles, CPRs are the richest sources* (Table 2.6.2).

Table 2.6.2: Number of Plant Species Providing Food in the Mountain Ecosystems and the Plains' Agriculture

Food Item	*Mountain Ecosystems**		*Plains' Agriculture***
	CPRs	Cropland	
Fruits	24	18	6
Vegetables	14	32	10
Cereals, Millets & Pseudocereals	–	12	4
Pulses	–	10	5
Oilseeds	–	7	4
Medicinal & Aromatic Plants	99	4	–
Fodder***	52	9	–

* Figures are based on a survey of Henwal Valley in the Garhwal area of the Uttaranchal Mountains.

** Figures are based on a survey of the plains adjoining Garhwal.

*** Livestock convert this forest biomass into human food, e.g., milk.

Source: Singh (2000).

Plantation of food-yielding trees, shrubs and herbs in the CPR areas would enhance biodiversity and the ecological stability of the farming system along with the food security of the community depending on them. Food products obtainable from trees are generally more palatable and of higher nutritive value than those provided by cultivated crops. Moreover, unlike the food grains and vegetables to come from the cultivated land, the variety of food occurring in the CPRs does not require cooking or any other processing.

The Superb Landraces

Himalayan mountains are a home to a number of landraces. Each landrace embraces unique characteristics. Specific ecological niches allow specific landraces to flourish with their superb traits. These landraces are the products of mountain farmers' continuous selection, breeding, experimentation, and on-farm conservation. Rice once was known for its very special landraces, which could grow up to an altitude of 2000 metres in the Himalayan Mountains. Himalayan valleys of Uttaranchal are especially famous for a variety of rice landraces, each with specific traits. Traditional rice varieties, like *Hansraj, Ramjawan, Kanguri, Bangway, Gòrakhpuri, Basmati, Thapachini, Jhumkya,* etc., thrive in lowland valley areas, while *Chawaria, Munjil, Jhailda, Lekmal, Kallao, Almunji, Chwatu,* etc., grow well in upland rainfed areas and at high altitudes. Some landraces can be grown even close to glaciers. Some landraces demand more water, some less, and some need no irrigation at all. Productivity of rainfed varieties is comparable with those of irrigated ones.

Table 2.6.3: Performance of Some Landraces of Rice in a Village of Uttaranchal

Name of Landraces/ HYVs	*Production, q per ha*		*Straw-Grain Ratio*	*Plant Height, cm*	*Days of Maturity*
	Grain	*Straw*			
Landraces					
Thapachini	54.00	96.00	1.8	140	140
Khushboo	49.00	80.00	1.6	125	145
Kali Mukhri	46.00	80.00	1.7	122	145
Agaria	49.00	78.00	1.6	125	145
Kanguri	38.00	54.00	1.4	115	120
Lalmati	45.00	64.00	1.4	120	140
Rikhwa	43.00	64.00	1.5	125	130
Jhumkya	50.00	80.00	1.6	130	140
Basmati Nagni	45.00	88.00	2.0	135	150
Utauli	36.00	64.00	1.8	118	145
Bangoi	40.00	65.00	1.6	125	140
Congressi	45.00	104.00	2.3	126	145
Anjana	29.00	48.00	1.7	125	145
Gajraj	33.00	48.00	1.5	126	150
Ghyasu	37.00	72.00	1.9	135	150
Lathmar	47.00	65.00	1.4	115	150
Rekhlya	43.00	70.00	1.6	120	140
Gorakhpuri	36.00	65.00	1.8	135	120
Hansraj	33.00	75.00	2.3	130	160
Bhagwandas	33.00	58.00	1.8	125	135
Nyuri	35.00	60.00	1.7	110	120
Palyopar	36.00	66.00	1.8	120	140
Basmati Doon	32.00	55.00	1.7	125	150
Nailchamya	43.00	72.00	1.7	120	145
Chawarya	32.00	60.00	1.9	122	135
Luakat	37.00	60.00	1.6	130	145

Note: Landraces were grown at the farm of a farmer in Jardhargaon. Organic manure was applied in all the plots at the rate of 250 q per ha.

Source: Singh and Jardhari (2001).

All Himalayan landraces are known for their characteristic size; the shape and size of the ear; colour, shape and size of seeds; palatability; aroma; cooking quality; medicinal value; etc. They also exhibit unique characteristics of drought-tolerance and resistance against diseases and pest infestation. Many of the landraces provide quite high grain and fodder yields (Table 2.6.3) and they have high acceptability amongst mountain farmers.

Landraces capable of thriving in harsh environments do not only satisfy people's hunger and contribute to food security, but they are also used in many rituals. All through the history of Indian civilization, these landraces have been used as potent symbols of religion and culture. These can heal the environment otherwise deteriorated due to insatiable requirements of chemical fertilizers and synthetic pesticides by the HYVs. The use of such chemicals has not only severely affected human health, but has also disturbed nature's food chain, threatening the delicate ecological balance. The landraces, indeed, can be used as a warrant for the arrest of hunger and malnutrition. And with them as an indispensable component of biodiversity-centred farming practices in the mountains, we can usher in a new era of agroecological renaissance.

Himalayan Waters

Himalayas are water towers for humankind. Uttaranchal mountains are especially rich in their water resources. This area is home to dozens of perennial streams and numerous other rainfed rivers along with innumerable rivulets, waterfalls, and ponds, etc. India's largest river system—the Ganga River System—also takes its origin in the Uttaranchal mountains. In Garhwal Himalayas, the largest glacier Gangotri, the origin of the river Ganga, has an estimated volume of well over 20 km^3 of ice, which is much more than even the maximum capacity of storage created by the Bhakra Dam on Sutlej, which is less than eight km (Sehgal, 1995). This glacier, unfortunately, now continues to recede. Apart from these streams and rivers, there are several lakes in the area as also the perpetual ice fields and glaciers.

However, due to maldevelopment, mismanagement, and continuous neglect, the Himalayas' aquatic resources are in hot waters. Dry spell can be witnessed all over especially in the summer season. In the land of plentiful water, most of the villages are suffering from the lack of drinking water. Majority of the people do not have easy access to potable water. Only some 10 per cent of the arable land is irrigated, and the rest 90 per cent depends on rain.

Uttaranchal's glacier-fed rivers are being seen only as a potential source of hydropower. Ruthless mismanagement of Himalayan waters might trigger potentially negative consequences not only in Uttaranchal, but also in the entire Indo-Gangetic Valley. Aquatic ecology in the mountains, on the whole, is in a bad state, affecting the integrity of the entire food production system.

All the water bodies in the mountains can be managed as a potential source of food production. The mountain water sources harbour a variety of food sources; fisheries and aquatic food plants being the most important. Water also has tremendous bearing on all components of the food production system. Water, in fact, is the most important element in the ecological integrity of a farming system. Its very wise use and conservation-based management is vital for sustainable food security in the mountains.

The Livestock Resources

Livestock form the core of livelihood systems of livestock-dependent mountain communities. They are not just an economic source, but are farmers' best companions serving them as manure providers, exploiters of wastes, sources of power, forms of investments, and in many more ways. They form a cultural identity of mountain people. By transferring nutrients from forest ecosystem to farmlands and maintaining cyclic flow pattern in the farming system, they contribute to the ecological integrity of the system (Singh, 1998a; Tulachan, 1998; Tulachan and Neupane, 1999; Singh *et al.*, 2001).

Many non-descript dairy animal breeds found in the region may excel the so called high-yielding crossbreeds or exotics, particularly in respect of some traits, like energetic efficiency, adaptability to the specific environment, feed conversion efficiency, resistance against certain diseases, draught ability, and the likes (Singh, 1998a). An economic valuation and description of the largely non-descript Hill breeds will contribute to conservation and further upgradation and development of the unique animal genetic resources in the region.

Traditionally, the Uttaranchal mountains are a region of milk-drinking culture. Plentiful availability of dairy products in this region has always been regarded as an indicator of a society's health, happiness, and prosperity. Small holder dairy holds great promises as one of the most acceptable land-based economic activities. Thanks to the contribution of small holder dairy farming that milk production, consumption, and economic returns from sale of milk have steadily increased over last few years (Singh *et al.*, 2001).

Cows and buffaloes are the only two recognised dairy species in

Uttaranchal. However, small holders and transhumant pastoralists in the high mountain areas own an overwhelmingly large number of goats and sheep. These are seldom used for dairy production. Some selective breeds of these that could be used primarily for dairy purpose need to be identified. Introduction of well-known dairy goat breed of Uttar Pradesh, *Jamnapari*, could contribute to milk production in the area.

Ecological Regeneration of CPRs

CPR areas, due to neglect and reckless exploitation, have undergone considerable ecological degradation in recent years. Ecological regeneration and enrichment of biodiversity of these areas will have enormous bearing on sustainability and food security in Uttaranchal mountains. Plentiful biomass harvests, especially of fodder and fuel wood from the CPRs, will strengthen organic linkages among the components of farming system, infusing health into the whole system. Cropping systems are more fragile than forest ecosystems. If there is crop failure due to an erratic weather cycle, for example, CPRs can fill much of the requirement of food. They also ease pressure on croplands. In their absence, more and more areas would have to be cultivated, which would be at the expense of the ecological balance in the region.

Efficient management controlling overexploitation through overgrazing and illegal felling would be a precondition to trigger the process of ecological regeneration. Large-scale plantation of trees, shrubs, and herbaceous species would accelerate the regenerative processes. Only site-specific vegetation must be allowed to re-grow. Climatic climax vegetation (*Quercus leucotrichophora* in the Middle or Lesser Himalayas, for example) must be in the first place, for this helps maintain the specific microclimate of the region. Monocultures of coniferous trees, mostly of *Pinus roxburghii*, are the most common scenarios of the CPR regimes in the mountains. This management also has negative implications on the performance of agroecosystems. Such areas must be developed into hetero-cultures of site-specific, soil-binding, and water-conserving indigenous plant species.

Institutional Intervention

Our current approach of agricultural production in Uttaranchal is just aimed at the quantitative flow of consumables. Natural resource base on which the very sustainability of agriculture and food security depends is being given less importance in our institutional policies and programmes. In a farming system, all elements and linkages amongst them are crucial for sustaining the performance (and increasing the out put whenever required) of food production. Our food production approach must focus on the farming system, rather than just on the commodity that has direct market value.

Protection of community's ownership on CPRs and people's participation in resource management must be ensured. Use of raw material extractable from the resource base under CPR regime has always been regulated through social sanctions in mountain areas. This system ensures protection and conservation-oriented management of natural resources.

Mountains' biodiversity is the most precious life-sustaining resource. A policy relating to its protection, *in situ* and on-farm conservation, and sustainable utilisation will be instrumental for food security. Revaluation of genetic resources—such as unique landraces and livestock breeds—will help their protection and conservation and continued development. There should be a concrete animal breeding policy that must ensure the conservation of mountains' unique hardy, adapted, terrace-negotiating, disease-resistant, energy-efficient, and multipurpose animal breeds.

Mountain agriculture should be valued against the quality of the diverse genetic resources in terms of the socio-culturally most desirable traits such as their palatability, nutritive value, medicinal value, religious value, hardiness, sturdiness, ecological services, and the likes. A Community Biodiversity Register with every *Gramsabha* will help understand the great measure of the valuable biological resources available for community welfare in an area.

A large number of Government and Non-Government organizations, voluntary agencies, *Mahila Mangal Dals*, *Yuva Mangal Dals*, apart from Village *Panchayats* are functioning in Uttaranchal mountains. All these bodies, despite differences in their opinion, have a great vigour to change the whole scenario. These can, and they should, work together for achieving the goal of food security in the area. A lack of coordination amongst them, however, often hampers attempts of a committed organisation by the other. There is an urgent need to promote coordination and harmony amongst the socio-cultural institutions that are the powerful engines of any desirable change leading to a state of sustainability in agriculture and food security.

The biodiversity and unique ecological niches of Uttaranchal and other Himalayan States could be pivotal in economic development and welfare of the mainstream areas, the plains. However, mountains have to have what is rightfully theirs. In the mainstream market system, they must get a fair deal. There must be an economic valuation of the Himalayan biodiversity in the context of global norms. Prices of varieties/ products of this biodiversity must be evaluated based on their direct values (consumptive use value, productive use value, etc.) and indirect values (non-consumptive use value, e.g., scientific research, recreation, etc., option value, e.g., value of maintaining options available for the future, and existence value, e.g., value of ethical feeling of existence of nature, etc.).

Institutional systems must learn to recognize, encourage, facilitate, and promote farmers' traditional strategies, innovations, and socio-cultural movements that invariably contribute to biodiversity enhancement, sustainability and food security.

References

Arora, R.K. and Nayar, E.R. 1984. *Wild Relatives of Crop Plants in India*. New Delhi: National Bureau of Plant Genetic Resources (NBPGR).

Jodha, N.S. 1990. *Mountain Agriculture: Search for Sustainability*. Mountain Farming Systems Discussion Paper No. 2. Kathmandu: ICIMOD.

Khoshoo, T.N. 1996. Biodiversity in Indian Himalayas: Conservation and Utilisation. In Pei Shengji (ed.) *Banking on Biodiversity*, 185-255. Kathmandu: ICIMOD.

Partap, T. 1990. Biological Diversity of Genetic Resources: Some Issues for Sustainable Mountain Agriculture. Paper presented at the *International Symposium on Strategies for Sustainable Mountain Agriculture* at ICIMOD, Kathmandu, September 10-14, 1990.

Quinney, J. 1984. Designing Small Sustainable Farms. *The Mother Earth News*, July-August 1984.

Reijntjes, C. B. Haverkort; and Waters-Bayer. 1992. *Farming for Future: An Introduction to Low-External-Input and Sustainable Agriculture*. Leusden: Macmillan and ILEIA.

Sehgal, K.L. 1995. Aquatic Resources of North-Western Himalaya. In Singh, V.; Sharma, R.J.; and Kumar, A. (eds.) *Ecological Carnage in the Himalaya*, 35-47. Dehradun: IBD.

Senanayake, R. 1993. There is a Link Between Biodiversity and Sustainability. *Ecoforum*, 17 (3), June 1993.

Singh, V. 1995. Biodiversity and Farmers in Mountain Agriculture: Experiences from Garhwal Himalaya. Paper presented at the *Beijer Seminar* held in Kota Kinabalu, Sabah, Malaysia from May 15-19, 1995.

Singh V. 1998a. *Draught Animal Power in Mountain Agriculture: A Study of*

Perspectives and Issues in Central Himalayas, India. Mountain Farming Systems Discussion Paper No. 98/1. Kathmandu: ICIMOD.

Singh, V. 1998b. Traditional Biodiversity Management Strategies in the Mountains: Farmers' Experimentation in Garhwal Himalaya. In Singh, V. and Sharma, M.L. (eds) *Mountain Ecosystems: A Scenario of Unsustainability*. New Delhi: Indus, 25-66.

Singh, 2000. Biodiversity: A Key Issue for Commons' Management in the Himalayan Region. In Marothia, D. (ed.) *Institutionalising Common Pool Resources*, 519-530. New Delhi: Concept.

Singh, V. and V. Jardhari, 2001. Landrace Renaissance in the Mountains: Experiences of the *Beej Bachao Andolan* in the Garhwal Himalayan Region, India. *An Exchange of Experiences from South and South East Asia: Proceedings of the International Symposium on Participatory Plant Breeding and Participatory Plant Genetic Resource Enhancement*, 87-96. Cali, Columbia: PRGA, IDRC, DFID, DDS, LI-BIRD, IPGRI, and ICARDA.

Singh, V.; P.M. Tulachan; and T. Partap 2001. Small holder Dairy Farms in the Mixed Mountain Farming Systems: A Case of Uttaranchal Hills, *Indian Journal of Animal Sciences*, 71 (10): 975-984.

Troll, Carl. 1988. Comparative Geography of High Mountains of the World in View of Land Scale Ecology: A Development of Three and a Half Decade of Research and Organisation. In Allan, N.J.R.; G.W. Knapp, and C. Stadel (eds.) *Human Impacts on Mountains*, New Jersey: Rowman & Littlefield.

Tulachan, P.M. 1998. *Livestock Development in Mixed Crop Farming Systems: Lessons and Research Priorities*. Issues in Mountain Development 98/5. Kathmandu: ICIMOD.

Tulachan, P.M.; and A. Neupane, 1999. *Livestock in Mixed Farming Systems of the Hindu Kush-Himalayas: Trends and Sustainability*. Kathmandu: ICIMOD & FAO.

Vavilov, N.I. 1951. The Origin, Variation, Immunity and Breeding of Cultivated Plants. *Chronica Botanica* 13: 1-364.

2.7

Concerns and Challenges

SONALI BISHT*

The formation of the new state of Uttaranchal has been the culmination of the hopes, dreams, and aspirations of the people living in the hill regions of the parent state of Uttar Pradesh. There has been fervent hope in the face of the increasingly difficult conditions of life and the push and pull to migrate, that life can be made worth living if mountain centred and mountain people oriented policies are made and decisions taken. The Terai regions of Uttaranchal and some of the plain areas are well endowed and part of mainstream development. Hence we will take into account here the concerns and challenges for a better life for people living in the hills and mountains which constitute the major part of Uttaranchal. Better life for the people of Uttaranchal is also the reason for the creation of Uttaranchal.

Hilly and mountainous topography dominates the landscape of Uttaranchal. Topography will always remain the greatest asset and the most challenging factor in the development of Uttaranchal. The difficult topography of Uttaranchal has been and will be a factor in infrastructure development and the cost of infrastructure development. Infrastructure development for transportation, communication, health, education and livelihood creation sets the foundation for an improved quality of life of the inhabitants. This is essential to give people the means to lead an active, healthy and fulfilling life in their own environs.

Concerns

The linkages between rural and urban areas are critical in the development of any region. The neglect of the villages and the rural areas in our

* INHERE, Almora.

country have lead to a spate of migration to the bigger towns and cities in which there is more investment and a spiral of growth in employment opportunities and incomes. It has also lead to mushrooming of slums with appalling conditions of life for those forced to live there. The hills and mountain regions of Uttaranchal are now also faced with a forced and dangerous urbanisation. Given the topography of the region, urbanisation has not been a natural phenomenon and the region can ill afford it.

The small towns of the region historically were either capitals of the erstwhile kingdoms and later hill stations created by the British to beat the heat of summer in the plains. After independence the district headquarters have bloated into ugly urban entities with tehsil headquarters and block headquarters following suit. Concentration of government offices, banks, roads, transport, communication, market, medical and educational infrastructure along with electricity and drinking water facilities in centres of administration with a sizeable number of government officials has been responsible for this.

The inhabitants of the hill regions are by nature conservationists with a good understanding of what is scarce and what is abundant in nature and how to use it. In an area of steep, hilly topography the flatlands of the valleys have long been cherished and protected. No house building took place in the rich, fertile valley lands which were carefully irrigated by a network of traditional irrigation canals called *guhls* which used the force of gravity to irrigate the fields. The *guhls* brought water from many kilometres and villages away using the gradient of rivers and streams. The *guhls* were carefully maintained by the beneficiaries for centuries till their rights and responsibilities were taken away by the minor irrigation department of the state government. The valleys have always been the small granaries spread across Uttaranchal which provided food security for the inhabitants. These granaries are now under threat from the government led urbanisation which sees them only as flat land for more buildings, institutions and amenities.

The valleys and flatlands where the administrative centres have been established consist of privately owned small plots of land which are highly fragmented in ownership. This means haphazard urbanisation with houses and buildings being built wherever land comes up for sale. Total absence of any tradition and hence knowledge of urban planning and the transitory nature of posting and stay of government officials has led to the emergence of small towns which are chaotic in nature and bereft of any sewage, sanitation or solid waste management and disposal facility.

The concentration of infrastructure and facilities in haphazardly growing urban areas which are also on the major arterial roads is leading to abandonment of homes in villages and shifting to the roadsides. Traveling across Uttaranchal everywhere one sees homes being built on the edges of the roads in clear violation of rules. This leads to children playing on the roads and its attendant dangers. It is also leading to the breaking up of the once cohesive village community and the growth of individualism. It is reflective of the growing class divide in a society which was homogeneous and lived in interdependency and harmony.

The houses and buildings built are themselves eyesores being a mindless imitation of basic houses in the slums and poor localities of the plains. The ban on stone quarrying, taking sand from the rivers and mining for slate as well as the difficulty in obtaining in obtaining timber have deprived the inhabitants of what were traditionally the basic building materials. With access to these materials and cooperation of the village any family, rich or poor could have a good quality home to live in. Now only the very well off can have new homes for which materials as well as labour are brought from the plains.

Environmental legislations have slowly but surely taken away traditional livelihoods of vast numbers. The wood carvers of Kumaon whose handiwork can be seen in all the traditional houses have disappeared with the years of ban on the tun tree which was used for carving. The nomadic sheep and goat rearers are a slowly but surely dying breed. The wool has to be brought from Ludhiana. The weavers find it difficult to compete with the machine made goods abundantly stocked in permanent markets and shops all over Uttaranchal. Agriculture is back breaking and does not yield enough for subsistence. The males are forced to migrate making life even more difficult for the families left behind. The new jobs and opportunities created are concentrated in the few urban areas which are also administrative centres. These jobs often need knowledge, skills and capital difficult for a local person who has no opportunities to obtain these.

Challenges

The major challenges before Uttaranchal are promotion of livelihoods to retain people through local employment and income generation and to enhance the quality of life of the people living in the villages. The opportunity to meet these challenges has been given history. The direction Uttaranchal takes and the road it makes will determine the destiny of this young state with a strong base of traditional wisdom which can be enhanced through the application of modern knowledge. Ultimately the yardstick has to be the quality of life and the quantum of satisfaction of its inhabitants.

Livelihood

The greatest challenge before the state of Uttaranchal is of ensuring livelihoods and livelihood security for all persons in the working age group. Thus no resource which can provide a recurring basis for livelihood or sustainable livelihoods should be allowed to be wasted. As Uttaranchal lives in the villages and the most potentially productive resource which can provide livelihood to the vast majority of the population is land, whether agriculture and/or forest land, land development activity should be the foremost investment. The land in Uttaranchal has been the most neglected resource and has suffered decades of abuse and degradation with half-hearted showcase attempts at improvement. We need to seriously and strictly apply and enforce the application of sound land and water improvement and conservation measures. Rational bunding on terraced fields should be made compulsory to check precious topsoil from flowing away with every rain. Bunding will also conserve soil moisture. Soil and water conservation with a watershed approach is very much needed in all lands, private, community or government to improve productivity of the land and to sustain it.

Good seeds suited to hill agriculture must be developed and made widely available. The soils and topography of Uttaranchal will not allow monocropping. This must be clearly recognised and accepted. Diversified agriculture is needed in Uttaranchal with a healthy mix of animal husbandry through cattle rearing, poultry, fishing, bee keeping etc., as per opportunity. In each of these areas emphasis should be on quality and sustained returns. We need to reduce our cattle population and increase its quality. Animal husbandry will always be important in the hills for food security as well as maintaining the productivity of the soil. In this context it is important to experiment with the spread the usage of technologies for composting organic matter to regularly enrich the soils and increase their depth in this stony and rocky terrain with a shallow soil cover.

Agro-Based Employment

There is a wide scope for agro-based employment through cleaning, grading and packaging of cereals and pulses grown exclusively in the hills for market in the plains. A vast amount of fruit in the hills goes un-harvested or gets perscribed and is sold at very low prices. Skills and support for processing and storing the fruit needs to be provided. Initially marketing support would also be essential. In fact no product should be allowed to be transported out of the hills in its raw state. It should go out semi processed and value added.

Non-Farm Based Livelihoods

The people in Uttaranchal hills are sorely lacking in skills. Opportunities for good quality vocational education are needed in order to provide its youth with non-farm employment. Uttaranchal needs to be able to provide its youth with employment and its people with a range of services in plumbing, carpentry, masonry work, repair of small machines, as well as technicians in electrical and electronics. A vast range of goods and services are available which are needed by the people but cannot be maintained due to lack of an adequate service sector. This vast potential needs to be tapped.

Livelihood Security

Livelihood security needs to be secured through promotion of the banking sector and the insurance sector. At present these are very poorly developed and confined to urban areas. Promotion and development of self-help groups can also give a measure of livelihood security and support in times of emergency. Banks and the government also need to play a supporting.

Village Access to Amenities

The investment in land and land based activities will not yield any result until the people can be retained in the villages. This means making the villages attractive places to live in. The villagers must have access to dependable and adequate source of safe drinking water, secure livelihood, a back up system for emergencies, access to good quality education for their children and vocational training for the young adults. They must have good communication facilities through telephone and internet in their village and access to transport facilities within a reasonable distance. Medical help must be easily available especially in times of emergencies. A mobile health care system which is available on call in time of emergency would be a great help. Some of the facilities will require state help while other can be created through community participation and organisation and entrepreneurship.

Maintenance of Infrastructure and Amenities

The maintenance of infrastructure and amenities is a big challenge in a mountainous topography. Yet the infrastructure built at a very high cost in challenging terrain also needs to be maintained. Systems need to be built and institutionalised which allow for proper maintenance and upkeep. As far as feasible responsibility for maintenance should be given to the users as they would also have the biggest stake in proper upkeep. In fact the prospective users need to be consulted from the planning stage itself and be involved in implementation for a sense of ownership to develop.

Education

The terrain of Uttaranchal will always limit the nature and scope of land based activities. Information Technology can be a boon for the problems faced by the people due to the difficult terrain and isolated habitations. To take advantage of the revolution in communication good quality education for the children of Uttaranchal is necessary. Education must be suited to the present and future needs of children. Good quality functional education suited to the environment in which the children will live and can be expected to earn their living when they grow up must be made available to every child.

2.8

Evolution of Van Panchayats

REKHA PAI*

Introduction

The concept of people's participation in forest management was discussed at the national level only after the National Forest Policy of 1988 made a mention of it. However, the concept was being practised in various parts of the country in some form or other much before. Existence of *Van Panchayats* in Uttaranchal state is one such example where communities have been involved in the management of forests. This chapter deals in brief about the evolution of *Van Panchayats,* their current status, introduction of new JFM model, and some emerging issues. An attempt has been made to analyse the reasons behind introducing a new model of JFM in an area where a well-established system was already in operation. This chapter has tried to focus on some areas of concern, which need attention to maintain the tempo that has been generated and to consolidate the gains made so far in the area of community forestry. Towards the end, few suggestions have been made for the future course of action.

Uttaranchal, the newly created Himalayan state, has come into existence with effect from November 2000 consequent to the reorganisation of the erstwhile state of Uttar Pradesh. The state has a total geographical area of 53,483 sq. km., which is mainly hilly terrain except the *terai* and *bhabbar* areas. The state is rich in natural resources and has preponderance of forests and biodiversity. The total population is 8.48 million (2001 census) of which, 76.88 per cent is rural and 23.12 per cent is urban. Details of the extent and kind of forest area are given in Table 2.8.1.

* C/o Inspector General of Forests, GOI, New Delhi.

Approximately two-third of the geographical area is recorded as forest area, of which 70 per cent is with the FD and the remaining with the Revenue Department, *Van Panchayats,* and others. These forests are an integral part of the socio-cultural and economic life of the people.

Table 2.8.1: Extent and kind of forest area in Uttaranchal state

	Area sq. km.
Geographical area of Uttaranchal	53,483.00
Population (in million)	8.48
Total forest area	34,661:52
Per capita forest area (hectare)	0.41
Total forest area as percentage of geographical area	64.81
Total forest area under management of the FD	23,988.76
Forest area managed by FD as percentage of geographical area	44.85
Details of forest area managed by FD according to legal status	
Reserved forests	23,826.87
Protected forests	103.79
Unclassed and vested forests	58.16
Other forest area	
Civil and Soyam forest areas with the Revenue Department	6,334.05
Panchayati forest	4,046.58
Private forests	62.36
Municipal forests	59.57
Others	169.20

Source: UPFD 2000.

Van Panchayats

Though the state is of recent origin, the concept of people's involvement in the management of forests is not new to the region. A well-established system of *Van Panchayats* where communities manage resources is unique to the region. It has been in operation for more than seven decades. These forests have the legal backup of the Uttaranchal Panchayati Forest Rules, 2001 (UPFD 2001a). Currently, there are 6,777 *Van Panchayats* managing 5,241 sq. km. area. District-wise details are given in Table 2.8.2.

It will be interesting to go a little into the history of the development of this institution. Before the advent of the British, people had unlimited access to forests. However, in the late nineteenth and early twentieth century, restrictions were imposed on the rights of people as the British undertook management of forests in these areas. There were wide and large-scale protests against these restrictions. This period saw great damage to forests as vast areas were burnt and deforested.

Table 2.8.2: Details of *Van Panchayats*

Name of district	*Number of Van Panchayats*	*Areas of Van Panchayats (sq. km.)*
Nainital	495	280
Almora	1,444	663
Bageshwar	454	343
Pithorgarh	1,046	1,240
Champawat	611	266
Total Kumaon	**4,050**	**2,793**
Chamoli	533	1,402
Dehradun	159	77
Pauri Garhwal	1,633	368
Rudra Prayag	249	166
Tehri	85	429
Uttarkashi	68	7
Total Garhwal	**2,727**	**2,448**
Grand Total	**6,777**	**5,241**

Source: Communication from District Magistrates.

This resulted in giving more freedom for use of forest produce and in certain areas even passing the management of these forest areas to communities. This gave rise to the institution of *Van Panchayats.* The first rules were framed in 1931 under the Schedule District Act, 1874. Subsequently the Van Panchayat Rules were framed in 1972 and then in 1976 under section 28 of the Indian Forest Act, 1927. Recently, these rules were modified and the Uttaranchal Panchayati Forest Rules, 2001 notified.

There are a number of *panchayati* forests, which have been managed in good condition whereas others have not done so well. Factors which helped the satisfactory functioning of *Van Panchayats* include leadership quality of the *sarpanch,* availability of funds, commitment on the part of villagers, proximity of villages to reserved forests, total area and quality of land of panchayati forest. Single-village *Van Panchayats* do much better than multi-village *Panchayats* (Saxena, 1995).

JFM

The Government of India issued a circular dated June 1990 in this regard asking state governments to involve village communities and voluntary agencies in efforts to regenerate degraded forest areas. It was only in 1997 that the erstwhile Uttar Pradesh Government framed the Uttar Pradesh Village Forest Joint Management Rules (VFJMR), 1997 under sub-section (2) of section 28 and section 76 of the Indian Forest Act.

This, combined with the launch of the World Bank Forestry Project in February 1998, in which JFM was conceived as a major intervention tool for process change, gave a real boost to the whole process. Thus, people's involvement in the management of natural resources, which started in the early twentieth century in the region, had its revival towards the end of the century.

The formulation of VFJMR 1997 provided a legal framework for JFM and thus a good start to the programme. However, the implementation of the same posed a great challenge to the FD. Over the years, the FD had developed a working style much different from what was required in the changed scenario. This needed to be changed. Coupled with this, were fear and scepticism in the minds of many whether the system would work or not. Therefore, the implementation of the programme was preceded by a period of preparation both for the people as well as officials. These measures are given in Box 2.8.1.

Box 2.8.1: Some initiatives taken by the FD to prepare all the stakeholders before the start of the JFM programme

- Seminars/workshops/conferences at state/district level to sensitise all levels of department and local communities—two major stakeholders.
- Training in participatory management, communication skills, group interaction for foresters as well as local people.
- Study tours/visits, etc., to successful sites.
- Formation of SHTs (one ACF, one Ranger or Deputy Ranger, two NGOs, one man and one woman).
- Involvement of NGOs through motivators in the SHTs, to act as an interface between the FD and local communities.
- Capacity building within the FD, particularly strengthening and upgrading training institutes, redesigning the course content, and so on.
- Amendment of the charter of the forestry training institute to incorporate training of *Van Panchayat sarpanches,* its members, the forest *Panchayat* inspectors and assistant development officers (Forest).
- Establishment of an autonomous society named Centre for Forestry and Natural Resource Management Development (CFD) in 1998 at the Forestry Training Institute, Haldwani. CFD has played an important role in imparting training to field staff and VFC members since July 1998.

Implementation Strategy

After sufficient ground preparation, the implementation process began. The implementation strategy had the following key elements:

- Site specific planning.
- Transparency.

- Decentralisation.
- Funds to be released directly to the VFCs.
- Creation of the VDF.
- Involvement of women.

- ***Site specific planning***

JFM rules 1997 provided for a three-tier system of village, range and divisional-level committees. The VFC had the most crucial role to play, being responsible for the preparation of the microplan and annual implementation plan. The FD provided technical assistance and guidance in the preparation of the plan whereas NGO motivators played the crucial role of mobilising people, particularly the women, using the PRA approach. The preparation of the microplan and its key elements are given in Box 2.8.2.

Box 2.8.2: Preparation of the microplan in two or three parts

The special features of microplanning include facilitation by the spearhead teams in the microplanning exercise and its division into two or three parts.

- Part one consists of forestry related activities, which can be directly funded by the FD.
- Part two enlists the entry point and other activities, which emerge during the PRA exercise and are related to rural development.
- Some villages also prepare a part three, which plans for the use of VDF created from the contribution of the villagers.

Key elements of the microplan include: (a) Bottom up planning; (b) Complete master plan for all-round development of the village; (c) Decentralisation; (d) Importance to "NTFP; (e) In-built flexibility for changes as the community gains experience; (f) Monitoring at the local level; (g) Poverty alleviation; and (h) Sustainability.

- ***Decentralisation and transparency***

Considered as the pillars in the programme, these two ingredients helped in getting effective participation of all as the element of mistrust was reduced to a minimum. Some of the initiatives that were taken to ensure decentralisation and transparency, are given in Box 2.8.3 and 2.8.4, respectively.

- ***Flow of funds***

Funds are released to the VFC on the basis of the approved microplan and detailed annual plan. All the accounts are required to be maintained by the VFC. As a precaution, the funds are released by the division level committee in two instalments after the microplan is approved. The second installment is released only after 65 per cent of the first instalment has been utilised.

> **Box 2.8.3: Decentralisation under JFM**
>
> - The VFC is a deemed forest officer which can institute and defend suits, make sale of forest produce, regulate grazing and even seize all tools or weapons used in committing forest offences.
> - The community is the body which approves the microplans for JFM. The VFC prepares and implements it.
> - The funds for JFM are released directly to the VFC which has full authority to spend it. The FD and the NGO just play the role of facilitators.

> **Box 2.8.4: Transparency in JFM**
>
> The details of microplans and annual implementation plan are read out and explained in detail in the general body and EC meetings. Details of the microplan and annual implementation plan, works to be done, money released and hames of persons responsible for the execution, are displayed on the walls of public buildings like schools, community centres to ensure transparency. Thus, even if somebody has not attended the meeting of the general body, she will still know what is happening.

• *Involvement of women in JFM*

One of the objectives of the National Forest Policy and JFM is to encourage and ensure active participation of women who are the backbone of the rural economy but have been marginalised in the process of decision making and implementation. In the hill areas particularly, women have a greater responsibility as men migrate to other parts of the country in search of employment. Besides the household chores, women spend a lot of time in collecting fuel and fodder from forests, fetching water, and looking after the cattle. In fact, women are more intimately related to and depend on forests. Therefore, one of the objectives of JFM has been to ensure active and effective participation of village women right from the conceptualisation to the implementation stage. Involvement of NGOs was a great help as female NGO workers could mobilise and initiate a dialogue with the women. Once the women were initiated into the programme, their eagerness to contribute was unbelievable.

• *Creation of the VDF*

This fund is made from money generated during the implementation of JFM on account of (1) savings due to voluntary labour contribution, (2) VFCs share of benefit from forest produce, and (3) fees/fine collected by the VFC. This fund is totally managed by the VFC, and the FD has no control over it. However, the rules do mention that at least 25 per cent of this fund should be spent on maintenance of the forest. The villagers are also being trained to use this fund as a revolving fund for income generation activities. The details of money generated for VDF is given in Table 2.8.3.

Table 2.8.3: Funds generated for VDF from different sources (as on July 2001)

Sl. No.	*Name of Scheme*	*Rs. (million)*
1.	Uttaranchal Forestry Project	18.81
2.	Other schemes	0.05
	Total	18.86

• *Status of JFM*

Table 2.8.4 gives the details of JFM committees constituted under different schemes. The 1,217 committees constituted under the World Bank forestry project are managing an area of about 2,118 sq. km. Of this, *panchayati* forests is approximately 783 sq. km., reserved forests 679 sq. km., civil forests 604 sq. km., and area under other forests 51.75 sq. km. JFM committees are also managing a large chunk of reserved and civil forests besides the *panchayati* forests, and there is no particular area being favoured or kept outside the purview of JFM (except protected area network where eco-development committees are being constituted).

Table 2.8.4: JFM committees constituted under different schemes

Name of the Scheme	*No. of VFC constituted*	*Area (sq. km.)*
World Bank Uttaranchal Forestry Project	1,217*	2,118
IAEP Project	38	179
Eco-committees under World Bank Project	98	–
Eco-committees under other schemes	10	–
Van Panchayat	6,048	4,458
Total	7,411	6,755

* This includes 729 *Van Panchayats* and 488 VFCs under JFM.

Another significant feature is that even in those areas where *Van Panchayats* have opted for JFM rules, the area under management of such VFCs is far beyond the *panchayati* forests that is the original jurisdiction of these *Van Panchayats.* One such example is Almora district where out of 1,444 existing *Van Panchayats,* 162 have opted to be managed under JFM rules. The total area managed by these *Van Panchayats* is 212 sq. km., which includes only 121 sq. km. of *panchayati* forests while the rest 91 sq. km. represents civil and reserved forests.

Unique Features of JFM in Uttaranchal

- Both *Van Panchayats* and VFCs are deemed forest officers which can institute and defend suits, regulate grazing and admission of cattle, and even seize tools, etc., used in committing an offence.
- Uttaranchal Forest Panchayati Rules, 2001 and VFJMR 1997 have been made under section 28 and section 76 of the Indian Forest Act, 1927. Thus, the *Van Panchayats* and village forest committees have legal backup.
- Involvement of NGOs through motivators right from the start of the programme. Each SHT has two motivators, one man and one woman.
- All categories of forest areas, that is reserved, protected and *panchayati* have been covered under the programme.

JFM versus Van Panchayat

From the forgoing it emerges that as far as JFM is concerned, Uttaranchal has a unique scenario. The state has a strong institution of *Van Panchayats,* where communities have been successfully managing the resources. The question is why then was the new model of JFM introduced in the hills, that too in *Van Panchayats.* As stated earlier. *Van Panchayats* are a creation from people's protest against restrictions on their rights. The FD played no significant role in the successful functioning of the *Van Panchayats.* It was the local leadership, basically, which resulted in the successful management of these *Van Panchayats.* Having said that, it is also important to bear in mind that all the *Van Panchayats* did not function well. According to a study conducted by The Energy and Resources Institute (TERI, formerly Tata Energy Research Institute):

- There has been a decline in the frequency of meetings over the years in most of the *Van Panchayats,* which is indicative of the fall in people's interest in the *Van Panchayat* as an institution.
- The *Van Panchayats* in Kumaon remain an exclusive male order, with no representation or participation (exceptions are both negligible as well as nominal) of women in meetings, elections, management committee, decision-making, conflict resolution or in the general functioning of the *Van Panchayats.* The participation of women is confined only to the utilisation and compliance of the existing regulations and norms.

Some of the reasons responsible for the ill health of the *Van Panchayat* are overall neglect by concerned departments, lack of administrative and technical support, paucity of funds, dual control, and lack of sufficient authority (Saxena, 1995).

Thus, there was a situation where the FD was preparing itself to work with local communities. At the same time, the *Van Panchayats,* which had some experience of managing the resources, were not functional. Thus, adoption of JFM in *Van Panchayats* was a step towards developing synergies between the efforts being made by the FD and the *Van Panchayat* in protection and development of forests. At this juncture, it will not be out of context to point out that as per VJFMR 1997, the FD *suo motu* cannot take up any *Van Panchayat* under the JFM programme. According to rule 3(2) of VJFMR "if a *Van Panchayat* by resolution decides that Panchayati forest under its management, be managed in accordance with these rules...the provisions of Uttar Pradesh Panchayati Forest Rules, 1976 shall cease to apply in respect thereof. Thus, it is only when a *Van Panchayat* decides to manage its *panchayati* forests under JFM, can further action be taken by the FD.

Moreover, the area covered under *Van Panchayats* is only 11 per cent of the total area, whereas the FD is responsible for 70 per cent of the forest area. If the FD has to adopt a people-centred approach in imanaging and protecting these areas, then it will have to adopt various options and methods available. JFM is one such approach. Thus, the reasons for adoption of JFM in Uttaranchal may be stated as:

- To provide working space for communities in the management and protection of forests.
- To strengthen existing *Van Panchayats.*

Four hundred and eighty-eight JFM committees (covering an area of only 1,338 sq. km.), which have been constituted outside the *Van Panchayat* areas represent the real increase in the working space for local communities. The figures may not be very impressive, but certainly show positive development. However, the functioning of most of these committees is a cause of concern. Based on the informal discussions with various field officers, it emerges that even in these freshly constituted committees the philosophy of JFM is not being followed in the true spirit. In majority of the cases, the working is not very different from departmental functioning. JFM is still being seen as another job employment programme with sufficient funds. In many villages, when asked how they would manage the project after the World Bank project got over, the reply was simple and straight—some other scheme would take its place.

In those cases where *Van Panchayats* opted for JFM, the response has been mixed. Some *Van Panchayats* have done well whereas others suffer from conflicts. One such instance is the Parbara Van Panchayat. Here JFM took off very well and acclaimed a success story. However, with the election of new *Van Panchayat,* there have been instances where the *gram pradhan* and *sarpanch* are from the same area and perceive each other as a threat to their respective positions.

However, these instances of failure should not shadow the successful cases where encouraging developments have taken place and the programme has been a success (see Box 2.8.5 and Box 2.8.6).

Box 2.8.5: Successful cases

Village Bhalson, District Chamoli

JFM was started in the year 1999-2000. So far the VFC has deposited Rs 157.000 in the VDF. The VEC has established an artificial insemination centre. Two bulls have been purchased. These bulls are being looked after by one family. The members have to pay Rs. 200 as fee for obtaining the services of this centre, Out of this amount, Rs. 175 is given to the family looking after the bulls, and Rs. 25 goes to the Village Development Fund (VDF), The villagers have purchased six Jersey cows. They have also set up a water mill, again managed by a local unemployed youth. A nominal fee is charged to pay the wages of this employee,

Village Sia Kemty

JFM started in 1998. There has been a perceptible change in the attitude of the people, particularly women. There has been an increase in the fuel and fodder collection. Milk production has increased from 40 to 45 million tonnes. People are switching over to using LPG. The status of the oak trees has improved considerably due to protection against grazing and heavy lopping.

Box 2.8.6: Some of the encouraging developments under JFM

- A general atmosphere for process change has been created. The concept has gained ground. Local people as well forest staff are talking about the concept and are ready to experiment.
- FD has built and developed its capacities. Training institutions have been strengthened, and the course content of various in-service trainings modified. Training of all the stakeholders, that is field staff, local communities, local bodies, and other related functionaries has been identified as an important ingredient for success of the programme.
- Participation of women at various levels (group discussions, planning, implementation) has improved considerably though much is still desired.
- Local communities are not only restricting themselves in managing and protecting forests but are also trying to establish linkages with other related departments such as agriculture, minor irrigation, horticulture, rural development, etc. They are taking up integrated approach to development of their villages.

No critical analysis of the factors responsible for the success and failure of the programme has been carried out. Based on the informal discussion held with some officers, factors which contributed to the success of the programme, came to light. Some of these are listed below:

- Location of the village: Villages which are easily accessible, particularly those situated on the main roads, have shown good results. This is mainly due to the fact that these villages are frequently visited by the staff as well as officers; hence, there is more interaction and effective monitoring.
- Leadership provided by the head of the JFM committee.
- Commitment and clarity on the part of field staff.
- Awareness and responsiveness amongst the villagers.

Serious efforts by the FD to implement JFM in the right earnest started just three years ago. This is a very short period to assess the success or otherwise of the programme of this magnitude, which involves a paradigm shift in workin-. However, acceptance of the concept amongst locals and forest officers can certainly be counted as one major perceptible achievement.

Areas of Concern

Sustainability of the Programme

All the areas that have been covered under the programme so far continue to receive a lot of support from the FD as well as NGOs in terms of finance, technical help in group formation, conflict resolution, skill building, etc. Sudden withdrawal of support may lead to a situation where committees find themselves helpless on various fronts as no exit policy exists. Linked with this is the problem of financial sustainability of the programme. Even those VFCs which have sufficient money in the VDF, are not using it effectively as seed money or revolving fund to take up economic activities in the region. Some VFCs have spent this money largely on works of public utility, such as construction of roads, school building, etc.

Others who adopted a cautious approach are using it as a bank deposit and utilise only the interest earned. There is a need for effective mobilisation of this money.

No concrete data is available to suggest what effective alternate measures were adopted to meet the fuel and fodder requirement. One area should not be protected at the cost of the other.

Greater emphasis must be laid and efforts made in areas such as SHG formation, micro credit, utilisation of NTFPs, with special emphasis on processing and marketing, so that employment opportunities are available and VFCs become economically viable. Adequate cooperation from other related departments such as agriculture, irrigation, animal husbandry, etc., to assist JFM villages to achieve overall integrated development of the area is easier said than done in the present setup.

High Cost and Slow Pace of the Programme

As stated earlier, out of the 1,217 committees constituted, only 488 committees have been constituted afresh. The remaining 729 represent the *Van Panchayats,* which have opted to be managed under JFM. Thus, only 488 committees could be constituted during the last year and Rs. 1,000 million allotted as cost of microplans prepared for these 1,217 committees.

Factors contributing to the expansion of area coverage in terms of creating more JFM programmes during the last three years are:

- Focus on the programme at all levels.
- Inputs in terms of regular fund flow, training, monitoring and evaluation.
- Some kind of pressure to develop and expand the concept as JFM is an important component of the World Bank project.
- Assured availability of funds for the programme.

After the World Bank project is over, these factors will disappear, and in such a situation, it may be difficult to propel the programme forward.

Relationship between Van Panchayat and Gram Panchayat

The Constitution (Seventy-third Amendment) Act, 1992, identifies the village *Panchayat* as institution of local self-governance at the village level. In Uttaranchal, the *Van Panchayat* represents the victory of local communities against the centralising tendencies of colonial rule, and holds a very sentimental and emotional value. The relationship of the two organisations should be clearly defined to avoid conflicts.

Future Course of Action

The concept of people's participation in the management of natural resources should be completely internalised in the functioning, thinking and policies of the FD. All work, as far as possible, should be executed adopting the philosophy of JFM. It has to be made very clear to the forest staff as well as the local communities that JFM is a process and not a project.

A comparative study on the functioning of committees formed in *Van Panchuyat* areas, outside *Van Panchayat,* and also some of the *Van Panchayats* which did not opt for the new JFM model is required to be carried out. This will help in understanding more clearly whether introduction of JFM has helped the working of the *Van Panchayat* or not, besides any adjustments, if required, in the existing model.

Arrangements should be made to ensure interaction amongst committees and formal networking developed at both division and state level. The existing *Van Panchayats* should be strengthened by providing them institutional as well as technical support. Serious monitoring of such cases where the FD has withdrawn from the areas, should continue.

References

1. Saxena, N.C. (1995), *Towards sustainable forestry in the UP Hills.* Centre for Sustainable Development, LBS National Academy of Administration, Mussoorie, Uttar Pradesh.

2. Tolia, R.S. (1998), *Land Forest and Village Community Studies,* Vol. 3: 111, Centre for Development Studies, UP Academy of Administration, Nainital.
3. GoUP (1997), Village Forest Joint Management Rules, 1997.
4. —— (1976), Van Panchayat Rules, 1976.
5. UPFD (2000), Uttaranchal State Forest Statistics (in brief) 2000.
6. —— (2001a), The Uttaranchal Panchayati Forest Rules, 2001.
7. —— (2001b), Empowerment of people through forestry (A status paper on JFM in Uttaranchal).

People Participation Formulae

"Go to the people
Live with them
Learn from them
Serve them
Love them
Plan with them
Start with what they know
Build on what they have
But of the best leaders,
When their task is accomplished
Their work is done,
The people all remark,
We have done it ourselves"

Adopted for Jimmie Yen,
Social Worker in China, 1945

2.9

Micro-Hydropower Potential in Uttaranchal

Yogesh Kumar*

The State of Uttaranchal is endowed with enormous hydropower potential. Large and medium hydropower potential in the state is estimated to be 20,000 megawatts. The state also has substantial hydropower potential for small, mini and micro hydropower development. According to an estimate the total potential including micro hydropower in the state is of the order of 40,000 megawatts. This is half of the required additional power projected to be realised during the next two decades for the entire country.

The survey figures (Table 2.9.1) indicate that nearly 20 per cent of the villages in Uttaranchal are not electrified. There are an even larger number of village hamlets that are not electrified. There are only 8,36,617 commercial as well as non-commercial connections for a population of 85,00,000; thus there is one connection for every 11 people. Since the family size is 6 on average, nearly 40 per cent of the population does not have electricity connections. Moreover, the per capita power consumption of the state is much below the national average of 450 units, which itself is very low by international standards (Table 2.9.2). Low power consumption is attributed to a large percentage of people below the poverty line, unregulated supply of power and unelectrified marginalized areas. The challenge is to use hydropower for development of the state and also for improving the quality of life of the people. Hydropower should bring economic development to the state and improve the purchasing power of the people.

* Consultant, New Delhi.

Table 2.9.1: Power Consumption in Uttaranchal

Connected load	:	1349 Mega Watt
Annual Power consumption	:	2660 million units
Number of Power Connections	:	8,36,617
Population	:	85,00,000 (estimated)
Persons per power connection	:	11
Per capita Power consumption	:	300 units (average)
Unelectrified villages	:	3193
Unelectrified Hamlets	:	Not Available
Total number of villages	:	15,620
People below poverty line	:	>50 per cent

Electricity brings dramatic changes in the lives of people. Increased illumination leads to more productivity, possibility for children to study till late in the night, income earning opportunities, value addition to local produce, improved irrigation, pumped water supply, better communication, TV and radio coverage and numerous other social benefits accrue from the availability of electricity.

Benefits of Power

Agriculture

Availability of cheap power can improve the economic condition of the people and also rejuvenate the environment. Agriculture, the mainstay of the economy, can get a boost with availability of cheap power by way of inexpensive water lifting systems for irrigation. The net irrigated area in the mountainous region of the state is only 25 per cent.

Agriculture/horticulture production under controlled conditions such as by using greenhouses where humidity and temperature can be controlled by use of cheap power can enhance yield at least two times. With such greenhouses, it is possible to grow high-value crops, medicinal plants, off season vegetables, high quality seeds and ornamental horticulture produce.

The state of Uttaranchal is highly suited to growing various medicinal and aromatic plants. Experiments conducted by HIMCON at Ranichauri have shown that scented Geranium can be cultivated on commercial scale. Similarly Bulgarian Rose, Chamomile and other flowers can also be commercially grown in the area. Cheap power can reduce the cost of extraction of essential oils from medicinal and aromatic plants, as well as save the biomass that would otherwise be used to provide the energy for the extraction process.

Cheap power can reduce the drudgery in daily life by energising agro-processing units such as milling, drying, threshing etc. It would make it possible for the cultivator to get crops processed in the village rather than going to distant places for the purpose. It will also help in increasing the production of selected crops.

Similarly cheap electricity can be useful in setting up small-scale processing plants in various parts of the state.

Fibre Processing

Traditionally, people in the state have been making their clothes using various fibres obtained from plants and animals. The processing of these fibres is very laborious and time consuming. The drudgery involved in the processing as well as lack of even limited mechanisation in this area has led to a steep decline in this cottage industry. Though a large number of families raise sheep, they are forced to sell the wool at a throwaway price since they cannot process this wool economically. Various processing activities such as carding, spinning, dyeing, drying, calendering, etc. can be mechanised with small-scale technology to reduce the processing time by at least three times. Availability of cheap power and appropriate technology for processing fibres at individual/community level can help people by enabling them to add value at competitive rates, thereby generating employment with its resultant economic benefits.

Similarly electricity can also be used in processing silk and tussar fibres. Uttaranchal has started production of mulberry silk as well as temperate tussar. Power is required for degumming, reeling, spinning, dyeing, drying etc.

Tourism

Tourism is an ever-growing industry. Uttaranchal is endowed with some of the most fascinating sites: high snow clad peaks, dense forests, historical and archaeological parks, religious places, etc. The state is among the most visited places in India, especially for pilgrimages, that often it is overlooked that Uttaranchal also has many other areas of tourist interest particularly for adventure and low budget tourism. Lack of infrastructural facilities has been a hindrance in this area. Low cost power along with accommodation in remote areas can provide the basic comfort that a tourist normally wants to have. Tourism can provide seasonal employment to a large number people in the state.

Household Needs and Protection of the Environment

Cheap power can be extremely useful in protecting much of the forest. If reliable electricity were available, at a sufficiently low cost, there would be an incentive for people to use it even to cook food and for heating. Firewood collection from the forest would stop, or at any rate reduce. On an average, the consumption of fuelwood is 2 kg. per person per day. Since 80 per cent of the people are using firewood, a total of 24 million tonnes of firewood be saved annually.

Difficulties in Supplying Power in Mountain Areas by Grid

Supplying sustained power to interior villages in mountainous terrain is very difficult and uneconomical due to poor load characteristics, adverse topographical features, harsh weather conditions and unusually scattered households. The main difficulties are:

(i) High cost owing to low density of population and concurrent increase in cost of transmission.
(ii) Difficulty in maintenance of power lines because of harsh weather conditions and undulating terrain.
(iii) Low revenue, poor load characteristics.
(iv) Difficulty in meter reading

The best alternative for electrifying marginalized areas is to set up mini-micro hydropower units that are not connected to main grid lines. If the situation demands, a local grid can be set up or the powerhouse can be operated in isolation or stand alone mode. At the government level, a number of micro hydro units were installed in Uttaranchal from 1890 onwards. Some of them have been successful and functional for a long period of time, whereas many of them have been shut down over time due to lack of spares of basically imported machinery and the financial crunch of State Electricity Board. Though a boon to local people, most of these 'stand alone' micro hydro units are not financially viable ventures for the state government. In the absence of rural industry, the power is solely used for lighting households for 4-5 hours a day, which translates into a plant load factor that is sometimes as low as 20 per cent. This is inadequate to generate enough revenue for maintenance of the power station and salary of the staff. Apart from these units, a few government owned indigenous micro hydro power stations have also been handed over to the community by the state government (now Uttaranchal) for operation and collection of revenue. But this transfer has not solved the basic problem of lack of adequate revenue generated and timely maintenance. It is clear that micro hydropower, especially as a stand-alone system, can only succeed if it is conceptualised as a composite scheme of generating power and using it for productive purposes. Which means that the power generated should significantly contribute to the development process.

Decentralised Power Generation in the Public Sector

The problems of such systems include lack of empowerment overing to lack of community participation in manpower mobilisation, planning, over-all management in construction, supervision, labour, post-construction maintenance of structures and equipment, and acquisition of necessary skills. Load characterises are poor as power is used only for lighting and the demand is limited to four to five hours in the evening/ night. The revenue generated does not even cover maintenance which is poor and after delayed owing to delays in government sanctions. In addition this power is expensive at Rs. 1,20,000 per kw.

Generation of Cheap Power by Community Effort

Micro hydropower is environment friendly and has negligible impact on the environment, and rarely involves any resettlement, unlike reservoir-cum-dam schemes. Community micro hydro schemes are usually meant for one village. If there are problems of land and water among the community, these can be resolved within the village. Micro hydropower could be very effective in far-flung areas or for small captive projects, but these are in no way a substitute for bigger schemes that generate power for densely populated urban areas and large industrial units. For a life of 15-20 years the cost of a community hydropower station, including distribution of the power in a compact village, could vary from Rs.50,000 to about Rs.70,000 per kw. It could be cheaper than the Government's as procedures are simpler, overheads are substantially lower and these are community-based facilities owned and maintained by the people. There can also be a greater scope for innovation and adequate utilisation of power by promoting local industry for development. In remote and marginalized areas where the purchasing power of the community is poor, community ownership and management of micro-hydropower system could be an ideal solution for electrification and development of the area.

In community owned hydropower stations of 20 kw set up by Foundation for Rural Recovery and Development (FORRAD), a national level NGO based in Delhi, the poor of the society, who normally cannot pay even a nominal sum for electricity connection and tariff for a government scheme, readily contribute labour and marginally cash as their contribution to their community's efforts in order to subsequently get access to reliable and cheap electricity. FORRAD has assisted in setting up two such power units.

1. An NGO at Budhakedarnath in Tehri-Garhwal, has been assisted with funds (Rs.3.5 lakhs), technical inputs and local support (in cash, kind and labour) worth Rs.5 lakhs. The NGO, Lok Jeewan Vikas Bharti uses this power for a hostel for underprivileged boys, residential areas and a cottage industry. This 20 kw unit is running for the last one and a half years and it is completely managed by the trained staff of the NGO.
2. A village community at Genwali in Tehri Garhwal district, located at 7,000 ft altitude and 15 km. from the nearest road, has been given cash assistance of Rs.5 lakhs, technical support and local contribution in cash, kind and labour. After commissioning a 20 kw hydropower unit and electrifying its houses, the village is now gearing up to process local produce such as wool, milk etc. with this power. This unit has a local contribution of about Rs.1,000 in cash and 45 man-days of labour per family. This accounts for nearly 40 per cent of total project cost.

Strategy

The process of setting up micro hydropower stations in the case of FORRAD is different from most others. First and foremost, even before the work on the unit commences, a village committee is constituted for management of the unit. The village identifies at least two local workers who are given rigorous practical training in household wiring, fault checking, assembly of alternators and turbine and their maintenance. The machines are not bought off the shelf, but fabricated involving the trainees so that they understand the intricacies of the equipment first hand and can repair it on their own if minor problems develop later.

Meanwhile, the village committee mobilises local manpower for transportation of goods and collection of construction materials. The villagers do all the construction work and installations, albeit under supervision. After commissioning, the unit passes into the hands of the by then trained grassroots engineers. Maximum efforts are made to increase the plant load factor by promoting increase in usage of power at household level and setting up village level industry. Initially, there is a desire to light rooms, then comes use of television sets, followed by ideas on electric fencing to prevent animals damaging crops, room-heaters, electric irons, power spinning and so on. The tariff, in cash or kind, is decided locally depending on the needs of maintenance and expansion of development activities. The possibility of collecting contribution in different forms such as cash, kind or labour is a flexibility that is unavailable to government owned system for obvious reasons. In these schemes the villagers accept greater responsibility entirely on their own, without having to be externally motivated to do so, as the unit has been borne out of their labour, and as a corollary of this 'ownership', they are fully aware that if it has to continue to work for them, it is to be maintained by them without outside support. *The key to success of these power stations is community participation, willingness to work persistently and the build local capability to maintain the unit and make full use of this power either by using it themselves or, if there are favourable changes in the Electricity Act of states, by selling surplus power to the national grid.*

A Connected Issue: Power through Water Mills

There are nearly 3,500 watermills in the state of Uttaranchal that can be improved to provide hydropower for scattered households and hamlets. A few watermills can be upgraded, and can also support electricity generation up to 5 kw. Traditional watermills work under a pressure head of 2-5 metres and use 20-200 litres of water per second. Therefore their output is dependent on water, which varies from season to season depending on the rains. The reasons why the scheme for upgradation of watermills is not getting popular support are:

If one water mill is upgraded, as a result of which it rapidly grinds flour, then other mills lose business and become redundant.

Most watermills are far away from residential areas and once these generate power, long power lines are needed for transmission – many hills means many crisscrossing and distant power lines.

Only a fraction of watermills are functional throughout the year, and very few can generate 5 kw of power continuously. A large majority of the mills are located close to the river and these are sometimes washed away in floods, whereas many of the mills are functional only during the rains.

Civil structure requirements for safety against floods, silt removal, automatic regulation, housing and power distribution tend to make it an expensive proposition.

A large number of watermills are jointly owned. Since all owners do not contribute regularly towards maintenance, the mills are abandoned.

A better way of using the mills could be by collecting the hydraulic head and water of all existing watermills that are found in a cluster, and installing one bigger unit instead of so many in a village. But this can only be possible if all the mill owners and the community in the village unite together. For instance in our project in Genwali (mentioned earlier), the village community was able to convince three watermill owners to abandon their sites for the common cause of a larger village unit. The other way could be that the mill-owners set up individual electricity generating units depending on the economics, and create a local grid for consumers.

Summing Up

In the state of Uttaranchal, there is a *fantastic potential for development of mini-micro hydropower generation.* Since such power stations are of extra small capacity, their maintenance is easy and comprehensive training can further enhance rural capacity to sustain such units. *Uttaranchal has reasonable facilities for fabrication of machinery for such units.* The micro hydro technology is simple and it can be transferred easily. People in remote and neglected areas can find employment and enjoy the benefits of power as most other citizens do, provided the state government recognises that community schemes of such low capacities can bring dramatic changes in the lives of people who are no doubt living in darkness but are willing to help themselves. *Involving the community in power generation can substantially reduce the cost of power.* Low cost power would not only improve the quality of life of people but also rejuvenate the environment in the hill state. It is beyond doubt that the *state government needs to involve people, communities, panchayats, NGOs etc. in micro-mini hydropower generation.*

2.10

Revitalising Ganga: The Sacred River

S.D. Garg[1], M.L. Dewan[2] and Piyush Rautela[3]

The views expressed m this paper are as a result of my irteractions with Dr. M.L. Dewan, Chairman, Himalaya Consortium for Himalaya Conservation, HIMCON in whom I have observed boundless love and concern for Himalayas and Parampujya Swami Chidananda Saraswati (Muni Ji), Chairman, Parmarth Niketan, Rishikesh who worships and surrenders to this sacred river the Ganga every evening by his devotional *aarti*. I have drawn inspiration from both these gr^at men. I cannot forget the evening prayers and *aarti* on the banks of the sacred river at Parmarth Niketan, Rishikesh. The perfect setting of the evening Sun with golden rays all over the sky with shining edges of the cloud. At that moment one can experience the phenomenon of merging with the nature and the role of flowing water of Ganges, its mystical sound and light from the sky to be in nothing but peace and bliss. A voice emerges from within—Hay Ganga, you are the mother of all rivers, you are the link between Heaven and Earth, the link between the human being and his true identity—the Atman.

About Ganga—The Sacred River

Rivers have been the cradles of human civilisation and are quite often considered sacred and the Ganga is a classic example of this—The Ganga, the 15th largest river of Asia and the 39th largest in the world, sustains the lives of over three hundred million people along its course.

1. Former-Senior Advisor, Council of Scientific & Industrial Resources, (CSIR), New Delhi.
2. Chairman, Himalayas Consortium for Himalaya Conservation, (HIMCON).
3. Sr. Coordinator, HIMCON, Himalaya Consortium for Himalaya Conservation.

The Ganga is the celestial river of India, the personification of the Indian spirit. In the Bhagavadgita Lord Shri Krishna declared, 'In rivers I am the Ganga', and this has for generations reassured the faithful that a dip in this holy stream guarantees salvation.

The waters of the River Ganga are believed to have miraculous properties. According to Ayurvedic works of reference the water has remarkable medicinal qualities.

Nowhere is the Ganga as enticing as in her mountain home. The Ganga and its head-streams present in the shadow of the snow-capped peaks and in deep valleys nature at its most sublime. It may be said without exaggeration, that one who has not known the Ganga in the hills has not known the river at all.

It was not long before Ganga captured the imagination of others. One among four major rivers of the world, it became a subject of romance and myth even for foreigners.

Megasthenes, has left for us an interesting account of Ganga. "Ganga is the greatest river on earth which neither the Egyptian Nile nor the Danube can compare with…Some have asserted that this river like the Nile rises from the unknown sources…while others trace its source to Scythian mountains".

Its Origin and Route from Himalayas to Bay of Bengal

Upto 1815 it was generally believed that Ganga originated from the lake Mansarovar forcing its way through the brow of the mountain or through an underground channel to the cataract at Gangotri. Fraser in 1815 followed by Hodgeson and Herbert in 1817 dispelled this notion and suggested that the western headwaters of the Ganga should be more appropriately located at the source of the Jadganga or Jahnvi, one of the tributaries of the Bhagirathi. The course of this river is marked with scenes of great grandeur and sublimity.

The Ganga river flows for over two and a half thousand kms. in India before merging into the Bay of Bengal. In addition there is another branch of this great river called the Padma, which separates itself 40 kms. above Farakka in West Bengal and flows through Bangladesh towards Bay of Bengal.

At its point of origin, i.e. Gaumukh (the snout of Gangotri glacier) in Garhwal Himalaya in Uttaranchal, the Ganga in known as the Bhagirathi. Receiving several hill rivers and streams such as the Bhilanagana, the Bhagirathi reaches Devprayag where it receives an important tributary, the Alaknanda. From this place onwards the river is called Ganga. The river emerges into plains at Rishikesh. In its further flow in Uttaranchal and the State of Uttar Pradesh the river is joined by the Ramganga, (left bank, near Kannauj), the Yamuna, Tons and Gomti. The Karamnasa river also joins the Ganga river after forming a border between UP and Bihar. Many tributaries from India and Nepal join this river, which is called by different names of Kali, Mahakali and Sarada. In its further march in the state of Bihar, the Ganga received several rivers—these include the Ghaghra, the Gandak, Kosi which joins the Ganga near Patna, Other rivers which join the Ganga in Bihar include the Sone, and Kosi.

The rivers which merge into the Ganga in West Bengal (fully or partially) include the Mahananda, the Dwarka, the Ajay, the Damodar, The Rupnarayan and the Haldi. In West Bengal the river a little below Farakka is called the Bhagirathi and further downstream after its confluence with Jalangi tributary, it is called the Hooghly. After Diamond Harbour the river flows southwards till it merges into the Bay of Bengal, Here the mouth of the river is about 25 kms wide.

The Special Quality of Ganga Water and its Purity

The faith in Ganga even gets the support of modern science when scientists confirm Ganga's unique self-cleansing abilities and the longevity of its water (it does not putrefy even after long periods of storage). If despite these highly remarkable qualities the Ganga water has become very polluted and is now seen by scientists as a major potential source of spread of infectious diseases, then clearly the destruction wrought by us has been quite massive.

From the above it appears that one of the secrets of Ganga water having miraculous properties may be due to such a large number of tributaries joining the Ganga from whole of the Himalayan range carrying with it the properties of mountain micro-organisms and minerals. Mountains are the home to an almost infinite variety of plants and animals and are precious reservoirs of biological diversities of food and medicine.

Ganga: The Present Scenario in the Himalaya

There was a time not very long ago when the hillsides in the birthplace of the Ganga were adorned with thick green foliage. The noble splendour of trees was spellbinding.

Atkinson himself confirmed this and has written: In many parts of the country Conifers occur in unbroken masses extending over many miles and present a scene of magnificent grandeur unknown elsewhere.

The majestic sight of tall pointed pines from which hung festoons of wild vines and fine specimens of chestnuts, walnuts and oaks as well as bamboo groves were enough to send any visitor into raptures. Holdsworth, who accompanied Smythe on the famous Kamet expedition of 1931 testifies in his journal to 'sprawling, aromatic junipers and bigger bush rhododendrons, graceful white birch trees and the dark gothic spires of silver fir and spruce. These were seen with thick stands of deodar and long leaved pines. Like the lush forests, flowering meadows have been a marvellous feature ornamenting the birthplace of the Ganga.

With good reason these alpine pastures have been named the garden of gods; *Nandan Kanan.* Not one but many valleys of flowers nestle on the banks of frolicking sisters of the Ganga, titillating one's senses. The fragrance of exotic blooms often proves intoxicating and the entire stretch of land is identified as the *Gandhnandan;* mountain of fragrance. It is here that the *Brahmkamal* (Lilly of Heaven) grows in profusion in the shadow of Kedarnath and in the vicinity of Hemkund. Another comparatively rare flower contributing to the riot of colours is the blue poppy which had bedazzled Frank Smythe who confessed. 'In all my mountain wanderings I had not seen a more beautiful flower than this primula. *The* fine raindrops clung to its soft petals like galaxies of seed pearls and frosted its leaves with silver'. All along the water course one can enjoy the splashes of scarlet *buransh* (rhododendron) which is an integral part of the Uttaranchal's cultural heritage and is celebrated in many a folk song.

Alas! All this is a thing of the past. Reckless anthropogenic encroachment upon nature has denuded the playground of the Ganga and her sisters. Ugly scars threaten to become festering sores and can play havoc with the fragile ecosystem of the entire Himalayan region. As a result once abundant wildlife has suffered great depredations. Sambar (a large antelope), Kankar (the barking deer) and Bharal (the fabulous blue sheep) and the legendary musk deer (*Kasturi mrig*) are all on the verge of extinction. The snow leopard has already moved from the realm of flesh and blood to the world of myths. The magnificent Monal with rainbow plumage is becoming increasingly difficult to sight and the Himalayan Quail exists as a hundred-years-old memory.

All hope is, however, not lost. There is growing awareness of eco-developmental issues and the call for conservation is coming from the grassroots. Given a brief respite nature may yet recuperate and nurse the once green hills of the Ganga back to health are the people home to help in this nature. At present there is a great deal of concern about pollution control on this great river. We may all pause to ponder whether the river can be kept in good health if its source and environs in the Himalaya are allowed to degenerate. Thus the need for a programme for 'Himalaya Rejuvenation and Greening'.

Ganga: The Scenario Downstream—The Source of Pollution

Comprehensive urban sewerage treatment and disposal systems came into vogue and were introduced in Calcutta, Bombay and Madras in the 1870s. Growth of these systems have failed to keep pace with urban expansion and in many cases have deteriorated on account of lack of maintenance. Half of Delhi, for example, has no sewerage facilities and the capital's wastewater treatment capacity is less than half of what is required today. The city's storm water drains, also carry sullage from unplanned and unauthorised colonies and empty these into the Yamuna. With ever-increasing abstractions of water for irrigation, even the mighty Ganga below Haridwar and Narora, where the Upper and Lower Ganga Canals take off, is reduced to a waste water drain in the lean season until replenished at the Holy Sangam at Allahabad by the Yamuna, which is itself only rejuvenated at Etawah by the Chambal.

River pollution, with a heavy load of untreated sewage and industrial effluents, has emerged as a major health hazard. On one estimate, diseases spread by Ganga pollution alone deprives the country of nearly 40 million man-days on account of ill health. The loss in terms of mortality and economic injury is incalculable. Concern over rising pollution in the Ganga became manifest with growing environmental consciousness in the 1970s.

Meanwhile, following a proposal in India's Sixth Plan (1980-85) that universities be associated with eco-development and study of environmental problems, a coordinated action research project fear the integrated study of the Ganga was launched under the auspices of the Planning Commission involving 16 universities situated on or near the Ganga from Garhwal to Calcutta and 14 scientific and technological institutions (March 1982). The river was divided into given reaches and the programme of studies included a baseline inventory of all natural resources and human activities, water quality and pollution, and ecological modelling.

A little earlier, the Central Board for the Prevention and Control of Water Pollution, Delhi, took up a study of the Yamuna and Ganga basins as part of its Assessment and Development Study of River Basin Scries. Three monographs were prepared by the Board; Part I pertaining to the Yamuna sub-basin (1978), Part II to the Ganga basin (1984), and Part III to the West Bengal stretch (1981).

Besides ingress of untreated sewage, wading by large herds of buffaloes, and mass ritual bathing on festive days introduce heavy bacteriological loads. On special bathing days, numbering over 20 per year, major fairs are listed "when thousands or sometimes even hundreds of thousands of people bathe in a congested stretch of river within the span of a few hours".

It has to be brought out to the planners and administrators of agriculture and irrigation that while meeting the rising irrigation requirements is extremely important, this cannot be done by diverting most of low water flows except at the cost of severe environmental degradation. The only practical approach is to store more and more of the monsoon run-offs both for various beneficial uses and for release in the critical reaches during lean periods. Such flow regulation and equalisation can be achieved either by building large, medium and small storage projects, or by ensuring enhanced percolation to the underground reservoir. A balanced mixture of both these is advisable.

The Ganga Basin Study (part II) also mentions the problem of very low seasonal flows, after abstractions for irrigation, in certain critical stretches below Haridwar and up to Kannauj where the river is joined by the Ramganga. Very large numbers of people bathe daily in the river at Rishikesh, Haridwar, Garhmukhteshwar, Kannuaj, Allahabad, Mirzapur, Varanasi and Nawadwip. From the point of view of water quality, the stretches from Kanpur to Patna and from Nawadwip to Diamond Harbour were found to give cause for concern. With intensive irrigated agriculture being practised in Western U.P., a rising salinity and alkalinity trend is evident in the river between Haridwar and a point near Badaun, However, on the whole, the salinity level in the Ganga is somewhat lower than what is found in the Yamuna.

The Ganga transports *83 million tonnes of dissolved solids*, the highest for all Indian rivers, and the Brahmaputra another 35 million tonnes to the Bay of Bengal. The Ganga is twice as saline as the Brahmaputra and it is said to account for 2.5 per cent of the global flux of sodium to the oceans (National Environmental Engineering Research Institute, 1987). Given adequate stream flows, the Ganga is able to dilute and assimilate sewage and other pollution loads within 20 kilometres of large cities except in vulnerable low-water stretches during the lean season and below major industrial urban and bathing centres. The river is resilient and belief in its purity is sustained by its unusually good keeping quality as testified by devout pilgrims who have taken home *Gangajal.* Faith in the curative quality of the water possibly stems *from* its high radon content (86.5 pci per litre at Jaduguda in Bihar).

River Pollution and GAP

River water quality (in mg/litre) is normally measured in accordance with three standards. The dissolved oxygen (DO) level should not be less than five, the bio-chemical oxygen demand (BOD) provides an index of pollution and should not be more than three, and the most probable number (MPN) of coliform or harmful bacteria should not exceed 500 per 100 millilitres of water.

The BOD at several places along the Ganga was found to be higher than the standard maximum of 3 mg/lt. It was 8.6 in Kanpur, 15.5 in Allahabad and 10.6 in Varanasi. In terms of DO the minimum standard of 5 mg/litre was met at all these three places in 1986 as the DO level ranged between 6.4 and 8.5.

The Ganga has a good DO rating averaging a count of 9 to 10. The BOD and MPN counts in vulnerable stretches however leave a great deal to be desired and is seldom within the permissible limits.

Concern over the degradation of the Ganga led the Department of Environment on the basis of the findings of the Central Pollution Control Board to prepare an *Action Plan to combat pollution in the river.* Addressing the nation early in January 1985, the Prime Minister lamented the pollution of the river and declared "we will restore the pristine purity of the Ganga. Thus was launched the Ganga Action Plan (GAP), one of the greatest and most significant river cleaning operations carried out anywhere in the world. A separate Central Ganga Authority was set up in February 1985 with a commitment of Rs. 291 crores for Phase I of the programme covering 27 Class I cities (with populations exceeding 100,000), Rs. 240 crores being earmarked for the Seventh Plan (1985-90). The Authority is a high-level body with the Prime Minister as Chairman, and the Chief Ministers of UP, Bihar and West Bengal, and the Deputy Chairman of the Planning Commission as members. Of the 692 towns within the Ganga basin, there are actually along the river 27 Class I cities, 23 Class II cities (population between 50,000 and 100,000) and 48 towns (less than 50,000 population). The Class I cities have been taken up first as 82.3 per cent of the total urban population living along the banks of the river from Gangotri to Sagar Island in the Bay of Bengal live in these centres which also generate 88.5 per cent of the total volume of sewage produced. Fifteen of these cities have at least partial sewerage and six of them sewage treatment plants. Optimisation of benefits from existing systems was therefore considered the best course to adopt

The *Ganga Action Plan falls into three broad categories.* The first is to intercept and treat the raw sewage flowing directly into the river causing gross pollution. The second is to ensure and enforce proper effluent treatment of industrial wastes. The third is to promote and assist programmes for supply of protected drinking water, drainage, construction or *conversion of existing dry latrines into sanitary pour-flush toilets*, renovation and improvement of bathing *ghats,* construction of electric crematoria, improvement and illumination of streets, plantations and limited erosion control measures, removal of unauthorised dairies, relocation of *dhobi* fifhate, development of facilities and services such as community toilets and washing places, lighting, water-front development, and establishment of river police units for *mela* organisation, life-saving and enforcement of pollution laws. These tasks are being carried out through local and State institutions and are linked, in part, to World Bank and other aid programmes.

261 Schemes were Sanctioned under GAP—88 schemes of interception and diversion of sewage, 35 of sewage treatment, *43 of low cost toilets*, 28 of electric crematoria, 35 of river front development and another 32 of miscellaneous category. Originally planned for just 6 years, GAP was later extended to nearly double this period and targeted for completion in March 1997. However there were further delays and a few schemes have spilled into 1998 and beyond.

Despite the fact that it was extended to almost double its original time span, the objective of bringing BOD and DO levels to desirable norms has not been fulfilled. According to official data for 1996. BOD level at Kanpur (4.1) and Allahabad (3.3) was still higher than the desirable maximum norm of 3 mg/lt. Although the situation had improved significantly compared to the 1986 levels. In Varanasi BOD level in 1996 had been reported to be below 3. The DO level in 1996 was higher than the desired minimum level in all these three places but significantly, the situation had become slightly worse in Kanpur where the DO level had gone from 6.7 to 6.4.

Another important task is monitoring the river for water quality throughout its length and undertaking, coordinating and collating a host of studies pertaining to all relevant aspects. Water quality is being monitored at both macro and micro levels for upto 42 parameters at 27 stations covering physio-chemical, biological and heavy metal indices.

The Central Pollution Control Board has fixed standards for different uses in India such as Class A (fit for drinking with chlorination), Class B (fit for mass bathing). Class C (fit for drinking after full treatment). Class D (fit for aquatic life), Class E (fit for receiving wastes). The object of the Ganga Action Plan is to *upgrade the river quality to Class B against the Class C and D quality* that largely prevailed at the commencement.

Though the waters of the Ganga would have been dirtier had there been no Ganga Action Plan, much yet remains to be done. Keeping in view this special cultural significance of river, any sincere effort to 'protect Ganga river', in particular to check its pollution and keep it clean, should evoke strong emotional feelings leading to large scale mobilisation of people for this task. Somehow, this has not happened and the pollution of Ganga river and most of its tributaries such as the Jamuna has reached alarming levels. What is needed is a missionary zeal and full participation of the masses.

Action Programme

Assessment of the level of pollution along the Ganga river is the first and foremost exercise that is required to be undertaken. In this task State of art technological know-how would be put in with the collaboration of various universities and technological institutions. Population distribution along the river course is a major factor affecting pollution and therefore needs to be documented, listing all habitations, and ascertaining their pollution contribution.

It is envisaged that the river Ganga can only be revitalised through active cooperation and involvement of the communities habitating its banks. Active partnership has therefore to be evolved with the masses. Apart from the masses, NGOs and other people's groups active in these regions have to be involved in this mission.

Initiating action at the source: It is observed that the catchment area in the Himalayan region contributes major part of the silt load while the plains contribute other pollutants. *Watershed management in the upper reaches of the river would be reducing the silt load significantly*. It is therefore required that watershed management in the Himalaya is promoted and sanitation and other sewage treatment facilities be provided to the masses, both in the hills and the plains.

Sanitation and awareness drive invoking the traditional religious motifs should be undertaken all along the river course and the masses should be sensitised of the urgency of cleaning Ganga. *Sanitary latrine construction should be undertaken on mass scale.* This besides reducing the pollution along the Ganga would also be improving the state of health of the masses. A *Massive Tree Plantation Programme* should be undertaken along all the stretches of the river. *Multipurpose; fodder, timber, fuel, fruit and medicinal plants be planted according to the need of the region and wishes of the masses.* This would be improving the farm productivity besides improving the state of the environment.

In order to enhance the river flow during the lean periods recourse should be taken to enhancing ground water recharge through a series of vegetative and engineering measures. A series of small reservoirs should be commissioned along the river course with the participation of the masses to store the monsoon runoff.

Organisation building: The CLEAN GANGA MOVEMENT relies on the strength of the masses and their support and thence all existing grassroots level organisations should be promoted and brought under the aegis of this movement. New voluntary brigades (Ganga Cleaning Brigade and Land Army) should be prepared along the river course.

Wealth from waste: Greener and innovative technologies are required to be put on test for Recycling every kind of waste material—household, urban, clinical and industrial. Compost, vermiculture and bio-pesticides need promotion so that *these can replace chemical fertilizers and pesticides.* Use of traditional farm related know-how would be useful in this regard.

Mustering technology: Technological institutions—National Laboratories, Universities, Colleges and Schools as also the grassroots level experience needs to be pooled for this mission in order to *make Clean Ganga a reality.* River cleaning missions have been undertaken successfully in the past in various parts of the globe and we must learn from those experiences and utilise the technologies and practices so evolved.

Principles of people's participation: People's Participation is the focal point of this programme and success of this programme would be dependent upon the level of motivation of the masses. People's involvement in Ganga Cleaning Action would be insured through an aggressive awareness drive through a series of publications, pamphlets in vernacular, television and radio programmes, *padyatras*, meetings, cultural shows and seminars. *All Melas would then be used as opportunities for inspiring people* to join in this action programme by volunteering. To add to it, the students would be inspired to participate in this movement. Attempt would be made to achieve the following in schools:

- Environmental awareness programme
- Voluntary course on pollution control
- Awareness regarding cause and effect relationship of our daily actions
- Awareness regarding the rising pollution levels in Ganga and effects thereof
- Awareness on how to control pollution
- Awareness regarding the state of other river cleaning programmes in the world

Clean Ganga Brigade: Short term volunteers be recruited from the schools to work towards a cleaner Ganga.

People's Movements

Villagers and nomadic herdsmen particularly in hilly catchment areas can be involved in forest protection programmes which protect the forests as well as their livelihood. Their efforts to oppose indiscriminate mining practices particularly in sensitive catchment areas should be encouraged. Nomads of hill areas can play an important role in giving information about any damage done in remote hill areas of rivers, particularly from landslides or anticipated landslides.

Action Plan

It is necessary to draw a well considered action plan for cleaning of GANGA. Some of the important aspects proposed are:

- Cleaning of Ganga from its source.
- Taking a stretch of river and assigning the responsibility to a willing organisation or an NGO to mobilise people's participation in keeping that stretch of river pollution free.
- *Preventive action*: Treatment of industrial, chemical effluent. Treatment of sewer, human excreta. Pollution due to human, animal dead bodies. Pollution by people during melas.

- Awareness campaign for educating children and people. Environmental education in schools.
- Courses on the need and benefits of clean drinking water for health. Importance of conserving water.
- Community toilets along the river Ganga will help in keeping it cleaner.
- For awareness creation a slot on TV/through news papers in the morning hours on the techniques on how to take up income generating activities would be very helpful.
- Action for creating wealth from waste is another important aspect which will require survey of the nature of waste available and training of those who are already collecting the waster value addition and earning a price from the waste.
- Introducing penalties for people who are responsible for creating pollution in the river.
- To provide pure drinking water involves treatment costs—the question is should the drinking water be provided free—*a token price may make people aware of conserving and utilising the drinking water more efficiently.*

Some of the NGO's like Himcon, Parmarth Niketan, Chirag, in here have already taken initiative to mobilise public opinion and have taken actions towards greening of Himalayas.

Some of these activities are:

- Rainwater harvesting structures, chals, check dams.
- Planting of trees—action for aerial seeding is being proposed.
- Promoting medicinal plants, nursery development and cultivation, and preprocessing.
- Introducing tissue culture techniques for preparing large scale plating material.
- Promoting fruits and vegetables farming.
- Promoting scientific techniques for milk production through dairy development, fodder cultivation, fodder trees.
- Introducing re-newable energies options by adopting solar, micro-hydel, bio-gas, bio-mass utilisation.

The above activities needs primarily Land and Water Care—Bio-industrial watershed development and management are the basic requirements. These activities require peoples' participation and inputs of modern science and technological developments. The present scenario in Uttaranchal poses a very depressing and challenging situation due to most of the youths moving out of the State in search of jobs at urban centres. Most of the working force is women. Therefore, a strategy needs to be developed.

The Mighty Himalayas

Seemed to

Symbolize

The Almighty himself,

AND THE GANGES

Looked as if

SHE WERE OVERFLOWING

WITH MILK

2.11

Ode to Ganga

M.L. DEWAN*

Just back from pilgrimage
With you. Mata, I address you
With Devotion, with love, with "DIYA"
You are the life line of India

We are working in the
Himalayas for over a decade
As Trees for Life, then Himalayan
Chapter of Trees for Life and
Now as Himalayan Consortium for
Himalayan Conservation Popularly called HIMCON

I saw on your Bank
And from Ashram like Parmarth Niketan
Van Prastha Ashram, Swarag Ashram in Rishikesh
Such Glorious views of your fury
Your Glory, Your Abundance, your speed
We prayed to you, your Aarti with lights, music,
People from all parts of the world, chanting,
Some in Trance, others with devotion

Your being in Hurry to
Race Towards Ocean
Through thousands of kilometres, of
Rural, urban and plains which you,

* Chairman, HIMCON, Himalaya Consortium for Himalaya Conservation Ranichauri-249199, Tehri Garhwal, Uttaranchal.

Mother Ganga built yourself
Over thousands of years
And now keep on depositing
Precious silt in the fields
Which give crops, Food and
With your water responsible
For livelihood of Millions

"Has something gone wrong with
Me now that you describe my fury"?
Asks GANGA MATA.
Yes, Beloved you bring Fierce
Floods, you bring millions of tons
Of Silt, which deprive your
Source, our Himalayas of precious
Soil Turning many parts to
Infertile Rocks and Barren Mountains

We, your children have
Excessively exploited, the Himalayas
Whereby you get excess silt, soil which
Is so important for saving &
Rejuvenation of Himalayas

My dear mother Ganga,
You have a long way to go to your destination,
The Sea like all of us merge in one superself PARAMATMA
And become one with Him. you become one with the ocean.

Sitting on your bank,
Singing among hundreds
Singing your praise and doing
Aarti at the dusk time
With lots of Diyas.
We sang about your splendour in your fury,
We have the determinatiom to help you
Reduce your fury & your burden,
The overweight silt May I share with you,
How we will continue to attempt reduction
Of Silt & floods & hopefully if all united to achieve some part
of it in the next decades, the following verses show.

As Himalayas getting damaged
Springs drying, trees cut
People abandon the sacred land
Slopes sliding
All causing floods today
Droughts tomorrow

Revered Himalayas—do not feel sad
It is not all that bad
As there is growing hope
And an expanding scope

People's action to save you
Planning programmes increasing
Where youth, children, women.
Volunteers local, national, international
All sharing the joy of planting
And fencing

Vowing to care for each plant
Growing more plants through nurseries
Schools, peoples, farmers, nurseries
With water from springs or ponds
Example recent eco-development camps in Ranichauri
And hundred others
O Himalayas, drying springs
Are on way to rejuvenation
Planting oaks, rhododendrons and other trees in
The catchment,
Storing their water through people's action

A full programme for spring restoration in the making
Which will make thousand other
Springs revive and
People ablaze with activity
Through harvesting water, your life blood.

Himalaya Institute just born
Though long way to adulthood
Yet keen to planned action

In your service
To save you
To green you
To invigorate you

Thus there is hope
In many of your domains
Women on the march
Children from schools determined

To save you
To serve you
To green you

All this beginning
Of a new surge
Yet many questions, problems
Still remain for example

–Big dams vs. small dams
Why subject you
To big stresses
Why not small beautiful water,

Many people getting polluted
Drinks, laziness, egoism
Though few but
Are like pollutants
Good young people often leaving

For plains for livelihood
For a handful of silver
Leaving behind the gold

Protection slow and not easy
Protection from axes
From the needs of cattle .

–Where are the green pastures?
Why tragedy of commons
Why no land of
Milk and honey?

–Let us all together work
Not slumber or shirk
Let people awake
For common good
For your good
With Namaskar to rising sun
Of Himalayas

Thus mother Ganga, you originating
From Himalayas, land of Shiva
In many branches, Rivulets
Streams, Mandakni, Alaknanda
Bhagirathi, all your daughters
Making **Uttranchal.**
Sacred Land of Rishis and Munis
Full of Medicinal Plants and
Resources which people from all
Over keen to visit Let us
With your blessings and of Himalayas
Make this challenging land a
Place of Joy, happiness, peace of
Mind and Resources utilized
For Benefit of All Working Together.

1. Nanda Devi (7817m) East

2. Kedarnath (6940m)

3. Shivling (6543m)

4. Trishul (7120m)

5. Summits of Panch Chuli Massif (6910m)

6. Deep snow conditions around Mana Massif (6795m)

7. Gaumukh – the snout of Gangotri glacier – the source of river Bhagirathi. In the background are – perennially snow covered Bhagirathi peaks

8. Zero Point – Pindari Glacier

9. Gangotri Temple

10. Yamunotri Temple

11. Hemkund Saheb (Lokpal)

12. Jageshwar Temple Complex near Almora

13. Inside Lakhamandal Temple near Chakrata

14. Nainital

15. River Bhagirathi near Harsil

16. Confluence of River Bhagirathi and Alaknanda at Dev Prayag

17. Laxman Jhoola at Rishikesh

18. Rafting on Ganga

19. River Ganga at Brahmakund, Har-ki Pauri, Haridwar

20. Pithoragarh (1650m), a mountain town bordering Nepal and Tibet

21. Picturesque Dogal Bitta Resthouse, Garhwal

22. Swami Narayan Ashram near Tanaghat

23. School children at Ukhimath

24. Local Lady at Dharchula

25. Adventure Sports – paragliding in snowy mountains

26. Bhotia Dance at Dharchula

27. Typical flora – Braham Kamal

28. Tiger at Corbett Park

29. Khamera landislide blocking Yamuna due to cloud burst in Sept. 2001

30. Mountain fires

31. Traditional Wisdom – A four storeyed firewood house (~200 year old) which withstood several earthquakes

32. New Residential Area

PART 3

NATURAL RESOURCE DEVELOPMENT, MONITORING AND EVALUATION

3.1

Natural Resource Policy: Some Related Issues

PANKAJ KUMAR*

Introduction

The hill districts of Uttar Pradesh have been formed into a separate state called Uttaranchal on 9th November, 2000. Uttaranchal was earlier made of eight districts of Almora, Nainital, Pithoragarh, Chamoli, Dehradun, Pauri, Uttarkashi and Tehri. In recent years, four new districts of Udham Singh Nagar, Bageshwar, Rudraprayag and Champawat have been created. The 2001 Census lists the population of the region at 84,79,562. Literacy rate for the state 72.28 per cent.[1]

The total geographical area of Uttaranchal is 53,331 square kilometres. The topography is characterised by deep valleys, high peaks and a wide variety of vegetation due to rapid changes in climate resulting from altitudinal variations. Elevations range from 300 to 7000 msl. Average annual temperatures range from 16 to 40°C although many parts face sub-zero temperatures in winter.[2]

Natural Resources of Uttaranchal

The two non-montane and four montane physiographic zones that have been identified in Uttaranchal are listed in Box 3.1.1 below.

The land use of Uttaranchal is shown in Table and Figure 3.1.1 below. As can be seen forests form the major landuse at 64 per cent total area. The extent of cultivable area is only12 per cent. Forests therefore play a

* Field Coordinator, SPWD, Dehradun.

pivotal role both in the ecology and the economy of the region. We therefore start by describing forests and their importance.

Forests

Importance of Forests

For historical reasons and due to natural resource limitations, a mix of agriculture, pastoralism and trade have traditionally been the major components of livelihood strategies in the Western Himalayas. Due to the steep topography and the high rainfall, percolation losses of rainwater from individual farmers' fields are very high. The soil does not hold water for long and in the absence of available soil moisture, agricultural crops would not do too well.

A traditional mechanism to combat this specific kind of problem has been the addition of large quantities of farmyard manure to the fields. While this is done in all agrarian societies in India, the important distinction in the Himalayas, is that here, the farmers are more interested in changing the soil texture in addition to soil nutrients. Thus soil physics becomes more important than soil chemistry. Farmers in almost all areas in Uttaranchal told us that holding of water is the single most important function that the addition of farm yard manure performs.[3]

This strategy is visible in the traditional management of Gools. It is the duty of the farmer whose turn it is to take water for irrigation to go up to the water source with two or three baskets of cow dung and to wash it into the channel. This gives a lining of cow dung to the channel and reduced percolation losses.

The importance of farmyard manure has remained even today. The standard method of preparing compost is as follows. Leaf litter from the forest floors is collected during one or two months in the fall (Jeth/Ashad) and stored in a heap with each household. Then a basketful or two of this leaf litter is scattered under the animals in the cowshed every day. This acts as a sponge and absorbs the dung and urine of the animals. After 2 or 3 days, the soaked leaf litter is removed and put either in a pit or in a heap.

This is done day after day for a long period (varying from a month to 6 months for a single heap or pit), which is then left to decay. Signs of vapours emanating from the heap/pit and the heap/pit getting warm are seen as signs of good composting taking place. This compost is then put into the agriculture field at the start of the agriculture season. Although this compost is not fully decomposed, it is allowed to decay further in the fields.

Box 3.1.1: Major Physiographic Zones in Himalayas

Non-Montane

Bhabhar: This is a level surface zone at the foothills of the Himalayas 34 km. wide where the Himalayan torrents rush down from the steep slopes and disappear under boulders and gravels due to the extremely porous soil type of Bhabhar.

Terai: Situated below the Bhabhar and parallel to it, the Terai is a marshy and damp tract (80-90 km. wide) containing fertile soils with good water retention capacity.

Montane

Sub-Himalayas: Called Sub-Himalayas because it possesses the least of Himalayan features, it consists of two zones, the Shivaliks—the youngest of the Himalayan ranges and the Dun (flat longitudinal structural valleys) to the north of Shivaliks. The Shivaliks extend in a narrow varying width of 6 to 30 km. with altitudes of 300 to 1000 m.

Lesser Himalayas: This zone extends in a varying width of 60-90 km. with abrupt rise in elevation between 1000 m to 3000 m. It contains two types of physiographic sub-units, (a) The Himachal ranges and (b) The Himachal valleys and lake basins.

Greater Himalayas: This zone has a varying width of 40-60 km. The altitude varies between 3000-7000 m. Except for lower valleys, this zone is perpetually covered with snow and is hence called Himadri. The region covers glacial landforms above 3000 m.

Trans-Himalayas: Also known as the Tethys Himalayas and Indo-Tibet plateau, the region is in the rain-shadow of the Greater Himalayas and is therefore a cold desert. It slopes down to the Yarlung-Tsangpo (Brahmaputra) river valley in Tibet.

Thus we see that agriculture is supported by nutrient transfers from forests (either directly in the form of manure from forest floors, or indirectly as leaf litter converted into compost). Without FYM, we have been repeatedly told, the soil would given negligible yields. Thus forest, livestock and agriculture form an interconnected and interlinked Mountain Farming System. (*See* Fig. 3.1.1).

In addition to sustaining agriculture, forests cover the tops of most ridges in the Himalayas, thus preventing erosion. The major source of energy for cooking and home heating (especially due to the prolonged and severe winters) is still fuelwood, which is also procured from forests. A widespread dependence on forests for grass (seasonally) and leaf fodder (in winters) is also seen.

Remoteness and inaccessibility have also given rise to a well developed indigenous medicine system based on herbs from the forests and trans-alpine pastures. The springs, which most villages depend on, for drinking water and irrigation are also nurtured by forests in catchments.

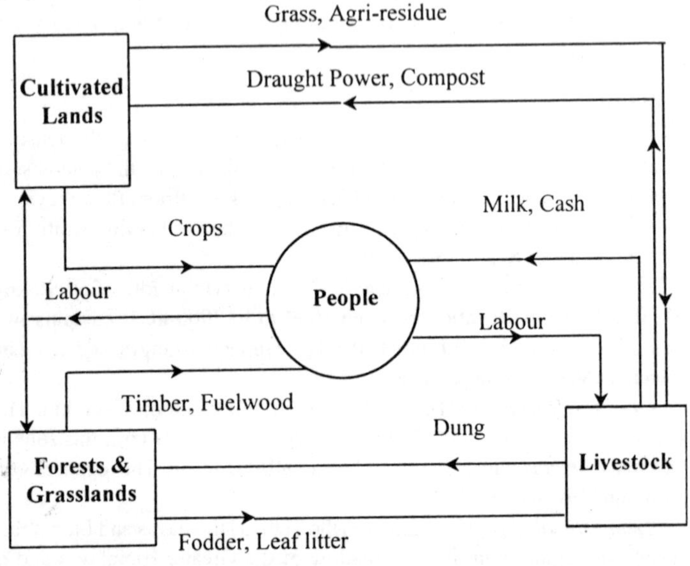

Fig. 3.1.1: Layout of Mountain Farming System

We thus see that Forests have been and still are the single most important ecological entity in the Western Himalayas. For most village people even today, life without forests is thus unthinkable.

Forest Types

The great variations in climate, altitude, rainfall, aspect and soil throughout Uttaranchal give rise to a rich floral diversity resulting in a variety of forest ecosystems. Near the snowline occur forests of creeping Rhododendron and Birch. These are succeeded down hill by forests of Silver fir, Spruce, Deodar, Oaks and Chir pine. On the foot hills and adjoining plains of Bhabhar and Terai occurs the most valuable Sal forests.

The major forest types based on altitude consist of four broad vegetation zones on the basis of climate and altitude with some overlapping of transitional features. (*See* Box 3.1.2).[4]

Box 3.1.2: Various Forest Types in Uttaranchal

(i) *Tropical* – Sub-Tropical Forests zone: Dominated by deciduous – Sub-deciduous types. Sal is the predominant species found up to an elevation of about 1300 m. Other prominent species are Khair, Semal, Kanju, Sissoo and Haldu.

(ii) *Sub-Tropical* – Temperate zone: Found at elevations of 900 m to 2100 m 'Chir' pine is the dominant coniferous tree with sub-Tropical to temperate shrubs.

(iii) *Temperate* – Sub-Alpine zone: Mixed coniferous forests of fir, spruce and birch are found between 1500 & 3300 m.

(iv) *Alpine forests and shrubs* – Found generally up to 4200 m of altitude. With increasing altitude, a gradual transition from larger flora to smaller fushes and Alpine pastures can be observed, beyond which there is a total lack of vegetal cover.

Source : 4

Distribution of Forests by Legal Type

The distribution of forests under major legal classifications is shown in the Figure below. As seen, the area under Reserved Forests is 69.12 per cent, Civil Soyam is 18 per cent and Van Panchayats is 11 per cent.

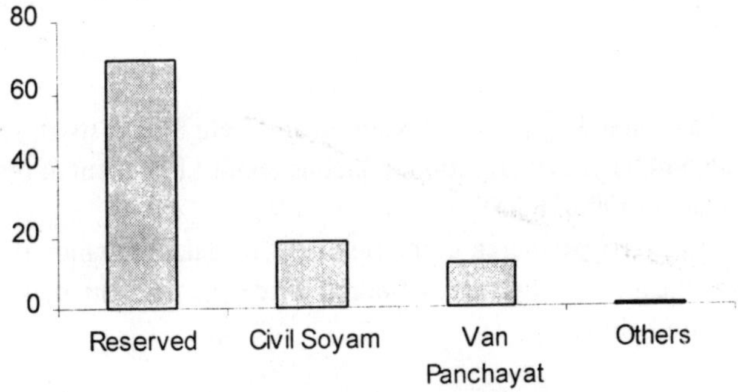

Fig. 3.1.2: Legal Ownership of Forests

Of the total funds spent on afforestation in Uttaranchal about 70 per cent are spent on Civil-Soyam lands. In spite of such massive investments, plantations taken up on Civil-Soyam are very poor.

The Van Panchayats face many problems such as duality of control, insufficient staff, poor budgetary support, lack of sufficient authority to Van Panchayats, encroachment on Panchayat lands, lack of training support, inadequate representation of women, etc.

The Reserved Forests face substantial pressure for timber and fuelwood. As a result of these problems, the actual forest cover is far below the legal area.

Actual Forest Cover

The distribution of actual forest cover shows a slightly different picture. Of the 63.7 per cent of the area that is classed as forests, only 77.24 per cent contains dense forests and represents 2.5 per cent of the total forest area or 11 per cent of the Open Forest area. Dense canopy cover forests exist in only 34.45 per cent of the forest area. The total actual forest cover is therefore only 44.31 per cent.[7]

Agriculture

Uttaranchal's economy is predominantly agrarian and activities related to agriculture account for about two-thirds of the region's workforce. The net sown area forms 12.5 per cent of the total area and the per capita cultivated area is only 0.89 ha. In addition to the small landholdings, most of the soil is infertile.[2]

Irrigation

Uttaranchal (excluding plains of Nainital and Dehradun districts) has an area of 55,544 ha under irrigation, which is about 11 per cent of the total net sown area (490,028 ha).

The gross irrigated area in the region is 1.0 lakh ha which is 12.85 per cent of the gross cropped area. Source-wise irrigation pattern is shown in the Figure below.[2]

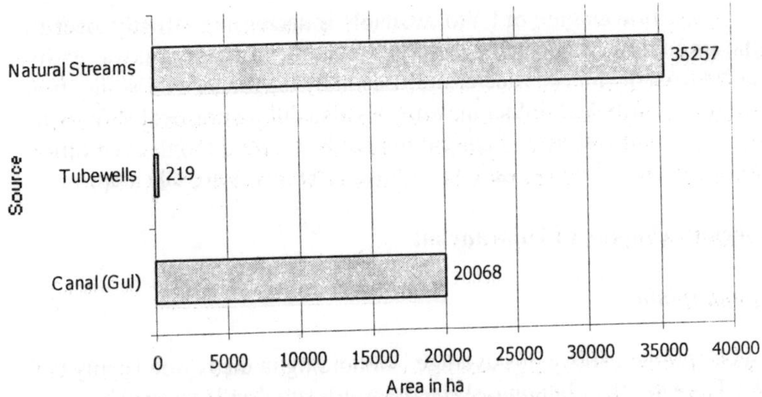

Fig. 3.1.3: Sources of Irrigation in Uttaranchal

As we can see, natural streams are the main source of irrigation. Water is conveyed to the fields using diversion channels (called Gools). Most crops are raised in rainfed conditions. This has serious impact on productivity. The yields can almost double if irrigation is provided as given in the Table below:

Crop	*Unirrigated yields (q/ha)*	*Irrigated yields (q/ha)*
Paddy	22.5	44.9
Wheat	13.6	33.0

Lack of irrigation also rules out improved agricultural practices such as the application of chemical fertilisers, pesticides, HYV seeds, etc. In addition to the poor productivity due to lack of irrigation and infertile soils, the average amount of FYM used is only about 3.5 kg/ha. The cow dung and animal bedding material is not properly placed in the pits and is generally heaped in an open area. This results in the loss of nutrients though volatilisation and rainwater. The FYM thus prepared is of poor quality and as such its application to standing crop serves the purpose of mulching rather than a source of nutrients.[2]

The irrigation potential of natural springs is decreasing as many are drying up due to deforestation of the region. A study by Valdiya indicates that in a little less than 50 per cent of the villages, springs have either ceased to yield water or do so only during the rainy season for the time when sufficient surface on rainwater is available. There has been a decrease in spring discharge ranging from 25 to 75 per cent resulting in a considerable decrease in water flow, estimated at 30 to 40 per cent in the last decade or two.[8]

Also, the amount of FYM available is decreasing—firstly, because the amount of compostable material (mainly leaf litter) that was earlier taken from the forest is decreasing. Secondly the fodder availability from forests (mainly leaf fodder in winter) is also falling drastically. In such a situation, productivity of agriculture lands is bound to fall even further unless efforts at conservation of spring catchments are taken up.

Social Economy of Uttaranchal

Landholdings

As mentioned above, the average landholding in the region is only 0.89 ha. Even this distribution is skewed towards small and marginal holdings. These holdings are also scattered in various locations and in the form of many fields. A sample survey of Chamba block (Tehri) revealed the following:[2]

Av. No. of fields/farm	:	16 to 42
Av. No. of locations	:	4 to 8
Av. Field size	:	0.038 ha in high hills
		0.034 ha in mid hills
		0.048 ha in valleys

Workforce

The workforce makes up about 36 per cent of the total population. For 92 per cent of the total population, agriculture is the main occupation. In effect, all operations except ploughing and sowing are done by women. The contribution of female labour is thus considerably higher than male labour in most crops (Figure below).

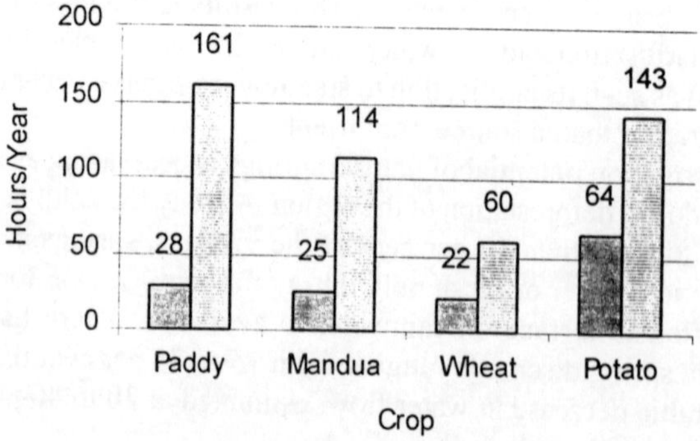

Fig. 3.1.4: Labour Input by Women and Men in Crops

Women are also burdened with the responsibility of managing the livestock as well as fetching fodder, fuelwood and drinking water. In hill farming system, it is anticipated that while two bullocks put in 1064 hours and men put in 1212 hours, women put in 2485 hours in a year. This is more than the hours put in by bullocks and men combined. Thus of the total energy spent in agriculture (-human + bullock), women put in 715 HP-hr (74 per cent). These estimates exclude women's contribution in other chores such as cooking, child rearing, sanitation, etc.[2]

Traditional Response of Farmers to Constraints

Through their power of observation and their innovative capacities, the people of the Himalayas have evolved economic activities and resource management strategies to suit the characteristics of their specific natural environment. Deeper enquiry into all indigenous practices reveals a sound logic aimed at sustainability. These strategies have internalised specific advantages and limitations of survival in mountain watersheds. The knowledge that grew out of hundreds of years of experience is visible in traditional practices such as shifting cultivation, terracing, use of medicinal plants, forest management for maximum production of specific biomass (such as fodder), transhumance transportation and management of water, etc.

Another response to environmental fragility and insecurity has been the practice of transhumance to Terai and Bhabhar (moving with large herds of cattle). This has been a traditional method of reducing grazing pressure on forest and reported as recently as 25 years ago in some parts of Uttaranchal. In almost all villages, cattle holdings have declined as grazing area in the vicinity of the villages has decreased. In the Terai and Bhabhar, previous grazing lands (designated by the title "Khatta") have now been almost completely colonised for agriculture by refugees from Punjab.

Considering the food production scenario in Uttaranchal, we have references of surplus production in historical times. Agriculture in precolonial times is reported to be very prosperous and instances of large amounts of export from this area are recorded. Exports from Uttaranchal were largely of Turmeric, Ginger, Chilly, Ghee, Honey, Walnut, Tea, Sheep, Goat, Tibetan horses, etc. alongwith other agriculture-forestry products such as wood, dyes, turpentine, gum, spices, herbs, etc.[3]

However, recent statistics indicate that this happy scenario no longer exists. Thus it is estimated that 75 per cent of Uttaranchal's food grains are imported from the plains.[9] The primary reason for this appears to be the lack of what Ashish calls "support" lands-forests and grazing lands available for the carrying out of agriculture. It is now well recognised that the agricultural economy of Uttaranchal depends heavily on forests for its supplies of fodder and leaf-litter (and hence manure). Each hectare of agriculture land requires sufficient amounts of support lands (forests, grazing lands, pastures, etc.) for sustained productivity. Thus these lands form an interlinked system. (*See* Fig. 3.1.2 above). Various estimates of the amount of support lands required for supporting agriculture in Uttaranchal (that is carrying capacity of Uttaranchal for agriculture) are available based on a number of studies and are discussed in the section below.

Carrying Capacity Calculations for Uttaranchal

The net sown area in Uttaranchal today is 669,000 ha. The total support land (Forests, Unculturable and culturable wastes, pastures and land under miscellaneous trees) is 8,964,000 ha. Thus per ha of agriculture lands, 13.4 ha of support lands are available.[10] Let us see how much support lands are actually required.

In a study of three village in Kumaon, J.S. Singh and Uma Pande found that for the production of one unit of milk and food grains, seven units of energy from forests are required. For every hectare of agricultural land, the amount of forests required for fuelwood, fodder and manure for three study villages came out to be 19.8, 31.97, 16.45 hectares.[11] In another study of 12 villages in Kumaon, Ery and Shastry calculated that for every hectare of sown area, 30.74 hectare of forests are required to meet fodder and manure needs.[12] On the same issue, Madhav Ashish states that for every hectare of sown area, 50 hectares of forest area is needed.[9]

Using 1980-81 figures, Shah calculates that for meeting current manure fodder and fuelwood requirements of Uttaranchal, a total land area of 40 lakh ha is required as against availability of 8.2 lakh ha. Similarly, while an area of 32,602 sq. km. of forests are needed for meeting current manure and fuelwood needs of the existing population, only 34,439 sq. km. are available (of which, portions under rocks or snow are unusable). Shah also points out that mechanisms such as transhumance, which were once effective in reducing pressure on the support lands have now been discontinued.[10]

On the basis of the above the total area available for supporting agriculture in Uttaranchal seems to be much less than what is actually required. This has led many to believe that it may be better for the ecology of the region to shift to permanent cover crops *such as horticulture or agro-forestry*. However, it must be remembered that in addition to food security for three months in a year, agriculture also provides *vegetables, spices, fruits, milk, employment and moorings* to a population that is increasingly called upon to migrate to meet the family's subsistence requirements. In a subsequent section we will see how migration is a major socio-economic response to Uttaranchal's food security needs.

Fruits and Vegetable Cultivation

Given the constraints in productivity of field crops, a shift towards high-value crops such as fruits and vegetables is taking place in the region. The varied agro-climatic conditions in Uttaranchal help in growing various sub-tropical and temperate fruits and vegetables. From 300 to 1400 msl, fruits like citrus, mangoes, litchi, bananas, guavas, papaya, strawberries and various vegetable crops are grown. Temperate fruits like apples, pears, peaches, plums, apricots, cherries and walnuts are grown between 1000 to 3000 msl.[2]

The production constraints which hinder adoption of horticulture crops are:

- Lack of high-quality plant material.
- The perishable nature of these crops.
- Lack of technical know-how with the growers.
- Poor transportation facilities.
- Lack of post-harvest processing facilities.
- Lack of storage facilities.
- Poor communication infrastructure.
- Lack of proper marketing facilities.
- Non-availability of suitable cheaper packaging material.

Migration as a Response

As a result of decreasing food security and due to the declaration of Uttaranchal people as 'Martial Races' by the British, a trend of migration started in 1920s that shows no signs of abating.[3]

Since ancient times, seasonal migration was reported to be an integral part of the life of the people of Uttaranchal. In fact, the Shaukas were a tribe whose primary livelihood strategy was trade between India and Tibet across the border. Thus seasonal migration in Almora was found to be 78 per cent and 98 per cent in Byans area in 1901 (mainly by the Shaukas of Byans). However, after the closure of Tibet trade (following the 1962 Indo-China war) and consequent settling down of the Shaukas, this seasonal migration has almost stopped.[3]

On the other hand, decreasing livestock population all over Uttaranchal has drastically reduced migration for transhumance. Therefore, the major type of migration found in Uttaranchal today is temporary migration for jobs. This trend accelerated after the 1962 Indo-China war, when a number of Army recruitment centres were opened in the area. Better accessibility and communication following the war and an increasing tilt towards commercialisation of the economy further increased the extent of migration into the army.

This situation has reached such a state today that it is estimated that out of a total population of 25 lakhs in Kumaon, 10.27 lakhs persons are employed in the military and paramilitary forces. On an average 1400 people every year join the army, thus one out of every 19 households in Kumaon has a person employed in the army.

In Pithoragarh district, this incidence is even higher with one out of every two households having a person employed in the army and one out of every three household having a pensioner. The profile of Garhwal is similar.

A study by S.S. Khanka found that the main reason for migration was insufficient income in 92 per cent of the samples studied. Unemployment (6 per cent) and unstable occupation (1 per cent) were other reasons. It was found that migration occurred mainly due to push factors rather than pull factors.

The majority of the migrants are reported to be between 15-35 years of age and largely with formal education. 85 per cent of the sample studied sent money orders back home, most of which is used for current use. In a large majority of cases the increase in the household income due to migration was found to be more than five times.

The study reports that the average labour required per hectare of land cultivated was 1.77 person units. Thus is household labour was in excess of this, the increase in productivity is only marginal. The author has worked out that the out migration from Uttaranchal (1981 figures) is 29.7 per cent.[13]

In spite of the above constraints, Uttaranchal does provide many opportunities for growth. The next section deals with opportunities that can be utilised for all-round development of Uttaranchal.

What Needs to be done for all-round Development of Uttaranchal

Uttaranchal has been recognised as an under-developed and backward area in national Government planning. A large amount of central assistance has been ear-marked for this region since the Third Five Year Plan. Since the Fifth Five Year Plan, separate development funds have been ear-marked for the region and 50 per cent of the state budget is borne by the Centre as Central assistance. In the early seventies, a Department for Hill Area Development was created. Current allocations for Uttaranchal are as follows:[2]

Plan	*Expenditure (Rs. Crores)*	
	Central Assistance	*Total*
5th V Year (1974-79)	104	204.02
6th V Year (1980-85)	350	658.87
7th V Year (1985-90)	671.99	1213.1
Annual Plan (1990-92)	364.02	614.89
8th V Year (1992-97)	1005	2105

However, such large allocations have not resulted in any appreciable difference in the conditions of either the hill folk or their environment. According to G.S. Mehta, a basic lacuna in the development plans for Uttaranchal has been the absence of an integrated and region-specific approach to thinking about and planning for the region.[14]

Thus environmental protection issues have been approached without due regard to the needs of the people, infrastructure was developed without considering its application to local development and sectoral economic activities were promoted through incentives without simultaneously developing backward and forward linkages. Diversity in mountain regions requires a highly decentralised area-based approach, which should be able to absorb local variations.[15]

The economic conditions in Uttaranchal show that while 92.7 per cent of the total workers in agriculture consist of women, only 49.74 per cent consist of men. In all, 89 per cent of women are engaged in agriculture compared to 42 per cent of men. The contributions to the net domestic output of Uttaranchal by other sectors is much less than agriculture as shown in the Table below:

Sector	*Share in NDO per cent*
Agriculture	66.77
Manufacturing	20.07
Forestry and Logging	8.78
Mining and Quarrying	4.20
Fishing	0.18
Total	100.00

Possible Approach

Uttaranchal offers a vast potential for economic growth in a number of areas provided the impediments to growth can be removed. In order to facilitate economic growth in Uttaranchal, we need to look at the agro-climate conditions within Uttaranchal and see what are the areas where the unique advantages that these mountains offer can be exploited. Given below is only an indicative list of some important points.

Recognise the Importance of the Mountain Farming System

Agriculture is the mainstay of the economy of Uttaranchal, involving 89 per cent of the women and 42 per cent of the male work force.[2] We therefore need to look at the Mountain Farming System and the interlinkages and flows in this sector carefully. As shown in Fig. 3.1.2, agriculture in Uttaranchal is heavily dependent on energy flows from "support" lands and livestock in the form of compostable biomass and cow dung from the agriculture lands. Fig. 3.1.5 on the next page shows the same Farming System in another layout. Keeping this interlinked nature of the Farming System in mind is very important in understanding why a single intervention in a particular field may not yield desired results.

On the other hand, development approaches generally start with interventions in a particular sector such as agriculture, horticulture, animal husbandry, forestry, etc. due to the sectoral nature of Government approach. In Uttaranchal, a sectoral approach is bound to lead to unbalanced growth, which may upset the dynamic equilibrium of the entire system. Fig. 3.1.4 shows possible interventions for strengthening the entire Farming System (Based on the author's experience in watershed development in Almora and Kangra district and may be further refined for other areas).

A balanced approach to the development of hill agriculture will necessarily involve interventions in areas such as grassland development, animal husbandry, irrigation, horticulture, vegetable promotion, appropriate technologies such as green houses, roof/spring/rainfall water harvesting tanks, compoting, etc.

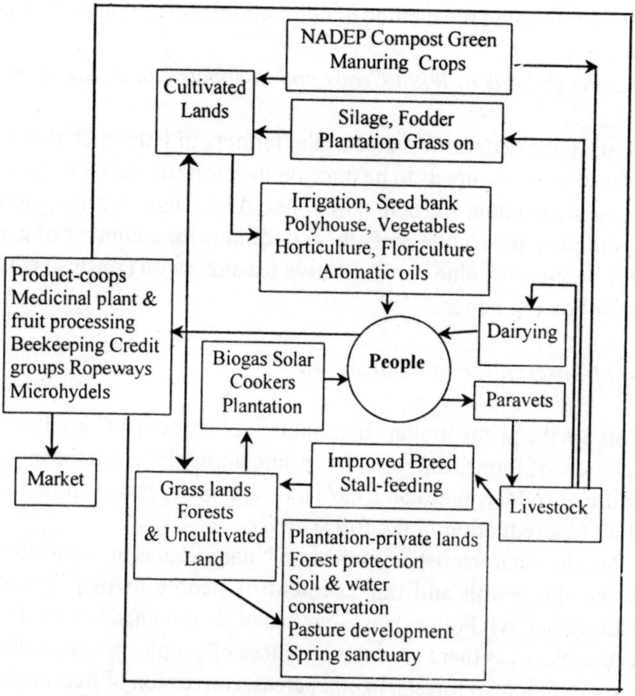

Fig. 3.1.4: Interventions for Strengthening the Farming System

An example of vegetable promotion will clarify the linkages. Introduction of improved vegetable seeds for increasing vegetable production may require water-harvesting systems to be developed first. Vegetable cultivation will also require large quantities of FYM, which cannot be obtained until improved composting methods are developed. This in turn would mean developing fodder availability.

One source for fodder is agriculture terraces. Improved grass plantation on terrace risers may therefore have to be taken up. Silaging of maize or Mandua stalks can also be taken up. Common lands may also have to be protected (and seeded) for improved grass production.

Vegetables are also prone to damage due to frostbite and low growth due to low temperatures. This may involve designing and implementing low cost green houses for growing vegetables nurseries. Thus we see that one single activity of vegetable promotion involves interventions in various fields for it to be successful. The conventional approach of distributing improved seeds of vegetables (probably supported with booklets describing the method of cultivation) will not serve the purpose.

Take a Fresh Look at What Crops and Products can be taken up

If boosting the economic status of the farmers of Uttaranchal is a focus, then fresh thinking needs to be done on the crops or activities that can be taken up in mountain Agroclimatic zones. As discussed earlier, mountains offer unique temperature and other conditions for a number of activities of high economic value. An indicative list alongwith constraints is given in the following pages.

Forest Conservation in Uttaranchal

Forests are the prime movers in mountain ecosystems. Conservation and enrichment of forests thus assumes prime importance. On the other hand, pressure of fodder, fuelwood, agriculture, timber, encroachments, etc. is leading to a reduction in the forest cover.

Another characteristic of forests in Uttaranchal is the wide dichotomy between the health and management of people-owned forests (Van Panchayat or Civil Forests) *vis-à-vis* that of state-owned forests. In remote inaccessible areas there are even instances of people managing Reserved Forests as their own forests. In other areas, conversion of Reserved Forests into agriculture land is taking place due to faulty rules regarding road construction.

If the forests of Uttaranchal are to be preserved, in addition to works in forestry, many works in the non-forestry sector need to be taken up in such a manner that the existing pressure on forests is reduced or diverted. We feel that for saving the forests of Uttaranchal, the following interventions are urgently needed:

(*a*) *Conservation of existing common land resources*: A number of initiatives have been taken up in recent years to involve the local people in protection and regeneration of common lands. Strategies such as Joint Forest Management (JFM) need to build on traditional mechanisms that exist for the same in the region (such as sacred groves, local Forest Protection practices, etc.)

(*b*) *Fodder and grassland development*: Private grasslands and terrace risers can be utilised for both grass and tree fodder to reduce pressure on forest lands. Silaging of maize and mandua stalks has been tried by various agencies in Kumaon and is a good option for free concentrates in the lean season.

(*c*) *Alternative sources of energy for cooking and room heating*: Use of alternative source of energy would reduce pressure on forests for fuelwood, which is the major source of energy for cooking and home heating. Biogas has often been suggested. However, poor performance has been reported due to the low temperatures in the region. Also, in the absence of adequate support infrastructure for maintenance, many plants are lying defunct, thus giving the farmer the impression that the technology is not viable. Using electricity for heating and cooking is one option that has a good potential, given the adequate amounts of MHP available in the region.

(*d*) *Other interventions*: Other interventions urgently required include streamlining of forest laws that prevent construction of roads, mobilisation of local communities for forest protection and regeneration, reducing drudgery of women by making available fuelwood and fodder near their homes and through technologies such as ropeway trolleys.

Promotion of Small Industries

Small industries based on raw materials available from an improved agriculture pattern are a must if local employment is to be generated. While the primary sector will provide raw materials for most enduse, such small industries will perform value addition before marketing the produce. Options available for such industries in Uttaranchal are:

- Fruit preservation, processing into pulp, jams, juices, concentrates, pickles, fruit packing etc.
- Processing and packaging of medicinal and aromatic plants and oils.
- Filtration and packaging of honey.
- Small industries based on bamboo and ringal – especially for flooring, furniture and utility and decorative items.
- Woollen products—sweaters, tweed, shawls, pattu, etc.
- Chilling and storage of milk, production of Khoya, paneer, etc.
- Packing and transportation of flowers.

Current Pattern of Government and Non-government Assistance

Since the Government is the major development agency in the region, we need to review the current pattern of assistance for development of the primary and small industry sectors. A detailed review would form the subject for a separate study. However, the gaps in the same are presented in brief below on the basis of the author's personal experience:

(a) *Gaps in Government Assistance*

Following are the major gaps in assistance by the Government:

- Partial credit for water harvesting tanks, loans for repair of defunct tanks and *Gools* are not available.
- Credit for agro-processing equipment, low-cost green houses etc. is not available.
- Low-cost farmer-level demonstration facilities for improved crops are not available.
- Technical support and credit for development of alternative sources of energy such as Mini/Micro Hydel Projects, Biogas, etc. is not available.
- Training and technical support for planting material, cultivation techniques, agricultural inputs, processing techniques, etc. to individual entrepreneurs is absent.
- Quality control, marketing support and credit to producers of both raw material and processed goods is not available.

All the above functions that the Government cannot/does not provide can be done very well by NGOs. However, this assistance by NGOs is not available due to the following reasons:

- Lack of training and technical (or even semi-technical) manpower with NGOs, most of which are small village level groups in Uttaranchal arising after the Chipko movement.
- Non-availability of working capital for initiation of such ventures.
- Inadequate scale of such ventures making them uneconomical.
- Lack of financial support for demonstrations and proving such technologies.
- Inadequate tie-up with Government technical and financial institutions.

Energy Demand

If a vision of the above agro-industrial set up alongwith an improved standard of living for hill people is to be made a reality, a large amount of decentralised energy would be required for running many such small units scattered in various locations. Energy would be required for the following domestic and industrial uses:

- Cooking, Home-heating.
- Transport of raw materials and local produce (for example through ropeway) and for better communication facilities.
- Drudgery (and time) reducing devices for drinking water, fuelwood, and fodder collection.
- Irrigation, post-harvest processing, etc.
- Collection of raw material, processing and running of various small industries, packaging, transportation, etc.
- Refrigeration of perishable product such as fruits, vegetable, milk products and flowers.

Expecting that the Government would undertake extension of the power grid so that these units are provided with required energy would be too expensive and unrealistic. Among the various alternate energy options that are available.

Profile of Household Energy used in Uttaranchal

The specific Agroclimatic conditions of the Western Himalayas are responsible for a unique demand-supply pattern of energy use. The severe and prolonged winters create a very high seasonal demand of heat energy for home heating and cooking on the one hand and on the other hand, the inaccessibility of the terrain requires very heavy public investments for successful extension and maintenance of options such as LPG, kerosene and electrical power.

Villages in Uttaranchal are characterised by poor accessibility and poor purchasing power. The share of commercial energy is therefore very low in the total energy consumed. The propagation of non-conventional energy sources such as Biogas and solar cookers has also not taken place to a very large extent. There is thus a very heavy dependence on the use of non-commercial energy.

A survey of energy use patterns in eight districts of Uttaranchal[16] covering 2004 families in 52 villages revealed that non-commercial energy formed 98.59 per cent of the total household energy consumed. Commercial energy formed only 1.41 per cent of the total energy consumed and consisted of kerosene and electricity.

It was also found that of the 98.59 per cent of non-commercial energy consumed at a household level, a staggering 93 per cent comes from fuelwood. On an average, the requirement of fuelwood per capita per year was found to be nine quintals. Thus for a family of five persons, a total of 45 quintals of fuelwood would be required per year. The general custom in the region is to collect most of this fuelwood in the free time after the kharif harvest and before the start of winters. The survey found that about 97 per cent of all families collected fuelwood for which no monetary value was paid as it was part of their forest rights. On an average two persons per household and 58 per cent of all women were engaged in fuelwood collection. The total number of hours spent every year per household in fuelwood collection was 485. The consumption of fuelwood in winter was much higher than that in summer. Eighty seven per cent of all household reported that they consumed 1.5 to two times the fuelwood that they consumed during summer.

It is obvious that since very large quantities of fuelwood are required, the pressure on forests is intense. The major sources of fuelwood were found to be as follows:[16]

Source	*per cent*
Reserved Forests	51.03
Civil Soyam	19.42
Panchayat forests	22.35
Private lands	7.20

This shows that all categories of forestlands are under pressure for fuelwood. As per S.L. Shah's calculations, a total of 32,602 sq. km. would be required to meet the fuelwood needs of the existing population of Uttaranchal. As of today, only 34,439 sq. km. is available of which a large portion is under rocks on permanently under snow.[14] As population increases, the demand for fuelwood would increase, thus putting an increasing pressure on the forests. In addition to fuelwood (most of which is fallen twigs or small branches lopped) are the commercial pressures on the forests. Thus from an energy angle, unless alternatives to energy for cooking, home heating and lighting are provided, the ecological future of Uttaranchal is bleak.

Lack of Energy for Sectoral Development

Lack of non-fuelwood energy for basic requirements such as cooking, lighting, home-heating, etc. is one dimension of underdevelopment in Uttaranchal. The second dimension is that of suppression of local skills, industry, productivity enhancement and income generating options. Following are the glaring examples that come to mind:

1. *Energy for Irrigation*: Productivity of hill agriculture can be increased tremendously if irrigation could be provided. However, although sufficient water resources are available,[19] in the absence of energy for water-lifting devices, irrigation cannot be made available. The Government has set up a Hydram Department in the area but its reach is severely limited. Of the cement tanks for water harvesting constructed by the Minor Irrigation and Soil Conservation Departments, 95 per cent in Dhauladevi Block were found to be defunct due to poor site selection. Due to these factors, only11 per cent of the total cultivated area is under irrigation in Uttaranchal. Even the recently started World Bank funded Drinking Water Project (SWAJAL) has focused only on tapping gravity flow for drinking water and has not explored the possibility of water lifting due to these reasons.[17]
2. *Energy for Fruit, Vegetable and Medicinal Plant Processing*: The disease-free and diverse agro-ecological conditions in the Himalayas generate an ecological niche for a variety of marketable produce such as off-season vegetables, fruits, medicinal plants, flowers, vegetable and potato seeds, mushrooms and angora wool. However, transportation and processing of these fruit, medicinal and other resources for income generation is another area where insufficient availability of energy is leading to a depressed development of local industry and has resulted in gross wastage of local resources.

As a result, although the total production of fruits in Uttaranchal is more than that in Himachal Pradesh, a large portion of this produce is wasted.[18] Thus, inadequate processing and marketing facilities have ensured that the horticulture industry in the area does not make a significant dent in the incomes of the local populations.

In addition, local agri-horti produce such as potatoes, fruits, flowers and medicinal plants as well as dairy products require energy for refrigeration and chilling plants, in the absence of which local produce is wasted.[19] Once again, adequate energy for local industries as well as availability of a proper marketing infrastructure are the constraints in the development of fruits processing industry. In the absence of a supporting infrastructure, farmers are averse to investing precious land resources in high value, high risk ventures.[20]

The conditions described above call for mountain-sensitive energy planning and implementation rather than blind imitation of policies designed for and by a plains oriented approach (the situation today).

Demand for Energy in Uttaranchal

Many villages have to adjust to a lower quality of life due to non-availability of larger quantity and a better quality of energy. However, if we plan for an Uttaranchal with a vibrant and developed economy, with a higher quality of life and substantial and gainful employment of the Hill people, we would have to plan for larger energy generation and consumption. Energy would then also be required for the following purposes:

1. *Cooking, home heating and lighting*: Demand for these enduses is by far the largest as of now. This demand is also likely to increase as population increases. The lighting load at current population levels would be about 240 MW. Similarly cooking would require additional installed capacity of 2400 MW and home heating another 2400 MW. Thus a total of 5040 MW would be required for the above purpose. The total energy required for these would be 78 per cent of the total Small Hydro Power installed capacity. However, the impact on the health of forests in the area would be tremendous.
2. *Transport of raw material and local produce*: Lack of transportation is one of the main reasons why farmers in remote locations feel hesitant in investing time, land and money in ventures that can fetch them good returns. Thus farmers in interior villages in Kullu district told us that even if they started growing apples, almonds, and the other such produce, the transportation cost using mules (Rs. 60 per trip in 1993) made the price of their apples too high for them to find a market.[20]

However, numerous options for transportation of goods from distant locations are available. The Forest Department uses non-motorised ropeways to transport timber from forests at remote locations. Slates are transported from quarries in inaccessible locations to the road head using simple gravity trolleys on ropeways in Himachal. However, such simple local technologies have not been used very extensively in Uttaranchal or Himachal for commercial applications. If such devices can be used to transport local produce (such as fruits, vegetables, etc.), this will give a boost to local production. Use of such simple devices can also significantly reduce the drudgery of women folk in the Himalayas in the collection of fuelwood and fodder. Motorization of such trolleys at strategic locations can obviate the need for roads that prove environmentally very damaging.

3. *Drudgery reduction technologies for drinking water, fuelwood/ fodder collection*: In addition to the very high levels of energy put in by women in agriculture, women are also responsible for collecting fuelwood, fodder, fetching drinking water and all household chores such as house cleaning, cooking and looking after children. For most of these tasks, technologies are available that can reduce the amount of time and energy required. The more strenuous tasks such as fetching of drinking water can very easily be replaced by a simple community-managed gravity or water-lifting scheme. Government schemes for drinking water do not cover all villages nor are they regular in their supplies. "Swajal" project in Uttaranchal has achieved notable success in setting up and handing over such schemes to village communities. Energy required for operation of such schemes is generally in the range of 50 to 100 Horsepower each.
4. *Energy for an agro-industrial set-up*: Unless inputs such as irrigation and post-harvest processing are provided, the agrarian economy of Uttaranchal can never generate sufficient income for the residents to stop migrating. The potential for processing of fruits vegetables, herbs, flowers and other products in the region is immense. The major bottleneck in the successful propagation of the same is lack of accessibility and decentralised energy. Various small industries can be based on the processing of produce such as potatoes, seeds, vegetables, medicinal plants, silage, medicinal oils, etc. Energy would also be required for supporting equipments that would support these activities. Thus

one can think of chilling plants for milk and milk products, refrigerated storage plants for potatoes, fruits, flowers, vegetables and other perishable products, etc.

Potential of Traditional Hydro-Energy Technologies

Historically, hill communities had developed technologies for their own survival in this fragile and inhospitable mountain ecosystem. These have included technologies of soil conservation (such as terracing), water harvesting (Gools, bawdis, etc.) and nutrient recycling. Owing to the difficult terrain, animal power cannot be used as extensively in the plains. In the absence of another alternative, human muscle power for mechanical work and biomass for cooking, heating and lighting has been used. However, this pattern of energy use has resulted in very high drudgery levels for the hill community in general and the rural women in particular whose working hours are sometimes from 4 a.m. to 12 midnight.

The Western Himalayas boast of a vast resource of hydropower energy from the many perennial streams and rivulets (fed mainly by snow or springs) that fall from great heights. Reduction of the drudgery in grinding of grain and carding of wool forced hill communities to develop and refine use of hydropower. Of these gharats, 65 per cent are in operation annually, 25 per cent are run seasonally and 10 per cent are reported to be defunct.[21] At a rough estimate of 1.5 KW per Gharat, these represent a total power potential of 90 MW in Uttaranchal alone and 375 MW in the whole of the Indian Himalayas at existing efficiencies (10 to 15 per cent). At improved efficiencies (60 per cent reported in improved Gharats), this potential would be 360 MW in Uttaranchal and 1500 MW in the whole of the Himalayas. By no means is this a small amount of energy.

In addition, upgradation of water mills represents a vast potential for taking up multi-dimensional economic activities that could present diverse economic options for income generation and local employment generation. A traditional water mill observed in Doiwala in Dehradun district is able to use water power for grinding of grain, powder medicinal plants for sale as well as generate 2 KW of electricity for the family's own consumption. The mill owner is planning to install an oil expeller, a porridge making machine and a 10 KW generator. Local industry based on such water mills could generate tremendous local employment as well as provide value addition to currently wasted resources.

Potential of Microhydel Energy in the Uttaranchal Himalayas

It is now recognised by national planning bodies that the Western Himalayas possesses a vast reserve of hydropower energy. Estimates suggest that the total potential of Hydropower in the Uttaranchal is as much as 40,000 MW. Of this, the potential currently being investigated and developed is about 6530 MW. Only a minuscule portion of this potential (1030 MW) has been exploited by the current schemes.[25] Even among these hydel schemes, the emphasis of the State and Central Governments has been on the development of small and large hydel projects. The large hydel projects give rise to problems such as displacement of local populations and reservoir induced or natural seismicity, and have therefore been the focus of much controversy by environmentalists due to their very size. Such projects also do not generate sustained employment for the local population (except sometimes as labourers during construction). The local population is very often not even the consumer of the power so generated.

Current Schemes for Development of MHP in Uttaranchal

As a result of this recognition of the environmentally benign nature of Himalayan Micro[1] Hydro Power (MHP), a number of projects for promotion of MHP have been launched both by MNES and by foreign donors. Among the various schemes for promotion of MHP development launched by MNES for the benefit of private sector developers are:[22]

(a) Support for survey, investigations and preparation of Detailed Project Reports.
(b) Capital subsidy of up to 50 per cent.
(c) Interest subsidy for MHP projects.
(d) Renovation and modernisation of old MHP stations
(e) Soft loans by Indian Renewable Energy Development Agency (IREDA), MNES' financing arm.
(f) Subsidies for upgradation of water mills.

So far nine states have offered sites with a total potential of 600 MW for commercial projects to the private sector.

The Uttaranchal Renewable Energy Development Agency (UREDA) is another major agency responsible for development of MHP in Uttaranchal. It receives funds both from MNES and the State Government and has installed 26 demonstration plants in Garhwal (data for Kumaon not available). The District Project Officer of UREDA has also been given the power to provide a licence for power generation and supply up to 3 MW into the grid to private parties after a clearance for the same has been obtained from Uttaranchal Power Corporation.

Foremost among the Foreign Donors to support MHP development is the GEF under the "UNDP-GEF Hilly Hydro Project" covering mainly the Himalayan States of India. The project has supported a mapping exercise by AHEC in 13 MW based on Toposheets and field surveys on a Geographical Information Systems platform. The project is also supporting upgradation of watermills, installation of about 100 projects of MHP and R&D into Load Management Systems, Energy efficient and Energy Storage End-use Devices.[22]

Another key player in the game is the Indian Renewable Energy Development Agency (IREDA), which provides financial assistance for individuals and agencies interested in setting up and promoting Small Hydro Power as well as other RETs.

Gaps in the Current Schemes

In spite of the various schemes operated both by the Central and by State Governments, as well as by foreign donors such as UNDP-GEF, Micro Hydro Power is yet to become a major source of energy in the Himalayas. A detailed analysis of the major reasons for the non-proliferation of Micro Hydro Power would require a separate study. However, listed below are some important reasons based on preliminary research:

1. *Load planning*: A common complaint of all agencies implementing Micro Hydro Power programmes (whether Government or Non-government) has been the under-utilisation of installed capacity in the rural areas where Micro Hydro Power plants have been set up. In fact, this under-utilisation is often quoted as a reason why electricity generated in remote locations should be sold to the grid to make these plants viable. However, a cursory look at the reasons for non-utilisation of the load reveals that very little policy or technical support is provided for ensuring that power generated is utilised locally. Even in sites where local consumption is easily possible (such as the tourists site of Sahastradhara), the excess power was observed to be dissipated as heat energy. Often, when load planning is

done, only the lighting load is considered. Possibilities of local processing industry would require organisation of local people into cooperatives and organisation of local level raw material collection, processing and packing. No Government agency would like to (or can) get into all these activities.

2. *Credit*: All the packages for promotion of Micro Hydro Power (such as MNES, IREDA, UNDP-GEF) provide credit and incentives for installation and maintenance of Micro Hydro Power plants. However, no credit is available for oil expellers, grinders, lathes and other agro-processing equipment. If credit could be made broad-based such as that done by BTI and ADB in Nepal, Micro Hydro Power plants can become viable as well as create local employment.
3. *Single window facility*: As seen in the case of Sahastradhara, under-utilisation of installed capacity and poor load planning were the result of the lack of coordination between UREDA and GMVN. This is the bane of all Micro Hydro Power plants currently being installed. If Micro Hydro Power is to serve as a means of rural development, Government agencies involved in rural development, cooperatives, small industries, agriculture, horticulture and dairy development have to be involved rather than only Non-conventional energy. The Government of Burundi, for example, has placed Micro Hydro Power under the Ministry of Rural Development. In case this cannot be done, at least a single window facility can be ensured to provide credit, training, maintenance and other facilities for Micro Hydro Power equipment as well as other agriculture-horticulture/forest products processing equipment.
4. *Either-or Syndrome*: In most Micro Hydro Power plants, the aim of the project is to supply electricity (primarily for lighting) either from the grid or from the Micro Hydro Power installations. Grid electricity is deliberately not supplied where MHP is available. Due to mismanagement of the Micro-Hydro Power plants, electricity is not available to these villages. They are also not able to avail of electricity from the grid. The village economic growth gets stunted and village people become increasingly disillusioned with Micro Hydro Power and want to opt out of it if given a choice. An intelligent alternative would be to provide grid electricity to the village and to satisfy agro-industrial demand from Micro Hydro Power. Over time, as

systems for reliable maintenance of Micro Hydro Power plants evolve through development of local skills, the village can shift to Micro Hydro Power entirely and may even sell surplus power to grid.

5. *Training*: In most plants installed, no steps have been taken towards training of local manpower and creation of a workshop or a team. This would have ensured that installation and maintenance of many neighbouring Micro Hydro Power plants is done by this local team. The pattern today is to appoint a person from the implementing agency who is not regular in running or maintaining the plant. Once again, the implementing agencies are not willing (or are not trained to) to put in the time and effort required to develop a team of grassroots level technical skilled workers. This component is very often not even part of the project design. However, both Nepal and Pakistan have shown how local skills, indigenous technology and incorporation of training into programme design can ensure smooth maintenance of Micro Hydro Power plants.
6. *Subsidies*: The current structure of subsidy is aimed at the organised private sector. Manufacturers of Micro Hydro Power equipment (such as turbines, generators, load management systems, enduse devices) are being encouraged through subsidies, moratoriums and other such assistance. This is a welcome sign and it is hoped that participation of the private sector will boost the efficiency which is currently poor or owing to the heavy dependence on the public sector and Government agencies such as UREDA. However, the current subsidy structure provides no scope for the rural entrepreneur to take up Micro Hydro Power as an economic activity. This will require subsidies and credit for other economic activities such as fruit processing, grinding, and transportation in addition to power generation. Once again Nepal has shown that a standardised package that incorporates two to three technologies for income generation can be implemented successfully.

Tariffs for other Sources of Energy

The major reason for electricity from Micro Hydro Power being costlier than grid electricity is tariff. It is a well-known fact that if all subsidies that go into the conventional energy sector are counted, electricity by

Renewable Energy Technologies turns out to be 8-10 times less expensive than energy by other sources. For example, Junejo found that subsidies by the Government to diesel resulted in a proliferation of diesel engines for grinding and oil extraction, seriously cut into the market for Micro Hydro Power. Therefore, unless promotion of Micro Hydro Power is done in tandem with appropriate pricing structures, Micro Hydro Power plants will continue to be unviable.

Action Required

In order to implement a Micro Hydro Power programme from the angle of development of the people of the Himalayas, in the author's opinion, the following approach needs to be taken :

1. *Design an integrated programme for Micro Hydro Power development*: An integrated programme for MHP development should ideally consist of the following
   - Treatment of the catchment of the source.
   - Load planning after incorporating potential and existing agriculture-horticulture-forest product processing in the area.
   - Organisation of local people into agro-industrial cooperatives.
   - Building of an institution for regular operation and maintenance of plants.
2. *Ensure proper credit and marketing linkages for the entire venture*: It is obvious that for running an integrated programme on Micro Hydro Power development such as the one envisaged above, the primary input would be credit at easy rates not only for MHP installation but also for other agro-processing equipment and raw material. Marketing support by a specialised body (such as NDDB for milk, F&V for fruits and vegetables) would be the other key component. The current legal and illegal trade of mountain products such as fruits, medicinal plants and vegetable seeds, shows the ample demand that already exists for these products.
3. *Investment in infrastructure*: In order to ensure that an agriculture-horticulture-forest based economy starts working in Uttaranchal, infrastructural support is required for transportation (ropeways on critical points), refrigeration and storage, processing, dairying, back-up support and such other facilities.

4. *Installation of Micro Hydro Power with people's participation*: The skills of the local people in designing and managing age-old irrigation systems can be effectively coupled with designing the layout of Micro Hydro Power schemes. If assured of a regular supply of energy that will lead to their overall economic growth, people would be willing to contribute to the scheme as well as take responsibility for maintaining the same.
5. *Training*: Training is perhaps the most important component that will lead to long-term sustainability of Micro Hydro Power plants. However, there exists no training institute in the entire Western Himalayas that can create a team of technical manpower from the large number of unemployed youth in the area.

Rough Energy Budget for Uttaranchal

The calculations of a rough energy budget for the Uttaranchal Himalayas is presented in Box 3.1.3 Assumptions that have been made in this calculation are listed below. Most of these have been taken on the higher side.

(a) Assumptions:

Total number of development blocks	= 80
Total population	= 60 lakh
Total number of households	= 12 lakh
Total number of villages	= 15,000
Total number of schools	= 9,000
Total number of hospitals	= 2,000
Govt. offices, other institutions	= 2,000
Number of small industries/block	= 20
Number of large industries/block	= 10
Number of refrigeration plants/block	= 10
Number of ropeways/village (15 KW)	= 1
Number of lift irrigation/village (15 KW)	= 1
Lighting load per household	= 200 W
Home heating load/household	= 2 KW
Lighting load per school	= 200W
Total load per small industry	= 20 h.p. = 15 KW
Total load per medium industry	= 50 h.p. = 40 KW
Total load per refrigeration plant	= 30 KW
Load per Govt. Office, Hospital, Institution	= 10 KW

1. *Energy Demand*: Box 3.1.3 shows that the total Annual Energy Demand of Uttaranchal comes to above 13,456,370 MWh.

2. *Energy Supply*: Assumptions: 2000 MW of Micro Hydro Power Potential has been developed.***

Total energy generated per year = 17,520,000 MWh.

Surplus energy available in Uttaranchal = 4,063,630 MWh or 406.363 crore Units.

If sold at Rs. 1 per unit, this represents a total revenue of Rs. 406 crore per annum. This is almost equal to the annual assistance by Centre and State to Uttaranchal during the Eighth Five Year Plan.

Thus we see that development of Micro Hydro Power in Uttaranchal will not only act as a prime mover for the village economy, but will also generate surplus revenue for the region. As time progresses, domestic consumption of energy within Uttaranchal will increase leading to a drop in surplus. However, this will be more than offset by the increase in agriculture, horticulture, forest and local industry-based produce. This approach would also generate more than adequate employment and prevent migration. In short, a "win-win" situation.

Investment in Development of Micro Hydro Power

The MNES uses a norm of Rs.50,000 per KW for installation cost of Micro Hydro Power. Therefore, for the undeveloped 1,400 MW, the investment that would be required would be – 1,400,000 × 50,000 = Rs. 7,000 crore. Assuming an investment of 3000 crore in infrastructure and industries, the total investment required would be Rs. 10,000 crore. This amount would be repaid in 20 years from the sale of surplus power itself. In the coming years the energy generated from Micro Hydro Power would have a multiplier effect as the industrial, infrastructural and economic set up starts paying back returns. Sufficient revenue would then be available to undertake development interventions on the lines outlined earlier. The net result would be the development of Uttaranchal's economy and of its people.

Impact on Uttaranchal's Ecology

S.L. Shah has calculated that a total of 15 lakh ha of forests are required to meet Uttaranchal's current fuelwood needs. Assuming that 50 per cent of this load is met from Micro Hydro Power, the saving in forest area would be as much as 7.5 lakh ha per year. In a period of 20 years, an area equivalent to 150 lakh ha of forests would have been saved which is half of the existing forest area. This would have direct spin-offs in preventing the sedimentation of downstream reservoirs and an increase in fertility of agriculture and horticulture in Uttaranchal due to increased fodder, water and manure availability. Thus a synergistic boost would be given to the path of development.

Box 3.1.3: Calculation of Energy Demand & Generation in Uttaranchal

1. Energy Demand of Uttaranchal

a. Lighting, Cooking and Heating Load:

Total lighting load of all household in Uttaranchal (12,00,000 × 200 W)	= 240 MW
Energy consumed in lighting for 6 hours/day (365 × 6 × 240MW)	= 5,25,600 MWh
Cooking Load of all household in Uttaranchal (12,00,000 × 2KW)	= 2400 MW
Energy consumed in cooking (6hrs/day) (6 × 365 × 2400)	= 5,256,000 MWh
Home heating Load of all households in Uttaranchal (12,00,000 × 2KW)	= 2400 MW
Energy consumed in Home heating for 8 hours per day for 4 months (4 × 30 × 8 × 2400 MW)	= 2,304,000 MWh
Lighting Load for all schools (9000 × 200W)	= 1800 MW
Energy consumed in lighting of schools (10 hours/day for 200 days)	= 3,600,000 MWh = 200x10x1800 MW
Total lighting load of Govt. Office, Hospital, Institution (4000 × 10 KW)	= 40 MW
Energy consumed in lighting of Govt. Office, Hospital, Institution (10 hours/day for 200 days) (200 × 10 × 40MW)	= 8,000 MWh
Total energy consumed in lighting and home heating	**= 11,693,600 MWh**

b. Irrigation & Transportation Load:

Irrigation Load for 15,000 villages at 15 KW per village	= 225 MW
Energy Consumed for irrigation for 3 months (3 × 30 × 24 × 225MW)	= 486,000 MWh
Total Transportation Load by ropeways for all villages (15W × 15,000)	= 225 MW
Energy consumed in transportation for 10 hours/day/year (365 × 10 × 225)	= 821,250 MWh
Total Energy required for Irrigation & Transportation	**= 1,307,250 MWh**

c. Industrial and Refrigeration Load:

Total Small Industrial Load (20 × 80 × 15 KW)	= 24 MW
Energy consumed for 12 hours/day/year (12 × 365 × 24 MW)	= 105,120 MWh
Total Large industrial Load (10 × 80 × 40 KW)	= 32 MW
Energy consumed for 12 hours/day/year (12 × 365 × 32)	= 140,160 MWh

(*Contd.*)

Total Refrigeration Load (80 × 10 × 30 KW)	= 24 MW
Energy consumed for 365 days for 24 hours (365 × 24 × 24)	= 210,240 MWh
Total Energy required for Industries and Refrigeration	**= 455,520 MWh**
Grand Total of Energy Demand of Uttaranchal	**= 13,456,370 MWh**
2. Energy Generation in Uttaranchal	
Total Small & Micro Hydel Potential	= 1365 MW
Assuming total Hydro Potential (Small, Micro, Gharat and existing Hydel Power Plants) of 2,000 MW	
3. Surplus Energy in Uttaranchal	
Surplus energy = 2-1 (above) 406.363 Crore Units	= 4,063,630 MWh or
If sold at Re. 1/- per unit, total revenue per year	**= 406 Crore**

Natural Resource Management (NRM) Policy for Uttaranchal

Nature of NRM Policy

Considering the resource use pattern and the socio-economic scenario described in sections above, any NRM policy for Uttaranchal must have, in our opinion, the following distinctive characteristics:

- The NRM policy should address the conflict between the need for economic development of local populations and the need to conserve the fragile ecosystems and biodiversity of the mountain areas. Such a policy would provide a framework for NRM policies of other mountain regions and would be Uttaranchal's contribution to the International Year of the Mountains.
- The policy should emerge from an exercise in identifying the gaps between existing NRM policy regime and people's aspirations and needs. Areas where existing policy regime needs to be modified or broadened for the ecological and economic well being of people of Uttaranchal therefore need to be pinpointed. The policy should also clearly outline the institutional and legal framework for sustainable management of natural resources in Uttaranchal.

Issues that Need to be Tackled for Formulating NRM Policy for Uttaranchal

We list below some of the major issues related to land, water and forest policy that need to be addressed for a satisfactory NRM policy for Uttaranchal:

Land

- Land availability for agriculture *vs*. fodder, fuelwood, conservation activities
- Land tenure and land distribution system
- Gap between land records and actual ownership/use of land
- Legal aspects related to land
- Land consolidation—impact of land fragmentation on agricultural productivity
- Permanent vegetation—need for agro-forestry or agri-horti based approaches
- Gaps between indigenous agricultural practices and modern approached/innovations for agricultural development
- Conversion of agricultural land into resorts, purchase of land by "outsiders" or real estate developers
- Horticulture—plant material, production, processing, marketing and institutional framework required for development of horticulture in Uttaranchal.
- Utilisation of the ecological niche that Uttaranchal provides for growing various economic crops and the legal, financial, technical skill support, transportation and marketing infrastructure required for the same.
- Irrigation infrastructure and laws for improved agricultural productivity
- Importance of Organic farming—can Uttaranchal be a decisive player in the organic field?

Animal Husbandry

- What kind of livestock composition can the state support?
- Legal and administrative structure governing animal husbandry
- Should sheep and goats be banned or are they beneficial for the overall health of Uttaranchal's grasslands and forests?
- Role of livestock in income-generation—wool, meat, milk, other products. Why is it that in an area where animal husbandry was the major occupation a few decades back, a significant dairy network has not been able to establish itself?
- Nature of animal husbandry services, considering that centralised government AH services have failed. For example—Dangar dais coupled with extension workers and a Veterinary doctor?

- Fodder management—what could be the approaches to achieve self-sufficiency in fodder?

Forestry

- Carrying capacity of forests of Uttaranchal in terms of demand on them for fuelwood, fodder, fertiliser, NTFP, commercial needs, etc.
- Alienation of people from forests—the case for and against state control over forests.
- Local subsistence needs versus commercial exploitation of forests—can there be a balance?
- Van Panchayats exist only in 65 per cent of the villages in Uttaranchal
- Role of traditional forest management systems and institutions in Uttaranchal, particularly Van Panchayats and Lath Panchayats
- Management issues in Van Panchayats, Civil Soyam and Reserved forests
- Rules, regulations and facilitatory environment required for production and marketing of NTFPs
- Impact of the World Bank Forestry project and its implementation in Van Panchayats or areas with good forest cover on forest institutions such as Van Panchayats
- Legal framework for Forest Management in Uttaranchal, for example, JFM rules, etc.
- Protected area management—participatory or enforced?

Water

- Legal framework on water
- Role of traditional water harvesting systems in providing drinking and irrigation water
- Experiences of watershed programmes in Uttaranchal—From Fakot to Doon Valley WS project
- Role of small water harvesting structures—Roof water harvesting, LDPE tanks, cement tanks, etc.
- Irrigation, water lifting, water harvesting, water diversions
- Stream stabilisation measures—the destructive face of water
- Decrease in forest area leading to decrease in spring discharges
- Community-owned microhydels

- Technology for harvesting water—
— *Modern*: LDPE tanks, Cement tanks, roof water harvesting tanks, infiltration wells, etc.
— *Traditional*: Water diversion (Gools), spring-based (naula, dhara); and water storage types – Chals/Khals.

References

1. Census of India, Provisional Population Totals of Uttaranchal, 2001.
2. G.B. Pant University of Agriculture and Technology, Ranichauri campus, "National Agriculture Research Project-Uttar Pradesh Hills", Vol. 1,2,3, 1989.
3. Kumar, Pankaj; Sandeep Chakravarthy & Pawan Kumar; "A Rapid Rural Appraisal on the Trends in Livelihood Strategies of People of Kumaon", Unpublished Study, 1993.
4. Champion, H.G. and S.K. Seth; *A revised Survey of Forest Types of India*, Govt. of India Press, Nasik, India, 1968.
5. Forest Department, 2001, *Uttaranchal Forest Statistics*.
6. Saxena, N.S., 1995, *Towards Sustainable Forestry in U.P. Hills*, Centre for Sustainable Development, LBSNAA, Mussoorie.
7. Forest Survey of India, 1995, The State of Forest Report-1995, Forest Survey of India, Dehradun.
8. Valdiya, K.S., *Uttarakhand Today*, Almora Book Depot, Almora, 1996.
9. Ashish, Madhava, "The Institution of Van Panchayats", Unpublished, Undated.
10. Shah, S.L., Undated, "Linkages between forestry and agriculture in Uttarakhand", Mimeo, Unpublished.
11. Singh, J.S. and Pande, Uma, 1986-87, "*Ecotantron ka Sambandh*", PAHAR 2, PAHAR Publications, Nainital, U.A.
12. Ery and Sastry, 1982, "Demography and socio-economic character of human population—An integrated ecological study of parts of Kumaon Himalaya with emphasis on natural resources": Second Annual Report, Kumaon University.
13. Khanka, S.S., *Paharoan Se palayan: Pravirti aur Prabhav*, PAHAR 3, PAHAR Publications, Nainital, U.A. 1986.
14. Mehta, G.S., "Development Experiences and Options in a Hill region: The case of Uttarakhand, U.A. India", Discussion Paper-ICIMOD, Kathmandu, Nepal; 1997.
15. Stone, Peter B. (Ed.), *State of the World Mountains*, Zed Books, London & New Jersey, 1992.
16. Nagarkoti, Diwan, "*Pahari Gaon Ka Urja Adhar*", PAHAR3-4, PAHAR Publications, Nainital, U.A. 1992.
17. Personal Communication—CHIRAG personnel (An NGO in Uttarakhand).

18. Rana, Raj Singh, "Correlation and regression Analysis of Horticulture in Uttarakhand—A specific study of Doon Valley". Dissertation submitted as Scholar, Deptt. of Economics, SGRRPG College, Dehradun, 1995-96.
19. Kumar Pankaj, "Development Dilemma in Uttarakhand—Can Microhydels be a solution?", *Wasteland News*, May-July, 1998.
20. Personnel Discussions; Farmers in the Great Himalayan National Park, Kullu during a Microplanning Exercise for World Bank funded Eco-development project, 1993-94.
21. "Splash", Quarterly Magazine of UNDP-GEF Hilly Hydro project.
22. Ministry of Non-Conventional Energy Sources, GOI; Circulars on MHP nos. 7/44/97 SHP, 6/1/51/95-SHP, 6/1/44/93-SHP, 6/1/23/93-SHP, and personnel Communication-Suresh Agarwal, PSO, MNES.

3.2

Approaches to Plant Biodiversity Utilization and Conservation

M.P. SHIVA*

Introduction

Uttaranchal is rich in flora and fauna and has fascinating scenic beauty for tourisms and recreation. Uttaranchal (created on 9th November 2000) comprises of thirteen districts, *viz.*, Pithoragarh, Champawat, Almora, Bageshwar, Nainital, Udham Singh Nagar, Uttarkashi, Chamoli, Rudra Prayag, Dehra Dun, Pauri, Tehri-Garhwal and Haridwar. The state lies in the Central Zone of the Himalayas and covers a geographical area of 53,484 Sq. Km. According to the 2001 census the total population of Uttaranchal has reached 84,79,562 of which 43,16,401 are males while 41,63,161 are females. Thus the sex ratio is 964 females per 1000 males. The literacy rate is 72.3 per cent with a level of 84.0 per cent among males population and 60.3 per cent among females according to the census, 2001. Over 70 per cent of the people are village or forest fringe dwellers. Agriculture is the main occupation. Forest cover is 62.31 per cent. Seven hundred and sixty-two thousand hectares land is available for agriculture (14.24 per cent) of which 40.66 per cent area is under irrigation. Eighty-eight per cent of the total geographical area is hilly region while 12 per cent is plain area.

The factors inhibiting the pace of development in Uttaranchal hilly areas include:

- Undulating topography
- Rugged terrain
- Varied climate
- Poor soil cover

*President, Centre of Minor Forest Products (COMFORTS), Dehradun.

- Very limited arable land
- Overwhelming percentage of small and marginal holdings
- Difficult agricultural conditions
- Shifting cultivation
- Severe soil erosion
- Deficiencies in infrastructure
- Inadequate institutional support
- Low investment

Specification of Uttaranchal Mountains

The Uttaranchal mountains are characterized by—Inaccessibility, Fragility, Marginality, Diversity, and Human adaptation mechanisms. The status of Uttaranchal Mountains in contributing to biodiversity, resource/environment, land use systems and biomass production is given in Table 3.2.1.

Table 3.2.1: General Characteristics of Uttaranchal Mountains

Mountain specificities and their operational implications	*Contributions to*				
	Bio-diversity	*Nutrient/ moisture circulation*	*Resource/ environ-ment stability*	*Land extensive system*	*Sources of diverse biomass*
INACCESSIBILITY Isolation, high cost of mobility, local resource focussed activity	×	×			×
FRAGILITY High vulnerability to degradation, low intensity (restrained resource use)	×	×	×	×	×
MARGINALITY Low potential, limited production possibilities focus on low cost, low productivity, high stability options		×		×	×
DIVERSITY Location specific, multiple production opportunities, diversified inter-linked local resource based activities	×	×			×
NICHE Potential for specific/unique activities, resource use options with comparative advantage	×				×
ADAPTATION MECHANISM Technological, institutional devices (e.g, Ethno-ecology, collective resource management etc.)	×			×	×

Rapid deforestation has aggravated the environment and ecology of the area. Unscientific management of natural resources and management of land use pattern has resulted in low productivity as well as depletion of floral/faunal bio-diversity and ecological imbalance.

Conservation of Floral Biodiversity of Uttaranchal

Uttaranchal or the Central Himalayas have plenty of resources of floral bio-diversity which if exploited sustainably would no doubt prove to be of immense economic value essential for its socio-economic and environmental development.

For the development of Uttaranchal, conservation of land, water and biodiversity is essential. The vegetal resources comprise of species yielding both timber and non-timber forest products (NTFP). The timber dominated forest management which has been in vogue is to be shifted to NTFP oriented need based sustainable forest management (NONBSFM). The meagre information about non- timber sources has been the main handicap for the foresters and policy makers in taking up NTFP oriented management. Hence, information on timber and non-timber sources is an essential issue for the conservation and development of the state. The Centre of Minor Forest Products (COMFORPTS) being the only organization in India and abroad working specially and exclusively on NTFP has been engaged in documenting and disseminating information and enriching MFP database with species specific information on various parameters for different user groups.

Lack of natural resource inventory has been the major impediment for proper Natural Resource Management. Inventory of Forest Resources for Sustainable Management & Bio-Diversity Conservation (with lists of multipurposes tree species yielding both timber and NTFP with shrub & herb species of NTFP importance) has been published in 1998 by Dr. M.P. Shiva, Adviser and Founder President, COMFORPTS. The book has proved to be a basic tool for forest managers, policy makers and other NTFP based entrepreneurs to accept the challenge of NTFP oriented need based sustainable forest management.

The state forest resources for both Timber and NTFP for 27 states have already been published by COMFORPTS. The same have also been prepared for all the newly formed states *viz.*, Uttaranchal, Chattisgarh and Jharkhand. The list of species with their uses have been provided in these books according to varied forest types, eco-floristic zones, and agro-ecological regions (Shiva and Shiva, 2001). The economic status of the species has been graded as A, B & C (A: common, large industry based and commercially important; B: local use and important for cottage and small scale industries; C: potentially useful). Both the inventory and State NTFP resources are highly significant for choice of right species for conservation, cultivation and commerce. These publications would be useful for the conservation and development of all the states with rich forest reserves.

Another book entitled Plant Biodiversity for Sustainable Community Development by Dr. M.P. Shiva & S.S. Bartwal provides the information about the flora of Yamkeshwar block, Pauri Garhwal and can be utilized for community development as well as conservation of forests of Uttaranchal for both plains and hilly areas (Shiva and Bartwal, 1998). These three publications provide all essential basic information about the floral diversity of Uttaranchal on the basis of which action oriented programmes on conservation, cultivation and commercial utilization of economic plant species can be planned and implemented.

Conservation Measures

Besides conventional conservation practices *(in situ and ex situ)* the unconventional method *i.e.* community conservation or 'on-farm conservation' is being given more focus today. Biodiversity Conservation Prioritization Project (BCCP) Report (1998) has identified the following classes of major threats:

- Human Interference
- Fragmentation
- Over exploitation
- Loss of habitat
- Harvest
- Trade
- Others

The report emphasizes that trade, unsustainable harvest, loss of habitat and over exploitation are the major causes of loss of biodiversity especially of medicinal plants. Whatever may be the cause, it has been felt that unsustainable harvest without proper replenishment is the major cause of threat to all the species. Hence *in situ* and *ex situ* conservation practices are very important. In Uttaranchal in particular, *in situ* conservation has been practiced on a very small scale. It needs extensive survey and collection of information regarding the actual state of the environment. It is always considered better to introduce the concerned endangered or threatened species *in situ* because these plants act as indicators of overall forest ecosystem health and their disappearance threatens the entire ecosystem. The forest department and ethnobiologists can do such intensive work.

In *ex situ* method plants are conserved in botanical gardens, seed banks, gene banks or in laboratories under cryo-preservation with the help of tissue culture and other bio-technological methods. But it requires extra establishment and additional investment that can only be borne by Government agencies and Universities and other research institutes.

In the third type of conservation termed as "community conservation" floral bio-diversity can be conserved, cultivated and commercially exploited more sustainably as in this process the plant species are included in cultivation. It requires selection of appropriate species and action oriented programmes. Growing awareness and improving technical skill is essentially required. Uttaranchal should follow this principle in a proper way to make utilization and conservation a real dream. This should be an integral part of national legislation in the field of bio-diversity conservation on plant variety protection (Swaminathan, 2000; Chakravarti and Shiva, 2001).

The actual production potential/productivity should be quantified and highlighted as a very important issue for conservation and utilization of bio-diversity of all the three resource rich states. This will call for an inventory of forest resources on a quantitative basis. But this work needs extensive survey and research as well as skilled manpower and financial investment.

Conclusion

Conservation of natural resources of Uttaranchal requires a multipronged strategy with an integrated management approach that should include the following steps.

(a) Proper inventorisation of forest resources both qualitatively and quantitatively.

(b) Use of information technology to acquire information, document and disseminate it for the benefit of different user groups. COMFORPTS'MFP Database can play a pivotal role in this sector. Its MFP database is enriched with information of about 3065 economic plant species.

(c) Choice of species for conservation, cultivation and commerce according to the State NTFP Resources published by COMFORPTS.

(d) Conservation of particular species in its natural habitat (*in situ*), outside their natural habitat (*ex situ*) or including integrated gene management, *i.e.* community conservation.

(e) Restricting denudation of forests and expansion of agriculture at the cost of forest land.

(f) Utilization of wastelands by planting economic species including multipurpose tree species of both timber and non-timber importance and shnubs and herbs of economic value.

(g) Social forestry plantation.

(h) Urbanization in an eco-friendly way.

(i) NTFP based enterprise development to preserve environment and to ensure socio- economic amelioration.

References

Anon, (1998), Biodiversity Conservation Prioritization Project (BCPP) Report on CAMP workshop on endangered species project.

Ministry & Environment and Forests. State Forests Report 1997 and 1999, Govt. of India, New Delhi.

Chakravarti, V., and M.P. Shiva (2001), Conservation and improvement of NTFP genetic resources for augmenting production: An important agenda for 21st Century (submitted in 4th SEANN Workshop at Manila, Philippines).

Jodha, N.S. (1922), Sustainability of Himalayan forests, some perspectives, *The Price of Forests,* Anil Agarwal, 285-290.

Pandey, P.N. (2001), Uttaranchal state and its development, *Yojana*, 45, (November 2001), 21-24.

Shiva, M.P. (1998), *Inventory for Forest Resources for Sustainable Management and Biodiversity Conservation* (with lists of multi-purpose tree species yielding both timber and non timber forest products (NTFP) with shrub and herb species of NTFP importance, Indus Publishing Co., New Delhi.

Shiva, M.P. and Bartwal, S.S. (1998), *Plant Biodiversity for Sustainable Community Development with Inventory of Timber and NTFP/MFP Resources of Yamkeshwar Block, Pauri Garhwal*, Surya International Publication, Dehra Dun.

Shiv, M.P. and Alka Shiva (2001), State Forest Resources, Yielding both and NTFP/MFP series, Uttaranchal.

Swaminathan, M.S. (2000), Government-industry-civil society: Partnership in Integrated General Management, *Ambio*, 29(2), 115-121.

3.3

Forests Resources: Regeneration and Conservation

M.L. Dewan[1] and K.D. Singh[2]

Uttaranchal forests and grasslands have been home to hundreds of plant, animal, bird species. This rich tapestry of natural assets have been protected and managed by the people of the state for centuries. However, so-called "scientific" forestry began with the advent of the British. That not only exploited the forests massively resulting in large-scale deforestation but also replaced many locally occurring species with the mono-culture of chir-pine, a commercially important species. Moreover, the establishment of the forest department (FD) has alienated people from the forests and has threatened their livelihood. Little wonder, while the FD continues to possess about 65 per cent of the state's geographical area, forests cover merely 42 per cent area and good forests with canopy cover exceeding 60 per cent are confined to less than 5 per cent. In short, today both the rich biodiversity and people's livelihood are facing a major threat despite 20 per cent of the state's forests, including reserve forests, are conserved by people themselves. These Community Conserved Forest Areas (CCA) are again, highly diverse and in a very good condition. They vary in form, legal structures and system of management. Most of them are Van Panchayats—a system of community management of forests— a right conceded by the British after a long struggle waged by the people in the early 20th century. Others are sacred groves, lath or traditional forest Panchayats, privately owned but communally managed forests and even reserve forests effectively conserved and managed by people.

1. HIMCON, Ranichauri.
2. Sr. Forest Economist, FAO (Retd.) also IFS [UP/Uttaranchal Cadre (Retd.)].

An active involvement of people in conserving and managing these CCAs has resulted in high biodiversity along with meeting people's biomss requirements. This fact has been established by an Uttarakhand-wide documentation of the CCAs carried out by the author along with PRAKRITI, an NGO based in Mussoorie, Dehra Dun. The study was sponsored by United Nations Development Programme under its Global Environment Facility Project that seeks to conserve biodiversity in fragile ecosystems like mountains.

Biodiversity Study

An extensive and in-depth study of 30 such areas all across the state has been done so far. All hill districts of the state of the state have been covered with at least two cases being taken from each district. Extensive discussions with the villagers and in-depth interviews with individuals were followed by comprehensive scientific studies to judge the extent of biodiversity of the area.

The broad findings of the study are:

(1) The reason why these CCAs have been established varies, but the common reason is a desire felt at the local level to protect their forests so that people face no problem to gather biomass so essential for their survival. Consequently, most CCAs are self-initiated although many of them needed some outside motivation and support.

(2) Hence, legal structures of these CCAs too vary. While most of them are Van Panchayat and have legal sanctity under Van Panchayat Niyamawali, many are not legally recognized. Some CCAs are joint areas with both Van Panchayats and reserve forests together forming one CCA. Still others are all three legal structures—Van Panchayat, reserve forests and civil and—combined. In some places where huge, multi-village Van Panchayats exist and are not functioning well, people of one or more villages have taken their own initiative and are protecting their parts of Van Panchayat and we have treated them as independent CCAs. Some are even sacred forests. Lastly, a few are forests owned by individual farmers but are managed and protected collectively.

(3) In most CCAs women are integral to the conservation and management. They are instrumental in enforcing rules and

regulations and patrol the forests, thus implementing a kind of social-fencing. Given the fact that mostly women go to the forests to fetch biomass in the state, this is not surprising. But in many places women have entered the formal decision making process, while they had little say in it until now.

(4) These CCAs do not have a uniform set of rules and regulations and they vary according to the needs of the people and geographical and climatic conditions of the area. However, these rules ensure a very regulated and scientific harvesting of biomass along with proper conservation and protection of the forests. Most CCAs also have the provision of punishing the offenders by imposing fines that are almost always double for outsiders.

(5) Almost all CCAs have been successful in their twin objectives of meeting people's biomass needs and protecting the forests. No CCA yielded less that half of basic biomass needs—fuel wood, fodder, Leaf litter, animal beds, thatching and timber—while 50 per cent of the CCAs studied met almost the entire bromass needs of people and another 25 per cent met about 75 per cent such needs. Only for timber and fuelwood up to an extent, people of these areas, depended on reserve forests.

(6) All there areas are rich depositories of biodiversity—both plants and animals. On an average a quadrate of 10m radius had 13 plant species, varying between 9 to 24 species. Broadleaved species like 'banj' (oak) dominates over conifers like 'chir' (pine) in these areas as the former are useful for people while the latter are of little uses. Similarly, there were at least five shrubs, four *flosses* and six herbs species in the specified quadrates. Every CCA has many animals (minimum five), birds (minimum six) and reptiles (minimum three species).

(7) Most CCAs have been otherwise beneficial to people also. With the availability of good broadleaved lead litter to make quality manure and enough fodder, the impact of protection on agriculture and livestock has been positive to an extent. Foodgrain and milk production have been increased in most CCAs. In most places the availability of drinking water too has increased with dried springs having revived in a few CCAs. While the impact on migration, children's and women's health could not be evaluated, in some place people claim of having a better rainfall than the surrounding areas.

(8) The most important impact has been social, especially on

women's lives. Their hardship and work load has been decreased to a great extent and their social status has been enhanced. Village unity too has registered a boost.

(9) The most noticeable negative fallout of the protection has been increased people-wildlife conflict. With the forests disappearing in most other areas, wild animals by-and-large have migrated to these areas and are destroying standing crops and killing domestic animals. Another negative outcome, in a few places, has been increasing conflicts with neighbouring villages that do no practice any kind of protection. However, there has been a good demonstrative impact of these initiatives with most neighbouring villages have either initiated such protections or are seriously contemplating over it.

(10) Lastly, in all *CCAs*, people think that their initiative has been a success as there is a better availability of biomass now and it ensures a better future for them and their children. But the only impediment—at some places—has been a dearth of sources and financial and technical support that is crucial to sustain such initiatives.

- Many areas can be reforested faster and less expensively (often 60 to 70 per cent cheaper) than conventional reforestation techniques if seedlings of tree species are naturally abundant and if the climate is favourable.
- Regenerated forests are much more diverse biologically than conventional plantations.
- Original vegetation and corresponding ecosystem functions are restored or maintained.
- There is minimal soil disturbance, thus soil structure is maintained and soil erosion is virtually nil.
- Employment is provided for local communities due to the labour.
- Hydrological integrity and biological functions are enhanced.

The experience should be utilized in Uttaranchal for a Sustainable Society as stated in the following page.

The physical systems of the Himalaya are naturally prone to a number of weaknesses: weathering, erosion and land degradation. Nature's regulatory mechanism to control the rate of this erosion is the vegetation cover and healthy humus-rich soils which match the character of the geomorphic agents. The rates of change brought about by these processes are altered by the human misuse of the system, leading to what we may call bleeding and crumbling Himalaya.

Humans have lived in this region for centuries but as far as is known, they have lived on sustenance basis. Their economy had always been of the subsistence type.

Over 40 million hectares in Indian Himalaya have been seriously degraded. Increasing population pressure and destructive land-use have resulted in the loss of fuelwood and fodder supplies, greater flood damage, intensification of drought, including drying of springs, sedimentation of dams and reservoirs and loss of crops and livestock.

Dream of Sustainable Himalaya

Can we sustain the Himalaya which is not bleeding, which is always green and full of springs with happy population working for the prosperity of the Himalaya and the people? BELIEF and VISION says that IT CAN BE DONE. We have to solve dilemmas, the people have to be involved fully. The dilemma of growth includes the tragedy of commons. When humans act freely in their own interest, exceeding the carrying capacity of an eco-system with over population and maximizing output of food and other goods, threatening the forests in the Himalaya and an unmanaged commons. One of the principles of Sustainable Society is "We cannot command nature except obeying her". Based on these lines, regenerative forestry and grassland have greater chances of success. In brief, we should temper our cleverness by studying and emulating nature. Nature has had millions of years to experiment and to find out what works. These forests will be completely consumed in another fifty years.

Forests are especially important for using excess CO_2 and for replenishing oxygen.

In the past, a stable balance existed between the two elements. At present this balance is in danger. What is the way out?

Principles and Practices of Peopled Participation

Strategies and concerted action for a Sustainable Himalaya are best implemented if the people who participate in such execution understand and see their own interest.

The creation of local institutional capacity to manage natural and other resources through collective action, not dependent entirely on the structure and authority of the state, offers an important alternative to bureaucratic approach if such capacity can become viable. It is quite unrealistic to expect participation by the rural poor when the style of programme administration curbs their initiative.

Raising People's Potential
Offer an important lead.

Humans are capable of doing much more than they are doing at present especially in India as evidenced by

(i) viability in the best the worst in government departments;
(ii) outstanding success of Non-resident Indians, especially the USA, Cananda and Europe; and
(iii) variability in industrial management.

Inspiration and Social Energy

Inspiration is the ability of the project staff to give farmers and land users the visions mentioned above. In this context, it is important to understand the concept of social energy. It is known that when people are determined and put their energy to work, unsolved and insolvable problems, find solutions. According to Prof. Norman Uphoff of Cornell University, social energy depends on: Ida, Ideals, and Friendship.

A Call for Action

PREVENTION is many times better than CURE. The arithmetic of prevention has two angles—

(a) how much will it cost to protect the fragile areas; and
(b) if not protected, how much will it cost in terms of misery and "disaster relief" Towards Self-Reliance of the Himalayan Communities.

It always takes time for simple communities to become self-reliant. There are three approaches that need to be taken:

- To have a vision of what needs to be achieved
- How to turn vision into reality
- Operational programmes and their contents

Practical Terms of this Vision

Transforming the vision to reality involves identification of socio-economic programmes in line with the strategies already developed such

Increased tree cover, regenerative forestry/grassland;
Conjunctive crops with fruit plus nut fruits, fodder, fuel and multi-purpose trees;
Continue Abstract here;
Water harvesting from rainfall, small ponds, check dams, roof water harvesting, perennial springs'
Income generating activities in small-scale non-polluting cottage industries;
Solar, wind, bio-gas, smokless chulhas, solar and pressure cookers, mini/micro hydel and related renewable energy technologies.

Promotion of Eco-Philosophy and Human Values in Himalayan Conservation and Development

As we stand on the threshold of the twenty-first century, we must be conscious that we have not done any justice to Mother Earth. We have ravaged, pillaged, destroyed and slowly drained it of vitality. We have to make peace with it now, else there will be nothing left to sustain life on this earth. This greedy mindset has to be returned to a caring, compassionate and participatory wave-length.

The earth is a sanctuary; so is the Himalaya. It is not an endless storehouse of materials to satiate human hunger for temporal consumption. We have to feel for our earth and for the Himalaya. We have to cultivate human values.

- The Right Action,
- Love,
- Peace Truth, and
- Non-violence.

These human values will make us all realize that trees are holy, forests are sanctuaries, Himalaya is sacred as also the Mother Earth which must be conserved and developed. We are promoting these concepts through writings, speeches, training and orientation programmes.

Action programmes through involving large number of people both as trainers and trainees and involvement of the communities form the backbone of this vision. An appeal to all the people is to recognize the sanctity of the Himalaya and soil and water conservation work for sustainability through participation and to enlarge and deepen the commitment of such participation.

Impact of Forest Fires

Fire is not new to the fragile Himalayan terrain as are other natural disasters and the fire season in the Chir pine forests begins in the first week of May or even earlier and ends in June, while in the Deodar zone the fire season starts in May and ends in June.

(i) *Local people*: Traditional belief of the locals that after a fire productivity of the grasses enhances very often leads to firing of the grazing fields in the hills.

(ii) *Natural/Accidental reasons*: Many a big fire are observed to initiate accidentally and these may well be attributed to accidents and human neglect of sorts.

(iii) *Conspiracy or cover up measures:* Some people are of the opinion that fires are a well planned conspiracy against the Himalayan people and they see it as a measure to destabilize the forest-farm interrelations, as also the local economy. These people assert that there exists a strong lobby that is bent upon teaching lessons to the hill community and in this background they see this fire as apart of their accumulated resentments.

(iv) *Mischief of the children*: Many people in the region argue that these fires are the product of childplay but unhabitated areas this does not explain fires. Whatever be the reasons, fires are a source of concern as they wipe out years of bio-diversity in a short period. Fuel and fodder become scarce, the hill sides become vulnerable to erosion and water sources dry up in subsequent years owing to loss of feast cover and its water retention capacity. Landslides become more frequent and tourism is affected owing to pollution and destruction of the pristine greenery of the mountains. Active co-operation of the local people is required to detect and control fires. The Forest Department may initiate youth groups to maintain fire free forests. Briquetting of biomss for commercial production of charcoal bricks should be promoted in the region as this practice has the potential of clearing the forest of inflammable material. The Forest Department can provide soft loans for this purpose to the local youth who would be gaining employment in return. The fire department should be adequately equipped to fight these large-scale fires and should ensure that their equipment is always in working order.

Mountains are fragile ecosystems. Their rich bio-diversity and the fact that they give birth to the mighty rivers which sustain life in the plains, makes it imperative that the eco-system is conserved and regenerated. Uttaranchal has been a rich repository of natures biodiversity. In recent years, galloping human and animal population have caused the forested area to shrink dramatically which in turn is reflected as hardship for the local people in terms of water shortages, decline in agricultural productivity, landslides, and other attendant problems.

3.4

Watershed Development: A Success Story

PIYUSH RAUTELA*

Disregard of mountain specificities and inadequate participation of the beneficiary population, together with neglect of traditional ecological conservation practices have prevented a large number of developmental schemes and projects from gaining momentum. Thus an observable change in the socio-economic condition of the masses of this region has not been brought about. TFL/HIMCON* realises the potential of watershed management strategy in providing a sustainable solution to the depleting resource crisis in the Himalayas and believes that in-depth understanding of socio-cultural dynamics of the region is a must before devising any locally relevant and socially acceptable tools for popularising watershed management resources.

The Area before Intervention

The twin village-watersheds (Lawadhar and Paturi), as also the entire Chamba block (Tehri Garhwal district), faced severe crisis of essential natural resources, namely, land, water, fodder and fuel-wood. The drinking water availability was very low and the females had to fetch water from far off places, specially during the summer. This took toll of their productive time and they were not able to participate in other productive pursuits. The scenario of health and sanitation in the villages was also pitiable. The literacy and general awareness levels, amongst the females in particular, were very low.

---

* Trees for life and Himalaya Consortium for Himalaya Conservation—An Environmental NGO in Uttaranchal based in Rani Chauri, Tehri Garhwal Dist.

When TFL/HIMCON decided to serve these communities, the resource management scenario was very poor. Though water availability was very low; there were no efforts from the grassroots level to address the problem. As the people did not have a good experience of co-operative work they were hesitant to participate in developmental endeavours. Improved agro-horticultural practices were unheard of in the watersheds. The traditional resource management system had broken down for lack of social solidarity without an alternative to adopt. Even grassroot level organisations were unheard of in these villages.

***The action plan*:** TFL/HIMCON initiated work in a slow but determined fashion, establishing entry point activities and working out a well thought out plan with thorough understanding of the socio-cultural dynamics of the society. TFL/HIMCON started its activities on a low key and in the first phase mass mobilisation was given the topmost priority. Discussions and meetings were organised together with thought provoking stage shows. These efforts soon started to bear fruit and two Mahila Mangal Dal (MMD) and two watershed management committees came into existence in these villages. The females of the villages started participating in the developmental efforts and in order to muster their internal resources Self-Help Groups (SHG) were organised within the MMD.

Entry points onwards: Water was the main problem of these villages and therefore water harvesting was accorded high priority in the watershed. Hitherto unheard of, rainwater harvesting, was undertaken by constructing recharge structures at higher elevations; and to reduce erosion, bunding was resorted to. Large-scale plantation was undertaken in the watersheds. Most of the plantation material was prepared in the nurseries of TFL/HIMCON. In choosing the species for afforestation the views of the masses were given high priority. Plantation of species providing fodder and fuel-wood was taken up in the degraded lands of the villages while many fruit bearing varieties were planted in agricultural lands.

As agriculture is the main economic activity of the watersheds and sole source of income, high value crop varieties were introduced through the Seed Bank managed by the MMDs. Seeds were distributed on returnable basis amongst the villagers.

Health and sanitation, as also animal husbandry were accorded priority and a series of meetings and training camps were organised. A large number of sanitary latrines were constructed and health camps were organised for routine check ups.

Philosophy Underlying the Project

This exercise is not the maiden attempt in watershed management and development in Himalayas or in this region; various agencies have been over the years engaged in developmental activities based on watershed approach, and many have been successful in fulfilling the project goals. There then ought to be some logic and reasoning for undertaking yet another exercise.

Firstly, the area chosen for present interventions by virtue of being cut off from the road head was hitherto grossly neglected by development agencies. Secondly, the initial surveys revealed the need for regenerative work in these watersheds. Lastly and more importantly, it was realised that there is a need for a demonstration project where principles of watershed management could be implemented with vigorous people's participation, so as to make it more meaningful and sustainable.

Perceived lacuna: Despite fulfilment of the objectives and serious efforts from different quarters it has been observed that the activities introduced during the watershed management exercise fail to become sustainable and die out once the project support is withdrawn. The main reason for this lies in failure of the project implementation team to enhance the motivation level of the masses and to make them aware of the benefits of the project activity. To add to it the masses are not, most of the time, involved in the project activity as equal partners and the project goals are fulfilled according to the pre-set action plan.

The underlying objectives: This project was therefore designed to be a people oriented demonstration exercise that could be replicated on a large scale. The project activities in the chosen village-watersheds were therefore undertaken with the full co-operation of the masses and major decisions regarding implementation at various stages were to be taken democratically and transparently in the forums of the people. In order to accommodate changes based upon emerging requirements, the structure of the project was deliberately kept flexible. In addition rather than replicating what is usually being done important innovations were incorporated into the project.

More than fulfilment of just quantifiable progress indicators, this exercise was aimed at changing the attitude of the masses (the beneficiary group) through awareness and exposure so that they could identify the project activity with their common good.

The sustainability of the activities introduced during the project tenure was therefore kept to be the primary measure of the success of the project but then, this could only be assessed in the long run. Quantifiable indicators no doubt reflect the quantum of progress made during project implementation and help in audit operations but these need not be taken as the success indicators, for sustainability is the main criteria.

THIS PROJECT IS AN EXPERIMENT; AN EXPERIMENT TOWARDS ENERGISING THE MASSES TO GAIN AN ATTITUDE OF WORKING FOR THEIR WELFARE ON THEIR OWN. INTERFERENCE IN THE PROGRESS OF THE PROJECT WAS THEREFORE MINIMAL AND ALL THE ACTIVITIES WERE SO DESIGNED THAT THE MASSES THEMSELVES DECIDE THE COURSE OF IMPLEMENTATION.

Details of the Area

Location

For the purpose of the present project activity the village-watersheds of Lawadhar and Paturi lying in the catchment of Henval river (tributary of Bhagirathi river) in Chamba block of Tehri-Garhwal district were taken up.

Raturi Khala and an unnamed *nala* form the drainage lines of these watersheds. Both these drain into Thelari Khala which is a tributary of Henval river. Both these streams are of second order and their courses are fairly straight, almost N-S oriented. In the toposheet Raturi Khala is depicted as being perennial but at present the stream has turned seasonal. This is attributed to various vegetal and landuse changes over time in the stream catchment. For the present exercise these watersheds are designated Raturi Khala watershed and Lawadhar watershed (drained by unnamed seasonal stream). These second order watersheds are narrow and elongated and their length to breadth ratios are high. Area of these watersheds is 0.936 and 0.643 square kilometres respectively.

Physiography and Meteorology

The watersheds fall in the sub-tropical climatic zone of the Himalayas. The altitudinal range of the watersheds is between 1150 and 1900 metres above MSL. The stream courses are fairly straight and the general slope of the area is low; 61 per cent of the area in Raturi Khala watershed and 74 per cent in Lawadhar watershed has surface slope less than 30°. The statistical detail of the land area under different slope categories is given in Table 3.4.1.

Table 3.4.1: Land under Different Slope Classes in Lawadhar & Raturi Khala Watersheds

Watersheds	*Area in (sq. km.) and per cent (in brackets) under different classes of slopes*				
	Flat (<10°)	*Gentle* (10-20°)	*Moderate* (20-30°)	*High* (30-50°)	*Steep* (<50°)
Lawadhar	0.0378 (5.9 %)	0.2133 (33.2 %)	0.2295 (35.0 %)	0.1517 (23.2 %)	0.0108 (1.7 %)
Raturi Khala	0.0548 (5.8 %)	0.2604 (27.8 %)	0.2595 (27.7 %)	0.3164 (33.8 %)	0.0452 (4.9 %)

Exact meteorological details for the watersheds are not available and therefore data available from the nearby Ranichauri Hill Campus observatory which is within the radius of five kilometres from the watersheds, is taken as representative for these watersheds.

Average annual rainfall in the area is around 1200 mm. The maximum temperature recorded in the previous decade is 26.7°C in June while the lowest recorded temperature is 2.5°C in January. During the winters the higher reaches of the watershed experience solid precipitation

The relative humidity is more than 50 per cent all through the year and 61 per cent of the annual precipitation of 1241 mm is confined to the four months of June to September. The minimum rains are experienced during October-November.

Landuse

Landuse relationships have an important bearing upon any watershed management exercise. The landuse/landcover details of the watersheds are as extracted from the Survey of India toposheets and updated with the help of the satellite data (IRS 1D LISS III multispectral digital data). The entire area has been divided into forest, agriculture and barren land and the landuse details are given Table 3.4.2.

Table 3.4.2: Landuse of Lawadhar & Raturi Khala Watersheds

Watershed	*Area (in sq. km.) and percentage (in brackets) under different landuse class*		
	Forest	*Agriculture*	*Barren*
Lawadhar	0.334 (51.9 %)	0.2406 (37.4 %)	0.0685 (10.7 %)
Raturi Khala	0.3138 (33.6 %)	0.3948 (42.1 %)	0.2277 (24.3 %)

Most of the agricultural land is on the lower part of the watersheds while the middle and upper reaches have most of the forest. Almost all the agricultural land is unirrigated.

Except for the upper reaches of the watershed where mixed *oak-buransh-kafal* forest is still thriving most area shown as forest land has a monoculture of pine and the crown density is low. Ever increasing demand for forest produce has degraded the forests close to the habitations. The State of the forest is however better in Raturi Khala watershed due to the efforts of the inhabitants of Paturi village.

Socio-economic Details

Raturi Khala watershed has larger geographical area and the slope characteristics favour agricultural activity. This fact is reflected in the population, socio-economic condition and the state of natural resources. The demographic details for the two villages are given in Table 3.4.3. The prosperity of Paturi is being reflected in the sex ratio in favour of females.

Agriculture is the primary occupation of the people but almost invariably it is supplemented by income from other sources.

Table 3.4.3: Demographic details of Lawadhar & Raturi Khala watersheds

Village	*Demographic details*			
	Male	*Female*	*Children*	*Total*
Lawadhar	58	56	76	190
Paturi	73	93	172	338

Despite sufficient rains in the area agriculture in the watersheds is rainfed. Intensive horticulture is not practised in these watersheds though there are fruit bearing plants in the area. This is attributed to the long gestation period, lack of resources, incentives and know-how. Wood is the main source of energy in both the watersheds though kerosene is also used. A number of multi-purpose trees (including medicinal plants) grow abundantly in the area and these are used for diverse purposes.

Details of the Work Undertaken

Building Organisational Capacity

Mahila Mangal Dal (MMD)

People's participation lies at the heart of watershed management and this involves organising the masses at the grassroots level. In the initial phases of the watershed management exercise the volunteers of TFL/HIMCON undertook a detailed door-to-door campaign for informing the masses regarding the benefits of having a grassroots level organisation in their villages.

These efforts resulted in the creation of MMDs with a Chairperson (Adhyaksha) in both the villages. Smt. Darshani Devi took charge of Lawadhar village, while in the absence of any active female member Shri Kunwar Singh took charge of Paturi village. It was decided that the affairs of Paturi village would be handed over to a female as soon as leadership develops amongst the females.

The MMDs hold regular meetings in the first week of every month (on 3rd in Lawadhar and on 6th in Paturi). The members discuss and debate upon various aspects of their social life at this forum and plan the shape of the things affecting them. Small disputes are also settled through this forum. It is thus adding to social solidarity and cohesion.

There are 63 members of the MMD at Paturi while the one at Lawadhar has 23 members. After the withdrawal of the project interventions MMDs would be responsible for the upkeep of the facilities created and smooth functioning of the other organisations at the village level.

Self Help Group (SHG)

In order to muster internal resources and also to help the needy both the MMDs organised a SHG. Membership of both the groups (MMD & SHG) is common and the SHG is envisaged as a people's co-operative. All the members deposit a fixed sum every month (Rs.10 in Lawadhar and Rs. 5 in Paturi) and the needy member's avail soft loans (at interest rate of 1 per cent monthly) from the revolving fund.

It is envisaged that the funds of the SHGs would in the long run be used for developmental initiatives in the villages. These efforts are bearing fruits and are reflected in the financial status of the SHGs (Table 3.4.4).

Members of the SHG decide on the mode of repayment on their own. The people avail loans for diverse purposes and the same are generally paid back within a short period.

Table 3.4.4: Balance sheet of the Self Help Groups of the two village—watersheds

Village	*Contribution* (Rs.)		*Interest earned on loans* (Rs.)		*Total deposit at the end of* (Rs.)		*Number of families availing loan* (Rs.)	
Year	*1998-99*	*1999-2000*	*1998-99*	*1999-2000*	*1998-99*	*1999-2000*	*1998-99*	*1999-2000*
Lawadhar	5,220	8,280	604	507	5,824	14,611	15	13
Paturi	18,000	20,170	8,000	3,600	26,000	49,770	62	27

Watershed Management Committee

In order to plan, implement and oversee the progress of the watershed management project, a watershed committee was constituted for the two villages. It was presided by Shri Kunwar Singh of Paturi village, while Smt. Darshini Devi of Lawadhar was second in command. All the members of the MMDs of the two villages were also the members of this committee that met every second month to review the progress of the work. It thus worked in the capacity of a planning and monitoring body of the beneficiaries of the project. Consequent to the completion of the project this committee has been formally dissolved and MMDs of the two villages have been imparted the responsibility of maintaining the structures so created under the supervision of this committee.

Seed Bank

Agriculture is the main economic activity of the two watersheds and in order to bring about a transformation in the economic condition of the people it was considered necessary to introduce innovations in agriculture. The masses in the two watersheds cultivate traditional low value agricultural produce. Despite massive advocacy for innovations in agriculture the level of accomplishment was poor. The villagers on the one hand did not have enough capital to invest in high yielding seeds, and technical know how to select and purchase the appropriate variety (even if the money could be arranged). On the other hand they had their suspicions regarding the results of these innovations.

Under the project guidelines TFL/HIMCON was to provide the required quality seeding material to the villagers but this would have turned them perpetually dependent upon external inputs. In order to make the agricultural economy of the watersheds self reliant, with regard to quality seed material, the idea of a Seed Bank was floated through the MMDs that readily accepted it. It was decided that the Seed Bank would be run under the aegis of the MMD and would be providing agricultural inputs to the farmers with a condition that they would return one and a half times the quantity so loaned at the time of harvest. It was envisaged that this activity once initiated would make the community self-reliant with respect to the inputs and in times to come surplus could well be traded for other varieties that the villagers would like to introduce. This would make the farmers self-reliant besides improving productivity.

Results at the harvest season left all the farmers extremely satisfied, though drought during 1998 resulted in partial waiver of the loans. The Seed Bank is also used for preserving the traditional seeding material that is fast disappearing due to decrease in the demand and introduction of new improved varieties. It is therefore contributing towards preserving the genetic diversity of traditional mountain agriculture. TFL/HIMCON plans to take charge of this stock for better preservation so that it is available for research or genetic engineering in future.

Health bank

Health related facilities are generally not available in this region and in the case of an emergency the people are forced to go to far off places for treatment. Ready cash is often needed in case of such an exigency. It is to cater to this need that MMDs of both the villages decided to launch a Health Bank with ready cash to help the needy. With this noble objective a monthly contribution of Rupees two is collected from each family. Fortunately none of the members required money from these funds.

Besides catering to exigencies the Health Bank is also envisaged to cater to the routine health requirements of the masses. A trained ANM from Kasturba Trust, Indore was initially catering to the health related issues in these watersheds and with her withdrawal from the project activities, a government ANM was engaged for this work for some time. At present a local dai is looking after these duties. She helps the expecting mothers in delivery and during 1998-99 she catered to 18 such cases.

In addition a qualified medical practitioner was engaged. Two health camps were thus undertaken in the watersheds and 115 people were examined. As per the report of Dr. G.S. Panwar more than thirty per cent of the people are suspected of suffering from tuberculosis and respiratory diseases. Large proportion of the children were malnourished while iron deficiency was common amongst the females. Children were vaccinated in these camps, and medicines were distributed. The chronic patients, together with those suspected of tuberculosis were advised to consult the district hospital for detailed medical examination and appropriate medication.

Awareness Drive

With the activities of TFL/HIMCON the level of awareness of the masses has improved. They now reflect on issues concerning the community in an organised and holistic manner. TFL/HIMCON's idea of awareness has been to initiate a thought process amongst the masses by which they can evolve a strategy for their common economic development. The process has been initiated and time would reveal its efficacy.

In the initial phases of the project activities TFL/HIMCON supported the literacy drive of Adult Health and Education and organised volunteers who conducted basic literacy camp for forty females of these villages. This lasted for six months. Further a regular adult education programme was carried out in both the watersheds. Ten females from Lawadhar and 17 from Paturi look advantage of this programme. TFL/HIMCON has also been undertaking regular training and exposures of various issues for the masses.

In May 1990 a two-day training programme was organised at Ranichauri on Health and Hygiene, which was co-ordinated by Dr. R.C. Bhalla. The participants were also sensitised on the issues of women's rights and vaccination, horticulture and the benefits of undertaking a watershed management exercise. This camp was attended by thirty participants. Training regarding the medicinal value of various indigenous plants was also imparted. This encouraged many participants to take up the organised cultivation of medicinal plants. This endeavour has been and is being supported by Swasthya Vatika (medicinal plant's garden) of HIMCON.

In order to demonstrate the effectiveness of improved farming practices as also the cultivation of medicinal plants a group of 15 females from Lawadhar and Paturi were taken for an exposure visit to the Himcon camps Ranichauri and Swasthya Vatika of Himcon, Ranichauri.

In October 1999 a two-day training was again organised at Ranichauri on Watershed Management and Horticulture which was attended by fifteen selected participants. The training included various aspects of horticulture, watershed management and the medicinal properties of various plants commonly found in their neighbourhood.

Enhancing Water Availability

Severe water scarcity during the summer increases the burden of females manifold as they have to negotiate long distances for fetching water. As atmospheric precipitation is the sole source of water (besides that pumped from outside) in any watershed, it was felt necessary to preserve whatever was received by diverse means. With thorough understanding of the hydrology of the region a multipronged strategy was worked out.

Rainwater Harvesting

Formal rainwater harvesting was hitherto unheard of in these watersheds. With the brainstorming over the meteorological details for the watershed (data of Ranichauri station extrapolated) it was perceived that the water collected from the traditional sloping roofs of the houses could be adequate for daily household purposes during most part of the year. It was therefore planned to erect LDPE and ferro-cement tanks for collecting roof runoff.

However, in the over-enthusiasm of producing innovative water harvesting practice in the watersheds due care was not taken in studying the nature of the bedrock. The rock types in the area are highly sheared and this rendered futile the exercise undertaken in construction of LDPE tanks, that were rendered unsuitable due to mass movement along the shears. All the structures erected for this purpose, except one, were rendered defunct by the end of the first year. Besides the geological complications the area is infested with rats that frequently damaged the lining. This exercise therefore had to be discontinued and the entire focus was turned to the construction of ferro-cement tanks.

With the LDPE tanks being rendered unsuitable TFL/HIMCON erected ferro-cement tanks but the cost difference between the two structures was very high and therefore additional resources were mustered for this work.

In the beginning of the project despite sound advocacy there were literally no takers for ferro-cement tanks due to the inhibitions involved in using the water collected from the roofs. In order to prove the efficacy of these structures to the villagers at this stage TFL/HIMCON had to erect this structure for collecting tap water for public use. At the same time recourse was taken to reduce the quantum of beneficiary contribution significantly.

After repeated persuasion through awareness campaigns and personal dialogue most of the people agreed that the water so collected can well be used for other household purposes.

After the end of two years ferro-cement tanks have become very popular in both the watersheds and are used for routine household activities.

Recharge Enhancement

It is the water percolating into the ground during the rains that appears in the springs. In order to enhance spring yield as also soil moisture a strategy of maximising groundwater recharge was resorted. Discussions with experts in the field suggested that maximum possible precipitation should be made to remain at a suitable high elevation for as long a duration as possible so that it had ample opportunity for replenishing the groundwater reserves.

For implementing this strategy, check-dams were constructed at suitable locations along seasonal streams. Suitable sites for these structures were selected after detailed hydro-geological survey of the watersheds. Besides these traditional recharge pits (chaals/khaals) were also constructed on higher reaches at the slope break. These were envisaged to enhance the productivity of traditional springs and add to the soil moisture besides reducing erosion. Two check-dams were erected in Lawadhar watershed and three in Paturi.

Four chaals were constructed on the upper reaches of the watershed in Paturi village and the silt from the old chaals was cleared. Besides enhancing recharge these provide water for the grazing animals.

These measures have started to show positive changes in a short time. Vegetation along the seasonal streams has increased significantly and erosion along the stream channels has reduced. The productivity of the traditional springs along the stream near Daula village (below Lawadhar) has been enhanced significantly and the same has become perennial subsequent to the construction of these structures.

Yields of the traditional springs at Paturi and Lawadhar have also increased. Encouraged by the results the people of Paturi renovated the traditional structure after decades of neglect.

Spring Rejuvenation

This strategy works on the philosophy that the water of the springs should not be allowed to flow but should be stored for productive purposes.

Work on these lines was initiated in Lawadhar that had a spring, which had become seasonal due to neglect and anthropogenic misadventures. TFL/HIMCON through its efforts in the recharge zone of this spring rejuvenated it and a tank with a capacity of 4,200 litres was constructed for harvesting the seepage. The villagers extended voluntary labour during the construction of the tank. The villagers use water from this structure regularly besides performing religious rites at this place.

Community Irrigation

Under the project an irrigation tank with a capacity of 1250 litres was constructed in Paturi with the support of the villagers. This place had a shallow dugwell that collected water during the rains, but now seven families living in the surrounding area are totally dependent upon this structure. Another similar structure of 10,000 litres capacity was commissioned in Paturi village.

Shri Bir Pal of Paturi owes his success in vegetable cultivation to the irrigation facilities provided by this tank. In one season alone he sold vegetables worth Rs. 2,150 in the local market at Chamba. Inspired by his success other villagers are also taking up vegetable cultivation. In Lawadhar village suitable land could not be located for the construction of such a structure.

Horticulture

Horticulture is not traditionally practiced in the watersheds on a commercial scale but the presence of various horticultural species indicate their viability. TFL/HIMCON approached this issue in a multi-pronged manner.

Firstly, the masses were motivated through personal contact and meetings to plant trees on a large scale. Economic benefits besides improvement of the environment were the issues that were highlighted in these meetings. Secondly, in order to disseminate the technical know-how necessary for commercial horticultural operations training programmes were arranged. Thirdly, the villagers were provided with suitable planting material. Lastly, attempts were made towards improving the productivity of the indigenous stock available through grafting of suitable and viable species. This is however a long-term process and the fruits of this activity would be visible only after a few years.

Species to be taken up for plantation were decided upon by the villagers and each individual was asked to furnish the quantity that he/she was interested in. They were then asked to prepare plantation pits and the plantation material was supplied only after the MMDs had approved the pits prepared. The survival rates of these plants are quite high and this reflects the level of motivation of the masses.

TFL/HIMCON has tried hard to propagate high value horticultural plants in the two watersheds. Motivation level of the masses has gone up but despite repeated perusal people are not willing to undertake this activity on a large scale. With a few scattered plants people do not have enough incentives to invest in inputs over and again.

Vegetative Bunding

Erosion is a major issue that needs to be addressed in the hills. TFL/HIMCON adopted the strategy of undertaking grass binding in the fields. This is envisaged to reduce erosion besides providing fodder in the vicinity and thus reducing the drudgery of the females. Both temperate and elephant grasses were introduced in the watersheds with the support of MMDs. In addition routine bunding of the fields was also undertaken in the watersheds and the retaining walls of some of the fields were also repaired.

Social Forestry

Environment protection is an issue that is dear to TFL/HIMCON and it has in the past been promoting afforestation in one way or the other. In the two watersheds the species to be introduced were decided upon by the MMDs. Care was taken to avoid introduction of alien plant species whose ecological impact is not well understood and the plants were so chosen that they serve the society to the maximum extent possible trees were planted both on private and common lands. The survival rates of those planted on common lands were discouraging in the first year but in the subsequent year the people were motivated and major plantation was taken on Van Panchayat land which is surviving well.

Income Generating Farm Products

The hill economy is sustained by remittances from outside and its no surprise that its often dubbed a money order economy. Not all the households are however lucky enough to have an employed member and a large number of families depend upon local resources.

More than thirty per cent of the households of Paturi village fall in this category. After the introduction of the watershed management programme in this region these families are taking special interest in cash crops. Details of the agricultural products sold during 1999 from Paturi village is given in Table 3.4.5.

Table 3.4.5: Details of the Agricultural Produce of the Watersheds Reaching the Market

Variety	*Estimated Produce*	*Families involved*
Pulses (Rajma)	45 quintals	15
Chillies	10 quintals	6
Lemons	4 quintals	3
Turmeric	0.5 quintals	5

Inspired by the capital gains consolidated by the Nepali labourers who are working on rented lands in the surrounding area some people of the watershed have taken to vegetable cultivation on their lands. Vegetables have a ready market at Chamba and the people engaged in this exercise are reaping good profits.

Animal Husbandry

The hill livestock is often written off as being unproductive, but this is the stock that is adapted to withstand the vagaries of the hostile nature and terrain of this area and provides the local people with daily consumables, besides rich manure. It would therefore not be a wise step to introduce alien stock whose adaptation capabilities are yet to be tested. Swayed by technology, in the initial project proposal artificial insemination was highlighted as being a potential area that could revolutionise dairy production in the region.

After much brainstorming it was decided to concentrate on improving the native stock (it would at least conserve our genetic biodiversity), rather than introducing alien stock. So selective inbreeding was the lesson that was propagated amongst the masses through awareness campaigns.

In order to look after the routine health of the animals five individuals were provided training in de-worming and curing common diseases prevalent amongst the hill cattle. This training was provided by Mahila Navjagaran Samiti, Chamba and the *dangar* (cattle) dais so trained are serving the animal population of the two watersheds.

For the people of the Paturi village pastoralism has been a traditional activity and therefore they have taken due benefit from these training courses. This village has a population of more than three hundred productive buffaloes and many families make a livelihood out of selling milk products. Details of the dairy products reaching the market from Paturi are provided in Table 3.4.6. This table is stresses the fact that hitherto unproductive hill cattle is capable of giving viable returns.

Table 3.4.6: Table Showing Economic Viability of Dairy Operations in the Hills

Product	*Produce reaching market (monthly)*	*Rate fetched (Rs./unit)*	*Average monthly income (Rs.)*	*Families involved*	*Average monthly income per family (Rs.)*
Desi ghee	25 kg	150	3,750	14	268
Milk	950 litres	10	9,500	10	950

Sanitation

Health and sanitation are closely linked to one another, and therefore emphasis was laid on making the masses aware of basic hygiene. Besides meetings and door to door contact programme, a two-day training programme was also organised on issues of health and hygiene. These efforts bore fruit and the surroundings of the villages reflect this change. Observing the interest of the villagers TFL/HIMCON approached the support agency for providing funds for the construction of sanitary latrines in the two villages. The request was accepted and thus a total of forty sanitary latrines were constructed in these villages.

Initiatives from the Grassroots

Pasture Development

Pasture development reduces the drudgery of the females besides reducing soil loss through erosion and adds to the recharge of groundwater. It is therefore an important activity. Though not specified under the original project proposal lead in this regard was taken by the MMD of Paturi village. MMD of this village through a consensus decision took steps towards development of protected forest in five hectares of community land. A watchman was arranged by the MMD to ensure that the land is not encroached upon by grazing animals. This patch of land is closed for all human interventions from May-June onwards. In the winter one member from each family harvests the grass which is equally divided amongst all.

This step of Paturi MMD inspired Lawadhar females to take up a similar exercise. In this village many influential families had grabbed the community land. The females through consensus decision got this land freed in 1999 and took steps towards the development of pasture on this land.

Van Panchayat

The main water source of Paturi village is situated amongst the mixed oak forest in the upper reaches of the watershed. It is this source that has always provided water to the villagers for diverse uses. It was a common experience of the villagers that anthropogenic interference in this patch of the forest adversely affected the yield of the spring.

Inspired by the awareness drive of TFL/HIMCON and understanding well the relationship between vegetal cover and recharge (that was disseminated through watershed management training and meetings) the villagers took recourse to formulation of a Van Panchayat that now protects more than 10,000 oak plants in the upper reaches of the watershed. This patch was socially fenced for any form of deforestation and a watchman was appointed to ward off unwanted intruders. The watchman is paid in kind by all the families of the village.

On the invitation from Van Panchayat TFL/HIMCON undertook plantation activity in this patch in 1999. Apart from other plant varieties 2000 ringal (bamboo) were planted. It is envisaged that bamboo plantation would help the people take up associated income generating activities (mat and basked weaving) in times to come. The survival rate of the plants in this area of the forest is exceptionally high.

Self-Appraisal

Every project document has two dimensions non-quantifiable and quantifiable. Non-quantifiable interventions incorporate organisation building, awareness generation and capacity building of the masses. Impact of these interventions is reflected upon other aspects but cannot be quantified in absolute terms and is adjudged subjectively based on certain indirect indicators. Quantifiable indicators on the other hand add weight to statistical analysis for summing up the progress of the project.

On the organisational front (a non-quantifiable progress indicator) both the village watersheds have fully functional Mahila Mangal Dals, Self-Help Groups, Seed and Health banks. Paturi also has a Van Panchayat. As the Watershed Committee has been formally dissolved on the completion of the project, the interests of the family groups have been interwoven with the smooth functioning of these organisations and therefore it is envisaged that these would be working viably and productively in future.

Financial and decision making autonomy is often used to decide the viability of these grassroots level organisations. A firm financial foothold has been provided to these organisations by finances mustered through the Self Help Groups while empowerment and decision making are reflected in the pasture development activity undertaken by Paturi and Lawadhar villagers. MMD of Lawadhar village even took the bold decision of evicting land grabbers from community land.

If voluntary group formation at grassroots level for a common cause reflects enhanced awareness level of the masses it can be stated that the masses of these village watersheds have acquired the acumen (that comes from awareness) of identifying their common good in a cause as secular as forest and pasture development. Though not quantifiable, these by any yardstick convey the message of success; the real viability of these institutions is yet to be tested through time.

As regards quantifiable measures all the targets set at the beginning of the project have been satisfactorily completed within the set time frame. In addition added workload undertaken in the second year (sanitary latrine construction) has also been completed within this time frame. As we perceive it today the project activity stands successfully completed.

Shortfalls

As in every learning exercise there always are some shortcomings and there exists nothing that cannot be done in a better manner, we do find some shortcomings in our work and have experienced difficulties on many fronts during the tenure of the work.

The targets set for animal husbandry in the first year could not be achieved. This is due more to our own dilemma regarding the shape of the things. Once we had decided to shed the issue of introducing alien stock things looked brighter and in the second year much progress was made.

As stated earlier, we underestimated the role of geological investigations in the construction of LDPE tanks and it was a gross failure. LDPE tanks had to be totally abandoned as a project activity.

Grasses introduced in the watersheds (both elephant and temperate) have not shown good results despite advice from the experts of the Hill Campus Ranichauri.

In the first year afforestation activity undertaken on the community lands showed low survival rates. In the second year more of the plantation was undertaken on the patches now reserved for pasture development and in the Panchayat area in Paturi village. The survival rates of these plants are encouraging.

Despite all preparations for water harvesting the weather behaved unpredictably in 1999. This led to severe scarcity of water in the area and raised questions about the acumen of constructing rain water harvesting structures. We are however convinced about the work undertaken and do not want to write off the good intentions on the basis of seasonal exceptions.

Adding to the fury of the dry weather, forest fires, damaged large tract of the forests during the summer of 1999. Afforestation has been undertaken on these tracts but it would take some time before the old state is regained.

TFL/HIMCON has been working in this region in health related issues for a long time. Despite regularly sponsoring motivated young girls for nursing courses, it found it hard to get a regular nursing staff for its own watershed management project. After experimenting with all the available alternatives, recourse was taken to regular services of the traditional Dai and in order to diagnose major diseases, health camps were organised in these watersheds.

Future Strategy

Experience across the length and breadth of the country reveals that two years is too short a time period for watershed management work. Most success stories in this field are consolidated over about a decade of continued and dedicated interventions. So it would be unwise to say that the watersheds can be left on their own to consolidate the gains of the activities introduced during the project tenure.

The formal interventions in these watersheds from TFL/HIMCON are however over, but the association is bound to continue for years to come. We have known the masses, interacted and worked with them for more than two years, so we would be continuing advisory support to them. Further, we would be continuing interventions in these watersheds wherever possible under the ambit of the other allied activities of the organisations.

This association is all the more important for gathering inputs on various vital issues regarding the impact of the project as also to assess the sustainability of the institutions and structures created by us under this project.

'Morals take care
of little things
Little drops of water
Make the mighty ocean
Little grains of sand
Make the beautiful land
Little monuments
Make the mighty eyes
Little pies and farthings
Make millions and crores
Little mistakes
Little unkind acts
Little evil thought
Will make you devil
Little worlds of love
Little act of kindness
Little good thought
Will make you saint
So says Sivananda
Morals take care
Of little things'

3.5

Prospects for Walnut Production

S.P. MALHOTRA*

Background

Uttaranchal is one of the small hilly states in India. The state have good potential for horticulture development since topographically and agro climatically there are wide range of variation which are suitable for growing large number of horticultural crops. Moreover grain farming is proving unremunerative in comparison to growing horticulture crops in the hilly undulating areas, which are devoid of irrigation facilities. Yet horticulture potential has remained unexploited although the Government of the Uttaranchal state has been making endeavours for the upliftment of the state. The location specific technologies generated so far, however, had limited applicability. Due to this horticulture could not be established as a major industry. Nevertheless, the economy of Uttaranchal is largely dependent on the horticultural production especially apples, nut fruits and off-season vegetables and the tourism. The hill zones of the state are one of the most economically backward regions of the country where the crop output level of most of the cereal crops is very low primarily due to lack of water resources, non-application of high yielding technology and lack of basic infrastructure.

Horticulture occupies a very important position in the predominantly agricultural economy of the State. Greater attention is being given to this sector because the terrain and topography of these hills are ideally suited for tree crops. Tree corps tend to bind the soil and prevent soil erosion, help in maintaining the eco-system, ensure optimum utilisation of the marginal and cultivatable wastelands and offer better returns.

* FAO (Retd.), New Delhi.

Among various fruit crops grown in the state, apples are most widely planted and are commercially the important fruit crop. Among the nut crops, according to one study walnuts are grown in the state. The available information about area, production and productivity of walnut in different districts of Uttaranchal is summarized in Table 3.5.1 below. These data are rather old and according to the Trade Sources area and production of walnut in the state have now declined considerably. Most of the quantities produced in Uttaranchal are now being used within the state, with no quantities sold for exports.

Table 3.5.1: Production and Yield per hectare of Walnut in Uttaranchal in 1985-86

District	*Area (Hectares)*	*Production (Tonnes)*	*Yield (Tonnes/hec.)*
1. Almora	1900	1120	0.58
2. Nainital	1300	1050	0.81
3. Pithoragarh	1850	1090	0.58
4. Pauri	1650	950	0.57
5. Tehri	1750	950	0.54
6. Chamoli	1950	980	0.51
7. Uttarkashi	951	680	0.72
8. Dehradun	1701	680	0.39
Total	13052	7500	0.57

Source: Tripathi, R.S. and Jagdish Kumar Nut Fruit Production and Marketing in U.P. Hills: G.P. Pant University of Agriculture and Technology, Hill Campus, Ranichauri, Tehri-Garhwal: Appendix II, March 1992.

Present Status of Walnut Economy in India

Walnuts in India are grown in four states with Jammu and Kashmir accounting for 82 per cent of the total production, followed by Uttaranchal (9%) and Himachal Pradesh and Arunachal Pradesh (the remaining 9%). Estimates of area and production of walnut in India vary considerably. Estimates put out by the National Horticultural Board (NHB), shown below, are almost three times higher than those given by the traders, FAO and the USDA. According to NHB total production of walnut in India is 90.8 thousand tonnes against 32000 tonnes given by other two sources. Both set of figures are presented to stress the need for a collection of reliable data on area, production and utilisation of walnut in India. Most of the discussion in this article is based on the FAO and USDA data, which give time-series on production, exports, imports and domestic utilisation.

Table 3.5.2: Area, Production and Yield of Walnut in India: 1999-2000

State	*Area (000 Hectares)*	*Production (000 Tonnes)*	*Yield (Tonnes/ha.)*
1. Jammu and Kashmir	59.4	74.9	1.2
2. Uttaranchal	16.5	8.5	0.5
3. Himachal Pradesh	5.8	7.3	1.2
4. Arunachal Pradesh	2.3	0.1	0.04
Total	84.0	90.8	1.1

Source: National Horticulture Board: Production Yearbook.

Large numbers of walnut varieties are grown in India. The state-wise cultivated varieties of walnut are as follows:

Jammu and Kashmir	:	Lake English, Drainovsky and Opex Caulchry.
Himachal Pradesh	:	Gobind, Eureka, Placentia, Wilson, Franqueffe, Kashmir Budded.
Uttaranchal	:	Chakrata selections.

Walnut Economy of Jammu and Kashmir

In Jammu and Kashmir trees generally grow along roadsides and riverbanks and areas, which are not suitable for other crops as well as on steep hillsides. The J&K State Horticulture Department, the Agricultural University and the Horticulture Processing and Marketing Corporation provide institutional support for cultivation of fruits and tree nuts. Although most of the walnut crop is concentrated in the southern districts of the state, production occurs throughout the state. Persian walnut and black walnut, the two most important temperate nuts, are grown in India. Three varieties of walnuts are grown in India; hard shell, medium shell and thin shell (kaghazi). In addition to earning foreign exchange, walnut production provides jobs for thousands of families engaged in shelling, lumbering, woodcarving and marketing of the fruit.

Although production is currently concentrated in Jammu and Kashmir state, according to experts, moist coniferous forests of the Eastern and Western Himalayas, Himachal Pradesh, Jammu and Kashmir, hilly regions of North and South, the Eastern hills, Uttaranchal and Arunachal Pradesh are most suitable for the cultivation of walnut. Total area under walnut is estimated at 36,500 hectares with annual production over 31,000 metric tonnes.[1] However, according to the NHB estimates area under walnut in Jammu and Kashmir is 59.4 thousand hectares with production of 74.9 thousand tonnes (Table 3.5.3).

Table 3.5.3: Area, Production and Yield of Walnut in Jammu & Kashmir: 1994-95 to 2000-01

Year	*Area*		*Production*		*Yield*	
	Hectares (000)	*% Increase over previous year*	*Tonnes (000)*	*% increase over previous year*	*Tonne/he*	*% increase over previous years*
1994-95	44.34	–	60.12	–	1.35	–
1995-96	49.46	11.54	63.87	6.24	1.29	-4.44
1996-97	52.43	6.02	68.88	7.84	1.31	1.55
1997-98	56.76	8.25	80.01	16.24	1.41	7.63
1998-99	58.38	2.85	81.36	1.60	1.39	-1.42
1999-2000	59.43	1.80	74.91	-7.92	1.26	-9.3
2000-01	59.84	0.69	83.29	11.19	1.39	10.3

Historically, walnut trees grew wild in the northwestern Himalayan belt. New walnut plantings in Jammu region are more structured. Actual harvested area is estimated at around 80 per cent of total planted area. The Jammu & Kashmir Horticulture Department brought additional area under walnut cultivation in Jammu and area has increased over time. There has been a gradual increase in area and production over the last few years. However, the rate of increase is slowing down and the productivity has also registered a declining trend over the period. This is due to adverse weather conditions and lack of proper orchard management techniques. As the entire plantation of the walnut in the state is of seedling origin, this causes great variability in production.

Among various districts, Anantnag has the largest area under walnut (12,715 hectares) and highest production (29,710 tonnes in 2000-01). In terms of area Doda, Kupwara and Poonch follow Anantnag. However, Pulwama with lower area than these districts, stood second in production for the entire state. This reflected the higher productivity in this district.

Climatic Conditions

Walnut tree flourishes well in temperate belts between altitudes of 900-3500 m. The production of good quality walnut crop is dependent on altitude, temperature fluctuations and humidity/moisture during fruit development stage. Walnut is sensitive to low temperature during spring and high temperature during summer. It should be grown under climatic conditions that are free from frost during spring and extreme heat during summer. Early front also injures young shoots causing them to fail to leaf out in the ensuing spring. At bloom, temperature of even 2-3°C below freezing results in killing of large number of young flowers. Nuts are sensitive let excessive heat, in summer, when the kernel is being developed: temperature over 27°C can darken or even shrivel kernels. Extreme low temperature can also severely affect production. When temperature is below -10°C, branch injury occurs on fully dormant trees. Adequate chilling is required to leaf out and bloom the tree.

An evenly distributed rainfall of 760 mm is considered the optimum for a good quality crop. The districts of Poonch, Rajouri, Doda, Anantnag, Pulwama, Srinagar, Budgam, Baramulla and Kupwara situated at higher elevations in the Himalayan ranges, is the concentrated pocket of walnut cultivation where it gets the congenial climatic conditions and sufficient chilling hours. These results in quality nut production with a light coloured kernel and thin shell. In the areas situated at lower elevations like in Kathua and Udhampur districts, the fruit tree do not get the required chilling hours resulting into brown colour of the kernel with a thinner shell.

The State of Jammu and Kashmir experiences a range of weather conditions during the growing season, some having a negative impact on crop development. For instance good moisture during the flowering and fruit formation period may be followed by hail in mid-March and at time flood in July. The hail may seriously damage walnut crop in important growing areas. Jammu and Kashmir receives approximately 750 mm of rainfall annually.

Inputs

Most of the walnut area is rain fed. Where canal water is available, farmers provide irrigation 7 to 14 days before harvest. This helps the shucks to open and remain suspended on the trees/dropping clean nuts on the ground. The application of fertilizer is somewhat random, although the Horticulture Department recommends increased applications beginning with 20 grams of nitrogen for a one-year-old tree to 2,000 grams for trees older than 20 years. In practice, phosphatic fertilizer applications vary from 20 grams to 1,500 grams per tree depending on the type of fertilizer. Growers find it difficult to implement the fertilizer recommendations due to lack of irrigation, the large size and old age of many trees and the rocky terrain. Some trees are several centuries old and have attained heights of upto 50 feet and girths of up to 36 feet. Leaf manure is commonly mixed in the nursery beds to improve soil fertility and drainage. Young seedlings are transplanted after 2 to 3 years in the autumn when growth ceases temporarily.

Varieties and Yields

Jammu and Kashmir is a rich source of walnut germ plasm with about 330 types catalogued. Out of this total, about 70 varieties are being propagated. Walnut yields have increased little over the years as producers continue to use traditional rearing practices. Problems include:

- Lack of standard cultivars.
- Poor propagation techniques.
- Problems associated with various pests and diseases.
- Trees are often scattered and very large which complicates normal maintenance.

The normal yield of a walnut tree during its productive life should be 45-50 kg/year, however the actual yield per bearing tree, as discussed below, is almost hall of this level. The current ratio between bearing and non-bearing trees is approximately 80:20 with an estimated total tree population of 1.6 million. Walnuts in Jammu and Kashmir have an average shelling percentage of 40 per cent. Thin shell varieties such as the Basksi variety reach 70 per cent.

Crop Quality

Unfavourable weather conditions early in the season leads to decline in the quality of the crop. On average, about half of India's crop is rated of superior quality because of its colour and thin shell. The quality of walnut produced is above average when common pests such as blister mite, stem borer, walnut weevil and aphids do not attack the crop and it is disease free.

Production Policy

The Department of Horticulture provides incentives for bringing new areas under cultivation of dry fruits. The Department's research programme on walnuts consists of surveying local quality strains, and introducing exotic types for growth under local conditions. Continuous attempts are being made to establish sound and successful techniques for budding and grafting walnuts under different conditions. In 1996-97 FAO had implemented a two-year technical project providing assistance for transfer of technology on Vegetative Propagation of walnut in Jammu and Kashmir state. Attempts are being made to dehull walnuts at proper maturity without affecting kernel quality by application of chemicals in the form of dips or sprays. J&K Horticulture Processing and Marketing Corporation looks after post-harvest handling, grading and marketing of walnut crop.

The USDA Agricultural Attache's Estimates

Apart from the NHB's estimates, the US Agricultural Attache's India Annual Walnut Reports give the time series data on Indian walnut economy. These data for the period 1993 to 2003 are summarized in the Table 3.5.3. It covers area planted, area harvested, number of bearing and non-bearing trees, yield per harvested hectare and per bearing tree[2], total supply and utilisation of walnut in terms of domestic consumption, exports and change in stocks. India does not import any walnut.

Since late 1980s area has expanded to some non-traditional producing areas especially in Jammu region where climatic conditions are similar to those in traditional growing areas. Trees in these areas are increasingly coming into bearing stage, which has resulted in higher production. The total planted area is estimated to have increased by 3.6 per cent from 35.2 thousand hectares 1993 to 36.5 thousand hectares in 1997 and has remained constant since then. However, the number of trees planted to walnut rose by 13.6 per cent from 1.39 million in 1993 to about 1.58 million, while the number of bearing trees during the last eleven years increased by 21.1 per cent from 1.08 million to 1.31 million. Although yield per harvested hectare increased almost by 50 per cent, the yield per bearing trees has increased only marginally from 20 kg in 1993 to 23 kg, in 2003. The current yields are less than half of the average normal yield of between 45-50 Kg/year, during its productive life of a walnut tree.[3] The low yield is partly due to the fact that most of the walnut area lacks irrigation and is dependent on rainfall. The application of fertilizer is somewhat random as growers find it difficult to apply recommended levels due to the large size and old age of many trees and the rocky terrain.

Production of walnut inshell basis increased from 22 thousand tonnes in 1993 to 31 thousand tonnes in 2003, over 36 per cent increase in eleven years. The annual growth rate comes to 2.9 per cent. The arrival of commercial volumes from the new production area in Jammu in 1994-95 surprised many in the industry. Production varies from one year to another, as the walnut trees experience alternate bearing cycle. Normally a bumper-output in one year is followed by lower crop next year. Moreover, unfavourable weather conditions at the time of blossom and fruit formation during March through May at times adversely affect crop. Walnut production in the Kashmir valley, the traditional walnut growing area, continues to be hampered by civil unrest. Area has not expanded and proper maintenance of existing trees has been neglected over the years. In addition, trees in some areas are being cut for firewood.

Walnut Utilisation Pattern

Domestic Consumption

Currently domestic consumption of walnut is around fifty per cent of the total output. Ample supplies, anticipated lower prices, the post harvest onset of the festival season spur up consumption. In the domestic market there appears to be keen competition between the price of imported Californian almond and of local walnut. For instance when reduced almond production in the U.S. increases almond prices in India, consumers shift to walnuts and cashews, particularly among poorer consumers. Walnuts are cheaper than other nuts (almonds/cashews/pistachios) and are often the preferred festival nut among lower income groups. Walnut use in the Indian confectionary, chocolates and ice cream industries is on the rise. About 5 per cent of domestic production is consumed in Jammu and Kashmir. Kashmiris also use walnuts as a colouring agent, extracting black and green dyes from the husk. Consumption for walnut oil extraction (only from rancid nuts) is 3 per cent of annual production. The oil extraction rate varies from 50 per cent to 60 per cent. Major consumers of walnut oil are the soap and cosmetic industries.

The domestic demand for walnut is influenced by several factors such as total supplies, export demand and level of prices *vis-à-vis* other nuts such as almond and cashew. For instance tight supplies, strong export demand and comparatively firm local prices could limit domestic consumption of walnut. Similarly low prices of almonds, due to the large U.S. crop (the major supplier to India) encourages middle class consumers and some institutional users to shift from walnut to almonds during the winter festival season. Walnut usage by the confectionary and ice-cream industry is expected to continue to increase. Total annual domestic consumption of walnut which varies considerably, rose from 9 thousand tonnes in 1993 to 16 thousand tonnes, representing an almost 78 per cent rise. The annual rate of growth in domestic consumption comes to 6.5 per cent. Demand for walnut in India like many other countries has been supported by the growth in the Indian economy and expanding middle class. Future prospects, discussed below, both for domestic consumption and exports appear to be good.

Projections for Domestic Utilisation

Long-term projections for availability of walnut for domestic consumption at the world level and for India are based on the standard methodology used by the FAO and other agencies. For instance the yearly estimates of availability for domestic consumption is worked out based on production, plus imports and minus exports. The time series data were analysed and in the first instance linear trends were worked out for major countries and for the world. These trends were critically examined and refined based on the available information of various parameters that affect demand for walnut and the domestic policies.

Global availability of walnut for domestic utilisation is projected to increase by 2.5 per cent per annum during 2000-02 to 2015 and by 3 per cent per annum from 2015 to 2020. World walnut utilisation would increase from an average of 1.2 million tonnes during the base period to 1.75 million tonnes by the year 2015 and 2.01 million tonnes by 2020. Consumption in India is projected to increase by 4.5 per cent per year during 2000-02 to 2015 and 5.0 per cent per annum during the next five years. Domestic consumption would total about 38.6 thousand tonnes by the year 2015 and 49.2 thousand tonnes by the year 2020. Consumption may even increase at a high pace than the projected one following the opening of the Indian market to branded ice creams, chocolates and processed food manufactured by the multinational corporations and if the targeted growth rate of GDP of over 8 per cent during the Tenth Plan and thereafter is realized.

Export Trade

World exports of walnut in-shell terms during the last three years averaged 239540 tonnes per year[4], valued at US$ 421 million. Of the total, exports of walnut in-shell averaged 88.3 thousand tonnes, worth about US$

140 million. In terms of volume exports of walnut in-shell represented 37 per cent of the total while in value terms its share was about 32 per cent. Exports of walnut shell accounted for the remaining 63 per cent in volume and 68 per cent of total foreign exchange earnings. Average world exports of shelled walnut (converted in term of inshell weights) increased from 74740 tonnes from 1990-92 to 151290 tonnes during 2000-02. The annual growth rate comes to 7.3 per cent against 3.1 annual increase in export of walnut inshell.

Walnut exports from India depend largely on domestic prices; export demand and competition from other suppliers especially from the eastern European countries, e.g. Moldova, Bulgaria, Hungary, and Romania. The world export market is dominated by the United States of America, which supplied over 57 per cent of the world exports. India average total walnut shipments of 17, 500 tonnes during the last three years represented 7.3 per cent of global exports.

India exports both walnuts in shell as well as in kernels. The share of kernel in total exports has increased steadily. During the last three years kernels accounted for almost 95 per cent of total walnut exports. Indian average walnut total exports expressed in-shell terms[5] increased from 11.93 thousand tonnes in 1990-92 to 17.86 thousand tonnes in 2000-02. In traditional European markets Indian walnut face intense competition from eastern European countries particularly from Moldova whose walnut crop precedes India's by a month and from Hungary and the United States. During the last three years or so Indian exporters managed to capture some of the markets by lowering export prices. Indian exports of walnut recovered following improved competition due to the decline in Indian rupees *vis-à-vis* US dollar. The value of Indian rupee compared to US dollar declined by 10-12 per cent during 2001-02 and 2002-03. Exports also increased in 2000-01 on strong demand from the EU. Major export destinations for Indian walnut are EU countries— Spain, France, Germany, Italy, Greece, Netherlands, Belgium, UK and Middle East and Far East countries.

Exports of inshell walnuts has declined (now to 5 per cent of total exports), as exporters are getting better returns on shelled walnut exports. India's "nitrogen flush vacuum pack" pouches (two pouches of 5 kg each in one carton) have become very popular in Europe. According to exporters, the shelf life of "vacuum packed" nuts is 7 to 8 months against the normal pack's life span of 4 months. Indian walnut kernels vacuum packed) continue to enjoy a premium of about $150/mt in the world market due to their excellent quality, which results from manual shelling. More than 80 per cent of walnut exports are currently in vacuum-packed pouches and the balance in cardboard cartons with butterlining. Most walnuts are exported from October through March with a bulk shipped during November-January. More than 95 per cent are exported as kernels (40 per cent light halves; 20 per cent amber halves/broken: and the balance as broken). Exports of walnut by destination for the last three years are shown in Tables 3.5.4 and 3.5.5.

Table 3.5.4: Indian Exports of walnut in-shell: 1998-99 to 2001-02

(Quantity in Tonnes: Value in Lakh Rupees)

Country	*1998-99*		*1999-2000*		*2000-01*		*2001-02*	
	Qty.	*Value*	*Qty.*	*Value*	*Qty.*	*Value*	*Qty.*	*Value*
1. Bahrain	–	–	9.3	6.2	3.8	2.62	–	–
2. Brazil	–	–	5.0	9.9	10.0	20.44	–	–
3. Denmark	20.0	31.5	90.0	140.4	69	91.43	20	30.58
4. France	104	91.8	57	64.4	84	95.63	22	29.92
5. Egypt	60	13.8	30	51.5	10.9	18.13	110	226.26
6. Spain	90	83.07	56	76.6	122	212.46	162.25	301.98
7. Germany	80.9	46.5	50	64.1	49.8	46.21	255.64	355.97
8. U.K.	39.1	12.02	80	77.9	34.8	45.64	96.32	119.58
9. Greece	11	58.9	43	45.1	10	11.13	64.9	93.18
10. Italy	86	58.9	–	–	14	26.94	–	–
11. Kuwait	–	–	3.5	5.5	9	15.60	8	7.38
12. Netherlands	54	69.4	41	56.3	41	54.97	91	156.15
13. U.A.E.	3.75	3.7	1.8	1.78	22	30.00	13	4.31
14. Others	145.8	247.1	9.3	72.6	183.2	125.61	143.65	220.80
Total	649.63	760.3	508.04	642.1	597.1	770.81	986.76	1546.11

Source: Government of India: Ministry of Commerce: Directorate General of Commercial Intelligence and Statistics: Foreign Trade of India; various issues.

In India there are no restrictions on walnut exports, and no export subsidies are given. Imports of walnuts/like most other dry fruits and nuts, are allowed without restrictions under the Open General Licence (OGL), and subject to an effective import duty of 40.4 per cent. Given the high tariffs and strong domestic production, opportunities for imports of walnuts are negligible.

There seems to be considerable scope to increase exports of walnut not only to the traditional markets but also to the new and emerging markets especially in the middle eastern countries. The future growth markets for walnut exports should include China, Korea Republic, Mexico, Egypt, Lebanon, Emirates, Mexico and Chile. India needs to increase its walnut production through improved productivity and also through expansion/establishment of new walnut orchards in other states such as Uttaranchal. The traders are experiencing considerable difficulties to get adequate supply of good quality walnuts especially from the Kashmir valley where orchard owners, as mentioned earlier, are unable to take proper care of their orchards due to disturbed conditions in the producing areas. The Horticulture Department of Uttaranchal should take the lead to encourage its farmers in their state to undertake walnut cultivation on commercial scale. For this the Department needs to provide some incentives such as seedling subsidy, cash and other concessions. The Department can in fact take a leaf out of the China's State Forestry Administration Pilot Conversion Programme initiated in the year 2000, allowing conversion of the cropland to cultivate economic trees, e.g. walnuts, pecans and other nut or fruit bearing trees. Farmers, specialists and the government officials consider walnut production as an ecological and economic alternative to cropland agriculture.

Table 3.5.5: Indian Exports of Walnut Kernels: 1998-99 to 2001-02

(Quantity in Tonnes: Value in Lakh Rupees)

Country	*1998-99*		*1999-2000*		*2000-01*		*2001-02*	
	Qty.	*Value*	*Qty*	*Value*	*Oty.*	*Value*	*Otv.*	*Value*
1. Australia	69.8	58.7	77.73	73.4	141.7	150.98	216.7	274.80
2. Belgium	47	6.1	21	24.8	76.5	98.49	59.0	82.08
3. Brazil	27	55.6	10	19.52	20	48.48	–	–
4. Denmark	194	260.3	116.1	169.2	178.8	286.3	325.8	533.70
5. Egypt	409	654.9	558.9	859.9	43	773.58	604.8	1191.60
6. Spain	748.8	1115.9	579.5	796.9	1518.8	2444.0	1514.6	2626.41
7. France	472.16	504.4	626.7	62.4	795.5	948.11	544.0	718.15
8. Germany	99.24	121.6	521.7	609.3	89.1	1176.6	663.1	977.01
9. U.K.	139.8	177.9	634.2	593.07	670.6	864.93	554.2	828.28
10. Greece	452	531.8	488.8	529.07	597.4	762.51	502.0	680.54
11. Italy	163	171.9	167.5	185.4	138.1	201.49	61.6	95.35
12. Netherlands	354	528	21-1	301.8	31.2	452.32	251.4	421.74
13. Portugal	53	69.9	42	45.3	75	108.1	53.0	82.78
14. Sweden	41	54.4	21	25.37	2.1	30	18.0	27.43
15. Switzerland	21	25.4	22.5	31.7	66	90.85	44.0	66.81
16. U.A.E.	64.3	76.6	63.1	11.19	109.6	179.06	81.1	140.91
17. U.S.A.	20.3	30.5	3.1	5.43	180.6	269.77	69.14	91.28
18. Others	1303.6	1687.2	509.8	1679.02	1600.8	1339.3	1852.76	1302.11
Total	4678-2	6131.12	4484.7	5413.4	7145.3	10222.9	6415.2	10232.16

Source: Government of India: Ministry of Commerce: Directorate General of Commercial Intelligence and Statistics: Foreign Trade of India; various issues.

Competitiveness Analysis

India faces a strong competition in the international market from other major walnut producing and exporting countries. In fact following the WTO Agreement on Agriculture, China, USA and France have become more aggressive in promoting their products especially in European countries, which is the important region for walnut imports. The comparative analysis of walnut imports in the major EU countries (presented in Table 3.5.6) indicates that Indian exports are generally competitive. The weighted unit import value of walnut in the six EU member countries studied comes to EUC 2.90 per kilogram, compared with ECU 3 per kg. for Indian exports to these markets. Due to higher freight and transportation costs Indian export prices are slightly higher than the USA, but these are lower than second highest rates. For instance in France Indian export price was ECU 3.01, against Chinese price of ECU 3.82 per kg., while in Germany, it was close to that of France. In the case of United Kingdom, Indian export unit value ECU 2.80 per kg., compared favourably with that of Chinese 3.07 and ECU 5 for Italy. India can improve its competitive position due to its lower labour costs. For this it needs to improve further its product quality and productivity, for which there is considerably scope. India can and should capture a much higher share of these traditional markets and penetrate into new potential

Table 3.5.6: Competitiveness analysis for walnut imports in IEU Country

Importing country/ supply source	*Imports*			*Importing country/supply source*	*Imports*		
	Qty. (Tonnes)	*Value (ECU 000)*	*ECU/ kg*		*Qty. (Tonnes)*	*Value (ECU 000)*	*ECU/ kg.*
I. Germany	**22,258**	**56,980**	**2.56**	**IV. Netherlands**	**6,947**	**15,700**	**2.6**
Imports from				Imports from			
1. U.S.A.	11,129	22,.814	2.05	1. U.S.A.	4,932	11,150	2.26
2. France	4,897	15,670	3.20	2. China	555	1,820	3.29
3. China	1,440	3,630	2.52	3. India	420	1,630	3.89
4. India	1,560	5,023	3.22	4. France	440	2,040	4.64
II. Italy	**15,824**	**33,230**	**2.10**	**V. U.K.**	**7,990**	**19,330**	**2.42**
Imports from				Imports from			
1. U.S.A.	12,180	35,380	2-04	1. U.S.A.	3,510	6,170	1.76
2. France	540	1,210	2.23	2. China	2,875	8,830	3.07
3. India	270	850	3.17	3. India	1,120	3,130	2.80
				4. Italy	110	550	5.02
III. France	**12,820**	**35,380**	**2.76**	**VI. Belgium**	**3,076**	**8,330**	**2.71**
Imports from				Imports from			
1. Moldova	3,460	10,034	2.90	1. France	1,780	5,380	2.88
2. China	3,200	12,220	3.82	2. Netherlands	400	1,120	2.80
3. India	1,250	3,762	3.01	3. India	73	290	4.00
4. Hungary	870	2,690	3.09	4. Italy	330	625	1.90
				5. U.S.A.	160	315	1.98

Source: APEDA Database: Euro STAT and National sources.

Far East is not as large market for walnuts as Europe. However, there could be the potential target markets for India, as the landing cost in this market for its main competitors, viz. U.S.A. and China is quite high. The main markets include Hong Kong and Japan. Hong Kong imports over 1,700 tonnes of walnut, worth HK$ 4.23 million (Rs. 296 million). The main suppliers are China (84%), supplying at an average rate of HK$ 24.7 (Rs. 173 per kg.). U.S.A. is the second major supplier, accounting for 12 per cent of import demand. Its unit export price is HK$ 21 (Rs. 151 per kg). Hong Kong could be a potential market for India, due to lower landing cost. India could supply walnut to this market at comparative lower prices than other major suppliers such as U.S.A. and China.

Japan: It imported over 260 tonnes walnut worth Yen 102 million (Rs. 30.6 million) at an average price of Yen 394 per kg. (Rs. 118). U.S.A. is the major exporters to the country supplying over 200 tonnes of walnut worth Yen 95.8 million at an average price of Yen 401 per kg. (Rs. 120).

U.S.A: Although it is the largest exporter of walnut, it is also a transit market for the fruit. Its imports have declined from an average of 3,420 tonnes during three years 1995-96 to 1997-98, to only 180 tonnes during the last three years. China is the biggest exporter to the USA. India is the second major supplier to U.S.A. market. India can target U.S.A. market in the months of February to May when there is fairly good demand in the market.

Imports of walnut by major importing countries and share of major suppliers are shown in Table 3.5.7.

Table 3.5.7: Walnut Imports m selected European countries

Country	*Imports In-shell basis (Tons)*	*Average price per kg.*		*Main Sources*
		ECU	*INR*	
1. Germany	22,258	2.5	107	U.S.A. (50%), France (22%), India (7%), China (5%), Others (16%).
2. Italy	15,824	2.1	88	U.S.A. (77%). India (1-7%), others (21.3)
3. France	12,820	2.8	116	Moldova (27%), China (25%), India (12%) (27%) Hungry (7%), Others (29%).
4. Netherlands	6,947	2.6	109	U.S.A. (71%), China (8%), India (6%), Others (15%).
5. U.K.	7,990	2-4	101	U.S.A. (44%), China (36%), India (14%), Others (6%)
6. Belgium	3,076	2.7	114	France (58%), Netherlands (13%), Italy (11%), U.S.A. (9%), India (4%), Others (6%)
Total	68,918	2.47 @	107	@ Weighted Average price.

Factors Affecting World Trade

The outlook for international trade in walnut is shaped by long-term and short-term factors. Some of the underlying long-term factors are the income growth of trading customers and increased market access stemming from trade liberalisation. Any deviations from the long-term trend are a result of short-term factors that can intermittently hinder or help trade prospects of producers. Examples of these short-term factors are changes in the U.S. dollar exchange rates in foreign markets and fluctuations in world supplies. Other factors, such as trade barriers and productivity changes from technological innovations may have a long-term or short-term effect.

To a certain extent, production of good crop of walnuts in 2000-01 and devaluation of Indian Rupees *vis-à-vis* US Dollar, pulled down prices for these commodities and, along with good quality, improved the competitiveness in the EU market. However, the Japanese yen had depreciated even before the financial crisis began in Southeast Asia and has adversely affected exports to that country. Despite the weaker yen, Japanese demand for Indian walnut remains strong. While Southeast Asia is currently a relatively small market for Indian walnut, there is considerable scope to increase exports to these countries, including China, Korea Republic, Japan, Malaysia, Singapore, and the Philippines.

Fluctuations in world supplies also affect the demand for Indian exports. The Indian exports to the global market increases when domestic supplies are large and/or traditional suppliers in the world market experience a decline in production. These supply factors are generally unpredictable, caused in most cases by unusual weather.

A number of barriers, both natural and artificial, diminish export opportunities for Indian producers. Depending on the nature of the barrier, the impacts to Indian exports could either be long term or short term. Examples of these barriers include costly transportation of products to far off markets and legal trade barriers such as government protectionist policies. Liberalisation of trade through multilateral, bilateral, and/or regional trade agreements are important in relaxing many of these existing legal trade barriers either by tariff reductions or harmonizing technical barriers to trade (TBT).

Technical barriers to trade, such as Phytosanitary requirements and labelling issues, are an example of a legal trade barrier. TBTs are not necessarily associated with developed or developing countries, but rather involve importing countries setting standards of quality or requirements, which potential trade partners must meet. Because the Japanese are very concerned about the spread of fire blight, codling moths, and other crop diseases, their government imposes rigorous and costly import requirements for shipments of agriculture produce. Another example is Brazil's mandatory fumigation at origin requirement for all U.S. walnuts and fruit entering their market, effective June 1997. This requirement was imposed following the detection of Pacific spider mite and thrips in some shipments. Mandatory fumigation-at-origin requirement may dampen prospects for future exports to these foreign markets.

Technological innovations can lead to achieving a larger share of the world market through a competitive advantage—either a higher quality product for the same price, or a lower price for a product of comparable quality. However, these technologies can be exported as well, and so any gains in export market shares may be short lived. The benefits of technology adoption for an exporting country are usually larger with proximity to major export markets. Example of this is Moldova walnut export to EU because of much lower transportation cost than shipment from India and the harvesting of walnut one month before Indian supply become available. India has successfully adopted vacuum packaging technology in walnut kernel, which has extended the shelf life of the produce. However, India needs to improve yields though introduction of better varieties, lower cost of production through improved field management practices and also to expand cultivation of walnut in other states to meet its increasing domestic consumption and for the increased exports.

Prospects in EU: EU is the biggest export market for Indian walnuts. However, India's share in exports to the large walnut importing countries such as France, Germany, Greece, Italy. During the last two years India's exports of walnuts to these countries averaged 10,720 tonnes, out of their total imports of 120,000 tonnes. The overall market of the European Union is a differentiated one, with each Member State market having characteristics that merit individual attention. Thus, although export business strategy for Europe is a must, tactics should be adjusted for each country. With approximately 370 million consumers, the EU is one of the world's largest importers of agricultural products, accounting for roughly 20 per cent of total world imports. The EU is the largest market for walnut imports. Consistent with the global trend, the market for consumer food products is a very promising growth area. While the prospects for different products vary from country to country within the EU, tree nuts are selling well in a number of EU countries.

In EU member countries walnuts, almonds, and pistachios are the biggest sellers in agricultural product category, but they face competition from local production in the Mediterranean countries. The walnut market in the EU is seasonal, with most imports occurring in the October-January period. As part of the Uruguay Round results, the EU is gradually cutting the tariff on tree nuts. Exports to the EU have been negatively affected by the continued slump in the European economies, but the long-term prospects remain bright as local economic situations improve. It is essential for India to increase exports to these EU member countries and also supply to the new markets such as Korea Republic, Japan, China and Switzerland. Increased competition from local producers can be expected. Exporters however should check on health certification requirements prior to shipment.

Long-term Trade Projections

The long-term projections of international trade in walnut has been prepared on the basis of the factors mentioned above along with the past trend, market shares, present and anticipated, of major exporting countries, prospects in major importing countries, the performance of the world economy and the policy aspects. World exports of walnut in-shell are projected to increase from an annual average of 88.3 thousand tonnes during 2000-2002 to 159 thousand tonnes by the year 2015 and 200 thousand tonnes in 2020. The annual growth rate would be 4 per cent and 5 per cent during the two projections period. Exports of walnut in-shell are projected to increased form 80.2 thousand tonnes to 125 thousand tonnes in 2015 and 152 thousand tonnes in 2020.

Indian exports of shelled walnut is projected to increase from an average of 6,845 tonnes during 2000-02 to 12,100 tonnes in 2015 and 15,480 tones by the year 2020. Average annual exports of walnut in-shell are anticipated to remain around 1 thousand tonnes. Based on the conversion ratio of 40 per cent of in-shell to shelled walnut, total walnut exports are projected to increase from 17,933 tonnes in the base period to 31,240 tonnes during 2015 and 39,700 tonnes in 2020. The annual growth rate comes to 4 per cent from 2001 to 2015 and 5 per cent from 2015 to 2020.

Supply Projections

Total requirements for walnut in India are projected at 69,800 tonnes by the year 2015 and 88,900 tonnes for 2020. It represents an annual 5.3 increase from 2001 to 2015 and 5.5 per cent from 2015 to 2020. To meet these requirements production projections were prepared based on the FAO Time series data and the USDA especially for India on area planted, area harvested, bearing trees and yield per harvested area and per bearing trees.

Based on the FAO series two alternative projections for the major walnut producing countries, including India and the world were worked out. The first alternative was based on the trend value for the period 1983 to 2000 and the second alternative was extrapolated on the basis of trend value for the period 1991-2002. Because of the faster growth during the period 1991-2002, projected production of walnut both for the world as whole and for most countries is higher compared to the much long-term 1983-2002 trend projections. The future walnut production may most likely follow the trend of the last decade. In fact with the improvement both in the field as well as management practices being implemented in some leading countries, production trend could be even better. Under alternative II the world walnut production is projected to increase an annual rate of 2.6 per cent during the period 2000-02 to 2015 and 3 per cent during 2015 to 2020. For India the respective annua growth rate is 4 per cent and 5.5 per cent.

India's share in the world production of walnut increased slightly from 2 per cent during 1980-82 to 2.4 per cent in 2000-02. However, China's share during this period has increased by almost ten points from 13.4 per cent to 22.7 per cent. It thus became the leading producer of walnuts in the world, surpassing the U.S.A., whose share declined by about over four points to 20 per cent. India's share in the projected world output would rise to 3.4 per cent by the year 2020.

Table 3.5.8: Walnut World and India's Production Base year and for 2015 and 2020

(Inshell basis Tonnes)

	Base period Av. 2000-02	*Alternative I*		*AltemativeII*	
		2015	*2020*	*2015*	*2020*
Production Projections					
World	1,246,629	1.578,140	1,708,520	1,835,250	2,113,620
India	31,000	45,050	54,100	55,450	72,550
India's total requirements	35,910	n.a.	n.a.	69,800	88,900

With the initial projected production India will not meet, as shown in Table 3.5.8, its total projected requirements for domestic consumption and exports, during both the projected periods. There would a shortfall of around 15,000 tonnes. Thus India would need to boost its production even higher than the initial projections to 88,900 tonnes, during the next two decades. This represents an annual growth rate of 5.4 per cent over twenty years, one percent higher than the initial projection. This would necessitate not only increase in productivity, which is very low, compared to its competitors, but expansion of area in traditional as well as other states, such as Uttaranchal, which seem to have a suitable agro-climatic conditions.

The revised projections of production for India based on total requirements are shown in Table 3.5.9. Based on the trend rate of growth in productivity, India's yield would increase from 1 tonne per hectare to 1.83 tonnes of harvested area by the year 2020. The harvested area is 80 per cent of the total area under walnut crop. With the projected yield level a production level of 88,900 tonnes would therefore require around 52,500 hectares under walnut, compared to 36,500 hectare currently estimated. The current yield per bearing tree in India is 25 kgs. against 50-60 kgs. in other competing countries. It is essential to increase the productivity per hectare as well as per bearing tree to their normal potential. It is also essential to uproot the old trees and graft the new high yielding varieties and increase the density of tree per hectare in the existing orchards. Even with the higher yields than projected, it would be necessary to bring in an additional 16,000 hectare walnut production to achieve the projected level of production. Because of scarcity of suitable land in Jammu and Kashmir State, it is essential to expand walnut production to other states, which has suitable agro-climatic conditions. This augurs well for expanding walnut production to other state, such as Uttaranchal and Himachal Pradesh. There is an urgent need for Uttaranchal to diversify its agricultural economy and the walnut growing offers good opportunity.

The fast increase in population in the hills in Uttaranchal has led to (i) reduction in arable land per family, (ii) deepening of poverty, and (iii) massive deforestation. The impact of these factors result in the vicious circle, in that the needs of the burgeoning subsistence population exerts increasing pressure on the forest cover leading to massive deforestation, which is the cause of accelerating rates of massive wastage.

In fact the pressure on land, the resource that is rather limited, is increasing immensely. In the past this pressure was partly offset by bringing in the forestland and slopes under cultivation. However, now

Table 3.5.9: Indian Walnut Planted and Harvested Area, Production and Utilisation: Actual 1993-2003: Projections 2015 and 2020

Item	*Unit*	*1993*	*1994*	*1995*	*1996*	*1997*	*1998*	*1999*	*2000*	*2001*	*2002*	*2003*	*Projection* *2015*	*2020*	*Annual growth rate (%)* *2001/1994*	*2015/2001*	*2020/2015*
Area planted	000 hectare	35.2	35.5	36.0	36.4	36.5	36.5	36.5	36.5	36.5	36.5	36.5	47.7	52.5	0.4	1.8	2.0
Area Harvested	000 hectare	27.5	28.4	28.8	29.12	29.95	29.95	30.5	30.2	30.2	30.2	30.5	40.5	48.6	1.0	2.0	2.3
Bearing Trees	000 Nos.	1082	1136	1152	1157	1228	1228	1305	1305	1305	1307	1310	1710	1910	1.7	1.8	2.2
Total Trees	000 Nos.	1387	1420	1440	1450	1496	1496	1565	1560	1570	1572	1575	2110	2330	1.3	2.0	2.0
Yield/hectare harvested area	Kgs.	800	986	868	996	834	1002	1016	1027	960	1060	984	1586	1830	1.7	3.0	3.0
Yield/bearing tree	Kgs.	20.3	24.6	21.7	18.5	20.4	23.0	23.0	23.0	22.2	24.5	22.9	45439	45.4	0.6	3.6	3.1
Beginning Stocks	Tonnes	4940	3390	5740	3200	6420	3620	6270	5270	3770	4770	3550	5000	7000	–	–	–
Production (October/Sept.)	Tonnes	22000	28000	25000	29000	25000	30000	31000	31000	31000	32000	30000	69800	88900	3.0	5.3	5.5
Total Supply	Tonnes	26940	31390	30740	32200	31420	33620	37270	36270	34770	36770	33550	75500	95900	3.8	5.1	5.5
Exports	Tonnes	14550	16050	16540	13780	15000	12350	14000	15500	15000	17220	15000	31240	39700	0.2	3.4	5.0
Domestic Consumption	Tonnes	9000	96000	11000	12000	12800	15000	18000	17000	15000	16000	16000	38560	49200	6.0	4.0	5.0
Ending Stock	Tonnes	3390	5740	3200	6420	3620	6270	5270	3770	4770	3550	2550	5000	7000	–	–	–
Total Distribution	Tonnes	26940	31390	30740	32200	31420	33620	37270	36270	32770	36450	33550	75500	95900	–	–	–

Source: For current data: US Embassy: Agricultural Attache's Annual Reports: India Tree Nuts: Various Years. Projections by the Author.

the opportunity for such expansion no longer exists, and thus individual land holdings are rapidly decreasing, with the average size being less than I acre. Nevertheless a large tract of arable land has been rendered as a waste and degraded land due to the negligence and lack of measures to harvest the rainfall through proper small irrigation works. As a result land is no longer able to sustain the growing rural population, and migration from rural to urban areas and other states is increasing. This is particularly the case in the hill areas, where people are moving to the cities like Dehradun and Haridwar in search of employment. At the same time, many people remain in the hill areas, where underemployment and unemployment are rife.

In Uttaranchal there is a considerable amount of wasteland in the state. This consists of forest-degraded area and non-forest degraded land. Culturable wasteland alone is estimated at over 350 thousand hectares. It constitutes over 25 per cent of the currently total cropped area. Destruction and degradation of forests are taking a heavy toll of soil with essential nutrients in the hilly areas being washed away each year. This seriously affects the economy of the sate. The degradation makes land less productive leading to impoverishment of the rural population. It is essential to regenerate degraded forest and wasteland. A programme of generation and restoration of eco-system will provide productive employment to a large section of rural population. The wasteland can be converted to grow tree and other crops, fodder and fuel. It is reported that an Ex-serviceman, Jagat Singh Chaudhry, from a tiny village of Kot Malla has successfully converted 1.5 hectares of wasteland in the hills of Rudraprayag district of the state, by planting various species of plants ranging from trees to medicinal plants. This experiments needs to be replicated on a large scale.

In fact, the varied agro-climatic zone of the state combined with generally a diligent peasantry offer good opportunities for producing horticultural products including walnuts. The development of walnut and other horticultural crops will not only help in the creation of employment opportunities and increasing income level of the masses, they will also provide permanent green cover to the soil besides acting as soil binder thereby prevent soil erosion to a considerable extent. Planting of trees also will help in bringing back the nutrients that are actually lost and cannot be used by the field corps as a result of leaching to the deeper zones of the wild. Moreover, the cultivation of walnuts and fruit crops is labour intensive compared to the cultivation of field corps starting from the stage of tree plantation to marketing. Thus the intensive cultivation of walnut tree could serve as a viable alternative strategy for the development of the hill regions. This would at the same time check the migration of the able bodied workforce and provide gainful employment opportunities within the region. Walnut trees seems to have good potential in the state, which are mostly grown in backyard garden, and no compact orchard exists. The existing walnut trees are of inferior varieties. Productivity can be increased by introduction of superior varieties. Preliminary results indicate that walnut, almond and Kiwi fruit, such low volume but high value fruit crops, will be of immense value and there is good scope for their commercial cultivation at higher altitude of the state. However, for this it is essential to undertake a comprehensive feasibility study on the promotion of walnut tree plantation and medicinal plants on commercial scale in the selected districts of the State.

Walnut orchard can provide full/part time employment to family labour. The human labour requirement on the maintenance of the orchard during the bearing and non-bearing stages is estimated to be around 1000 days per hectare. The gross return on walnut comes to around Rs. 64,800 per hectare. This is based on a yield of 1,830 kg. per hectare and farm price of Rs. 60 per kg of walnut in-shell. After deducting the out-of pocket expenses of the farm, assumed to be 40 per cent of the gross return, the net income of the farmer comes to Rs. 38,900 per hectare. It is essential, however, to stress that the establishment of walnut orchard involve heavy cost, which most of the farmers cannot bear and also there is a time lag of 5 to 6 years from planting of walnut tree to the bearing stage. To introduce/expand walnut growing on commercial stage in the state, the government would need to provide the financial incentives on a large scale to the farmers, in addition to the Hill Campus of G.B. Pant University of Agriculture and Technology, located in Ranichauri, providing technical guidance and the necessary extension service.

Realizing the need for the introduction of new tree corps and the importance of good quality planting material and seeds TFL/HIMCON, a voluntary organisation, has during the last few years or so introduced new high value horticultural crops and medicinal plants in the selected hill areas of the state. Walnut, Kiwi and Almond are being promoted together with granium, brahmi, aswagandha, shatavari, kuth and kutki. It seems that walnuts can be successfully grown between the elevations of 1000 to 3000 metres above sea level. Walnut production in the state, as mentioned above, has declined considerably and most of the produce is currently being consumed within the state. However, traders and exports are experiencing difficulties to get adequate supplies of walnuts from the Jammu and Kashmir to meet increasing demand for exports as well as domestic consumption. They are interested to diversify the source of supplies.

Although a good start seems to have been made to distribute walnut stems among farmers in the Ranichauri areas. There is however, need to carry out a proper feasibility study which should cover soil analysis at the farmer's fields and provide him the proper technical guidance for planting and caring of the pants say upto three years or so. At present the farmer is left to himself and he does not plant walnut tree in a scientific manner. Also most of these farmers are not aware of the type of the walnut stems supplied to them. Walnut orchard, like other tree crops plantation, has a long gestation period. The tree starts bearing fruit after 5-6 years and net economic return accrues to farmer almost after 10 years of planting. This involves a considerable amount of risk by the farmers. It is therefore, essential to carry out a proper scientific research by the Horticultural Department of the Hill Campus of G.B. Pant University of Agriculture and Technology, on the soil, water and the type of walnut trees which can be grown successfully in different areas of the state, before undertaking a large scale walnut planting campaign in the state. Otherwise, there are chances that the experiments undertaken on trial and error bases may not yield good viable results. This will have in turn a negative impact and would shake the confidence of the farmers in the state to undertake any new venture in the future.

"We may
Often
Give
Without Love
But we Can
Never
Love
Without Giving"

3.6

Resource Conservation as a Tool for Economic Development

P.K. SAMANT AND L.M.S. PALNI*

Introduction

Uttaranchal, the 27th state of the Indian Republic, was created on November 9, 2001. Administratively, the state consists of thirteen districts, namely, Almora, Bageshwar, Nainital, Udham Singh Nagar, Pithoragarh, Champawat, Uttarkashi, Chamoli, Rudraprayag, Tehri Garhwal, Dehradun, Pauri Garhwal and Hardwar. With a geographical area of 53,485 sq. km., it supports 84,79,562 persons (Census of India, 2001) who constitute about 0.83 per cent of the total population of the Indian Republic.

The people of Uttaranchal like elsewhere in other mountain eco-systems, are largely dependent for their living on their immediate natural resources and production from primary sectors such as forestry, agriculture and livestock. Bio-resources, are undisputedly, critical to the survival of the people of Uttaranchal. India is one of the centres of diversity of plant genetic resources and Uttaranchal constitutes part of the sub-centre called Western Himalayas. Further, twenty-six "hot-spots" have been identified in India where there are high rates of deforestation and endemicity. One of these is the Himalayan belt as a whole constituting one mega hot-spot; eight areas in the Himalayas are specially critical and Uttaranchal is one of these eight critical areas. The state is home to a number of crop plant species in addition to many species of wild economic plants. Such plants offer age-old vocation and a source of income to the local people. The continued dependence of the ever growing

* G.B. Pant Institute for Himalyan Environment and Development, Kosi, Almora.

population on these resources without option for other viable avenues of livelihood and technologies to enhance production to meet their needs, is depleting and marginalizing these scarce resources effecting productivity and affecting poverty. Further, enhancement of production through the replication of modern technologies in this ecosystem is restricted to a large extent by mountain specificities, viz. inaccessibility, fragility, marginality, diversity (heterogeneity), niche (natural suitability) and adaptability (human adaptation).

For economic development of the state and the very survival of its people, the finite resources, particularly bio-resources, need to be conserved. Conservation, dealing with effective management of resources for sustained use, essentially means doing three things—(i) maintaining essential ecological processes and life support systems, (ii) preserving genetic diversity, and (iii) utilising species and eco-system sustainability (Palni, 1993). It is indeed a holistic concept and encompasses the whole spectrum of activities from *in situ* conservation dealing with population, communities and ecosystems on the one hand, and on the other it deals with *ex situ* conservation involving botanical gardens, arboreta, biological banks, etc. (Khoshoo, 1993). *In situ* conservation aims at conserving bio-diversity in natural habitats on a holistic basis more as a system than as separate individuals. The first and foremost system under *in situ* category are the watersheds which are not only rich in biodiversity but are also intertwined with long-range ecological security (Khoshoo, 1993).

The most widely used method of conservation is by seed storage. However, in a number of cases seed storage is difficult or impossible. To circumvent these problems, *in vitro* methods developed initially for the propagation and genetic manipulation of plant species, are presently being adapted for germ plasm conservation (Palni, 1993). Conservation ensures constant supply of genes for maintaining future possibilities of evolution of the biota, in addition to eco-development. Eco-development stands for economic development based on ecological principles (Khoshoo, 1993). Therefore, conservation and wise management of biological diversity must receive due importance in the planning process, and economic development of Uttaranchal must be based on sound ecological considerations (Palni, 1993).

Primary Resources of Uttaranchal

Forests are the prime natural resource of Uttaranchal being the very basis of life of its people. On the other hand, these forests also have a national ecological importance as protection of the catchments of the major rivers of north India (Anonymous, 2000). It is reported that forests occupy more than 60.0 per cent of the total geographic area of the state (Table 3.6.1). Classification of land under forests by ownership in Uttaranchal shows that about 69.24 per cent of the forests belong to the forest department; 23.30 per cent are Civil Soyam while 6.89 per cent and 0.57 per cent are Panchayat forests and private forests, respectively (Shah, 1996).

Table 3.6.1: Area under Important Landuse Category in Uttaranchal* (in percentage)

Category	*1976-77*	*1980-81*	*1985-86*	*1990-91*	*1993-94*
Forest	65.2	64.6	63.8	63.9	64.0
Barren and uncultivable land	4.5	5.5	5.6	5.6	5.5
Land put to non-agricultural use	2.1	2.2	2.3	2.5	2.6
Culturable wasteland	5.6	5.9	5.9	5.9	5.9
Permanent pasture and grazing land	3.8	4.1	5.0	4.2	4.2
Land under Misc. tree cover/groves	3.8	3.5	3.9	4.2	4.1
Current fallow	0.5	0.4	0.2	0.1	0.1
Other fallow	0.6	0.6	0.8	1.2	1.2

* Excluding Haridwar district.
Source: Singh & Lal, 1996 and Joshi, *et al.*, 1999.

Though, it is claimed by the forest department that the area under forests in the region is above 60 per cent of the total area, many studies report the area under forests to be much less (Tiwari *et al.*, 1985; Saxena, 1995 and Singh & Lal, 1996). The forest cover, from 1972-75 to 1980-82, reduced by 10.15 per cent for the Indian Himalayas and by about 18.8 per cent for Uttaranchal (Planning Commission, 1985). Tiwari, Saxena and Singh (1985), using Landsat-1 images for the year 1972, have estimated that the total forest cover in Uttaranchal was only 24.9 per cent. Good forests (with a crown cover of more than 60%) cover only 15.4. per cent of the forested land and 4.4 per cent of the total geographical area.

Distribution of forests as interpreted by Landsat imagery for the years 1980-82 showed that only 28.63 per cent of the total area of Uttaranchal is under forests; out of this good tree cover exists only on 15.45 per cent of forest land, medium (with 30-60% of crown cover) and poor tree cover (with 10-30% crown cover) exists on 52.32 per cent and 32.23 per cent of forest lands, respectively (Saxena, 1995). The State of Forests Report, 1991 of the Ministry of Environment and Forests, Government of India estimated the forest area of Uttaranchal as only 44.08 per cent of the total area (Singh & Lal, 1996).

Agriculture is the dominant sector of the economy of Uttaranchal with nearly 85 per cent of the people dependent on it for their survival (Anonymous, 2000). Agriculture in the state, apart from being labour intensive, is strongly related to ecological specificities and socio-economic and cultural conditionings. The agro-ecosystem is holistic in composition including agriculture, forests and livestock. Agriculture is also largely influenced by altitude, size of farm, and availability of uncultivated support land (forests). This uncultivated land (forests) surrounding a village supports cultivation by supplying organic matter and plant nutrients to cultivated land and, therefore, has been defined as support land (Ashish, 1982). A topo-sequence is maintained with forests or uncultivated land or support area at the top, the village in the middle and the agricultural lands below the village on terraced spurs in slopes ranging from 8-45 degrees. Agriculture is sustained by a flow of organic matter and plant nutrients from support land to cultivated land and by the recycling of organic matter and plant nutrients in crop residues. The livestock is dependent on green leaves obtained from forests as fodder and the cultivated land is dependent on animal dung used as compost, apart from animals (bullock) being used for ploughing. The dry leaves, also obtained from forests, are used as bedding of the animals which are also used as compost in cultivated land. Indirectly, by supplying firewood, the forests also support cultivation; in the absence of which livestock dung must have been used as fuel, seriously interrupting the flow of organic matter and plant nutrients to cultivated lands (Jackson, 1985).

By and large the agriculture system in Uttaranchal is complex and diverse. Further, the agricultural system is characterised by a number of sustainable practices such as cropping pattern, crop rotation, multiple and mixed cropping, that vary considerably along altitudinal gradients. While the people in the lower elevation grow crops like wheat and barley as winter crops, and buckwheat, rice, maize, potatoes, etc., as summer crops, the people at high altitudes have to be content with one crop per year, and "transhumance" communities have also evolved as an adaptation strategy, with intricate resource use and management practices and need driven animal breeding system. Within a given landscape, the farmers of the state have a variety of landuse systems contributing towards bio-diversity at all levels ranging from sub-species, through species, population, and the ecosystem. Further, farmyards maintain a large number of plant species of immense value as food supplements, medicines, fodder, fuelwood, fibre, spices and condiments, for their own use and for economic gains. Uttaranchal is one of the important centres for the origin of crop diversity and is known to be home to several cereals, pulses, fruits, oil and sugar yielding plants, and their close relatives. In addition, the state is a "storehouse" of many under-utilised and potential future crops.

The population of major types of livestock in Uttaranchal, has either increased or remained constant in the last 30 years (Table 3.6.2). In absolute number, the increase in livestock population is about 1,23,000 from 1961 to 1993. However, after converting the animal type to a standard animal unit, the absolute increase of units is 2,42,000 which is almost double of the increased livestock population. This is due to increase in buffalo population which is stall-fed and the green fodder for which is usually obtained from forests and grasslands.

Table 3.6.2: Livestock Population in Uttaranchal* (in thousands)

Livestock Type	*1961*	*1972*	*1978*	*1988*	*1993*
Cattle	2056	2110	2030	1941	1900
Buffalo	583	647	700	827	846
Sheep	383	353	410	348	352
Goat	757	736	950	902	799

* Excluding Hardwar district.

Source: Saxena, 1995 for the years 1961 and 1972; Jackson, 1985 for the year 1978; District Statistical Abstracts, 1991 for the year 1988 and Joshi *et al.*, 1999 for the year 1993.

Resource Conservation: Constraints

The state is experiencing major difficulties in sustaining its growing population on its environmental resources—land, forests and grasslands, water resource, etc. Much of the environmental degradation is governed by mountain specificities and growing population, which is nearly doubling in 27-30 years. Irrespective of differing data on the area under forests, it is commonly agreed that the health of forests, in term of crown cover, is deteriorating under growing anthropogenic and livestock pressure. It has been established that each unit of agronomic production in the state is obtained at the expense of about seven units of energy from the adjacent forests in terms of fodder, firewood and leaves for manure. Against the requirement of 18 hectares of forest land, including 5-12 hectares of well-stocked forests, per hectare of cultivated land, the ratio of forests to agricultural land is only 1.33:1 and the ratio of well-stocked forests to agricultural land is only 0.84:1 (Singh & Singh, 1985).

State policies and Forests Acts alienated people, particularly from reserved forests which is visible in increased incidences of forest fires, illicit felling and encroachments resulting in deterioration in quality and quantity of forests. Even, the Civil Soyam forests, under the control of the Revenue Department, are severely degraded due lack of management systems, population and cattle pressure and their proximity to agricultural land, etc. Civil Soyam forests are either managed by traditional Lath Panchayats in whichever village this traditional institution exists or in its absence, individually by villagers. The Panchayat forests are being managed by Van Panchayats. There are about 5000 Van Panchayats in Uttaranchal; these Panchayats, apart from lacking proper management plans with well defined monitoring mechanism, are experiencing gradual erosion in control and management power over forests under state interventions (Prabhakar, 2000). Conflicts between the Forest Department and the Revenue Department is another major reason responsible for deterioration of the physical health of Panchayat forests.

Decrease in protective vegetal cover against the optimal 60 per cent, has increased the rate of erosion in the catchments of rivers of Uttaranchal. The rate of erosion has increased five times compared to that in the geological past; the present rate being upwards of one millimetre per year (Valdiya, 1985). The rivers are carrying large amounts of sediment at the rate of 16.5 hectare-metre per 100 sq. km of the catchment area per year (Valdiya, 1985). Further the loss of forests has reduced the capacity of mountain slopes to absorb and infiltrate rain water leading to drying up of springs and consequent dwindling of water resources. A survey in the Gaula river catchment in Nainital district of the state revealed that about 45-46 per cent of the springs have gone dry or become seasonal (Valdiya, 1985). The drying up of streams has resulted in more work for women as they have to walk longer distances for collecting water for domestic use. This has adversely affected their quality of life. In some villages, in order to collect water, fodder and fuel, women travel about 10 km everyday. Even if very crudely calculated, an average women in Uttaranchal travels roughly 3000-3500 km in a year which is more than travelling from the Himalayas in the north to Kanyakumari in south in India. Looking at fuelwood requirement, about 25.04 lakh mt is required annually against the availability of 13.20 lakh mt (Singh & Lal, 1996).

While, there is substantial growth in human population in the state, the area available for cultivation is not increasing proportionately, rather it shows a declining trend. The per capita land holding from 1980-81 to 1990-91 decreased from 0.15 ha to 0.11 ha. The net area sown is only 12.57 per cent of the total landuse; more than 80 per cent of the cultivated area is rainfed, and nearly 71.0 per cent of the operational holdings are owned by marginal farmers. The per capita cultivated land in Uttaranchal is lesser than that in the Himalayas (0.16 ha) and India average (0.20 ha).

Though all the major rivers originate from Uttaranchal, hardly 30.0 per cent of its cultivated area is irrigated because of geo-morphological factors. In 1980-81, the percentage of irrigated area was 28.5 per cent which increased to 31.31 per cent in 1993-94 registering an increase of only 2.89 per cent over a period of fourteen years. The traditional varieties in the state are under threat of depletion as studies have indicated alarming decline of traditional crops. Once a local traditional cultivar is displaced, its unique characteristics are lost for ever.

The intensity of grazing is very high. With present level of production from grasslands, each ha can support only two units of livestock while cattle/ha in Uttaranchal is 7.99. Considering the number of livestock in the region, the green fodder requirement has been estimated to be 259 lakh mt per annum. However, present production is only 52 lakh mt both from forests and agriculture (Singh & Lal, 1996). At present substantial portion of the gap is met from extensive lopping of trees.

Resource Deficit: Impact

The population pressure has resulted in decrease of forest cover, per capita availability of cultivated land, and other life supporting resources like water and non-renewable energy sources. The impact of population growth can be best represented through the equation:

$$I = PAT$$

where I stands for Impact, P for population, A for affluence (Per Capita level of material living of consumption), and T for technology to sustain that affluence (Ehrlich & Ehrlich, 1990).

The three factors PAT interact in multiplicative fashion, that is, they compound each other's impacts (Myers, 1993). In Uttaranchal, there is continued increase in population from year to year, so also their affluence, whereas there is minimal or no technological intervention and/or replication to enhance the production and sustain the population. While the population during the decade 1981-91 grew at the rate of 24.23 per cent, the food production during this period registered a growth rate of 12.10 per cent. Further, while population is keeping on increasing, food production is gradually decreasing. From 1,326,432 tonnes in 1980-81, food production increased to 1,506,897 tonnes in 1989-90. However in 1990-91 it decreased to 1,486,943 tonnes.

Thus, the impact of population growth rate in the state is resulting in loss of forest cover, loss of timber harvests, loss of habitat, biotic extinctions—flora and fauna, climatic instability, loss of topsoil, loss of yield, loss of fuel and fodder, reduction in water sources, deterioration in quality of life and multiplying the tragedy of the commons thus leading to poverty. Poverty has a larger socio-economic consequence resulting in migration, and adversely influencing the gender division of labour that includes productive, reproductive and community labour, and also access to and control over resources and benefits.

Resource Conservation: Prospects

Resource conservation as a tool for sustained economic development in Uttaranchal should include use of natural regeneration processes, multiple use, local availability, indigenous knowledge, simple technologies, biotechnologies, education and awareness, realisation of local milieu in population control, and people's participation (Anonymous, 2000). In addition, it has to take into account mountain specificities and adaptability of people which is governed by socio-cultural principles. People and population dynamics such as population growth, population distribution, population density, in-and-out migration, etc., have vital responses to resource conservation. Moreover, since demographic behaviour is related to productivity, understanding of specific demographic issues would help increase productivity and conserve resources.

Understanding how local and indigenous people are associated with resource use and conservation, their needs and uses, their economic relations with the resources, etc., will help increase the productivity and result in better conservation of the resources. Identification of social, cultural, economic and political issues such as gender, poverty, education, land tenure, legal rights, trade, debt, and so on, will help in understanding how they affect productivity. There is a necessity to know how gender is related to population-resource relationship, and to identify women's role in development and planning to enhance productivity.

Since as much as 65.0 per cent of the area of Uttaranchal is under forests and out of this 65.0 per cent is already conserved as reserved forests, either to bring more area under forests for conservation or more forests under reserved category would be an inappropriate proposition. Rather, proper use and conservation of forests in Uttaranchal is fundamental for its economic development. The traditional economy of its people is primarily built around the forests, since they extract a major portion of their food, fodder, fuel, fruits, edible roots, etc., from the forests acting as support land to agriculture. Bringing forests and forest products under systematic management of the state resulted in conflicts arising on the traditional use of the forests by the locals and the state's long-term interest. The Indian Forest Act of 1876 and the first forest policy which came into effect in 1894 envisaged equal benefit to the whole body of taxpayers. However, they invested higher authority on forest officials who curbed, limited and regulated the rights of the locals on forests. The forest policies were changed in the Forest Act of 1952. Under these changes, the traditional rights of the local people were no longer recognised as rights. In 1894 they were considered "rights and privileges", but in 1952, they became "rights and concessions" only (Hasnain, 1990). However, the Forest Conservation Act of 1980 had given priority to non-forest and subsistence needs and 1988 forest policy emphasised the need of the local people and environmental conservation. It is reported that currently about 20 per cent of the total forests in Uttaranchal are protected; however people are unaware of the laws of the protected areas and their implications. Even the Van Panchayat rules have been amended restricting the power of the people in management. The Van Panchayat Rules came in 1931 and were subsequently amended in 1972 and 1976 in which the powers of the Van Panchayat Institutions have been reduced and the power has been centralised in the state (Bisht, 2000).

Therefore, it is strongly argued that effective conservation of forests is possible through modification of working plan and changing the organisational structure, rules and management mechanism of the forest department. The afforestation programme needs to take into account selection of appropriate species that will improve fuel and fodder supply, enhance income and help *in situ* conservation of water. The actual area under forest is nearly 40 per cent, though the desired area under forests is 65 per cent. Therefore, *efforts should be made on priority basis to bring the desired area under actual forests.* Further, only 15.45 per cent of the actual forest has good crown cover, which should also be increased manifold. Another issue which needs consideration in the forest policy is to give permission to villagers to cut a stipulated number of old plants to be used for fuelwood which will help in saving a large number of young species, easy to cut illegally and clandestinely to meet the fuelwood requirement of the villagers.

Secondly, there is also a necessity to give importance to non-timber products in the forest policies, as these products support the livelihood of the locals catering to their various needs. Some of the major non-timber products are processed crude drugs, extracts, herbal medicines, cosmetics from medicinal plants; essential oil, spices etc. incense which have the potential of being metamorphosed to small industries which will promote self-employment and help the local economy (Sarin, 2000).

The third and most important component of effective forest use and conservation is ensuring people's participation. People's participation, being a social phenomenon, takes a long time to evolve. Participation involves decision making, implementation, sharing of benefits, monitoring and evaluation. A number of factors, like physical and biological, economic, political, social, cultural, and historical are generally encountered in the process of participation. Further, lack of commitment or development agents such as forest departments to adopt a participatory approach, unwillingness of officials to give up control over management, mistrust between stakeholders (people and the forest department), vested interests, lack of committed leadership to motivate the villagers, etc. are other critical factors that affect people's participation in forest management (Samal and Sharma, 1997).

Forest management programmes that anticipate people's participation need to have potential to increase production and productivity. The programme should also have tenets like gainful employment, self-reliance, equity and ecological balance. Focus should be on gender equality, use of indigenous technology and development of local capabilities.

A good forest cover would result in (i) long-range ecological security for the conservation of climate, water, soil and biodiversity, (ii) meeting the needs of goods and services of the people, and (iii) amelioration of degraded areas and wastelands so as to enhance the productive capacity of such derelict lands and many others (Khoshoo, 1993). Since forests in Uttaranchal play a vital role in ecological and even food security of the people of India elsewhere, and particularly in the Indo-Gangetic plains, the states which are benefiting should compensate for conservation of forests in Uttaranchal. As rightly said conservation without compensation is only conversation (Swaminathan, 1991). The destiny of nearly 40 per cent of the people inhabiting the Gangetic plains depends on the management and conservation of the Himalayan hydrologic estate (Swaminathan, 1991).

Improved economy through higher returns from agriculture will decrease pressure on forests. Though, only 12.4 per cent of the reported area is under agriculture, it is not possible to bring more land under it, as such land does not exist. Additional land under agriculture could be brought only by encroaching forest land which is not advisable. The options to improve agriculture yield or at least to maintain the present level of production is possible through S & T inputs, conservation of soil and restriction/prohibition of agricultural land to be converted to any other use, particularly built-up areas for construction.

In Uttaranchal, the degraded lands where biological potential of the soil has diminished owing to a variety of human induced causes, need to be restored. Soil conservation should be given priority in agriculture which is possible through measures such as erosion control, control of soil loss, and drainage line treatment. Erosion control will include gully plugging, brushwood check dams, vegetative barrier spurs, contour trenching, and safe water disposal channels; control of soil loss will include silt retention structures, dry-stone masonry check dams, silt observation posts and monitoring of soil loss; drainage line treatment would include stream bank protection, landslide treatment, gully stabilisation and gully catchment treatment. Soil conservation will ensure reduction in soil loss and water run-off, protection of agricultural fields, and improvement in soil cover resulting in arresting degradation and improving the vegetative cover. Application of SWEET (Sloping Watershed Environment Engineering Technology) package for the rehabilitation of degraded/wastelands and SALT (Sloping Agricultural Land Technology) will bring unproductive land under production, conserve soil and promote the economy. Bio-engineering practices, use of any form of vegetation either alone or in conjunction with other physical measures have assumed significance in landslide hazard mitigation, torrent control, rehabilitation of mine-spoils, and slope stabilisation. The whole exercise will ultimately improve agricultural production leading to economic development.

There is also a necessity to conserve and develop water resources which could be possible through *in situ* moisture conservation practices, surface water development through water harvesting structures and instituting water users' committees. *In situ* moisture conservation is possible through contour tillage, strip cropping, mulching and contour bunding/terracing; water harvesting structures will include tanks, farm ponds, village ponds, lift irrigation, check dams, sub-surface harvesting, khuls and minor irrigation. Pani Panchayat (Water Council), a traditional institution that managed water resources in villages of Uttaranchal, is fast disappearing; it needs to be strengthened through appropriate policy intervention.

There has to be a total package of incentives and S & T inputs for conserving traditional crop genetic resources. Agriculture to be productive needs introduction and replication of suitable traditional/ modern inputs and technologies for improved agricultural practices, consolidation of land holdings, efficient marketing system, introduction of agro-forestry and agro-horticulture, biological maintenance and improvement in soil fertility. Besides richness of traditional crops, the people of Uttaranchal have considerable knowledge of wild-edibles, as a supplement or substitute, of their staple food. The nutritive value of some of these are comparable to that of cultivated/domesticated plants. This suggests the potential of these plants for diversifying the food base of people; this is vital to the future food security and work on value addition of these green products may also result in alternate livelihood options. The neglect of traditional food crops has weakened the household nutrition security system in addition to preventing Uttaranchal becoming the home of the health foods of the future (Swaminathan, 1991). In order to ensure higher incomes from agriculture, there is a strong need for diversifation. This can be achieved through promotion of horticulture in suitable locations. The constraints on agricultural production can be overcome by diversifying to horticulture and setting up efficient marketing and processing facilities. Formation of long-term horticultural plans, cultivation of off-season vegetable and seeds, promotion of floriculture, effective marketing system and institutional back-up for promotion of tissue culture, and other such measures would make horticulture more productive (Anonymous, 2000).

The biodiversity of farm animals in the Himalayas is also immense and represents unique genotypes that have evolved through natural or intentional breeding and selection over generations. These have been serving communities for specific needs necessitated by specific agro-climatic regions over time. A systematic and judicious study focusing on documentation of traditional techniques of management, breeding, feeding, medical care, and development would ensure future continuity of this valuable resource base. Improved animal husbandry would include plantation of fodder trees, shrubs and perennial grasses, improvement of pastures, institutional strengthening of dairy development and other such measures.

Added to the knowledge of supplementary food resources and traditional techniques of management of farm animals, the people of Uttaranchal have wide understanding of medicinal plants and vast knowledge on ethnomedicine. Conservative estimates indicate that Uttaranchal is home to more than 700 species of medicinal plants out of the 1748 species reported in the Indian Himalayan Region (IHR) and 2500 species of medicinal plants in India (Samant *et al.*, 1998). Unscientific and non-regulated collection of medicinal plants have threatened their regeneration and habitats. Though there are regulations and restrictions introduced by the government in the use of medicinal plants and many a medicinal plant has been banned for use, clandestine collection of such banned medicinal plants is a regular practice which has threatened the survival of many such plant species (Samal *et al.*, 2001). Ineffective management control over the sale of medicinal plants has resulted in over extraction (Horowitz, 1988; Farooquee & Saxena, 1996; Samant *et al.*, 1998). Today most of the medicinal plants are being harvested for pharmaceutical industries from wild populations; this has adversely affected the very existence of these species. Seventeen Himalayan medicinal plants, more than half of them from Uttaranchal, are listed in the Red Data Book of Indian Plants (Samant *et al.*, 1998). In addition, several other taxa, although not listed, have reached the critically endangered stage. *Podophyllum hexandrum* is an example.

The biodiversity could effectively be conserved through selection of seed provenance of economically important plant species, development of seed orchards, seed banks and decentralised nurseries of important species, transfer of available technologies at grassroots level, survey of endangered species and their subsequent multiplication and cultivation, demonstration and development of tissue culture techniques for mass multiplication of medicinal and endangered plants for trade and value addition, establishment of alpine/temperate botanical gardens/zoological parks, research and development work on indigenous food and medicinal plants and education and awareness campaign on the role of biodiversity conservation for the state (Anonymous, 2000). In order to realise the economic potential of herbiculture, a major initiative would be required for undertaking intensive research for developing reproducible propagation protocols. A successful herbiculture programme with conservation in focus must incorporate scientific input compatible with social needs and aspirations (Purohit, 1997).

Tools and Measures of Resource Conservation

Population Control

The primary task in resource conservation is to control the population growth. The factors which need to be emphasised in population control are education and awareness, and socio-economic and cultural principles. Studies carried out in the state have established that literate women have lower fertility than these who are illiterate (Anonymous, 1995; Anonymous, 2000). It has also been found that the knowledge and use of methods of contraceptives are more known to literate women than illiterate women (Anonymous, 1995). Therefore, priority must be accorded to female education as it promotes adoption of effective family planning programmes. Studies in the state have also revealed that scheduled castes and tribes have a larger number of surviving children than the other groups (Anonymous, 1995; Samal *et al.*, 1996). The state is largely inhabited by caste Hindus (91.84% of total population) including scheduled tribes as they also consider themselves as Hindus, a small population of Muslims (4.85%) and Sikhs (2.68%). Since, the scheduled caste and the scheduled tribe population in the state constitutes only 13.0 per cent and 3.54 per cent of the state population respectively, in comparison to 16.73 per cent and 8.08 per cent for India as a whole, the state is in an advantaged position that these minority groups will not aggravate the growth rate and it will not be very difficult to control the growth rate in these communities. The fertility rate in urban areas of Uttaranchal was found to be lower than that of rural areas; considering the lower percentage of urban population, it is important to create awareness among the rural folk about contraceptives.

Indigenous Knowledge, Innovations and Practices

In their efforts to survive in remote places having inadequate or no infrastructural facilities, the people of Uttaranchal have evolved unique indigenous knowledge, innovations and practices based on locally available bio-resources, which play a pivotal role in promoting the economy and in conserving resources. Understanding of the indigenous knowledge, innovations and practices (KIP) of the native societies of the state is an important aspect of resource conservation. The Convention of Biological Diversity (1992) has recognised indigenous knowledge as a tool for resource conservation through Article 8(J) which reads "to respect, preserve and maintain knowledge, innovations and practices of indigenous and local communities embodying traditional lifestyles relevant for the conservation and sustainable use of biological diversity..." Article 10(c) of the Convention also reads "protect and encourage customary use of biological resources in accordance with traditional cultural practices that are compatible with conservation or sustainable use requirements". Indigenous knowledge, innovations and practices of the people of Uttaranchal revolve around traditional values of resource use that include subsistence values (food, clothing, housing medicine, energy), socio-cultural values (ritual, spiritual, aesthetic, educational, psychological), economic-commercial values (agricultural, industrial, pharmaceutical, tourism), and traditional practices of resources use (agri-diversity, wild edibles, medicinal plants and ethnomedicine, forest and grasslands, ethnoveterinary, etc.). However, they are being threatened and eroded by the growing tide of commercialisation and therefore, they need to be preserved. It is also necessary to explore possibilities for value addition and validation through appropriate science and technology inputs which would rejuvenate and enhance the efficiency of the products and improve their economic potential. Value addition could ensure conservation through enhanced income generating potential of bio-resources.

Simple Technologies

In Uttaranchal as much as 70.0 per cent of the population are engaged in the primary sector, namely, agriculture, livestock, forestry, plantation, etc., for their livelihood. However, for enhancement of production in this sector, advanced technological inputs are either not available or if available are not ecologically appropriate. The application of advanced technological inputs, so far, remained confined to agriculture in the form of high yielding varieties, pesticides, insecticides and chemical manure. In addition to modern technologies, there are simple and cheaper technologies already in use in the state that have potential to promote socio-economic development of the people and ensure regeneration of degraded mountain lands, blending development with conservation (Palni, 2000). Some of the income generating simple technologies are medicinal plants, tea cultivation, apiculture, mushroom cultivation, floriculture, cash crops like cardamom cultivation, apiculture, season and off-season vegetable cultivation and integrated fish farming. Some of the yield increasing simple technologies that would promote economy and help conserve resources are bio-composting, vermicompost, bio-fertiliser, polypit, polytrench and polyhouse. There is enormous scope for promoting the economy by improving under-utilised lands/wastelands through silvi-pastoral practices and multipurpose tree planting. Simple technologies like hedge-rows, agro-forestry and bio-fencing will help conserve soil, and increase income. Value addition of some traditionally practised technologies by the villagers in water harvesting, fermentation of foods and products of bamboo will also help economic development. Other simple technologies include zero energy cool chambers and bio-briquetting.

Biotechnologies

In the process of resource conservation in Uttaranchal, biotechnological applications can be of immense use in agriculture, resource recovery and food and fuel-energy production (Palni & Pandey, 1994). Genetic engineering or *in vitro* genetic manipulation develops improved crop plants in agriculture, which have characteristics such as adaptability, higher yield, resistance to disease and pests and higher nutritional content. The benefits to be derived from biotechnology applications are many; major ones are disease free stock, new varieties of plants that are normally difficult to propagate can be produced and mass multiplied rapidly; plant propagation round the year; development of genotypes with respect of disease and pest resistance, abiotic stress, and yield enhancement (Palni & Pandey, 1994). In biodiversity conservation, biotechnology can play a pivotal role in tissue culture/*ex situ* techniques, cry preservation and resource conservation can even be taken up at the molecular level (Palni & Pandey, 1994).

Sloping Watershed Environmental Engineering Technology (SWEET)

This technology is suited to 'V' shaped watersheds in the midaltitude zone (500 m–1500 m amsl) which is most thickly populated and also most severely degraded. This package addresses the degraded land including abandoned agricultural land owned by individual farmers and degraded community lands owned by the villagers.

Bio-fencing or stone walls are to be preferred over "barbed wire enclosures" to bring fragmented land under one workable unit. Plugging of gullies with biological/physical means is also carried out.

Alleviation of water stress is a prerequisite for enhancing the pace of regeneration of natural or introduced productive processes. Rainfall regime is highly variable; depending upon the location, surface flows are harvested by constructing water tanks. Size, number and distribution of tanks is decided depending upon the rainfall regime, water balance, soil properties, topography of the watershed and size of the area to be reclaimed. Surface run-off should be diverted through 'V' shaped temporary channels to siltation pits and finally to underground tank(s) whose inner walls should slightly slope outwards. UV stablized polythene lining (black) of 250-300 micron thickness is used to minimise seepage. Waste water from perennial sources can be diverted through PVC/GI pipes, placed at a depth of at least 30 cm. below the soil surface to guard against biotic disturbances/forest fires.

Physical as well as biological treatments of degraded lands are essential for enhancing their productive potential. Transplantation is done in pits filled with gravel free soil, mixed with well composted farmyard manure Biocomposting of weeds and agricultural wastes can be utilised to supplement FYM.

Surface irrigation, once a fortnight during dry spells, together with periodic harvests (rather than open grazing) would increase fodder yield by 5-10 fold, depending upon the level of existing degradation. Plantation of *Thysanolaena, Arundinaria, Crotalaria,* etc., on the margins of terraces and along risers prevents erosion and provides quality green fodder and/ or green manure. Maggar bamboo can also be planted as windbreaks and for fodder/culms.

Conclusion

To act as an effective tool for economic development, resource conservation must integrate population dynamics such as growth rate, migration, urbanisation, wasteful consumption and production practices, etc. They, in fact, are among the main causes of resource loss. Understanding of the resource consumption pattern of the local people and the nature of their association and economic relations with natural resources will contribute to resource conservation. It is strongly argued that the rich and unique biodiversity of Uttaranchal has the potential for sustained economic development of the state, if it is used and conserved properly.

Since, in Uttaranchal, it is neither feasible to bring more area under forests nor more forests under reservation, appropriate changes in management of forests which would improve the economy is the key to resource conservation. Soil conservation should be given priority in agriculture which is possible through erosion control, control of soil loss, drainage line treatment etc. Adoption of bioengineering practices would help in stabilising hill slopes and achieve resource conservation. Conservation and development of water resources through *in situ* moisture conservation practices, surface water development through water harvesting structures and instituting water users committees will result in higher agricultural yield ensuring economic development. To be more productive agriculture needs the introduction and replication of suitable traditional/modern technologies, consolidation of land holdings, efficient marketing system, introduction of agro-forestry and agro-horticulture, biological maintenance and improvement in soil fertility, and change in policies. Improved animal husbandry would include plantation of fodder trees, shrubs and perennial grasses, improvement of pastures, institutional strengthening of dairy development and other such measures. Development programmes with conservation in focus must incorporate scientific inputs compatible with the social needs and aspirations of the people. Many of the constraints in conservation of primary resources of Uttaranchal could be overcome though appropriate changes in management practices and application of measures and tools such as population control, indigenous knowledge, simple technologies and biotechnologies and application/replication of packages/techniques like SWEET (Sloping Watershed Environmental Engineering Technology) and SALT (Sloping Agricultural Land Technology).

The Conservation policy in Uttaranchal should be guided by the principle "think Himalayan but analyse and act locally" (Swaminathan, 1991). In brief, the intrinsic and ecological, genetic, social, economic, scientific, educational, cultural recreational and aesthetic value of biological diversity can only be promoted through conservation (WWF, 1992). Restoring and sustaining integrity of soil, water and bio-resources and the linkages between them and meeting the needs of the people through efficient and environmentally sensitive production and conservation of resources are the key to economic development in Uttaranchal.

References

Anonymous (1992) Action Plan for Himalaya, G.B. Pant Institute of Himalayan Environment & Development, Almora, India, p. 68.

Anonymous (1995) Pithoragarh: District Level Baseline Survey of Family Planning Programme in Uttar Pradesh, SIFPSA, Lucknow; The Population Council, India and Indian Institute of Health Management Research, Jaipur, p. 96.

Anonymous (2000) Role of Science & Technology in the Integrated Development of Uttarakhand, G.B. Pant Institute of Himalayan Environment & Development, Almora, India.

G.B. Pant Institute of Himalayan Environment & Development, Annual Report (2000), Almora, India, p. 80.

Anonymous (2000) Proceedings of the Seminar on Sustainable Forest Management in Uttarakhand. Society for Promotion of Wastelands Development, New Delhi, p. 27.

Ashish, M., (1982) "A suggested statement of problems", Paper presented to the Task Force for the study of the eco-development in the Himalayan Region, Planning Commission, New Delhi.

Bisht, A.S., (2000) "Problems and opportunities in the implementation of JFM project in Uttarakhand", Paper presented in the Seminar on Sustainable Forest Management in Uttarakhand", February 22-23, 2000, organised by Society for Promotion of Wastelands Development, New Delhi.

Dhar, U., (1997) "Biodiversity studies—existing mindset and real issues", In: Dhar, U. (ed.), *Himalayan Biodiversity—Action Plan*, pp. 5-10, Gyanodaya Prakashan, Nainital.

Ehrlich, P.R. & A.H. Ehrlich, (1990) *The Population Explosion*, Simon & Schuster, New York, USA, p. 320.

Farooquee, N.A. & Nautiyal, Annapurna (1990) "Traditional knowledge and practices of Bhotia pastoralists of Kumaon Himalaya: the need for value addition", *International Journal of Sustainable Development and World Ecology*, 6:60-67.

Hasnain, Nadeem, (1990) *Tribal India Today*, Harnam Publications, New Delhi, p. 336.

Jackson, M.G., 1985 "A strategy for improving the production of livestock in the hills of Uttar Pradesh", In: Singh, J.S. (ed.), *Environmental Regeneration in Himalaya: Concepts and Strategies*, The Central Himalayan Environment Association & Gyanodaya Prakashan, Nainital, pp. 130-154.

Jackson, M.G., Madhav Ashish, & S.L. Shah, (1997) "The concept of sustainability in village resource management", In: Shah, S.L. (ed.), *Sustainable & Replicable Eco-Development in Central Himalaya/ Uttarakhand*, Shree Almora Book Depot, pp. 87-126.

Joshi, A., Garia, P.S., & I. Hasnain, (1999) *Uttarakhand Update: A Statistical Profile for Development Planning*, Kanishka Publishers, Distributors, New Delhi, 404.

Khoshoo, T.N. (1992) "Plant Diversity in the Himalaya: Conservation and Utilisation" II Pt. Govind Ballabh Pant Memorial Lecture. GBPIHED, Almora, India, p. 129.

Khoshoo, T.N., (1993) "Himalayan biodiversity conservation—An overview", In: Dhar, U. (ed.), *Himalayan Biodiversity: Conservation Strategies*, pp. 5-35, Gyanodaya Prakashan, Nainital.

Myers, Norman, (1993) "Population, environment and development", *Environmental Conservation*. 20(3): 205-216.

Palni, L.M.S. (1993) "Conservation of plant genetic resources: the role of biotechnology", In: Dhar, U. (ed.), *Himalayan Biodiversity: Conservation Strategies*, pp. 481-496, Gyanodaya Prakashan, Nainital.

Palni, L.M.S., (2000) Preface: *Potential Technologies for Hills*, GBPIHED, Almora, India, p. 53.

Palni, L.M.S. & A. Pandey, (1994) "Plant biotechnology: opportunities and challenges", In: Somvanshi, R. & R.R. Lokeshwar (ed.), *Current Advances in Veterinary Science and Animal Production in India*, pp. 174-188, International Book Distributing Co., New Delhi.

Planning Commission (1985) *The Report of the Working Group on Hill Area Development Programme,* Planning Commission, New Delhi.

Prabhakar, B. (2000) "Forest management in Uttarakhand—what is wrong and where", Paper presented in the Seminar on Sustainable Forest Management in Uttarakhand, February 22-23, 2000, organised by Society for Promotion of Wastelands Development, New Delhi.

Purohit, A.N. (1997) "Himalayan medicinal plants—focus on Uttarakhand", In: Dhar, U. (Ed.), *Himalayan Biodiversity—Action Plan*, pp. 91-110, Gyanodaya Prakashan, Nainital.

Samal, P.K., R. Fernando and D.S. Rawat (2000) "Influences of economy and culture in development among mountain tribes of Indian Central Himalaya", *International Journal of Sustainable Development and World Ecology*, 7 : 41-49.

Samal, P.K. Y.S. Topal & M.S. Chauhan (1996) "The causes for the declining sex ratio in Central Himalaya: an analysis", *Journal of Human & Environmental Sciences*, Vol. 1(2): 41-61.

Samal, P.K. & S. Sharma (1997) "Institution building at community level: understanding the constraints in it from a micro-analysis", In: Shah, S.L. (ed.), *Sustainable & Replicable Eco-Development in Central Himalaya/ Uttarakhand*, pp. 179-195, Shree Almora Book Depot.

Samal, P.K., Y.S. Topal and Pushpa Pant (2000) *Van Rawats: A Tribe in Peril*, Gyanodaya Prakashan, Nainital, p. 132.

Samal, P.K., A. Shah, S.C. Tiwari & D.K. Agrawal (2001) "Indigenous animal health care practices and their relevance to bio-resource conservation in Indian Central Himalaya, *International Journal of Sustainable Development and World Ecology* (in press).

Samant, S.S., U. Dhar, and L.M.S. Palni (1998) *Medicinal Plants of Indian Himalaya: Diversity, Distribution, Potential Values*, Gyanodaya Prakashan, Nainital, p. 163.

Sarin, Y.K. (2000) "Restructuring of forest management to promote local industries and self-employment in Uttarakhand", Paper presented in the Seminar on Sustainable Forest Management in Uttarakhand, February 22-23, 2000, organised by Society for Promotion of Wastelands Development, New Delhi.

Saxena, N.C. (1995) *Towards Sustainable Forestry in UP Hills*, Centre for Sustainable Development, Lal Bahadur Shastri National Academy of Administration, Mussoorie, India, p. 79.

Work

Without

Faith and Prayer

Without

Sincerity

Are Like

Artificial Flowers

Without

Fragrance

PART 4

VISION AND ACTION PROGRAMME

4.1

Vision and People's Participation Programme for Development of the New State

M.L. DEWAN*

A new State of Uttaranchal took birth on 9 November, 2000. The people look forward to a better economic and social order. The expectations are large, the challenges of being a hill state are many and concerted efforts are required both from the Government and the people to lay the foundation of a strong and vibrant economy.

Uttaranchal is populary known as Dev Bhumi. Even after this introduction, I give the data about this state and also a poster designed by HIMCON with photos taken by the world-known Himalayan Photographer Shri Ashok Dilwali and including *5 Dhamas*— religious and spiritual centres all located in Uttaranchal.

Permit me to start with a personal note of love and affection for the mountains. Born in the small town of 'KOHAT', 'KOOH' in Persian & Urdu means Mountain, in NWFP of undivided India, now in Pakistan, brought up in Dehradun where my parents made their home after partition, The made their home in Haridwar known as Kohati Dharamsala)—thus belong to Uttaranchal with start from Dehradun, home in Haridwar and now at Ranichauri. As a Soil Conservationist, I worked in the field of Land and Water Development in FAO of UN for 31 years (including Chief of Programme Development, Regional Bureau for Asia). I worked in three countries, Iran, Italy & Bulgaria and have been associated with the Asian countries including China, which I visited eight times. During this period and in 1975, I had the privilege to prepare "Land and Water

* Chairman, HIMCON, Ranichauri.

Conservation and Development as a Regional Programme for Himalayan Region". Being fond of the Himalayas I visited them once in 1979 from FAO, Rome for looking at the FAO Mushroom Project in Himachal Pradesh. I was asked by the then Vice Chairman, Planning Commission, Dr. M.S. Swaminathan to give impressions of the Himalayan Ecosystem. I traveled and reported, Himalayas are bleeding, Himalayas are crumbling, we must protect them it is a great challenge to all of us". A Task Force was formed under the Chairmanship of Dr. M.S. Swaminathan which prepared a Report submitted to the then Prime Minister in 1982 with a recommendation to invite me from FAO as "Chief Programme Coordinator-Himalaya Eco System Development". On early retirement I came back to India with the task of Member, Land Use & Conservation Board of GOI. I don't wish to share my bio-data with the readers of this introduction but share the background, & good luck to continue to work in the Himalyan Region. In the last year of my work with FAO, ICIMOD—International Centre for Integrated Mountain Development was being considered & FAO asked me if I would be agreeable to be nominated as the Director General which I politely declined saying younger person of other nationality (other than Indian) for posting in Kathmandu, Nepal) be invited. However I have continued my informal association with ICIMOD.

I retired and returned to INDIA on 1 October, 1983 and joined the Centre for Policy Research, New Delhi as a visiting Professor. In 1985, I was invited as Chairman of FAO/ICAR KVK (Krishi Vigyan Kendra) Mission of GOI which I lead for a year. During these visits, I visited KVK at Ranichauri Hill Campus of Pant Nagar Agriculture University for the first time and was so inspired by the location that I decided that I would like to spend my retirement years to serve the people and build a home—an Ashram for service to the People of Himalayas. I was lucky to have that opportunity and since 1991 I have a home in Ranichauri—popularly called "Ashram" from where "Tree for Life" (TFL) & Himalayas Consortium for Himalayan Conservation (HIMCON) have been operating.

I have had the privilege of promoting and sometimes leading some projects all essentially in Land & Water Development, Watershed Management & Land and Water Care. Tree Planting was an important part of the task with the Mahila Mandals, the Schools and Inter Colleges.

During these years I have developed and helped others to develop a Vision for the Himalayas—a Plan of Operation for Rejuvenation of the Himalayan Environment. Several books were written and programme developed from the "Shivranjini" a name also of a *Raag* dear to Lord Shiva) which my wife Darshi Dewan and her Guru in Music Pt. Mani Prasad gave to this cottage where we spent a good portion of our time. The books are all related to Himalayan Ecology and several projects prepared jointly with the people and my young colleagues. What is Vision ? You can visualize what is needed what should be done and how and with whom. The clear vision emanates from a sense of Mission of Services, as Gita teaching, "Nish Kam Karam"—not to expect returns, expect save the Environment and stop the bleeding and crumbling of the Himalayas, that is, Himalayan Rejuvenation with Peoples' Participation in Land & Water Care which would serve the Himalayan communities on a sustainable basis. This in turn would help the Himalayan Communities serve themselves and stop or slow down the migration of male youth to urban places and all determined to work and serve the Himalayan Region staying with the Central Region now called Uttaranchal State, the Hill Districts of Uttar Pradesh.

In this process, I am quickly to have young colleagues who are devoted and determined to learn, work hard and take greater and greater responsibility in these operations. The principles are clear and simple.

1. The Himalayan Environment is rather degraded
2. It must be protected and saved
3. People themselves, namely Himalayan communities should be at the centre of such programmes. They have lot of wisdom experience and hence they should indicate their preferences and priorities
4. Training is needed which can be imparted by the government and the NGOs.

The vision is of a healthy, literate, committed state in service of its people. A state with considerable land, water and plant resources. In brief:

(a) Natural Resources including:

- Land Rsources
- Water Resources
- Agriculture Resources
- Forest Resources
- Animal Resources
- Wildlife Resources

(b) Human Resources

- Literate Population
- Educated People
- Healthy People

(c) Development Potential

- Renewable Energy including Solar
- Biomass
- Hydropower
- Wind Energy
- Animal Energy
- And above all Human Energy
- Youth Energy
- Women Energy
- Energy of all People Young and Old
- Tourism Potential including—Eco Tourism
- Religious Tourism
- Sport Tourism

In this connection, I would like to share with the readers what many of my colleagues both in HIMCON and the villages we are serving have assured that their tasks are to meet a part of our vision.

Our vision in brief is "A healthy happy Uttaranchal with an environment, conserved, inspiring, stimulating and communities living harmoniusly, working hard staying predominantly in Uttaranhcal and involving their brothers and sisters living in other parts of India and the world, welcoming all to co-enjoy the environment and resources. Utilize but not exploit and promote/work towards a peaceful efficient state. This vision is quantiattve and quantified in the following people. Partnership programmes rather action programmes which run parallel to what the Government has indicated in the statements enclosed in the annex.

1. Literacy–Complete–Almost hundred percent–In all ages.
2. Elementary, primary education for all in age group 6-14 years.
3. Vocational, agricultural and horticultural colleges and universities—To bring the farmers, ruralites and even urbanites to love plants, trees and adopt such vocation.
4. Small scale industries such as land and water resource based, plant resource based, renewable energy, mining, bio-mass.

5. Tourim promotion—Welcoming peoples from all parts of the country and the world.

Under NRM (Natural Resource Management)

1. Bio-industrial watershed.
2. Integrated programme for water harvesting including surface runoff, spring rejuvenation, chals, in large numbers.
3. Wasteland development.
4. Rejuvenatton and greening of Himalayas (summary of programme enclosed).

Human Resource Development

(a) Role of Volunteers—Volunteer Brigades, Local, District, State, National and International-Leading to a Land Army of Volunteers
(b) Combination with tree planting program including nut fruits vegetables and medicinal and aromatic plants and flowers
(c) Commercial Horticulture
(d) People's plant nurseries
(e) Tissue culture and hardening units
(f) Emploment generation such as
- Biomass
- Bamboos
- Mulberry
- Neem

And medicinal/aromatic/herbal plant processing and ayurvedic family health kits, and other ayurvedic medicines.

5. Serious thought be given to aerial seeding for greening movement, especially for inaccessible areas
6. Plan/Agro based industries for processing of
   - Fresh Fruits Vegetable
   - Medicinal and Aromatic Plants
   - Dairy and Milk Products Industrues
7. Cottage and small scale non wood forest based industries including
   - Silk

- Honey
- Mushrooms
- Rengal
- Bamboo
- Khadi and Village Industries
- Herbal Teas

8. Forestry and Agro forestry, Social and Farm forestry.
9. Training, inspiration and cooperation programmes in all spheres indicated in the vision and Peoples Participation Program (PPP) should be given special attention by Government and training institutes as well as NGOs. These include awareness and organisation building through
   - Self-help Groups
   - Mahila Mangal Dals
   - Seed Banks
   - Grain Banks
   - Van Panchayats
   - Milk Cooperatives
   - Medicinal Plants Cooperatives
   - Plant Nursery Cooperative Marketing
   - Panchayhati Raj Systems
   - Computer Training Groups
   - Information Technology Groups

10A. Various chapters of the book give
   - Views
   - Advice
   - Experiences of various experts and also non-expert citizens

10B. Many proposals, projects and programmes will need to be framed, their Techno-economic feasibility studies done and then executed.
   - Cooperatively
   - Through individual enterpreuners
   - Jointly with the Government and or NGOs

10C. Examples of such programme could be
   (a) Rejuvenation and greening of Himalayas (could be jointly between Uttaranchal and Himachal)
   (b) Commercial Horticulture, Fruits, off season Vegetables, Flowers

(c) Export zones of walnuts, medicinal, aromatic and herbal plants and ayuvedic formulations including if possible kesar (saffron and musk deer)
(d) Milk and milk products
(e) Rabitry, wool and wool products
(f) Aquaculture—Fresh water fisheries
(g) Bamboo, rengal and their products
(h) Execution and support organisation for Mini Micro Hydel Projects
(i) Provision of renewable enrgy through commercial organisations like Tata BP Solar, arsh electronics Solar shops etc.
(j) Tourist corporations, Tourist homes, Tourist sport groups, Eco-tourism, Camps, Hotels, etc.

Consortia of NGO can help in a significant way

11. Resource Mobilisation and Fund Raising

As far as possible locally but from all sources such as

- Himalaya conservation fund
- Small scale industries
- From Non-resident Uttaranchalis—Many of whom have formed organisations in other parts of India and abroad.

In short:

- ***Himalaya Mountaineers and Sportsmen***
- ***Himalaya Lovers All Over the World***

4.2

Bio-Industrial Watershed Development

J.S. Bali*

A better India would be India without poverty, hunger, disease and malnutrition. It would be India with better human environments, purchasing power and happiness. It would be India wherey every project or scheme is evaluated on the test whether it has helped the poorest of the poor to live better. It would be India without ecological, economic, social and electoral exploitation.

Such a transformation can come from development, care and sustainable use of our Land, Water, Plant, Animal and Human resources. It has to be based upon soil and spiritual energy. It has to be a joint effort of the Government and the People. Non-Government Organisations can act as catalysts in this process, which must be spearhead by the community/volunteers.

As an example of such a joint effort, three Bio-industrial Watershed Management Projects are being pursued by HIMCON and the Government of Uttaranchal, under the umbrella of the Land and Water Care Movement launched by M.S. Swaminathan, Research Foundation of Chennai, namely

I. Bio-Industrial Watershed Development and Management for Medicinal Plants (Thrust Area: Upper Elevations)

II. Bio-Industrial Watershed Development and Management for Vegetables, Fruits, Nuts and Agro Forestry (Thrust Area Middle Elevations)

III. Bio-Industrial Watershed Development and Management for Milk and Milk Products and Animal Care (Thrust Area, Lower Elevations)

* Human Environment Action League, (HEAL) Delhi.

The present scenario is apparently chronic poverty characterized by low yields, partial or no employment, low family incomes and migration or even lowest type of jobs. Even this is dependent upon the unsustainable exploitation of government owned forest lands or village commons which are consequently in a sate of degradation. The result is low incomes, leading to malnutrition, ill health, disease and high level of morbidity and children suffer the most. Adult males, even grown up male children leave the villages to find work. Women are left behind for the arduous work or not only looking after the family chores but are also responsible for all the agricultural operations besides fetching water, fodder and faelwood from long distances . The Himalayan plant wealth of forests and medicinal plants are exploited for the benefit of plains. Even water and electricity from water which could be a great source of local wealth, appear to benefit only the people of the plains. Himalayas and the Himalyan people, where our Vedic civilisation originated, are today crying for help. The Himalayas are in danger-bleeding and even crumbling. How can they be saved? Save the Himalayan people and the Himalayas would become safe again.

In simplest terms, this can be done by producing more consumable and saleable products per hectare, and per person, and in the words of M.S. Swaminathan "more crop per drop of water". But unless the food lasts for all the twelve months and unless the saleable products are well graded, processed, packed and marketed, incomes do not rise and the people remain poor. Then the basis of production is the soil which is prone to erosion and needs to be conserved. Soil Conservation which includes rain water conservation and harvesting and better forest care and management is therefore to be the foundation of environmental, food and employment security for the Himalayas. Plant and animal wealth its sustainable high production, safe storage and consumption, processing and commercial marketing, generation of rural jobs and higher incomes are thus links in the chain of Himalayan Conservation.

All these environmental, economic, employment, electoral and social security concerns have been integrated in the rural transformation model called Bio-industrial watershed Management for Eradication of Poverty. (Electoral exploitation has been mentioned here to indicate that true democracy cannot flourish without economic prosperity and social equity. Democracy and disparity cannot exist together).

Bio-Industrial Watershed Management

The Foundation Land and Water Development: This means people collecting together into cooperative association to provide themselves the economies of scale when the individual holdings of land and associated natural resources are small. This also implies WATER conservation in diversions or "ghouls", in small storage structures, spring development, lift (by pumping) from nearby streams harvesting water from the fields and roof-tops or simply conserving the rainwater where it falls and allowing it to percolate into the soil to benefit plant growth. The first step is Land and Water Care Development and Management on soil and water conservation principles, within the natural units of watersheds. This includes use of sprinklers and drip irrigation if the crop economy demands it and permits it. It means bench terracing of hill lands property. It means rectification of faulty terraces, diversion channels, contours ditches or simply contour farming.

Sustainable Production Systems

On this environment foundation of Land and Water Development and Management we erect superstructures of sustainable production systems for the benefit of the people based upon PLANTS and ANIMALS and their numerous products. It means sustainable agriculture with highest yields which can be obtained perpetually as well as sustainable horticulture, vegetable culture, farm forestry, kitchen gardens keeping of cows, buffaloes, goats and sheep or other animals, or any other combinations which can be maintained without diminishing the inherent productive capacity of the soil and the environment. Animal care without proper fodder development and management throughout the year would be meaningless. The whole chain of production and productivity is thus taken care of. High yields are not possible without modern inputs of quality seeds with hybrid vigor and disease resistance. It regenerates people and not mere singing praises of traditional practices and sustainability which have resulted in extreme endemic poverty.

Large areas within the watershed may comprise village common and the forest and village common land can be protected for greater growth of fodder grasses, bushes and trees. The poor in the village greatly depend upon these lands, their proper protection and scientific utilisation for the lower strata would form an important plank in the operations for poverty alleviation. Poor people's animals must have adequate fodder and water from these lands all year round.

The forest land is normally isolated from the villagers and is managed by the Forest Department often in conflict with the local people. This is the biggest area of conflict management in the Indian villages. If the village cooperative envisaged under Bio-industrial Watershed Management is also entrusted with the management of the forest land, all natural resources could be integrated into the chain of ameliorative measures to improve ecology, economics, employment and equity. Joint Forest Management only partially answers the need of the people. People must manage the forests themselves and be responsible for their protection as well as have the entire right to use the food, fodder, minor products and even the timber themselves. People protect what they own. Forests inside the project area should at least be handed over for integrated watershed management to the common watershed cooperative or any other association created for the purpose.

Processing and Marketing and Backward and Forward Linkages

The above described measures of Land and Water Development and Conservation Farming, Agriculture/Horticulture and Forestry are being included in the ordinary Watershed Management projects. What is the new in the Bio-industrial Watershed Model is the inclusion of Processing and Marketing as a responsibility of the project management. These essential tasks have to be done directly or through Entrepreneurs who would not exploit the people. In India five per cent or less of the fruits are processed. For Uttaranchal the figure may even be less. Proper vegetable production and marketing can revolutionize the life of the villages and remove poverty within a short time span. Processing and Marketing co-operatives producers could provide forward linkages, backward linkages such as seed, water equipment, fertigation, land preparation as well as Technology to the farmers and landless to give them inputs of knowledge and materials.

Rs. 1.00 lakh per Hectare from a Vegetable Project

In project area in Kuppam Block of Andhra Pradesh (District Chittoor) supervised by Israeli experts and under the direct watch of the Chief Minister have grown vegetables and marketed successfully to Europe bringing profits as large as Rs.1.00 lakh per hectare per year. The system consists of grading the fields into ridges and furrows with agricultural machinery, planting seeds obtained from reputable national and international companies, fertigating them (combined irrigation and fertilizer application) with drip irrigation equipment (installed near wells on the sells). Grading and processing of vegetables in nearby modem plants (freezing them to minus 40 degree (centigrade) processing and packing in suitable containers and exporting them to faraway countries at international prices. This system is good for selected areas but may not have general replicability However, each project must have this system installed on a suitable part of the project land in order to demonstrate the ultimate potential of production and incomes to the poverty-ridden Indian villages. In Uttaranchal the system could be installed in ashram lands, hotel lands, or on other lands in the valleys and the foothills where people themselves demand it and are prepared to invest in the equipment and the inputs. This would be the ultimate system when excess population is attached to far off industry and the rural areas are left for fewer but richer farmers as elsewhere in the world. In other areas, even national marketing or local marketing done systematically, can increase income levels several-fold.

Facilitating Milk Marketing

In Patudi village of Tehri district of Uttaranchal which this writer had the occasion to visit after a 3-hour steep climb, each of the village families had one or two buffaloes. Their main income was sale of milk or money order from the men working outside the state. As animals are the mainstay of the poor any project in the area must include a component for improving and facilitating the marketing of milk. It may consist of cooperative collection of milk, chilling and transporting to remunerative market like Dehradun, Rishikesh or Haridwar.

Cooperatives

The people of hill areas in general and Uttaranchal in particular favour cooperation. Thrown into the harsh mountain environments, cooperation is their survival tool. Cooperative processing and marketing in the bio-industrial watersheds therefore could have a better chance here. In Gujarat and Maharashtra cooperatives have done well. Elsewhere, especially in U.P. and Bihar, politicians are known to have exploited the cooperative movement leading to large scale failure. The present Cooperative Act needs amendment reducing the power of the government functionaries for intervention in the democratic set-up. Some safeguards are, however, necessary. Considerable cooperative experience has been gathered in the country. It is believed that Cooperatives have not failed the people, it is the people who have failed the cooperatives. As a unique amendment to the Farmers Cooperative Act farmers could be given shares in the privately owned processing industry to the tune of 40 per cent so that the management remains in the lands of private entrepreneurs. This is a suggestion from well known entrepreneur Mr. V. Ramasamy.

Bio-Village

The M.S. Swaminathan Research Foundation have been implementing a project named Bio village for a decade. It promotes soil and water conservation, and multiple livelihood for the people. For example some households w ere successfully growing mushrooms to enhance family income. Some marketing difficulties were being experienced by the people as the Project did not have a marketing component. It is based on micro-enterprises backed by micro-credit organized by Self- Help groups. It is replicable model. If marketing is added and processing industry is introduced for tapping the more remunerative markets. It becomes a Bio-industrial model. Also it is village based. Since our watersheds also consist of villages completely or some partially. The Bio-village concept is indeed the first preparatory stage for the Bio-industrial Watershed Management model which is being proposed for Uttaranchal.

Knowledge Centres

A more directly adoptable feature of the Bio-village was the computerized knowledge center. It gathers information from books, publications and experts and disseminates the same to various villages in the Project. More importantly it culls weather data from the US-satellite systems and provides it daily to the fishermen warning them against storms. Agriculturists would also find the knowledge centre useful for the precision farming which is promoted by Dr. M.S. Swaminathan. Multiple livelihood and job-oriented rural development are the special features of both Bio-villages and Bio-industrial Watershed Management.

Infrastructure

Nobel laureate Amartya Sen advised that Government should provide health and education, and the people would do the rest. These essential items could be the entry point of any project in Rural India. If people remain without medical aid and their children without education, they would be right in rejection of all other peripheral programmes. As Dr. M.S. Swaminathan proved with international facts and figures at the Lady Irwin College Lecture at New Delhi recently, malnutrition is hampering the mental development of the children in India and other developing countries. No integrated project should therefore neglect these components. The project itself may not have funds for health and education, but must be ensured that government and non-government sources provide the project area with adequate health and education facilities before the people should listen to anything else.

Mini and Micro Hydro Power solar and wind energy and geothermic energy sources (e.g. Hot springs) also need development. Without energy, no development can be sustained. Biomass brick making has been introduced recently by HIMCON in Grahwal.

Roads are another vital need of Uttaranchal. Some development experts feel that the Government should concentrate on roads, communications, energy, and other infrastructure, and forget about thousand other items where money is being spent without making a dent on poverty. Cable ropeways, trolley bridges and such other devices are useful in mountainous regions for transport and marketing. For example, milk supplies could come down to the roadside from the above mentioned Patudi village through a ropeway on the other hand road would be atleast 10 kilometres and ten years away.

Rural Tourism

Travel into the Indian villages and around is an experience which most of the Indians and foreigners would like India offers cultural tourism opportunities of a high order. They have remained unexploited because there are no facilities for safe drinking water, hygienic living spaces, and sanitary conditions for living in the Indian villages. No tourist would like to develop dysentery or filaria and malaria while touring the countryside. India thus scares the foreigners. The Singapore gets ten times more tourists than India. But they spend also fifty times more on it (in terms of proportion of the GNP). What is wanted are some practical steps in each rural area project which aims at poverty education, for Rural Tourism infrastructure. This would mean a few rooms with sanitary bath rooms and a grove of trees around in on near a village. Grants/ incentives could be given to villagers specially on important roads for them to add a room or two extra in their houses for tourists. These rooms could have the safe and modem sanitary facilities. Urban architects could take up the challenge of providing modem amenties for tourists in the "Panchayat ghars" and Community Centres. If a pond or tank is built in the village, its periphery could be beautified to provide a Tourist Spot. Of course, foreign tourists are welcome and many would like to be in the village India rather in the Five-Star cities which are similar all over the world. India is different and hence attractive to the outsiders, only in the villagers. What is said above is doubly true for Uttaranchal which has a unique scenic beauty besides being the "Abode of gods" and hence a source of eternal spiritual energy and inspiration.

Project Components

People's Entitlement to Government Schemes

Based upon the foregoing concept, the following components, among others, would normally from the major ingredients of the Bio-industrial Watershed Management Project. The components are listed here in order of their timing in initiating the activities. This would not exclude attention to other components simultaneously. As suggested by Dr. M.S. Swaminathan, the first step in the project should be to give the right of knowledge to the people. (The people do not know, no one has told them to what benefits and under what schemes they are entitled), in one instance it was found that the people were entitled for benefits from 140 schemes. They were not aware about them. Vested interests not only deprive them of the benefits but even the knowledge of the schemes is denied to them. Such are the problems of people's illiteracy and neglect by the very same who were supposed to deliver. And what is being delivered by the Government's delivery system? "Fifteen paise out of a rupee" that was the estimate of no less a person than Rajiv Gandhi when he was the Prime Minister

Can NGOs Deliver?

But can the people look after themselves now? Can the NGOs deliver knowledge, inputs and services more efficiently and genuinely? It depends upon the NGO. There are NGOs and NGOs. The scale has a vast range, may be zero to hundred. Government has an army of "experts" who receive salary but little funds for works. On the other hand, even clean and motivated NGOs have difficulty in mobilizing the expert services required to deliver agricultural, horticultural, processing, marketing and management services. China succeeded in spreading the revolution of development to the rural areas rapidly, but their methods of governance were different from India's. NGOs in India have succeeded here and there in establishing and validating some innovations. But the projects have to be converted into bulk programmes before all the people and areas benefit. Can the NGOs do it? Obviously not alone. It is for the Government which can act as the genuine representative of the people. But the Government of late seems disinclined to activate its vast field machinery to deliver a truly agrarian revolution of sustainable rural development within the bounds of environmental, economic and social values.

Intellectual Vacuum

There is no acceptable philosophical framework of poverty eradication in the vast rural regions of the country which are increasingly lagging behind. There is an intellectual vacuum. There is no coherent bond between technologies, services and public policies. NGOs often present an unseemly spectacle of begging around for funds—from the Government, from Trusts, from Companies and from Foreign sources. NGOs might attempt to become self-reliant which can succeed in providing effective models. But who will encourage them up to extend to the whole country. None at present. Government waits for the magic that the process will be self-sustaining. People will do it alone. But without massive governmental investments in Rural Infrastructure of Health, Education, Power, Roads, Communications etc., no rural project, whether through government or NGOs will become self-spreading ONLY A PARADIGM SHIFT FROM URBAN BIAS TO RURAL CONCERNS CAN BRING IN HOPE.

Till this happens inspired individuals and informed NGOs must continue to create workable models of poverty eradication and real rural prosperity. Bio-industrial Watershed Management promises to become one such model.

Before listing the components of the project, a few fundamentals have to be kept in mind.

1. It is a poverty eradication project.
2. Poverty means lack of purchasing power, lack of income, which again means lack of gainful employment throughout the year: including a guaranteed employment scale.
3. With small landholdings, currently there are no marketable surpluses. They can be created by increasing yields several fold in a sustainable manner.
4. Animal products play a big role in helping the poorest of the poor to survive. Their yields and marketing need to be improved.
5. A kitchen garden is a must for nutritional improvement
6. Forests occupy a large proportion of land in the watersheds, but they do not at present contribute adequately to the requirements of the local people. Forest management must pass to the responsible communities.
7. High yields of food crops will release land which can be put by individual holders to cash crops like vegetables and fruits.
8. Land and water development and forest care are fundamental to all development. This has to be done on Soil and Water Conservation Principles Foundations are built first.
9. It is a community based programme and projects. Community workers, paid or unpaid have to be organized. Cooperatives, Self-Help Groups and others are an essential step towards action.
10. Government finance, staff, universities, institutes must be tapped and utilized for such projects. Dr. Swaminathan indicates that there are 140 specific government programmes for promoting rural development through various Ministries, Departments etc.
11. Safe Drinking Water is the foremost necessity even before food.
12. As Professor B.D. Dhawan says a successful WATER STORAGE STRUCTURE is the secret of the success of a watershed project (result of analysis of successful projects).
13. MARKETING (improved and profitable) will be the source of success of the Bio-industrial Watershed Projects.
14. Guaranteed employment (on gainful works within the project) must be introduced.

Pillars of Economy

The Agro ecological conditions of the area should play a crucial role in selecting the sustainable activities and goals. In Uttaranchal Economy the role of the following pillars must be kept in mind.

A. Forests
B. Land
C. Water
D. Electricity
E. Himalayan Medicinal Plants and Herbs
F. Fruits and Nuts, Vegetables
G. Animal Products
H. Cooperative people
I. Himalayan Sacredness
J. Rural Tourism

Project Structure

1. Based on intensive reconnaissance and contact with the people identify ENTRY-POINT ACTIVITIES (help in milk marketing; a school or dispensary building; community Food Bank; a milk collection and chilling center; Road bringing benefits of ENTITLEMENT to EXISTING GOVERNMENT PROGRAMMES etc.
2. Explaining the Project to the PEOPLE and forming Watershed Association, or Coorperative.
3. Opening a Kisan Cafeteria as a Cooperative Venture to provide inputs for production and also help in marketing surpluses.
4. Starting work on the major water harvesting structures so that employment guarantee may be tied up to productive works.
5. Taking up Bench Terrace Rectification and new Bench Terracing, Landslide Control and other Soil and Water Conservation Works.
6. Bio-Village Activities } On the Pondicherry pattern of M.S.
7. Knowledge Centres } Swaminathan, Research Foundation
8. Enhancing FOOD CROPS YIELDS
9. Starting work on
   A. Himalayan Medicinal Plants Herbs Programme (Regulation of collection, study of Agronomy of Herbs, and starting Production Centres, Processing Centres and Marketing activities).
   B. Fruits, Nuts and Vegetable Production (Ashram lands and other bigger land sites to be put under the Kuppam model of vegetable production).
   C. Milk and Milk Products (To be coordinated with the

Government Project, and subject to feasibility to be determined by the National Dairy Development Board).

10. Forest Management.
11. Processing (starting from the Product identification, setting up of the main plant and distribution of semi-processing work to the village sites as far as possible).
12. Marketing (this is the crucial work on which project success depends people's incomes must be increased on a sustainable basis to eradicate poverty. Marketing to be developed for local surpluses of fruits, milk etc. according to the Marketing Sub-Plan to be prepared).
13. Infrastructure (Government schemes to be tapped for building access roads, power projects, communication network etc.
14. Monitoring, evaluation to be part of the project so that periodic corrections may be introduced.
15. It is repeated that IT WOULD BE A PEOPLE'S PROJECT and each work will be taken up only when the people reach a stage of DEMANDING the activity rather than someone doing it because it is part of a project prepared by someone else.

How this or these projects will transform from an NGO drafted (HIMCON AND HEAL) Document with people participating in the PEOPLE'S OWN PROJECT will be a test before the Project Initiators.

The Project will be financed by the People, Government, State, National and International Trusts and Bodies.

The basic structure as depicted below remains the same as:

Presented earlier:

Uttaranchal Land and Water Care Movement.

Bio-industrial Watershed Development and Management in Uttaranchal for Fruits Nuts and Vegetables and Forestry Himalayan Herbs and Medicinal Plants and Milk & Milk Products

I.	Foundation Components	Soil and Water Conservation or Land and Water Development, Water the foremost priority, land to be developed for erosion-free safe cultivation of other land uses. All land including forest land to be surveyed for any soil consecration needs. Landslide and stream bank erosion works to be component All water sources to be developed.
II.	Superstructure of sustainable production systems	Plant-based • Increase yield of food crops several-fold • Develop whole crop systems or fanning systems as per needs, introducing researched models of Agriculture, Horticulture, Agro forestry. Fodder Development; Agronomy of Herbs and Medicinal Plants to be developed and practiced. Nurseries to be developed- • Forest Management and use for People's needs of food, fibre, fuel, fodder etc. Animal based • Breeds of buffaloes and other animals to be improved, services provided. • Milk and Milk Products to be produced at enhanced yields. Mixed land use patterns to be tried
III.	Processing	Local village and main centre levels, this component to be the major introduction for Value Addition for poverty eradication.
IV.	Marketing	Marketing of all surplus watershed product to be taken up as the high priority component.
V.	Infrastructure	Health, Education, Roads, Ropeways, Power, Communication etc.
VI.	Non-conventional sources of energy	Fuel-bricks from organic wastes, solar, wind, mini hydro, geothermal biogas etc.

4.3

Mountain Tourism for Local Community Development

R. SREEDHAR*

Background

Considering the diversity of environments and the massive changes taking place in the lives of local communities, "Mountain Tourism" *senso stricto* is nebulous and is difficult to orthogonally pigeon-hole touristic resources and tourists. In Uttarakhand, any tourism that occurs is often considered as mountain tourism and therefore we need a flexible and dynamic approach to the definition of Mountain Tourism. We focus *on the motivation for travel in the* region *and underline the importance of local community development as a critical feature of tourism.*

Overview of Tourism in the Region

The Himalayas and particularly Uttarakhand has been long revered as the land of the divine—'*Dev Bhumi*'. This epithet is best pronounced in the gateway to Uttarakhand—the pilgrim towns of Haridwar and Rishikesh, which draw the largest number of visitors, mostly pilgrims, anywhere in the world. Pilgrimage has been the prime motivation for travel in the region from time immemorial. Legends abound and the recorded history is only of recent times and the history of specific destinations, *Sthalapuran,* reflects the devotional, mythological attributes and pilgrimage of times when written word perhaps did not exist! So much has been the influence of the motivation for pilgrimage that it has given rise to a new class of tourists who follow sites referred in

* Managing Trustee, Academy for Mountain Environics, Narendranagar.

mythological legends, such as the *Mahabharata Trail* of the Dutch travellers. Needless to state, pilgrimage draws the largest number of people to the State and will continue to predominate.

The focus of travellers to the other destinations in the region truly came in with the British. The British developed hill stations and alternate centers of power such as summer capital and cantonments and here they devised mechanisms to translate their aspiration to live in their native environments—Mussoorie, Chakrata, Ranikhet and Nainital are places which have almost for a prolonged period of the year climates similar to places in Britain. The growth of tourist inflow into these hill stations is a later phenomenon and the destructive foray of the urban neo-rich from the adjoining cities and metropolis has been predominant. The long-weekends are now almost a nightmare to towns like Mussoorie when tourists, almost twice its resident population, climb up the hill.

Himalayas continue to pose the greatest challenge for mapping and research in various aspects of the earth and human endurance. There have been legends written about how the '*Pundit Explorers*' mapped several parts of the Himalayas. The development of the theory of isostasy has been largely attributed to the work in the Himalayas. The discovery of vertebrate fossils in the region has lead to a large number of fossil hunters and researchers in the last two centuries to piece together information on human evolution. The recent understanding of global warming and a variety of extreme weather events and its implications, the need for understanding the rich biodiversity and cultural heritage and the continued enigma that earthquakes makes research an important reason for a particular class of travellers into the region. Oddly enough the devastating earthquake of 1991 and the more recent quake of 1999, brought in a heavy influx of official and business tourists and volunteers into the region.

The symbiotic relationships of the Himalayan communities with those from the plains, such as the *Gujjars*, a semi-nomadic community, who make the high altitude Himalayan meadows the summer homes for themselves and their cattle and the trade and exchange with communities in the Tibetan Plateau were specific movements which were well integrated with the social economy of the Himalayan people and no where near the concept of tourism and particularly so as a profit-making industry! The protected areas in the region is as follows:

Region	*Approximate Area (km²)*
Rajaji National Park	820.03
Corbet Tiger Reserve	520.82
Nandadevi National Park	630.33
Nandadevi Biosphere Reserve	1200.00
Valley of Flowers National Park	87.50
Gangotri National Park	2390.00
Govind Pashu Vihar	472.08
Govind Pashu Vihar Wildlife Sanctuary	957.00
Sona Nadi Wildlife Sanctuary	301.76
Askot Wildlife Sanctuary	600.00
Kedarnath Wildlife Sanctuary	957.00
Binsar Wildlife Sanctuary	45.59
Total Area (km²)	7692.11
Total Forest Area (km²)	18272.66

Source: Forestry Statistics, 1995; ICFRE, Dehradun.

While the problem of people living in protected areas is that even some of the environmental activists are in favour of the exclusion of people without recognising the implications for the conservation of these areas. The dependence of people on the resources within the protected areas is significant and has already brought them in conflict with the Forest Authorities. All the high altitude alpine pasture lands which would now lie in the protected areas will eventually degenerate as has been the case of the Bhyunder Valley, now the Valley of Flowers National Park. It is recognised that limited grazing and manuring improve the quality and diversity of the species in such alpine meadowlands (Kharaks, Marora, Bugyal). These are now devoid of any grazing. Further, the alienation of the local people who depended upon these meadows enables poachers and other vested interests to gain entry and control.

It is in this context that we have to place tourism today and given the opportunity of the new federal State identify a continuum of policy-programme-project action strategy to utilize the touristic resources of the State to effectively contribute its might to the sustainable development of mountain communities.

Problems Affecting Local Community Development

There are several problems that impinge upon the traditional methods of sustenance of local communities and some of these will require specific attention beyond the modern sector of Tourism. We highlight some of them:

(a) Lack of basic needs such as Water, Fuel and Health Services;
(b) Population Growth and Expansion of Settlement;
(c) Lack of Occupational Niches and Employment Opportunities;
(d) Improper Planning and Implementation of Development Programmes;
(e) Lack of local investment potential and poor government efforts;
(f) Threats of Natural Hazards including Earthquakes; and
(g) Impact of economic reforms and liberalization of the economy.

Issues in Mountain Tourism

The results of several studies and analysis point to several specific issues and problems in the development of mountain tourism as a significant mechanism for local community development. These are:

(a) *Exploitation of and Impingement on Natural Resources Beyond Resilience of Mountain Ecosystems*

The mountain ecosystems of the Himalayas are experiencing severe crises. The rapidly expanding population, the poor opportunity for employment leading to selective male-migration, the increasing burden of meeting basic needs of food, fuel-wood, fodder, water and sustaining agricultural productivity which is now a back-breaking burden for women has almost become characteristic of the region. The nature of the causative forces are diverse, yet at the root of the crises is the degradation of resource base.

Current tourism activities and practices accentuate this problem, for instance, the urban pockets particularly along the major pilgrim routes are in utter decay. Large proportion of the pollution load, most of which reaches the venerated rivers, is a direct consequence of mass tourism. Rudraprayag and Kamaprayag are themselves two sad examples.

Similarly the high altitude meadows, such as the Valley of Flowers, Har-ki-Dun etc. have been pushed beyond the point of resilience of natural systems. The expansion of weeds in these meadows is no longer a matter of threat it is a reality. Together the *Bugyals* of Uttarakhand can claim to present the largest variety of world's most beautiful flowers and yet the dramatic decrease in their biodiversity is a matter of grave concern. Unless carefully designed and sincerely implemented, tourism can be a devastating activity.

(b) *Lack of Linkage of Tourism with Local or Regional Production Systems*

Sustainable non-farm employment needs to be opened up and mountain tourism is undoubtedly a critical livelihood source as agricultural productivities are declining with progressive division of land over generations and dispersal of farm plots. Tourism has remained an activity of the tourist and it has yet to develop adequate linkages with local production systems. Therefore tourism remains a peripheral seasonal appendage to the local economic systems. There are a number of products and services that can be exchanged by the local communities with the tourists. Fruits and Nuts, Handicrafts, Herbal Medicines, Arts and Crafts, Music and Theatre are some of the host of goods and services that could be exchanged. These are suffering from lack of proper planning, under valuing of local materials, natural resources and skills and if some of the attempts have yielded products they are badly produced and are improperly marketed.

(c) *Lack of Retention of Benefits from Tourism*

The issue of lack of linkages to local production systems is twinned with the flow of goods and services from people outside the region and thus the benefits of tourism in the region drains away. In Uttarakhand, most of the goods and services are provided by larger national enterprises and services by agencies in Delhi and State Capitals wherefrom the tourist originates. The local people undertake the least remunerative tasks and in these services also there is a stiff competition from the more poor migrant rural workers from the plains of Uttar Pradesh or from poorer regions of Bihar and Orissa.

(d) *High Level of Seasonality*

This is an intrinsic character of the region and though there is a scope of expansion of the travelling season. The mechanisms for coping and the limits to dependence on tourism as a contributor to the local economy must reflect these constraints.

(e) *Lack of Policy and Poor Efforts towards building Quality Institutions*

The relative insignificance of the region in the larger context of Tourism in the erstwhile State, there was no policy pronouncement on Tourism.

The adhocism in developing a destination or a fiscal incentive has neither engendered a secure environment for investment nor an expansion of the local economy. On the contrary the policy and legal position of the State is marginalizing local communities from these tourism destinations.

Government owned Tourism Corporations have remained a poor replica of the Private Industry rather than a creative Public Enterprise with a strong Social purpose. The inadequacy of institutional development is not limited to these institutions. It is widespread from University curricula to Community Based Institutions, however in the field of Tourism the overwhelming role of the State in investments and development of infrastructure makes it a critical factor in the nature of evolution of the tourism in the State and the relative role of the community and the private sector is defined by its activities.

Sustainable Development: A Statement of Reason

Sustainable Development has become a cliche over the past two decades in which the term has become popular. The concept of sustainable development has offered a challenge to find the unifying principle for human organisation. Some efforts to present a perspective has been briefly summarised here:

1. Sustainable Development at the broadest level could be conceived in terms of the Bruntland Commission's Report as a process of using resources that do not deplete the options for the future generation—more crytically—it means *generating more alternatives while conserving existing options.*
2. If the processes for Sustainable Development of a community have to lead to its being in harmony with its ecology. Atleast four principles have been clearly identified which characterise sustainable development, viz.
    - It has to be *environmentally sound* and demonstrate the potential to renew;
    - It has to be enabling the evolution of a more *equitable* community;
    - It has to be creating a community which is self-reliant or *endogenous* in accessing its needs and investing into its future; and
    - It has to be *economically-efficient.*

It is also widely recognised that all these principles have to be concurrently adhered to and addressed at various *scales* (individual through community to the global scales) and different *levels* of human intervention (policy, programme and practices). The current impasse we are really faced with arises out of the precarious situation that exists with widespread poverty and squalor and the feeble impact all these collective efforts are making.

The real challenge is to hone our skills, choose our technologies and build our resources in such a manner that it provides for the human needs of Food, Clothing and Shelter and enhance the quality of Water, Energy and Biomass systems. This demands determined action and we cannot any longer hide behind ideologies and financial intentions.

We have to walk beyond institutions to seek solutions and this can only happen as an accretionary process. While in several parts of the region, the production problem does not seem to still worry us unduly, the management of resources are injudicious despite knowing many of the answers. The Community, Government and Markets have colluded only as far and mutually destroyed the unified Society that represented the best of the republics of the past. Community, Government and the Market should be able to provide Health, Education and Occupation as the basic inputs for a sustainable society.

The contextual role in the promotion of such a development process belongs to people who have been through the process and those who have knowledge about aspired and achieved levels of success of investment programmes. Programmes in India have shown how the entire process of designing and implementing through the existing mechanisms consistently draws it away from the original objectives. It is therefore we suggest a new way of looking at Mountain tourism and tourists, beyond the jargon of 'eco-tourism', soft-tourism' and so on, so that the future is more consistent with the goal of creating a sustainable society.

Towards Mountain Tourism for Community Development

On the basis of the plethora of existing underpinnings for the development of tourism, the task of engendering growth in absolute terms at the scale envisaged by the government appears to be more than merely formidable. We present here a strategy based on the current situation of high-volume low-value tourism and to identify the high-value low-volume opportunities. This means

- broad-basing of the tourist profile, both economic and geographic;
- proportional decline in environmental threats with increase in number of discerning tourists;
- enlargement of the tourism 'cake' bringing in its wake the potential for greater quality based services that the local people can be trained to offer.

The tourism activities associated with the tourists on the basis of which the specific policies and programmes could be drawn are identified as:

Mass Tourism

A large number of tourists visiting the state annually are from this category. Tourism of this kind 'happens' more without any design and actually requires no promotion. The social and environmental costs of such marauding tourists are indeed incalculable. Evidence of damage wrought by such tourists is visible in places like Mussoorie and Shimla as well as those centres enroute the Chardham.

This kind of tourism fulfils none of the objectives such as;

(a) generation of local employment and industry,
(b) appreciation of the unique socio-cultural conditions of the State,
(c) using tourism as an input to improve the environmental conditions of the destination.

On the contrary it breeds all the ills of the large industry—influx of outside commercial interests, widening of economic disparities, lopsided distribution of income between the local and the outsider and depletion of natural resources and contortion of social values.

Mass tourism's insensitivity to the environmental concerns, both physical and cultural, is itself a sufficient reason for arresting the growth of this kind of tourism. An important factor that is missed is the fact that the revenues accruing at macro-level to the State and the large private enterprises, which is argued as a reason for its promotion, is not proportional to the high levels of investments made for creating and sustaining the infrastructure.

Thus if investments in infrastructure is redirected towards creation of a wider range of destinations, with multifarious improvements the tourist spending will increase and be spread wider. Among these the budget tourists are the hill-station visitor and tourists on long-weekends or on 'Leave-Travel-Concessions', while the high spenders are the Corporate Conferencers and Elite Holiday seekers in Tourist resorts. It is clear that the level of environmental concerns and social responsibilities are low and while there has to be measures to raise their awareness, the Mass Tourist also needs punitive measures to keep their destructive impact on check. Some of these measures like the enactment of laws against use of plastics, littering and stricter implementation will go a long way to stem the impact. In fact, the State needs to dissuade the growth of such tourism.

Class Tourism

The Class Tourist is better oriented to the range of destinations and is more often travelling on a purpose. The Class Tourists range from the culturally educated Mass Tourists who have not ventured beyond the identified destination for lack of sufficient information to tourists exploring the art and culture of the region. A well-developed network of information centres with trained personnel to guide at these centres can convert the marginal Mass Tourist into a Class Tourist.

Among the low-spending Class Tourists are the pious pilgrims, trekkers, amateur skiers, mountaineers, motor-cycle riders, spiritual sanctuary seekers with the numerous ashrams while the high spending Class Tourists are those holiday makers seeking hygienic space Club Class Businessmen seeking relative solitude for planning and strategising, Heli-skiers and aero-sports lovers.

Given the greater sensibilities and discerning nature of the Class Tourist, a band of honest and efficient guides and local tour operators could grow to service them. Professionally managed Training Centres which have the ability to devise various packages using the knowledge of the local environment, such as designing Botanical and Ecological Tours, Cultural tours based on the nuances of the visitors will be necessary to be developed to generate many more tourism 'products' for such tourists.

This would also involve wide-ranging inputs to the local entrepreneurs and will require more care and attention in developing their skills rather than mere investments. Some of the destinations such as hot-spring locations, the large number of Protected Areas in the region offer an excellent opportunity to consciously promote this kind of tourism.

Investment in this sector will not be capital intensive and can be an area for exploring and implementing alternate technologies and the return on investment will be far larger than in the case of those provided for Mass Tourists, both financially and in terms of lower environmental and social costs.

Value Tourism

At the apex of our classification is the value tourist, who is a veteran climber or trekker, researcher, high-altitude flora and fauna enthusiast who have traversed his way through the world and is almost romantic about the Himalayas. The Value Tourist needs no persuasion from image-makers and advertisers and is willing to replace anything that is needed in his travel with local material provided they meet the high quality standards they demonstrate in their own activity. These are travellers who completely merge with the Himalayan identity and are extremely conscious of the risks to the local ecology and culture.

The needs of such travelers are also highly personalised depending upon their backgrounds and particular focus on a specific tour. This would require:

(a) creation of a string of high-calibre professionals who can aid the Value Tourist with more intense and deep knowledge of the area and thematic aspects;
(b) creating a exclusive club that would serve as a meeting ground for these reclusive travellers;
(c) create a schedule of fairs and festivals some of which are less known but bring to the fore the spirit and elan of the local people; and
(d) create conditions for aviation so that helicopters could ply to points where it could be viably operated and to those destinations where the value tourists could charter.

Specific Measures that are Needed

Mountain Tourism can flourish only when consistency of policy and processes from the Central Government to the local level and there is a continuum of activity—Policy-Programme-Projects—to deliver the objectives of sustainable development. In the current context, we should consider the following:

Policy Level Action

1. Evolve an National Tourism Policy for Mountain Regions
   Mountain regions are different in their characteristics and therefore demand evolution of specific policy perspectives. Though the policy for special areas and hill area development plan suggests that a fresh impetus must be provided for Tourism development, this is not likely to shape unless a coherent policy is evolved for Mountain Tourism.
2. Review of Policies in Other Related Sectors
   Development of Tourism is critically dependent on concurrent changes in policy in other sectors and therefore there is a need to review policies with respect to
   (a) Infrastructure Development in Mountain Regions,
   (b) Existing security related policies which hinder information dissemination and movement including those related to National Parks and Sanctuaries,
   (c) Policy on Civil Aviation,
   (d) Urban Development, and
   (e) Forestry.
3. A cogent environmental policy should be developed for tourist centres including creation and management of facilities in national parks and sanctuaries.
4. Develop a consistent policy for private sector participation, which is transparent and simple.
5. Eliminate inconsistency in Policy Directions.

Any follow-up of policy can only occur if the basic elements of the policy remain consistent. The inconsistency as the one seen from the policy objectives of 1982 to the central concerns of the National Action Plan of 1992, shows considerable deviation from the policy objectives.

A review of the existing policies in all sectors that impinge on tourism to act as a tool for local community development is called for particularly with a view to understanding the disparities caused by the existing set of policies, programmes and projects.

Programme Level Action

While a consistent set of polices are put into place, specific programmes must be promoted in order to understand the following issues:

1. Use the new interest among European and American Travellers of visiting places of mythological importance such as the "Pandava Trail" which could involve mountain and rest of the country.
2. Promote centres that could be counter-magnets to the over crowded hill stations or develop them as a corridor, such as the Mussoorie, Dhanauti-Chamba ridge.
3. Encourage different states in the mountain regions to develop collaborative programmes rather than promoting in isolation.
4. Develop a programme to intensify electronic connectivity through wireless and broad-band communication systems.
5. Develop air-routes within the mountain region so as to enable faster communication.
6. Develop a programme to identify the 'carrying-capacity' of different destinations including mechanisms for continuous monitoring.
7. Devise programmes that can enable participation of poorer sections of the society. Programmes such as financial support for creating 'guest-accommodation', which has been initiated and needs to further developed for wide-spread implementation.

Plan Level Priority Tasks

(a) Develop a detailed strategy for data-collection and incorporation of such information for policy formulation, planning and monitoring.

(b) Develop realistic plan programmes, which are evolved from specific area plans that are consistent with overall policy objectives.

(c) Strengthen institutions at the District level and at specific tourism centres including NGOs and CBOs so as to train the local people to increase their earnings from tourism related activities.

(d) Integrate Tourism with District level plans, schemes IRDP, TRYSEM etc.

(e) Encourage production of goods sought by tourist and emphasise on quality.

4.4

Productive Ageing: A Step Towards Socio-Economic Empowerment of Rural Elderly Women

AABHA CHAUDHARY*

Introduction

Ageing in India

Since time immemorial, older persons in India have been accorded a place of honour and importance in the family and community. Ancient literature in India is replete with reverent references to the elderly: Long life was cherished, old age was viewed with deference and the elderly played an important role of advisors and counsellors. On the other hand. the family and community looked after them regardless of their productive capacity (Khan, 1989).

To a society and culture, that has long prided itself in its veneration of the elderly, the existential reality of the aged may come as a surprise. Our older citizens, on a daily basis, are reminded both of their expendability as also of the deepening coarseness society displays against them. Be it the way they are treated within the family, the woeful inadequacy of the healthcare provisions or glaring problem of economic security and financial sustenance—it is evident that modern Indian society is ill prepared to meet the challenges posed by the graying of its population.

* Founder Secreatry-Anugraha, B-33, Arya Nagar Apts., 91 I.P. Extensions, Patparganj, Delhi-92.

India, a developing country, is in the grip of fast demographic transition. According to an estimate every minute about 23 Indians become old. Almost 50 per cent of the world's elderly live in Asia alone and out of which 23 per cent live in India. The important statistics reveal that in 1991. the population of elderly in India was 57 million and is estimated at 71 million in 2001. The proportion of elderly to the total population has been rising from 5.3 per cent in 1951 to 6.7 per cent in 1991. India remains predominantly an agrarian society with 80.8 per cent of total elderly population living in rural areas. Over 78 per cent of the elderly workforce is engaged in agricultural activities. In case of elderly female workers, the figure is over 84 per cent.

The situation appears grimmer when one notes that the dependency ratio is 1:2. The percentage of elderly under the poverty line is high at 25.8 and 90 per cent are not covered by any social security provisions or pension schemes. The data collected on economic dependence of the rural elderly depicts 70.6 per cent of rural aged females as fully dependent on others.

The 1991 census survey reports show that the life expectancy of women at 60 (16.8 years) is greater then that of men (15.0 years) and they constitute a larger group than that of men. As a result there is a greater proportion of older women suffering from widowhood, economic hardships, functional impairment, disabilities and dependency on breadwinning sons.

With an increasing proportion of India's population living for longer years, we are now confronted with the problem of not knowing what to do with our elderly citizens. The joint family, long held out as answer to this problem, is neither as widespread as popularly believed, nor does it seem capable of accommodating the pressures created by the demands of a modem urban industrialized lifestyle. Far worse is the expression of social neglect and unconcern giving rise to the feelings of loneliness and worthlessness among the aged.

In particular, we need to direct our attention towards the special problems of rural aged women, living in hill regions and facing the brunt of enormous socio-economic and psychological stress and strains.

This presentation highlights some of the important issues, namely; demographic position, socio-familial status, economic security and various dimensions of productive ageing and empowerment as applicable to rural Himalayan communities.

Position of Aged Women in Rural India

Ageing for women in rural areas, brings with it dependence, insecurity, ill health and loss of control over one's life. In an already fragile social security system of rural areas, ravaged by poverty, unemployment, malnutrition and population explosion, aged women constitute a vulnerable group, which is often subject to insult, injury, exploitation inequality, injustice, and suffer multiple morbidity.

In a socio-cultural milieu, which is by and large hierarchical, rigid and patriarchal, majority of women are rarely educated, married early, not encouraged to take up employment and their public participation limited, there is a growing number who face a situation of "triple jeopardy" that of being "old, female and poor." (Prakash, I.J. 1994).

Majority of older women are dependent on others economically, as they were not employed gainfully earlier. There is no comprehensive social security system to cover all needy women in rural areas. Seventy-four per cent of women spend their lives without a spouse as the chances of widowhood increase with age and remarriage of widows (especially in older age) is not prevalent in rural areas. Fifty per cent of older women are illiterate and seventy-five per cent of them suffer from at least one chronic condition. Majority of them live with children and the quality of their life solely depends on the sentiments, resources and inclination of their carers (Kumar, Vinod, 1996). For them to internalize and maintain a sense of self-worth is difficult. At times, they feel depressed, maladjusted, deprived and without any sense of selfhood.

Most of the elderly women stay with their married sons and their interpersonal family ties in relation to the former are becoming increasingly brittle (D'sousa, 1993). This also manifests growing negative attitudes towards the elderly in the younger generation of Indian society. The adjustment of the aged is positively associated with the sound financial condition, good health status, educational and occupational level, non-interfering attitudes, hobbies, interaction with friends and kin, overall activeness and social integration.

These studies show economic security as one of the significant determinant for well being of the aged. According to 1991 Census, out of 60 million elderly, 53 million were in unorganized sector. Those retiring from unorganized sector do not possess any social security system. In the name of social assistance, state governments do have a few schemes for the destitute elderly, main among them being 'Old Age Pension Scheme'. This scheme also, due to its stringent conditions like age.

domicile, absence of means of livelihood etc. remain out of reach for many needy elderly.

Focusing on economic aspect of elderly females, M. Deva Sahayam (1988) in his study on 'Aged females: the most deprived among the deprived' finds that more females are working for meager wages in their old age (16.4%) as compared to (11.6%) males. Economic dependency is high among females (86%). Also, 17 per cent women receive a share in their husband's property and that 90 per cent do not have any independent income or property (Prakash, I.J., 1989).

Himalayan Context

The Himalayas is the largest mountain system in the world. Spanning across nine countries, it is a multiethnic and multilingual region. It has rugged topography of the terrain and some areas in high altitudes are inaccessible. Due to undulating topography, there exists wide variations in altitudes, rainfall, vegetation, social structure and density of population. The area under study, located in Garhwal Himalayas, is marked by harsh winters, scarce arable land. scattered population, poor health, educational and transport infrastructure. Primary occupations are agriculture, cattle breeding and related agro-industrial work. As land is not fully able to support the population, adult males in large numbers take to migration to urban-industrial centres in search of work. At any rate the income level is low. The data reveal that only 47 per cent of the households are found to be having a regular income, average being $ 67 a month (household size 6.5 persons). Taken on the whole, life in rural Himalayan regions is rather hard and demanding.

Social Status of Elderly Hill Women

The social context of the Himalayan areas involves diversity in family size. ethnic and caste hierarchy, racial, religious and cultural diversity and inequality in status. In fact, a broad correlation does exist between the degree of inequality in society and inability of the rural poor, particularly the elderly women, to participate in the development processes.

In the majority of the rural Himalayan regions, the existing social and economic structure pertaining to rural women has itself become a cause of poweriessness. Symptoms of disempowerment include disintegration, exclusion, ethnic unrest and lack of social security.

Aged women living in these areas have a poor quality of life as physiologically, psychologically and socio-economically. They age earlier than their counterparts. A recent study conducted in selected villages of Himalayan region brings to light the existing phenomena of premature ageing among the women.

Several factors contribute to their poor health condition, such as; multiple pregnancies, poor nutrition, cultural and social practices, self neglect, poor health infrastructure catering to scattered sparse population at high altitudes, lack of roads and transport facilities in rural hilly areas.

What sets a woman in the hills apart from her rural counterpart in the plains, is the terrain. The unique topography of the mountains aggravates a woman's vulnerability to poor health. In the hill regions, the consequences of ill health for poor and marginalised older women are often tragic. Their ability to work is essential to their survival, as vast majority has no other source of income. When their health fails totally, they become entirely dependent on their families for care. In such inhospitable conditions, the families are unable to provide any support to the aged who become unproductive and non-effective. When disability or chronic conditions prevent contributions to the family chores and livelihood activities, older women are considered unproductive and a liability. In an environment of scarce resources and poverty, they feel unworthy of using resources for their own well-being. Care for chronic problems and pain is unavailable or unaffordable, so older women suffer in silence and pray for death so as not to burden their families.

The resilience of these "skilful survivors" is commendable as they continue to work till functional disabilities cripple them. In fact, there is no retirement for her till either her death, dementia or disability claims her!

The joint family system remains a primary agency of social support to the older females. They are attached to family to the extent that they would prefer to stay with the family even if they undergo some physical or emotional hardship. Elder women perform the role of an affectionate and care giving grandmother. Majority of them (83%) are consulted in taking decisions on various household matters—children's education, marriage and rituals, buying household goods. Among other things, consultation on matters of consequence indicates the status of aged women in the family. Their role and status in the family is to a great extent determined by their contribution in different household chores like rearing of children, washing, cooking, cleaning, milching cattle, fetching fuelwood, fodder, water, spinning, grinding, as well as engaging in agricultural activities. It was found that the women irrespective of their advancing age continued to perform indoor as well as outdoor activities. The consistency of elderly hill women in the daily routine activities during all the three seasons reflects their drudgery.

Work participation level and age of respondent

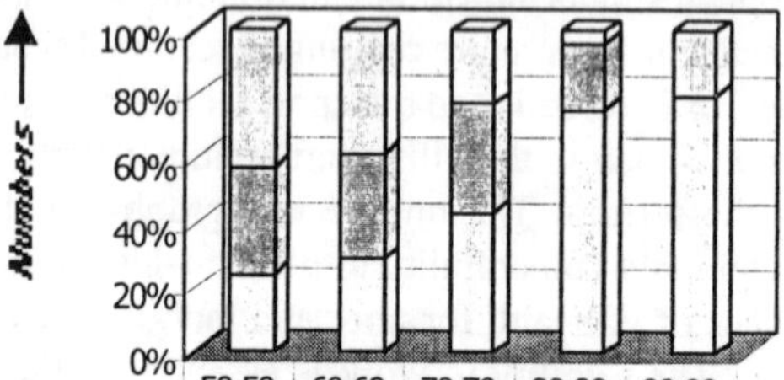

	50-59	60-69	70-79	80-89	90-99
High	111	181	31	2	2
Medium	86	156	46	11	0
Low	64	139	59	40	8

Age in Years →

The above diagram depicts that most of the respondents in the age group of 50-59 years (42.5 per cent) and 60-69 years show a high level of work participation. In the age group of 70-79 years, 39.4 per cent women are active. It is obvious that with the increase in age, energy level decrease and there is low work participation in higher age groups.

Apart from the family, village level community based organisations—women's groups, youth groups, institutions of local self-government etc. have become an important structure for grassroots development. Participation of women in these bodies puts them in a position of decision making, making them aware and empowered about their rights and responsibilities. However, it was observed that only 27.6 per cent of aged women in the study area are holding membership of these bodies. It was a cumulative result of overburden of daily work (16-18 hours a day). low level of education (94% illiterates), lack of awareness and independent status in the family and of course the advancing age, which account for low participation of older females in village level organisations.

The social status of woman is decided both by endogenous and exogenous variables. While the endogenous forces emanate within the family and from her immediate surrounding with which her personality interacts, the exogenous forces emanate through both governmental and non-governmental interventions. In addition, the present value system of society has an important bearing in deciding and reserving a role and status for women.

The study revealed that the development programmes of aged women are more or less absent, especially in the remote and inaccessible villages of the hills.

The presence of large number of old destitute women in hilly regions is due to several reasons such as desertion by the husband, out migration of sons, death of children, having no children and in few cases breakup of joint family. They constitute a vulnerable group, living in an impoverished state without any source of income or support structure, dependent only on the charity of the village community.

Widowhood is a curse as it results in social isolation and restrictions, economic dependency and high morbidity among the females in a traditional rural setting.

Realities surrounding women's lives in Himalayan areas have changed considerably—both for the better and worse. Voluntary initiatives and recently, state legislation like Local Self-governance Act have increasingly urged women to step in to new roles organizing self-help groups, women's groups and now, local-self governance. While these 'well meaning' initiatives may have given women some foretaste of things yet to come. They have burdened her already busy schedule and frail health tremendously. Armed with inadequate skills and scarce time, lacking appropriate support systems—traditional or otherwise, she has become the victim of mere tokenism and patriarchal manipulation.

In the past decades, a trend of men moving away from homes pursuing livelihood started. On the surface, it would seem to provide women more psychological space, more visibility and decision making powers. Instead it has only increased her stress. Major decisions still have to be deferred to husband's return. "In such instances where men have *de jure* control over land, cash and other productive resources, and are socialized to interact with institutions and personnel of the 'outside world' male migration actually reinforces women's dependence on men (Jetley, 1987)" (Mehta, 1995).

On the contrary, all that men were doing at home earlier, is now having to be done by women. Men's mobility has brought in many destabilizing influences, such as: information and exposure to 'plains' (city) culture; rampant alcoholism, a real risk of STDs and AIDS, a subtle pressure to migrate to plains.

The present social and economic status of elderly women has its seeds in the socio-cultural tradition. The status of women starts from the household where she takes birth, grows and lives, accordingly her outlook and perception are influenced. A majority of womenfolk are at the receiving end right from the time of their birth. Discrimination is observed in all walks of life, the magnitude, however, varies accordingly to personality, role and status enjoyed within the family and outside. Under pressure and force of traditional, cultural and historical factors, women have been ignored and denied opportunity for participating in the process of development and sharing its benefits. Despite the high status of women during the vedic period, gender bias is entrenched deeply in cultural heritage of not only India but also in other societies globally. Gender bias is part of social value system, which has roots within the family. Gender discrimination sits at the very root of work allocation and distribution arrangement.

Women are undoubtedly the most productive unit in a hill society and occupy a unique position by virtue of their productive power—both biological and work related. Yet when question relating to the improvement of their socio-economic condition and overall role and status are asked much remains unanswered due to male-biased social values. The social-cultural values and ethics take long time to change as they are non-economic parameters. Mere funding and state legislation can do little in terms of influencing the household behaviour. Some invisible work in the form of sensitisation and awareness generation can help in influencing such endogenous value components.

Economic Status of Elderly Hill Women

In recent years, the proportion of older population especially women is going up steadily due to their lower mortality. The older population is and continues to be dominated by women who are mostly widows. A majority of elderly women in India are being forced to live at the margin of survival and most of them work in agricultural and unorganised sectors with low paid wages, long hours of work and without any formal facility or security. Since most of their jobs need physical strength and motor coordination. Younger persons often substitute the elderly who are weak and slow. Added to this, the introduction of modern farming methods and mechanisation in the agricultural and industrial sectors have adversely affected the elderly in work participation. Thus the displacement of elder women from their bread winning jobs due to marginalisation causes economic and social hardships to them. Due to decreased activity in work place during old age, more and more elderly stay back at home and are engaged in household chores. Their economic value is invisible in a sense that it is neither remunerated nor acknowledged. Thus their productive role in the domestic front is unnoticed, unaccounted and are not viewed as a resource in national development (Ramamurti, 1991). Women sink into greater poverty as they age, mainly because they have very little to start with and have no way of compensating for what they have lost.

In view of the above changed conditions at the work place, most elderly females in the lower socio-economic groups who are landless labourers find it difficult to have even a semblance of livelihood. Though some of them are capable, their potentials are underestimated, underutilised and they are kept away from the mainstream of national development (Jamuna, 1998).

"Women constitute the backbone of the Himalayan economic system as hill agriculture is totally dependent on them. Women generally work for more than 15 hours a day, attending to agricultural work, cattle, toil and trudge daily across mountain gradients to fetch fuel, fodder and water as well as the normal duties within their homes. The hard work of the hill women can be interpreted as their enterprising nature based on culture and community perception of shared need." (Aiyappan, 1975)

The role of women in agricultural operations is very significant and their contribution works out to be more than three-fourth of the labour required for agricultural operations. Even the aged women participate in almost all the agricultural operations, viz. land preparation, manuring, sowing, transplanting, weeding, hoeing, applying fertilizers, harvesting, threshing, carrying the produce from farm to home, storage of foodgrains and so on. Following diagram depicts the relationship between the old women's age and her dependence in agricultural operations. The dependence level of the aged woman shows an increase with advancing age of the elderly women. It is to be noted that 35 per cent of women in 70-79 years age group and 22 per cent women in the age group 80 years and above are involved contributing actively in agricultural operations.

Age of respondents and involvement in the farm based activitiess

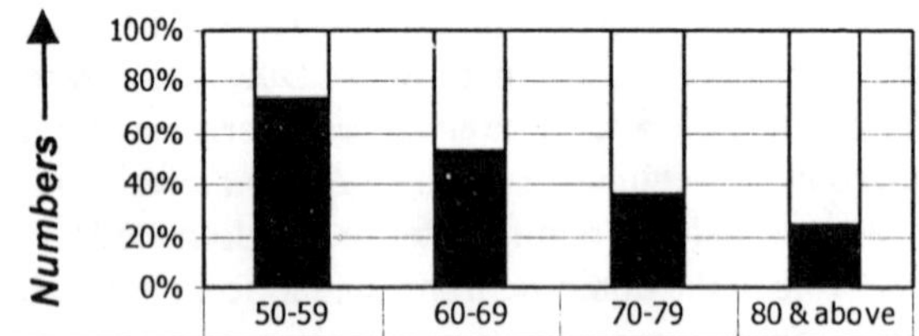

	50-59	60-69	70-79	80 & above
□Needs help	55	165	64	25
■On her own	160	191	36	8

Age group (In years) →

Contribution of a mountain woman in dairy production system is enormous. She harvests fodder from the forest, feeds and looks after the animals, milks the cattle, processes and markets the milk and does almost everything related to the dairy production. The diagram shown below depicts that even the women belonging to age group 80 years and above are involved in pastoral care.

For the collection of water, fuelwood and fodder, women in some villages have to cover a distance up to 8-10 kms. The sight of young girls aged 5-6 years, carrying small bundles of wood and pots of water, assisting their mothers, is common in rural hills. This activity is life long for them, continuing as long as their limbs are functional and support them.

Age of respondents and dependence in pastoral care

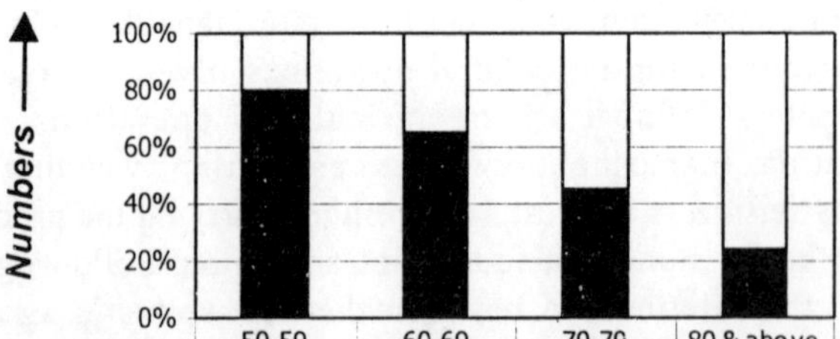

	50-59	60-69	70-79	80 & above
□Needs help	46	130	53	28
■On her own	186	244	44	9

Age Block (in years) →

Such activities consume not only the significant portion of their time but also have an adverse impact on their health. The medical observations reveal high incidence of ankle, joint pains, backache, fractures, fatal injuries and prolapse of the uterus by the time women reach middle age. Given the tough hilly terrain, severe cold conditions, rainy season, inadequate footwear, danger of wild animals, the problem of collection and bringing a heavy load can be well understood. Further factors like family size, family composition, land holding size, number of animals, distance from forest, level of education in the family generally determine the hours of daily work and workload on aged women in rural households in the hilly region.

Large-scale migration of young men to urban areas for employment compels women to do the lion's share of work. Money remitted by these non-resident earners forms a significant part of the financial resources at the disposal of their families staying in the villages. It was also observed that for many elderly persons, this "money order economy" was the only means of cash support. Their heavy dependence on outside monetary support, which is uncertain and irregular, further makes their situation vulnerable.

The main reason for rural poverty and backward hill economy, inspite of women working the year round has to be traced to the way women's "work" is defined. In rural India, where most production is family based and for home consumption, women's contribution is not quantified. No monetary value is attached to her work participation. Since most of the rural women are illiterate and work in agricultural or unorganized sector, there is irregular income and economic compensation in the old age. Barely seven percent of the older women interviewed in the study area have a regular income and it is too meagre $10-$12 a month. Thus, there is a "graying feminization of poverty" (Prakash, I.J. 1994).

For their sustenance, the few uncertain and irregular sources of income available to these aged women are:

1. Only one-third women aged 60+ are the recipients of the Old Age Pension given by the state government, which amounts to about $3 per month, disbursed after every six months.
2. Money remitted by the migrant son (about 40 per cent recieve upto $15 per month).
3. Selling grass (9.6%) and milk (8.5%).
4. Very few women, only 37 had any cash saving in their name.

This data highlights the drudgery and misery old women have to face, despite being " productive" for more than five decades of their life. There are several contributing factors in the current situation, which make the need for cash incomes for the elderly an imperative. These are briefly:

(i) Growing monetisation of the economy forcing cash transactions;
(ii) Nuclearisation of families, often leaving elders to fend for themselves;
(iii) Breakdown of community care of elderly;
(iv) Uncertainties in incomes from children living outside; and
(v) Problems related to old-age pension scheme;

Due to low literacy and awareness levels and prevalent socio-cultural taboos poor older women face many obstacles related to lack of access to land ownership, greater difficulty in obtaining bank loans, less technical assistance and training and restricted employment opportunities.

If permanent changes are to take place in the status of women that gives them control over their destiny, then due attention must be given to involve womenfolk in income generating projects. It should be supported by structural and institutional changes which allow them to acquire skills, self-discretion and decision-making for their economic independence.

Need for Productive Ageing

Against this backdrop, promoting methods of productive ageing may prove helpful for these women in gaining a sense of self worth, social respectability, economic security and above all a sense of holistic well being.

Intensive elderly participation in productive activities is important as it helps reduce the impact of many problems associated with aging. Involvement in useful work curtails boredom, encourages social interaction, enriches social life, generates income and reduces economic dependence.

This involvement, in turn, must bring about empowerment for them in social and economic fields. Here, the concept of 'empowerment' is not only linked to the real transformation of the system but also the true transformation of their attitudes and thinking patterns, their actions and perceptions of their environment and all of their relationships.

The national policy on older persons, formulated by Government of

India. considers 60+ as a phase when the individual should have the choices and the opportunities to lead an active, creative, productive and satisfying life by viewing their experience, skills, time and wisdom as a resource in national development. Strapped for funds and unable to provide basic services to all its elderly population, developing countries like India, have practical reasons to encourage productive ageing.

Productive work dimensions cover physical, mental, social, or even spiritual components and these are not separate watertight compartments. The term "productive activities" does not necessarily mean or is only confined to commercial, business or monetary benefits. These extend to personal, social and developmental activities also.

The term productive ageing covers:

- *Physical aspects*, i.e. a healthy mind and a healthy body, emotional and spiritual well-being.
- *Economic aspects*, i.e. commercial, business, monetary benefits, gainful employment suitable to age and local habitat.
- *Social aspects*, i.e. participation in family's and community's activities to the satisfaction and advantage for herself and for the society, (Kumar, V., 1996).

This concept redefines older populations as asset rather than a liability, a vast resource and repositories of tradition, culture, knowledge, wisdom, and skills. The vast majority of older persons make vital contributions to their family and society as workers, caregivers, volunteers, mentors and as active citizens. Their physical capacity might have declined but their mind is usually sturdy.

Out of choice or out of necessity, many of the rural aged women in the hill regions remain active and vital contributors to the communities in which they live. Women are perhaps 'invisible' contributors to the development and social cohesion. Older women, in rural societies, continue to serve as care givers to young and to old. They are the crucial agents of socialization, education and cultural transmission. Taken together, they are certainly superannuated, yet they are far from being burnout (Khan, 1989).

As stated earlier, despite the handicaps of tough terrain, severely cold climate and poor health status, the older women in Garhwal contribute significantly in the social and economic spheres and manage to age gracefully. These odds compel them to be *productive while ageing*. Productive ageing is not a matter of choice but is a matter of compulsion in order to ensure their survival.

The vital question here is whether despite their continuing inputs, they are empowered. Are the 'productively aged' women independent to make choices and take decisions, and triumph over physical and social constraints? Do they have access and knowledge about the socio-economic, educational and other opportunities? Do these aged women possess a positive self-image and confidence in their own potential to take action in areas affecting their own lives?

Empowerment is about people—both men and women—taking control over their lives; setting their own agendas, gaining skills (or having their own knowledge and skills recognized), increasing self-confidence, solving problems and developing self-reliance. It is both a process and an outcome (European Commission, 1988). It is an enabling process of building capacities and confidence about participating effectively in taking decisions that affect women's lives at the family, community and social levels.

The empowered women become agents of their own development, are able to exercise choices, set their own agenda and are capable of challenging and changing their own position in society.

Empowerment is about Emancipation and Equality

The process of empowerment for the rural elderly women has to deal with the widespread negative attitudes towards old age, such as, feelings of low self-worth, self-esteem, helplessness, dependency, depression and discouragement. Bringing attitudinal changes among the rural women in particular and society in general is imperative for them to be considered as unique, special persons, leading meaningful lives.

Giving them social stature, enabling them to be self-confident and making available opportunities to translate their skills into monetary returns may bring about empowerment of this group.

This in view in, the intervention plan for the rural aged women in hill regions should aim at

> *Initiating a set of coordinated activities so that disadvantaged conditions which surround older women and which hamper their fuller participation in family and community life are reduced, paving the way for enduring psycho-social fulfilment, economic security and holistic well-being.*

The intervention plan will have following strategic concerns:

- Services envisaged under the plan are to be provided to older women at their doorsteps to have their fuller participation.
- Services are to be provided without disrupting family structure or ties (these are to supplement family-care rather than supplant it).
- The cost of these services is to be kept as low as possible.
- The formation of community-based organizations (CBO). comprising older women, is to be given the utmost priority.
- CBOs are to be involved right from the beginning, be it planning of services or programme implementation.
- To network its activities with government agencies and Non-Government Organisations.
- Problem-solving in approach, it is to assume and pursue 'advocacy role', wherever needed.
- It is to have a built-in component of withdrawal and start preparing locals during the last phase of the programme.

The above is likely to maximize the impact and ensure the sustainability of the programme.

Linkages among the Actors

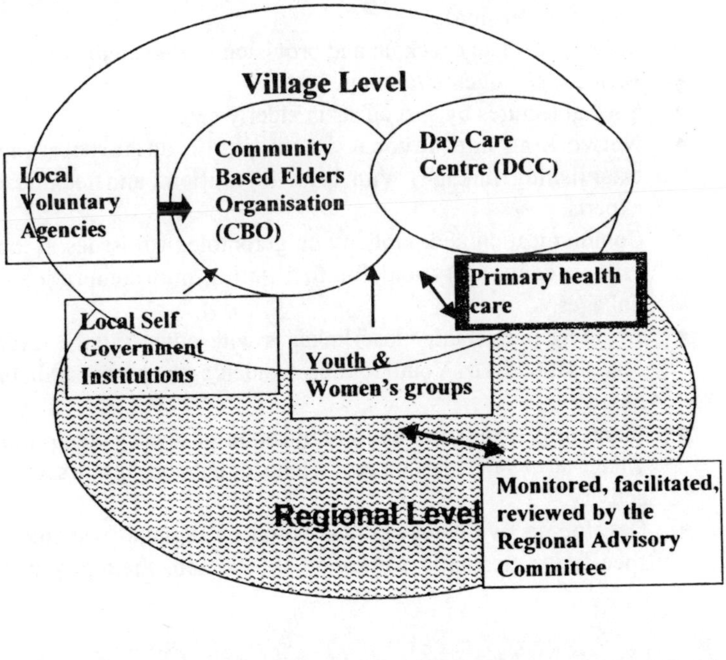

Basically a two tier coordination for the implementation:

1. *Local or village level*: Day care Center/Community Based Elders Organisation.
2. *Regional level*: Regional Advisory Committee will mobilize resources and services at regional level and provide overall supervision and guidance to the village level bodies.

Local Coordination at village level will be done by two nodal agencies—individual *Community Based Elders Organisation (CBO) and Day Care Center (DCC)* of the village. Day-to-day technical support could be provided through Local Voluntary Agencies. Community Based Organisation will be an elected body consisting of elderly population of a village. CBO and Day Care Centre will be responsible for local activities and organising various events in the village etc. These two bodies will perform the following activities in the social and livelihood development sector:

- Extensive mobilization for associational activities and close community level interaction.
- Directed workshops on emotional and interpersonal problems.
- Counselling services for government schemes meant for elderly (Old Age Pension).
- Weekly medical check up and provision of free medicines.
- Periodic get together/outings.
- Special lectures by specialists in elderly care.
- Networking and advocacy with public authorities and establishing linkages with local institutions and technical experts.
- Communication and publicity on gerontological issues in the village community and for facilitating multigenerational linkages.
- Evolving partnership/close linkages with other Village level organisations, viz. Youth forums, women's groups, ex-soldiers board etc.
- Awareness generation and mobilization of aged women into village level Self Help Groups (SHGs) for initiating group saving activity.
- Developing livelihood options based on regional resources/ specificity, aesthetic values of old women, their physical

capacity and interest, e.g. milk dairy cooperatives, mushroom cultivation, poultry, vegetable/fruit cultivation, medicinal plants nursery.

- New activities will be a step towards diversification of the current traditional framework.
- Encouraging multigenerational linkages in income generating programmes.
- Establishing continuous support structures for financial, institutional and technical inputs, flow of low volume and high value products in local/external markets.
- Evolving a mechanism for instilling entrepreneurial skills among aged women, making them stake holders in an enterprise-based model.
- Integrate ecological and health benefits along with the financial benefits to the target group.

Conclusion

For Indian women, ageing is not a trauma. It is the disadvantages that ageing brings with it that is dreaded by them. Otherwise, Indian culture has enough buffers to promote natural acceptance of the process of ageing. Religious and cultural ideas about birth and death cycle as ever recurring, tradition of respect for the aged mitigates the socio-psychological problems associated with the ageing to some extent. But ignoring the sweeping changes in socio-economic and cultural ethos will be a pathological denial of reality.

Why is ageing a liability for women, especially those living in remote rural areas? When they offer substantial contribution in food production, but have no access to land ownership; when they are worked to death in unrecognized and unpaid jobs; when the development programmes fail to deliver goods, naturally they grow old with a load of disadvantages. Experience shows that women do not lack the ability to improve their lot, given a fair chance. Efforts to create space for women in decision-making bodies in political field have paid good dividends.

If women are not to become a liability in old age, prevention has to begin much in their lifecycle. Equal opportunities and access to education, employment. and compensation for their homemaker role go a long way in reducing vulnerability in old age. Prudent nutrition, awareness building programmes, screening for and identification of diseases, improving home care services will add life to years. More than anything else, finding ways in which older women can feel in control of their lives will go a long way in reducing the helplessness that older women face.

These measures, one hopes would go a long way in initiating the process of empowerment for the "productive aged" womenfolk in the rural Himalayas.

We the "productive" segment of society, can not help but see the "unproductive" (elderly) segment of society either as consumer (better geriatric services...) or producer (more income generation projects for the elderly...). This is the dominant view. But there is a parallel perception where old are seen as repository of wisdom and capable of offering critique of the "dominant order, of the productive segments of society. Production and consumption do not exhaust all realms and realities of a human being.

This we think, is a sufficient justification for working with and for the elderly.

The Secret of Success
Behind All Men of
Achievement,
Lies in the Faculty of
Applying their Intellect
In all their Activities
Without being misled
By any Surging
Emotion or Feeling
The Secret of
Success in Life Lies
In Keeping the Head above
The Storms of the Heart

4.5

Sustainable Environment through Cooperative Action

IFFCO*

India's Forest Resources

India's forest resources are estimated at 640,000 km^2 or about 19 per cent of the country's land area. This is well below the 33 per cent recommended in the national forest policy. India recognises that sound, environmentally sustainable management of its forests is crucial in maintaining long-term economic and social development. To increase the area of the forests, India has targeted wastelands and marginal lands for reforestation.

Need for Establishing a Cooperative Society

Tree growers cooperatives have proven to be an effective way to encourage the sustainable development of natural resources. Cooperatives are people's self-help organisations. They are active in the sectors of agricultural production, its distribution, processing and marshalling food resources for a vast number of people throughout the world. A variety of farm inputs are handled including warehousing and transportation of food stocks. All these activities are closely linked to environmental factors. Here are the responsibilities, which cooperative institutions have to discharge to be in harmony with the environment. Cooperatives are partners in development. Development, to be sustainable, should be carried out in a sustained manner so that the development of cooperative institutions and their character is preserved and sustained, on the principle of equity representing the aspirations of the people.

* Indian Farm Forestry Development Cooperative Ltd. (IFFCO), New Delhi.

The General Membership of Cooperative Institutions

As for the role of women in the protection of environment through cooperatives, they can play an important role as: (i) equal partners in the process of development, and (ii) as promoters of family welfare programme. Women, as members of cooperative institutions, are co-owners and co-managers of these institutions. Women can also contribute to this movement by coaxing, persuading and even "enticing" their husbands to have restricted families.

Environment should not remain the concern of governmental and non-governmental organisations alone. No doubt, large-scale industrial pollution can be prevented by the State (through effective legislative means and executive orders) and organised people, but every individual can do something towards this earth in its natural form and glory. People are the main actors in this arena. If the problems of people as identified by themselves are to be solved to their satisfaction, then the people have to be encouraged to participate in the decision-making process. Cooperative institutions are the organisations which they own and operate for themselves on democratic lines.

Objectives

For establishing a cooperative, the objectives should be:

- Mobilising community support,
- Assisting in obtaining land,
- Providing finance for cooperatives,
- Training of cooperative members,
- Creating workable structures,
- Integrating forest product production with management, marketing and processing systems and
- Strengthening the economics in the project villages.

Conservation of Energy

Keeping in view the current levels of energy of consumption, it is not too far when the fossil fuels would get exhausted. There is need to develop and exploit other sources of energy. In some of the cooperative institutions solar energy has been used for lighting and heating, but is this still on an experimental basis and serves more as a showpiece. Further bio-gas, wind energy or solar energy have not been used on a large scale.

In the cooperative sector not much has been done to conserve energy or to utilise or exploit other sources of energy although there are a large number of industrial units and housing complexes in the cooperative sector. Some instances of successful application of alternative sources of energy have been noticed within the Indian Cooperative Movement, for example gas from biogas plant used as fuel for the distillery of a sugar cooperative. Dairy cooperatives are promoting solar cookers, wind mills, solar panels and bio-gas for a variety of uses; and even recycling empty plastic pouches.

Rural Development and Environment

Due to multi-agency involvement in rural development, without attempting a proper coordination, the development inputs do not adequately include environment concerns and activities. Cooperative institutions could be used by development agencies to undertake rural (rather village) development programmes on an integrated basis keeping in mind environment concerns.

Cooperative institutions, which are engaged in processing, industrial and other manufacturing activities should voluntarily go one step further to undertake environment - related activities. This initiative is lacking and cooperatives tend to "shirk" their responsibilities, perhaps due to ignorance, fear of over expenditure or indifference. There is a need to create awareness among the cooperative members and the general public that environment-friendly activities are of use to mankind.

Cooperative Extension Activities for Improving the Rural Environment

- creating awareness among the people on indiscriminate mining and digging up soil for brick kilns etc.
- creating awareness among the people on the consequences of flow of wastewater in village streets.
- educating farmers on the use and handling of chemical fertilisers, insecticides and pesticides *e.g.*, DDT.
- educating people on the importance of washing vegetables and fruits before consuming them.
- informing people on the use of alternative sources of energy for cooking, heating and lighting and the increasing use of bio-gas for domestic use.

- encouraging people to develop social forestry programmes.
- encouraging people to participate in community development programmes, *e.g.* rural sanitation, cleaning of schools premises, cleaning of village streets, repairing of leaking water taps, discussions with the nearby factories for mills, developing modest rural health programmes, better management and regreening of waste land etc.

Cooperatives Promote Human Values – Need for Environment Friendly Culture

Cooperatives promote cooperation among fellow members of their organisation. Mutual respect for each other, joint efforts for a common cause, equity, brotherhood, practice of democracy, truthfulness, honesty, caring and sharing the plight of each other are prominent values inherent in cooperation.

Human cultural values are set not merely at individual, or family level, but indeed at community level. A community organisation is at the eco-system level. If we are to realise a sustainable world, we must act at a local level—the eco-system level. In the same way, to realise a sustainable society, we must begin to act at the local community level. Here comes the role of a cooperative which can help in creating a sustainable environment.

Cooperatives for Empowerment of People: Both Men and Women

Cooperatives have a potential to generate employment for women by engaging them in local handicraft work, tailoring, and collection of forest products. Men can also equally work in marketing and processing of agricultural and forest produce. Generation of income and its distribution by members of a cooperative society in an equitable and democratic manner is a dignified way of living and empowering themselves. Besides, cooperatives can create credit facilities for their members to fulfil their needs. Consumer protection is very much needed in hilly and tribal areas. The members can set up consumer cooperative stores where essential consumer goods would be available at the right price, good quality and right quantity. The local poor people could be saved from adulterated goods and unreasonable prices. This would be a big advantage.

Dairy cooperatives are yet another venture which local people can adopt and reap fruits mutually.

Planting of Trees by Cooperatives

Cooperatives of all types have been set up all over the country. Cooperatives at primary village level can undertake the work of educating their members and others by explaining the environmental need for planting of trees in the villages and thus creating effective awareness. This programme can be implemented on a project basis for a group of villages by a district Cooperative Bank or some suitable non-governmental agency or even by an international agency. Such a programme is very much needed in hilly areas where deforestation has taken place on a large scale.

IFFCO and NDDB, the national level cooperative organisations, are already in this field for quite some time and have helped interested communities to organise their own tree growers cooperatives. The National Tree Growers Cooperative Federation established under the guidance of NDDB at Anand helps the Cooperatives secure land tenure. It provides technical assistance in successful plantation and nursery management and effective extension methodologies. It also provides physical inputs such as tree stocks, sets up demonstration plots and publishes a members' newsletter. Their help can be taken to implement tree growers cooperative projects in selected areas in Uttaranchal.

Cooperative Efforts to Sustain Environment

The Need

As has been mentioned earlier deforestation is one of the most serious and widespread environmental problems facing India. Each year 15000 km^2 of forests are lost at tremendous environmental cost. The consequences of deforestation are the loss of ecosystems, irreversible soil erosion, soil compaction, loss of fertility, local climate change, downstream flooding and loss of biodiversity. It has therefore become very crucial to save forests. Considering the importance of environmental development, peoples' organisations engaged in socio-economic development activities have come forward to contribute their efforts to sustain the environment.

Initiative

The National Diary Development Board (NDDB) at Anand, the prestigious organisation which brought about the White Revolution in the country and the Indian Farmers Fertilisers Cooperative (IFFCO) at New Delhi, the other equally important farmers' organisations have taken the initiative to form suitable cooperative organisations to strengthen India's capacity to reclaim and manage its wastelands in a socially, economically and environmentally sustainable manner.

NDDB's Initiative

The tree growers' cooperatives have proven to be an effective way to encourage the sustainable development of natural resources. The National Tree Grower's Cooperative Federation (NTGCF) has been organised at Anand with the aim to help organise tree growers cooperatives. It has already organised cooperatives in the states of Gujarat, Andhra Pradesh and Karnataka.

Purpose

The overall objective of the NTGCF was to design and implement a forestry and agriculture production system which would generate employment, revenue and long-term sustainability. The Tree Growers Cooperative Project, which was begun in late 1993, has been assisting the NTGCF to establish 300 village-based tree growers' cooperatives in the three target States. The total number of direct beneficiaries is expected to be 35,000 cooperative members and their families.

Focus

The main focus of the Project is to organise villagers to reclaim marginal lands and wastelands by planting trees on them, and then to set up facilities for processing and marketing the wood and non-wood products harvested from these plantations.

Cooperative Movement in Uttaranchal

Uttaranchal cooperative movement and the NGOs can follow the above example and attempt some such projects in the State. The Ranichauri project and such other projects running successfully for the benefit of the local people may attempt to organise cooperatives in their area of operation.

IFFCO's Initiative

The other important example of sustained efforts made to promote farm forestry on a large scale on wastelands and integrated farming system for maximizing economic gains to the members is that of IFFCO. This farmers Cooperative Organisation has helped in organising the *Indian Farm Forestry Development Cooperative.* This is a multi-state cooperative society which was registered in 1993 and started implementing its work in April 1995. The important feature of this organisation is to *assist farmers specially women to promote afforestation on wastelands and marginally productive lands and thus making it a peoples' participatory programme.*

New Concept

To make it really a people's participatory programme the concept of organising self-help groups has been introduced by IFFCO. Self-help groups are functional in almost every Primary Farm Forestry Cooperative Society (PFFCS). The concept is first introduced to the rural women who are motivated to join with the aim to improve their economic condition and also to make them independent in other aspects of life. Certain norms have been prescribed to ensure the smooth functioning of the group.

Benefits

Self-help groups provide an opportunity to their members to make their own decisions regarding the functions of the group, this certainly helps in improving decision-making power. Self-help groups are also committed to improve communications skills and the organisation's sense of togetherness. This approach helps in minimising the communication gap and boosting relationship amongst members. This is needed to improve their economic and social condition.

The Group actually benefits its members by encouraging income generation and providing needed monetary support, for instance to buy cattle, sewing machines, bicycles, seeds and fertilisers, agricultural equipment and to open cloth stores, cosmetic shops etc.

Efforts in Uttaranchal

The information given above would be useful to prospective organisers of Farm—Forest development cooperatives in Uttaranchal.

References

Indian Farm Forestry Development Cooperative Ltd., Udaipur—A Profile CIDA, Tree Growers Cooperative—Forestry Profile.

Prakash, Daman, *Sustaining Environment through Coöperative Action.*

Umre, R.S. (1995), Survival of Cooperative Values in New Millennium, Paper read at the International Conference on Cooperation held in Saskatoon, Canada.

Dewan, M.L. and M.L. Chilana, *The 'Human Values'—A Task for All*, 1998 (Reproduced in 2002).

Disappointments
Come only to those
Who make appointments
With future
Do make appointments,
But only with the presents.
Then disappointments
Can never, never come.
He who seeks
Happiness Outside
Himself
Will never find
Satifaction.
It is an illusion
To think
That
More Comfort
Means
More Happiness

4.6

Role of Science and Technology in the Integrated Development

GBPIHED*

Introduction

The Bruntland Commission Report (Our Common Future, 1987) has made it clear that our existing patterns of development are simply not sustainable. We are confronted with a perpetuation of disparities between regions and within the nations, a worsening of poverty, hunger, ill health and illiteracy, and continuing deterioration of the ecosystems on which we depend for our well-being. These problems can be overcome if we integrate developmental concerns with environmental ones. Greater attention to them can lead to the fulfilment of basic needs, improved living standards for all, and better protected and managed environment for a mere secure and prosperous future. For achieving this, global partnership is required (Agenda 21 of the Earth Summit at Rio de Janeiro in 1992).

The situation in the Himalayan region of India is no different. Though much of its problems are of natural origin, yet they are exacerbated by mountain specific anthropogenic activities. For instance, present rates of exploitation of natural resources are much higher than their regenerative capacity leading to deterioration in environmental quality in terms of deforestation, poor biological productivity and utility potential, accelerated soil erosion, hydrological imbalances, increasing natural hazards and socio-economic inequities caused by improper developmental planning (Action Plan for the Himalayas, 1992). There is, therefore, an urgent need to reorient development planning for hills in a manner that preserves the fragile ecosystem while meeting the aspirations of the people for a higher standard of living.

* Govind Ballabh Pant Institute for Himalayan Environment and Development (GBPIHED), Almora.

The Himalayan region occupies an important place in the economy of the country. Its forest resources provide timber, fuelwood, fodder, medicinal herbs, and a number of minor forest products. Its water resources are used for generating hydro-electricity and providing irrigation and drinking water. Several major rivers including the Ganga and its tributaries have their origin here. The high mountains of the Himalayas also control the climate of the country and provide a natural protection against the icy cold winds from Siberia in winter. Historically, the region has been famous for its calm and quiet environment. Culturally it is a major attraction for pilgrims as numerous important shrines and temples are located here.

Unfortunately, in spite of its importance to the rest of the country, the Himalayan region continues to remain economically backward and under-developed. Perhaps this is largely due to the fact that we have, as yet, neither a policy frame nor a strategy to bring about the balanced integrated and sustainable development of the Himalayan region. What is really needed for an *all-round development of the region* is a comprehensive strategy based on an integrated and area-specific approach. This write-up is a modest attempt to outline the principles and major elements of such a strategy for Uttaranchal.

The Region

The Himalayas constitutes a unique geographical and geological entity comprising a diverse social, cultural and environmental set up. The region is more than 2,800 km in length and 220 to 300 km in width. In India it is spread over the states of Jammu & Kashmir, Himachal Pradesh, Sikkim, Arunachal Padesh, Nagaland, Manipur, Mizoram, Tripura, Meghalaya and parts of Uttar Pradesh, Uttaranchal, West Bengal and Assam. It has a total geographical area of 591,000 km^2 (18 per cent of total geographical area of India), its population as per the 1991 census was about 51 million (6 per cent of total population of India).

Himalayas being the youngest mountain chain on earth, is still evolving and has not stabilized from a geomorphological and geological point of view. Any alteration in the environment, therefore, is likely to have cascading effects not only for the region but also for other areas.

Uttarakhand (now Uttaranchal) Himalayas is primarily a mountainous and hilly region. The economy of the region is predominantly agriculture based, which tends to be subsistence oriented largely due to physical, geographical and other limitations imposed by nature. Despite being subsistence-based and uneconomic, agriculture remains the life line of a majority of the inhabitants of the region. This is primarily due to non-availability of alternative income and employment opportunities.

Specific Problems of Uttarakhand

- Environmental degradation caused by excessive denudation of the forest wealth in the region in general, and mining — legal as well as illegal — in specific locations.
- Over dependence on agriculture (despite constraints on agricultural development as a result of terrain and topographical conditions) in the absence of a developed industrial sector.
- Lack of adequate infrastructure facilities to promote all-round development of the region.
- Insufficient avenues of gainful employment for the people leading to large-scale out-migration of able-bodied youth in search of employment.
- Heavy burden of work on women resulting from out-migration of men.

The Policies

National policy on the approach to, and strategy of, development in the Himalayan region has gradually evolved over the years. In the initial years, specially up to the Fifth Five Year Plan (1974-79) the approach to the development of the Himalayan region was no different from that of the rest of the country. No special problems or development needs of the region were recognised. The Fifth Plan for the first time came to accept that the development issues, needs and problems of the hill areas were distinct, necessitating a different set of policies and programmes. This understanding has continued to inform national, and now increasingly state level, policy perspectives on the development of the Himalayan region. In recent years the need to integrate development with environmental concerns has come to be accepted and articulated in policy documents with greater frequency.

The experience of development planning during the period before the Fifth Plan has increasingly underlined the realization that unless adequate programmes were evolved for conservation and proper utilization of the resources of the hill areas, not only would the problems of these areas continue to remain unsolved, but the economy of the plains may also come to grief. There was, therefore, the paramount need for conceiving an integrated strategy for development of the hill areas based on sound principles of ecology and economics. It was in consideration of this need that special Hill Area Development Programme (HADP) was initiated during the Fifth Five Year Plan (1972-77).

Various commissions and working groups constituted by the Government of India and the Planning Commission from time to time to recommend policy measures and programmes for the development of Himalayas generally concur with the view that the Indian Himalayan Region does not constitute a homogenous region and variations on the basis of terrain, climate, altitude, rainfall, topography, soil conditions, proximity to plains and various other factors called for different strategies for different regions. Some of the more important of the Commission's Committees and working groups are:

- National Commission on Development of Backward Areas under the Chairmanship of Sri B. Shivaraman which devoted one volume of its report to development of backward hill areas;
- Task force for the study of Eco-development in the Himalayan region under the Chairmanship of Dr. M.S. Swaminathan (1980);
- The Group for deciding strategies for eco-development of the Himalayas with special reference to north-west Himalaya (1987);
- Expert Group on National Policy on Integrated Development of Himalayas chaired by Prof. S.Z. Qasim (1993).

A review of the state of policy formulation at the national level related to the development of Hill areas highlights a few interesting features which merit some comment. Firstly, it needs to be stressed that as yet, no clear policy frame has emerged for integrating environmental concern with development issues, specially for these areas. The discussion is limited to the level of rhetoric. Various working groups, Commissions, committees, etc. appointed by the Planning Commission to make recommendations on development of hill areas have underlined the urgent need to integrate the two ideas. Many of them have also made some useful suggestions to achieve this objective.

During the Seventh Plan (1985-90), a working group was set up give its report on development of hill areas. The working group gave due consideration to the fragile ecosystem of the region and formulated its strategy for making integrated rural area development plans. In the following section, a set of such principles is presented.

Strategy and Approach for Development of Hill Areas

- The focus of development planning should be on (i) complementarity of the hills and plains within a regional and national frame and (ii) integrated approach encompassing ecological, economic and sociological dimensions.
- Developmental plans should be made at two levels, *i.e.*, the region and sub-watersheds within the region.
- The strategy of development should include people's (especially women's) participation as a central feature.
- Agro-forestry and pasture development should be given due importance.
- Forests being the single largest land-use category — development of forests with emphasis on increasing productivity of reserve forest, *Proper Management of Community Lands and Plantations in Waste Lands with People's Participation* should be given due importance.
- Increased agricultural productivity through the use of appropriate technologies that are profitable, labour intensive and dependable as a major means of increasing the purchasing power of the people. Land consolidation should be attempted keeping economic and ecological conditions in view.
- The pivotal role of women in the process of development should be recognised and the education, training and extension programmes should be designed so that these can reach out to them.
- Provision of infrastructure facilities such as roads, water supply, hospitals and other services should be an integral part of all development plans.

In the early nineties the Planning Commission decided to constitute an Expert Group for a comprehensive examination of the issues and to suggest a policy within the framework for an integrated development consistent with the conservation of the fragile ecology of the young mountains. After several detailed deliberations it was felt that the unique ecology of the Himalayas which has such an extensive and pervasive influence on the life of our people, needs to be preserved, conserved and qualitatively upgraded. Moreover, the socio-economic life and the living standards must be improved in the region. The report of the Expert Group has clearly emphasized the need to create an administrative mechanism, and further recommended the setting up of a High Powered Himalayan Development Authority and the creation of a Himalayan Environment and Development Fund to support innovative actions and programmes. The report also seeks to provide an insight into the major problems of the Himalayan region as a whole and recognizes that socio-economic development is only possible through the active participation of the people in the formulation and implementation of the plans. It is only through a process of sustainable development that poverty can be eradicated and prosperity ushered in.

Priorities and Desired Actions for Uttaranchal

Uttaranchal, like the rest of the Himalayas and other mountain areas of the world, is characterized by inaccessibilty, fragility, marginality, diversity and which constrain its development as well as provide opportunities. The region is facing a complex set of problems, which includes population pressure, subsistence level farming, deforestation, land slides, soil erosion, floods, water scarcity, out migration, drudgery of women and poverty. The fragility of the mountain ecosystem is manifested in different forms. Some important issues are listed below and discussed. Each priority issue is followed by some important action points (in block).

Geo-resources

Water Management

Although a number of important rivers and their tributaries have their origin in this region, water is not available for irrigation in most parts of the region and is often not easily available even for drinking and other household purposes. High lifts, undulating topography and lack of appropriate water harvesting technology are some of the impediments in the availability of water. Ground water, in most areas, is out of reach because of hard rocky strata. As a consequence, only about 10 per cent of the total net area sown in the region is irrigated and the rest is exclusively rainfed. In stark contrast to this fact the present agriculture policies are focused on irrigated areas.

- Integrated watershed based development.
- Decentralized drinking water supply system.
- Rain and excess water harvesting through storage and revival.
- Exploration of ground water resources.
- Development of spring sanctuaries.

Land Management

Land resources are subject to gradual degradation over time as a result of mismanagement. Immediate attention is required to develop and conserve these resources so that they may contribute more efficiently to the objective of increased productivity. Proper land management requires knowledge and application of appropriate soil and water management techniques.

- Large scale mapping of land, water and forest resources through state of the art methods and micro-planning based on latest data.
- Plantation of trees for slope stability.
- Control of erosion and water recharge and conservation.
- Consolidation of land holdings.
- Capability classification of land according to local conditions and bringing degraded land under production.

Energy

Energy resources of the region have not been harnessed to capacity except for 1000 MW of hydroelectric power of available 20,000 MW. This calls for judicious use of all forms of renewable energy sources. For example, if the full potential of hydel energy is realized, over 75 per cent of power generated can be exported and provide a major source of revenue for the region. Harnessing the full potential of hydel energy, would however involve mobilization of resources on a large scale, as the capital cost of hydel power plants are fairly high. There is also an urgent need to promote the use of non-conventional sources of energy to reduce the pressure on bio-resources.

- Further exploitation of hydel energy resources.
- Proper harvesting of wind, solar and thermal energy with suitable institutional backup.
- Establishment of decentralized mini and micro-hydroelectric

projects with the involvement of the local for population electrification of remote areas.

- Availability of LPG connections on priority basis and of finance on easy terms for purchase of LPG connections and energy efficient/clean appliances.
- Improved technologies such as inflatable rubber dams for energy production.

Management of Natural Hazards and Disasters

Every year the region experiences a number of major and often destructive natural hazards like earthquakes, landslides and flash floods. Besides, the region is seismically active which further accentuates the problems and calls for sound and systematic mitigation measures.

- Development of methodology for hazard prediction and management.
- Popularization of earthquake resistant buildings/shelters.
- Forecast systems for hail storms, lightning, cloud burst and avalanches.
- Development of biological and simple physical methods of mitigation.
- Institutional set-up for disaster mitigation and management and preparation of district disaster mitigation and management plans.

Bio-resources

Forests

Forestry is the major land use in the region. The forest cover is depleting and the natural habitats are severely affected. The restriction on forest resources has further aggravated the conditions of the local inhabitants. Moreover, the present conditions have resulted in conflicts in forest management.

- Massive afforestation of mixed/broadleaf species, especially bamboo.
- Comprehensive plan on forest fires.
- Promotion of wild edible fruit trees and seed collection centers.
- Arrangements for processing and marketing of forest produce.

- Promotion of small-scale industries using raw materials from the forests.
- Afforestation of multi-purpose and nitrogen fixing trees based on the perception and requirement of local inhabitants.
- Utilization of forest debris (*e.g.*, pine needles etc.).
- Promotion of NTFPs including medicinal and aromatic plants.
- Integrated development of grasslands and pastures.
- Involvement of people in forest management — Joint Forest Management.
- Cultivation of perennial crops under forest trees.
- Establishment of weather monitoring and prediction centres.

Agriculture

Agriculture is the dominant sector of economy of the region with about 85 per cent of the people dependent on it for their livelihood. Most of agricultural activity is labour intensive and is carried out under rainfed conditions. Since rainfall varies greatly across time and space, there is a corresponding fluctuation in agricultural productivity. The increasing pressure of human and livestock population on land is further compounded by the fact that steep slopes, inherently unsuitable for agriculture, are being brought under cultivation. There is a total lack of incentives and science and technology inputs for conserving traditional crop genetic resources. In order to ensure higher income from agriculture, there is a strong need for it to be diversified. This can be achieved through promotion of horticulture in suitable locations and setting up efficient marketing and processing facilities. Animal husbandry is another important sub-sector of agriculture in the region. The main constraint here is that the productivity of local breeds of milch cattle is very low – about 2 litres per day per buffalo and one litre per day per cow. The buffaloes are generally stall-fed and cows are mainly open grazed and only partly stall-fed. There are few institutional arrangements for supply of feed, veterinary services and marketing of milk, especially in the interior areas.

Crop Husbandry

- Introduction and replication of suitable traditional/modern technologies.
- Consolidation of holdings; reserving the trend of abandonment of agricultural land.

- Efficient marketing system; encouragement of traditional crops as organic health foods.
- Policy modification for rainfed agriculture and R&D initiatives on traditional crops and varieties.
- Biological maintenance and improvement of soil fertility.
- Multiplication, domestication and cultivation of medicinal plants and other cash crops.

Animal Husbandry

- Protection and improvement of pastures.
- Plantation of fodder trees, shrubs and perennial grasses.
- Stall feeding and regulated grazing; improvement of local breeds; establishment of cottage industries.
- Bee-keeping, sericulture, etc., as economic activities.
- Institutional backup and promotion of Embryo Transplant Technology (ETP) for upgrading milch cattle.
- Institutional strengthening for Dairy Development by constituting. Uttarakhand Co-operative Dairy Federation, to cater to all hill districts.
- Strengthening and expansion of Central Cold Water Fisheries project to include all hill districts.

Horticulture

- Formulation of long-term horticultural plan.
- Cultivation of off-season vegetables and seeds.
- Promotion of floriculture; introduction of superior varieties.
- Establishment of cold storage and fruit processing units.
- Effective marketing system; processing of culled and lower grade fruits at household level.
- Improvement in mountain specific farm implements.
- Institutional backup for promotion of Tissue Culture, Poly-house technology on commercial lines.

Infrastructure, Communication and Connectivity

Transport and Communication

The region is poorly provided with both basic and supporting infrastructural facilities and services such as input supply systems, institutional credit facilities, processing, storage and marketing facilities, extension education service, transport and communication and rural electrification. The absence or inadequacy of these services and facilities has not only hampered the modernization of agriculture but has also discouraged entrepreneurs from establishing agro-based industries in the region. As a consequence, the potential of agro-industrial development in the region remains by and large untapped.

- Traffic flow/volume based road construction and cable-way as alternative transport system in remote areas.
- Careful formulation of road network with emphasis on green road technology.
- Expansion of satellite communication and Internet technology.

Tourism

Tourism is a major income generating activity for the region, but suffers from lack of infrastructure support. Although the region provides opportunities for all types of tourists, *viz.*, adventure, pilgrimage, aesthetic, etc., this potential has not been adequately addressed. In this context the identification of new tourist attractions should accompany resource mobilization.

- Development of new tourist destinations.
- Building on pilgrimage tourism.
- Promotion of adventure and ecotourism.
- Skill development of local manpower and resources.
- Declaration of tourism as an industry.

Industry

Uttarakhand shows low levels of industrialization largely owing to its lack of accessibility on the one hand and the absence of a large enough market due to the relatively small size of its population on the other. The low level of industrialization is reflected in the data on contribution of the industrial sector to state domestic product (from commodity producing sector) and distribution of employment by industrial categories. We find that the share of industry in both, net state domestic product from commodity producing sector and in employment is rather low and most of it is concentrated in the category of small and household industries. The few medium and large size industrial units that exist in the region are located in the Tarai (Udham Singh Nagar district) and Doon Valley. There are hardly any units in the hilly upland areas. Expecting any major change in this situation may turn out to be overly optimistic. However, possibilities of establishing small industrial units for processing, and thereby adding value to local produce, which at present is being traded in unprocessed form, can be fruitfully explored. At the same time, the potential of the plains in the Terai and the Doon Valley for setting up new industrial ventures, especially in the areas of agro-processing (especially in Udham Singh Nagar District) and non-polluting, knowledge-based industries (especially in the Doon Valley where there are severe restrictions on establishing pollution industries) should be fully explored. All this calls for an appropriate policy framework and supportive systems.

- Formulation of an industrial policy for Uttarakhand taking into account the special needs and situations of different locations.
- Creation of appropriate support structure and institutions for advice on industrial potential, environmental clearance, credit and finance, etc.
- Promotion of small scale industries and foot-loose processing plants for low volume/high value products.
- Encouraging value addition at local level.
- Promoting IT and knowledge-based industries in selected locations.

Socio-economic Issues

Education, Health and Sanitation

There is widespread poverty, unemployment and under employment prevalent in the region. This, in addition to the lack of basic amenities of life, has resulted in large scale migration of people from the region in search of means of livelihood. The existing social and economic institutions and organisations in the region are also not geared to meet the needs and challenges of a growing economy.

- Establishment of vocational training centres and professional institutions.
- Proper storage and supply of potable water.
- Introduction of improved smokeless chulhas.
- Emphasis on proper nutrition of children and nursing/pregnant mothers.

- Encouragement of traditional medicinal systems and human resource development.
- Low-cost technology for the disposal of garbage and sewerage.
- Reduction of drudgery of women.
- Increase in outreach of health care.
- Mobile medical teams with specialist services and awareness programmes.
- Government intervention to mitigate pulmonary (lung) aliments, TB, Goitre, etc.
- For women's empowerment, at least three more districts may be added under Mahila Samakhya Programme.

Indigenous Knowledge

The traditional knowledge of people is under threat due to modernization. Documentation of this knowledge is important for development of the region alongwith appropriate benefit sharing mechanism.

- Documentation and utilization of indigenous knowledge.
- Strengthening the knowledge on fermented foods and beverages.

References

Anonymous, 1992. *Action Plan for Himalaya,* Himavikas Occasional Publication No. 2, G.B. Pant Institute of Himalayan Environment and Development, Kosi-Katarmal, Almora.

Bandyopadhyay, J. 1998. *Approach to Sustainable Human Development in the Indian Himalaya with speicial focus on the Himalayan Areas of Uttar Pradesh.* Unpublished Concept paper prepared for UNDP Workshop in New Delhi.

Dhar, U. (Ed.) 1998. *Biodiversity Action Plan.* G.B. Pant Institute of Himalayan Environment and Development, Kosi-Katarmal, Almora.

Joshi, A. Garia, P.S. & Hasnain, 1999. *Uttarakhand Update : A Statistical Profile for Development Planning,* Kanisha Publishers and Distributors, New Delhi.

Joshi, S.K. 1996. *Some Issues Related to the Sustainable Development of the Himalayan Region,* 6th G.B. Pant Institute of Himalayan Environment and Development, Kosi-Katarmal, Almora.

Joshi, B.K. 2000, *Statehood and Beyond : Revisioning the Future of Uttarakhand.* Centre for Himalayan Development and Policy Studies, Dehradun.

Khoshoo, T.N. 1992. *Plant Diversity in the Himalaya : Conservation and Utilization,* 2nd G.B. Pant Institute of Himalayan Environment and Development, Kosi-Katarmal, Almora.

Kumar, K., Dhyani, P.P. & Palni, L.M.S. (Eds.) 1996. *Land Utilization in the Central Himalaya : Problems and Management Options,* Indus Publishing Co., New Delhi.

Mehta, G.S. 1998. *Development Experiences and Options in a Hill Region : The Case of Uttarakhand, U.P., India.* Mountain Enterprises and Infrastructure Division Discussion Paper 1997/4, ICIMOD, Kathmandu, Nepal.

Mohan Ram, H.Y. 2000. *Plant Resources of the Indian Himalayan Region : Some Points for Action.* 9th Pandit Govind Ballabh Pant Memorial Lecture, G.B. Pant Institute of Himalayan Environment and Development, Kosi-Katarmal, Almora.

Planning Commission, Government of India, *National Policy for Interated Development in the Himalaya.* New Delhi.

Pokhriyal, H.C. 1999. *Mountain Development : Whose Priority? (A Case Study of Uttarakhand Himalaya in India).* Unpublished paper prepared for ICIMOD, Kathmandu, Nepal.

Purohit, A.N. 1998. *Science and Technology based Programmes for Environmentally Sound Development of Special Areas (A Case Study for VIII Five Year Plan).* High Altitute Plant Physiology Research Center, H.N.B. Garhwal University, Srinagar, Garhwal, U.P.

Qasim, S.Z. 1995. *Some Major Socio-economic and Environmental Issues of the Himalayan Region.* 5th Pandit Govind Ballabh Pant Memorial Lecture, G.B. Pant Institute of Himalayan Environment and Development, Kosi-Katarmal, Almora.

Rajagopalan, V. 1993. 3rd Pandit Govind Ballabh Pant Memorial Lecture, G.B. Pant Institute of Himalayan Environment and Development, Kosi-Katarmal, Almora.

Rao, U.R. 1994. *Space for Sustainable Development with Special Emphasis on Himalayan Region,* 4th Pandit Govind Ballabh Pant Memorial Lecture, G.B. Pant Institute of Himalayan Environment and Development, Kosi-Katarmal, Almora.

Swaminathan, M.S. 1991. 1st Pandit Govind Ballabh Pant Memorial Lecture, G.B. Pant Institute of Himalayan Environment and Development, Kosi-Katarmal, Almora.

Valdiya, K.S. 1997. *Developing a Paradise in Peril.* 7th Pandit Govind Ballabh Pant Memorial Lecture, G.B. Pant Institute of Himalayan Environment and Development, Kosi-Katarmal, Almora.

World Commisison on Environment Development, 1987. *Our Common Future.* Oxford University Press, London.

4.7

Technological Empowerment for Sustainable Livelihood in Mountains: Some Initiatives and Experiences in Participatory Technology Development and Transfer

SUNIL K. AGARWAL*

The Himalaya are not merely a geographical feature, a mere chain of Mountain ranges. They epitomize a people's civilization that goes back to the DAWN OF HISTORY. The mountain community developed the traditional technologies to cope with their problems. These technologies were environment friendly as well as efficient for the requirement of the village society. With changing time and condition, these technologies were set aside and technologies were brought in without making them suitable for mountain environment. This resulted in environmental degeneration, unemployment, migration of people, etc. Lack of communication and interest for upgrading technologies is one of the major reasons for such problems in mountain regions. Other limitations are inaccessibility, low level of awareness, and lack of communication Science Technology (S & T) inputs in these traditional mountain technologies are the cost effective way to improve the lifestyle of the inhabitants.

In mountain societies, women are responsible for most of the farming as well as the nurturing of future generations. Their importance is not reflected in their access to education, social services, credit, land and

* Scientist, Science & Society Division, Department of Science & Technology, New Delhi-110016.

other assets, and technologies. These disparities begin in childhood and continue through their lives. Women are mostly engaged in low-paid and labour intensive activities; they cannot obtain credit even when they are the main producers; and rarely have major decision making roles outside their families, or benefit equitably from inheritance. A central focus of S&T based mountain development initiatives should also be to decrease these inequities, aiming at gender-balanced development requiring actions from all of us.

The Need: Appropriate Technology and Linkages

Thus, there is a need to address the above challenges, conserving and managing mountain resources to ensure access to basic minimum needs for the inhabitants living in this marginal and fragile ecosystem. For this purpose sustainable and appropriate technologies must be developed to harvest conventional and unconventional resources into utilitarian products and a means for employment generation. This can only be achieved by thinking afresh about human resource development and technologies appropriate to mountain ecosystem, which can lead to sustainable development. In this context, role of developmental agencies and voluntary organization become more vital here. These groups are the crucial link between mountain people and developmental work. Sensitization of these voluntary organizations with Science and Technology (S&T) base will facilitate appropriate technologies to enter into mass use. Keeping these facts in view, the need was felt to initiate specific programme to fill this gap, which can help mountain and hill people, focusing on following aspects:

- To promote traditional knowledge and wisdom in the light of new developments in S&T;
- Environmental sustainability and poverty alleviation through appropriate and sustainable technology;
- Sensitization for appropriate and sustainable technology;
- Coordination in different projects of in this region;
- To identify, sensitize and generate field based projects in different thrust areas of mountain-ecosystem;
- To rope in different centers of excellence and research institutes for S&T needs, projects, assessments and other various assistance like lab facilities etc.; and
- To organize regional workshops for regular discussion, input and feedbacks from partner agencies.

In this endeavour, Science and Society Division of the Department of Science and Technology has catalyzed and developed the concept of TIME (Technology Intervention for Mountain Ecosystems) based on the deliberations amongst the different stakeholders. Under this programme, a separate mechanism has been executed for sensitizing technology-based development of the mountain and hilly regions through involvement of science and technology based field groups/voluntary organization. The specific areas have been identified for skill upgradation in different developmental sectors for human resource development, sustainable utilization and conservation of local resources. The TIME programme focuses on innovative approach of network system of technology implementation. With this approach in mind to reach majority of the people, several grassroots level organizations with scientific and technological capabilities can provide the crucial link between the emerging new developments in knowledge and technology and the local economy, help in the utilization of local resources, and upgrade the skills of artisans, landless labourers and other disadvantaged sections. This programme is, therefore, specially conceptualizing time bound innovative projects for developing fine tuning/simplification/transfer of technologies for specific conditions with new as well as with more conventional approaches to address the specific developmental challenges in the mountain areas due to complexities of rural livelihoods.

Systems Approach for Participatory Technology Development and Transfer (PTDT)

For sustainable development in mountain and hilly areas, there is a need for development and introduction of appropriate technologies coupled with sound delivery system having systems approach for need identification, technology choice and appropriate scaling, technology modulation/innovation, economic and ecological sustainability and optimum use of local resources and material with emphasis on technology capacity building amongst local people. The process of technology development and transfer for direct benefits to weaker sections, women and other backward category of society has some unique features which are quite different from the issues and the processes of the standard method of such transfer mechanisms from research laboratory to industry. The success of technology development and application oriented programmes of societal nature clearly indicates that more than technology development it is the total system which is important for acceptance by the people leading to creation of sustainable livelihood.

In above process, technology choice can have a critical impact on many aspects of mountain development, especially the ways we choose it, the way we innovate and design them and the way we deliver them to masses. Therefore, technology must be carefully chosen to enable local people to acquire and imbibe knowledge of technologies appropriate to their needs and environment. *The technologies should be such as would upgrade their traditional skills and capabilities; minimize fatigue and reduce drudgery; be innovative and capable of easy assimilation; generate significant and assured added value to existing methods of operation; generate employment and use local resources both men and materials; need low capital investment and should result In low cost production of goods; be capable of replication and adoption and should blend harmoniously with existing eco-systems leading to tangible improvements in the living conditions and self-sustained development of the mountain and hilly areas.*

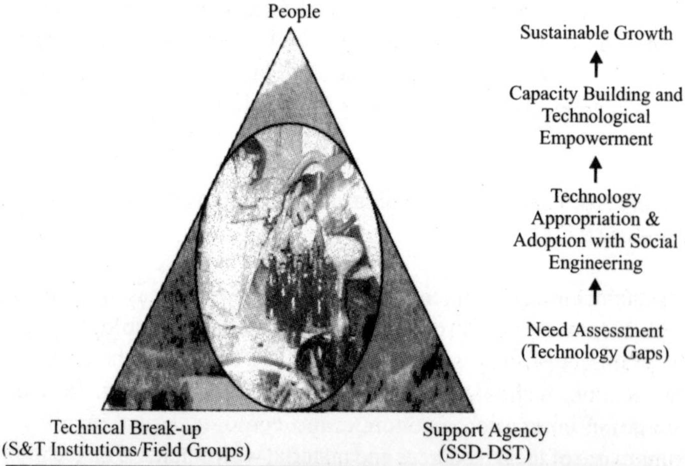

Systems Approach for Technological Empowernment

It is, therefore, necessary to develop and introduce 'appropriate' or so called 'Green' technologies coupled with sound delivery systems which ensure economic and ecological sustainability and optimum use of local resources emphasizing on capacity building and technological empowerment amongst mountain and hill communities particularly disadvantaged groups. *In this endeavour, institutional linkages and active participation amongst voluntary agencies/science and technology based field groups, R&D Institutions, financial agencies and above all people who are the primary stakeholders—become crucial for improving the quality of life in remote and rural areas to achieve long-term sustainability.* However, success in development and dissemination of such green technologies lies in participatory systems with down to earth approach for effective percolation of technology from people's acceptance point of view as well as to make proposed intervention sustainable to be managed by them. In order to ensure this, one must think about appropriate and effective mechanisms with systems approach in development and transfer of appropriate and sustainable technologies as per user needs in the mountain and hilly areas.

The salient features could be summarized as under:

- The need of technology is assessed from the people with the assistance of NGOs/S&T based field groups usually science and technology field groups. The NGOs concerned then look for an ideal technology option keeping in mind the availability of local resources and skills.
- Technology is developed with their in-house capability or with assistance of nearby technical institution. Thereafter, the technology is appropriated to a scale and level, which is acceptable to the people, and also which will be suitable in the local conditions for long-term sustainability.
- For a period of 2 to 3 years the people are trained to handle the technology that is being developed and they are also trained in maintenance, service and repair. During this period, technology back up through continuous landholding is provided by the NGO concerned, if necessary, with assistance of the technical institutions.
- The NGOs/S&T based field groups in the meanwhile also sets up the process for backward and forward linkages both for production as well as marketing for long-term sustainability.
- Once the system is placed with the total package of sourcing of raw material, processing, final product preparation, packaging, marketing, etc. the NGO gradually withdraws giving the entire responsibility to the locally formed people's organization or groups for further dissemination.

With the systems discussed above, appropriate technological interventions can be made at the grassroots level to improve the living conditions of disadvantaged people by reducing their drudgery; improving their health and environment; generating significant and assured added value to existing methods of operation using local resources; requiring low capital investment and capable of replication and adoption. Such interventions can bring lifestyles of local people and can have multiplier effects in other parts through some appropriation as per local needs with technical backup support of its technology generator/provider groups. It will also help in forging partnership for cross-fertilization of ideas and experiences to work towards a socially responsible and environmentally sustainable development in mountain and hilly areas through available green technological options.

Thrust Areas for Technological Intervention in Mountains

Looking into various limitations, disabilities and priority needs of the mountain, thrust areas were identified for immediate and long-term intervention ensure involvement of the local community through network of developmental field groups in technology empowerment.

Promoting Sustainable Agriculture

Agriculture in mountains is considered to be a marginal activity as it pays scarcely. But at the same time it is the most important activity as it is directly linked with the villager's sustenance. The limiting factors are unirrigated land, poorest land productivity and poor cultivation practices, etc. The intervention in mountain agriculture should be envisaged from different point of view. It must be looked as not high yielding but as mountain specific such as:

Off seasonal vegetable and seed production

The Agro-climate of hill areas has the advantage of being suited to off-season vegetables, which can fetch better prices. In addition, seed production and low cost nursery raising of economically important plants, appropriate technology packages offer immense potential for income generation.

Organic farming

Heavy litter fall cause forest fires. This can be prevented by using litter for compost. This can highlight unproductive mountain contours organic, farms. This use can also discourage cattle thus, preventing free grazing. Formulation of plant based herbicides and pesticides is an important area for intervention.

Non-perishable cultivation (NPC)

Perishable products generally do not fetch better prices due to various market intricacies. The mountain agro-climate offer tremendous potential for non-perishable products mainly the spices, pulses, oil-seeds etc.

Horticulture

One of the major resources of the mountain region is horticulture, however, the income from such produce has always been very poor due to lack of:

- Transportation facilities.
- Storage and preservation know-how.
- Processing facilities.

This major resource in mountain has been largely ignored. On the other hand human association with horticulture produce is very old and deep as wild fruits have been used as food for ages and fruit plantation is followed in the recent culture of the inhabitants. Appropriate resource utility through development of human skill is important in this context through the following:

- Natural preservation of fruits for off-season use.
- Efficient storage, processing and packaging of produce for local and commercial use.
- Processing of produce for local and commercial utility with quality control.
- The technologies for preservation/drying of the produce for the affluent market.

Cover Management

Green cover in mountains is important to maintain the environment of the country whereas it is more important *in situ* to meet local need. Thus it is very essential that green cover with appropriate bio-engineering plantation management be considered. This necessitates strategy of promoting vegetation with immediate and long-term value. Proportion of shrubs and grassy will have to be increased as these are immediate and paying. Smaller land holdings mountains require this kind of cover, resistant to environmental stress but with higher energy content.

Animal Husbandry

In the past, thrust has been on raising exotic breeds of animals. But scarcity of fodder has discouraged this. This suggests that animal husbandry in mountain should be based on fodder resources available locally. Thus goats and poultry emerge as most amenable husbandry in mountain areas. Since there are only a few tree species, which are used as fodder, the possibilities of making leaf concentrate of unpalatable species bear a large potential. This can, provide supplementary fodder.

Energy

Traditional use of water power

The two important resources for the mountain ecosystem are Water and Energy. Large dams are proposed or are under construction throughout the Himalayas but the upgradation of traditional water mills, thresher huller and carding devices have not been adequately thought out. A rough estimate reveals that over 5 lakh traditional waterpower use systems which directly help the hill society are functioning in the Himalayan zone. A complete strategy for upgradation of these systems must be a part of future plan. Above all, it is being felt that energy saving options should score over energy generation techniques. More and more efforts are required to develop sustainable technologies for harnessing and conserving renewable energy like water lifting devices, solar lanterns and dryers, etc.

Non-wood energy

Cooking fuel is one area where adequate attention is needed. In regions the possible major source of fuel may be waste biomass. Chir pine cone/needles/weedy biomass can be explored for the purpose. Appropriate stoves to use such biomass for cooking is an essential area of intervention.

Disaster Management and Landslide Control

Following areas need intervention for capacity building and technological empowerment of local people to meet the disaster related challenges:

- Mountain risk engineering: Botanical-cum-mechanical treatments; and
- Pre and Post-Disaster Management: Preparedness for quick relief and rehabilitation.

Artisans

Artisans are the important element of the hill economy. Due to several chronic problems being faced, many of them no longer want to pursue their traditional activities. Thus. there is a need to look into this aspect closely. It is felt that there is a need for upgrading of technologies in terms of improving their tools and implements which in turn may increase their efficiency/reduce drudgery and hence better earning through innovative skill development, training programmes and adaptive R&D. Artisans Guides may be created which could cater to the various needs of the artisans both in terms of forward and backward linkages.

Water Management and Harvesting

Increasing scarcity of drinking and irrigation water is one of the ironies of the hilly areas particularly when mountains are the source of water shedding to the country. For instance, in Uttaranchal out of 13 districts, seven are in acute water crisis. Only seven per cent of the land is irrigated. Same is the scenario for other parts. Following areas need specific intervention:

- Technology for recharging of springs.

- Low cost water pumps technologies.
- Specific rainwater harvesting both for drinking and irrigation.
- Surface water harvesting for irrigation.
- Technology based sustainable watershed development and management focusing on land, water and bio-engineering plantations.

Non-Timer Forest Produce

The entire mountain system is supposed to be covered with forest. For this purpose our biomass use strategy must be clear and technically defined for society. Since biomass is the only renewable source, our step into this resource forms the priority area. The various category of biomass like unutilized, under-utilized and invasive in village access should be planned for use *in situ* for local and commercial purposes. The NTFP will have two major sectors:

Herbs

Medicinal plants occurring in the mountain have a great national and international market. Growing awareness towards herbal therapy gives scope of developing herbal industries in mountains focusing on cultivation, processing and marketing of herbs. Primary processing of medicinal plants for value addition of their product should be promoted locally and local people should be trained about the latest cultivation practices.

Other Biomass

The other non-timber produce of the forest has a great value in economic development. This requires:

- Identification of resource,
- Value addition, and
- Appropriate market outlet.

Since a large area of the mountains are under forest cover, utilization of minor forest produce can be a sound option for mountain economy. This involves oil seeds, natural dyes. herbs, aromatic plants, fibre etc. Appropriate agro-forestry design and system should also be developed, by identifying species to be grown with respect to health, nutrition, fuel, fodder, water, ornamental etc. This is one of the most important sectors where direct community dependence is possible. The appropriate utilization of MFP can be a sustained activity in mountain areas.

There are region specific MFP in different mountains. Their status, utility etc. will have to be found out. The major biomass available as MFP that can be subjected to utility are:

- Non-conventional fruits
- Oil yielding
- Fibrous
- Other uses

Human Resource Development (HRD) in this case can easily be organized as this wisdom traditionally exists among the forest dwellers. The following specific inputs will have to be ensured:

- Documentation of indigenous knowledge, development of skills for cultivation and processing herbs with scientific validation of practices;
- Exposure for patenting rights, benefit sharing; and
- Skill development for market.

Health Care and Sanitation

Health of the population in the hills is another important aspect, and facilities for healthcare is one such area that needs to be addressed. The need for technology intervention in the area of rural sanitation should be accorded high priority. Introducing the right kind of vegetation with medicinal value for cultivation as a part of farm foregetry/agro-forestry therefore needs to be encourage.

Tourism

Tourism and travel forms the basis of the economies of many mountain regions. If proper linkages between the development of mountain communities and mountain tourism is established, tourism benefits would spread to them, and hence adoption of technologies would also increase improving the return they will get as in the case of production of value added products from local horticultural produce; fibre based fancy articles and organically grown food products etc.

Experiences in Uttaranchal

The above approach has been adopted for technology development and transfer in different parts of the mountain regions by some field-based S&T field groups/NGOs involving small and marginal farmers, women, weaker sections, Scheduled Castes and Scheduled Tribes. In this direction a group of scientists from HESCO, Chamoli, Uttaranchal working on a project *technology upgradation for fuel/fodder needs* of women in Garhwal hills has been able to train hill women from three selected villages of Chamoli in appropriate techniques for cultivation of forage crops/grasses, silage making, stall feeding and efficient use of non-woody fuel in monsoon season to mitigate the problem of fodder/fuel scarcity. HESCO has also developed new carrying devices using *Agave fibre,* upgraded harvesting tools and stove which are more efficient, in use, and helping hill women who are overburdened by daily chores in time saving. Training in construction and management of silo pits for silage making and and appropriate storage and preservation of grass/fodder techniques has helped a lot to avoid the hardship faced by women in hills during monsoon season and lean periods.

Intervention made by HESCO in *improving traditional water* mills through new S&T inputs for better outcome and multifunctional activities like grain milling, local electrification etc. may be seen in Box 4.7.1.

In a recent initiative to address the problem of natural resource management and human resource development, efforts are being made by this group to establish a *Women Technology Park (WTP)*, a live technology model exclusively for women at Dehradun, Uttaranchal. WTP will provide demonstration and training on need based selected technologies and promoting rural entrepreneurship amongst mountain community specifically to women in and around the area. The park is essentially to show case location specific technologies relevant to women, provide training and also backward and forward linkages so that women would optimally be able to use these technologies to improve their living conditions and minimize hardship faced by them in day to day activities. The main objective of the WTP is to serve as a common platform to document, develop afnd transfer proven technologies as per women's needs in the mountain regions. It will also facilitate increased participation of women technology innovators.

Box 4.7.1: Improved Water Mills

Problem/Need Assessment: The Western Himalayas are dotted with rivers, rivulets, streams, lakes etc. Larger rivers are being tamed for electricity generation through huge hydel projects. Micro-hydel projects and small gharats (traditional water mills), which work on run-of-the-stream power, have also been successful. This region is rich in gharats developed by local inhabitants thousands of years ago using simple techniques and which served them well. In the simplest water mills, energy differentials due to the Himalayan terrain are used to produce shaft power primarily used for grain milling. Later, more complex machines were also used for spinning and carding. The ancient designs did not pose any major problems earlier but now, with the advent of diesel/electric flour mills and also the increased workload of villagers due to various reasons, the low output of the gharats, although at a cheaper rate, has become a major deterrent causing villagers to abandon them. Another factor is the limited function of the gharat as grain grinder only; for rice husking and oil expelling villagers have to resort either to manual labour or use the services of diesel/electric mills.

Approach/Strategy: Studies conducted by HESCO revealed that the gharats can become functional, using appropriate technology, and can be improved in terms of output/efficiency and also be rendered multifunctional. With little effort, these improved gharats can then be made an important hub of the rural economy.

Technology Package: The following modifications have been made to the traditional water mill:

- High velocity of water makes the surface rough and causes excessive turbulence in water flow at the flume, leading to loss of energy by friction. To avoid such losses, Gl sheet covering the inner surface of the flume was placed.
- The wooden runner has been replaced by a cast steel runner. The diameter of the runner is 500 mm. with 16 blades. The complete runner is of one piece casting throughing about 32 kg.
- The flat blades of the water wheel on which the water jet strikes have been provided a curvature, so that maximum pressure energy could be harnessed. This would prevent splashing losses, besides lessening disturbances to the incoming water jet.
- A bearing has been introduced at the bottom of the water wheel allowing more free rotation.

Economics: The additional input involved is Rs. 4500-6000, which improves the efficiency up to 140 per cent. The costs recovered or income from this technology is locally considered in terms of bhagwari, i.e. the part of the flour paid by the customer to the owner for their service. Such intervention has led to a large number of abandoned water mills being/operational not only in Uttaranchal but also in J & K.

Major focus under this park is to make science and technology visible and accessible to rural women folk through demonstration and application of knowledge in a form, which they can apply in their day-to-day activities. Technological empowerment and skill training of people, convergence of income generating activities and creation of sustainable livelihood through the structure by people's institutions are major and critical components of the WTP. Other support services like health, counselling, marketing and credit will be taken care of with the support and linkages of other financial/technical institutions to make the proposed intervention sustainable. Some of the technology packages being delivered to women through the Women's Technology Park are—mushroom cultivation, floriculture, animal husbandry, natural dyes, vanilla bean cultivation, medicinal plant cultivation, nursery raising, fibre utilization, sustainable fodder management, utilization of conventional and non-conventional fruits, organic farming, post harvest technology, solar energy utilization, processing and weaving of local wool, women's health and information technology.

The concept of WTP will also provide a nucleus of science and technology for technological empowerment of poor people in nearby areas in terms of appropriate technology back-up and management support/services in various sectors like information, organization and planning; watershed management; agro-forestry processing; sustainable agriculture; horticulture and bamboo farming; energy application and environment; and non-farm activities covering simultaneously the social engineering aspects with low cost appropriate technology packages.

Such WTP model is serving as a help desk and allowing women to use resources and facilities of WTP appropriately to develop them as individual/group entrepreneurs. Number of women's groups from Uttaranchal and Himachal Pradesh have benefited from this WTP.

In another initiative an S&T based field group, Janaadhar Society was able to implement a project in the upper Yamuna valley of Uttarkashi district focusing on income generation programme through transfer of *appropriate technologies to disabled persons* in the project area. The training on 3 activities, i.e. rural technical services, fibre based technologies and fruit processing and preservation were provided on the basis of these categories. About 100-disabled persons (men and women) were trained to initiate their own income earning activities. Some of them opened their own shop and are earning their livelihood. The programme has been able to encourage the ignored disabled persons in the project area.

In an innovative work, Indian Institute of Community Development were able to train ragpicker women in Rishikesh area for re-utilization of waste poly bags collected from the community waste. The women have been trained in weaving mat and making others decorative material through appropriate designs leading to income generation. Thus. such an intervention has shown potential to address the growing problem of *appropriate waste utilization of non-destructive plastic waste* in the mountains.

Some other potential areas like cultivation of off-season vegetables, need-based cultivation of herbs for local and community utility, technology based micro-watershed management, preservation and processing of horticultural produce with quality control have shown promises for sustainable utilization of local resources in hills and better livelihood opportunities to local people in mountain production system. If proper networking amongst different stakeholders in terms of technology, credit, and social engineering based on location specific need is ensured from planning to implementation stage, it certainly helps in percolation of technology at the grassroots level and post project sustainability.

Conclusion

The experience clearly indicates that the "bottom up" approach for participatory technology development starting with the people and with lateral contribution from Science and Technology Institutions and close interface with voluntary organizations can provide sustainable models for technology development and transfer. A new sense of accomplishment by way of new skills and earning independent incomes generate confidence amongst people to bring about other reforms in their lives. Application of a systems approach in development as well as appropriation of available traditional technologies with proper networking and linkages amongst people and institutions as described above—can certainly change the lives of the mountain people through technological empowerment and capacity building at the grassroots level putting in place sustainable systems, which are managed, by the people.

Note: The views and opinions expressed in this article are those of the author, not of the organization to which he belongs. The author gratefully acknowledges the inputs provided by above-mentioned Field Groups/NGOs.

References

1. *TIME Newsletter*, DST Publication. Vol. III, pp. 1-22, October. 2002.
2. *Technology Models for Rual Application*, DST Publication, p. 114, 2001.

"True Knowledge
Enables a Man to Realize
That he is
The Soul with a Body
Now, in his Ignorance, he
Thinks
That he is
A Body with a Soul"

"You are Successful
and
Creative only when
You see
An Opportunity
in Every Difficulty"

ANNEXURES

Annexure 1

Uttaranchal at a Glance

I. General

Formation day	:	09-Nov-2000
Area	:	55,845 sq. km.
Population (Appx.)	:	7.045 million
Capital (interim)	:	Dehradun
High Court	:	Nainital

District	*Area (sq. km)*	*Population*	*Headquarters*
Pauri Garhwal	5438	682535	Pauri
Chamoli	9126	454871	Chamoli
Dehradun	3088	1025679	Dehradun
Tehri Garhwal	4421	580153	New Tehri
Uttarkashi	8016	239709	Uttarkashi
Nainital	6794	1540174	Nainital
Udham Singh Nagar	3358	914861	Rudrapur
Almora	5385	836617	Almora
Pithoragarh	8856	566408	Pithoragarh
Hardwar	2360	1124488	Hardwar
Bageshwar	1626	224172	Bageshwar
Rudra Prayag	2439	200451	Rudra Prayag
Champwat	5	N.A.	N.A.

II. Important Mountain Peaks

1. Abl Gamin (7255m)
2. Baljori (5922m)
3. Bandarpoonch (6316m)
4. Barte Kanta (6579m)
5. Bethartoli (6352m)
6. Bhagirathi-I (6856m)
7. Bhagirathi-II (6512m)
8. Bhagirathi-III (6454m)

9. Bhrigupanth (6771m)
10. Bhrigu Parbat (6041m)
11. Chandrashila (4090m)
12. Changabang (6864m)
13. Changuch (6322m)
14. Chaukhamba-I (7138m)
15. Chaukhamba-II (7068m)
16. Chaukhamba-III (6974m)
17. Chaukhamba-IV (6854m)
18. Devtole (6788m)
19. Changkhal (6050m)
20. **Dantu-Dugtu-Sipu Region**
    1. Chhitia (5252m)
    2. Chhota Kailash (6191m)
    3. Chikulawe (6038m)
    4. Devtoli (6788m)
    5. Gilding (5629m)
    6. Ikuwalari (6059m)
    7. Kuchila (6294m)
    8. Mangron (6568m)
    9. Nagling (6041m)
    10. Name-Chaudhara (6510m)
    11. Nandakhani (6029m)
    12. Nandagond (6315m)
    13. Nandamanas (6236m)
    14. Nandapal (6306m)
    15. Nitalthaur (6236m)
    16. Rajramba (6537m)
    17 Sakram (6254m)
    18. Sin Teela (6333m)
    19. Sipu (5629m)
    20. Sutilla (6373m)
    21. Trigal (5983m)
    22. Yungtangto (5945m)
21. Devisthan (6680m)
22. Doonagiri (7066m)
23. Gangotri (6674m)
24. Ganesh Parbat(6351m)
25. Ghori Parbat (6590m)
26. Hanuman Parbat (6070m)
27. Hathi Parbat (6727m)
28. Jogin I (6465m)
29. Kagbusand (5830m)
30. Kalanag (63&7m)
31. Kalanka (6931m)
32. Kamet (7756m)
33. Kedamath (694®m)
34. Khatling (6387m)
35. Kholi (6114m)
36. Kirti Stambh (6402m)
37. Kunaling (6509m)
38. Longstaff Col. (5910m)
39. Mahalaya Parbat (5970m)
40. Maiktoli (6303m)
41. **Mana Peak** (7272m)
42. Mem (6660m)
43. **Milam Region**
    1. Hardeval(7151m)
    2. Trishuli (7074m)
44. Mrigthuni (6565m)
45. Mukut (7242m)
46. Nanda Bhanar (6236m)
47. **Nanda Devi**
    (Main Summit–7816m)
    (East Summit–7434m)
48. **Nanda Devi Sanctuary Region**
    1. Burfu Dhura (6334m)
    2. Chhringewe (6559m)
    3. Kalabaland Dhura (6105m)
    4. Kalganga Dhura (6215m)
    5. Sulitop (6300m)
49. Nanda Ghunti (6309m)
50. Nanda Khani (6020m)
51. Nanda Khat (6611m)
52. Nanda Kot (6861m)
53. Nar Parbat (5831m)
54. Narayan Parbat (5960m)

55. Neelkanth (6596m)
56. Nilgiri Parbat (6475m)
57. **Panchchuli Range**
(I-6904m, II–6355m III-6312m IV-6334m,V 6437m)
58. Pangarchulla (5183m)
59. Panwali Dhar (6663m)
60. Rataban (6166m)
61. Rishi Pahar (6992m)
62. Saife (6161m)
63. Satopanth (7075m)
64. Shalang Dhura (5678m)
65. Shivling (6543m)
66. Sudarshan Parbat (6507m)
67. Sumeru Parbat (63 50m)
68. Sphetic Prishtwan (6905m)
69. **Sunderdhunge Region**
    1. Baluni (4877m)
    2. Malktoli (6803m)
    3. Sunderdhunga (6663m)
    4. Tharkot (6099m)
70. Swargarohini-1 (6252m)
71. Trimukhi Parbat (6422m)
72. Trisul-I (7120m)
73. W.Ibi.Gamin (7376m)

III. Important Lakes

1. Arwa Tal (3980m)
2. Baghani Tal
3. Bedni Kund
4. Bekhar Tal
5. Beni Tal (near Adi Badri)
6. Bhainkaltal (2744m)-near Mundoli
7. Bhimtal (1371m) 31
8. Bore Lake (6 km from Gailgarh, near Kuari Pass)
9. Brahm Tal (3507m)-near Wan
10. Chorabari Tal (Gandhi Sarovar)
11. Deoria Tal (3289m)
12. Deotal (5684m) - The source of Saraswati river, near Manaa Pass
13. Dodital (3307m)
14. Devi Kund (3587m)
15. GohnaTal
16. Hemkund Sahib (4329m)
17. Homekund (4061m)
18. Jhola Tal
19. Kabhusand Tal (5230m)
20. Kashni Tal
21. Kedar Tal (4425m)
22. Khara Tal (3420m)
23. Masar Tal (3675m)
24. Masap Tal
25. Maindagall Tal
26. Massar kund-2 km from Kalamuni
27. Nachiketa Tal, near Chaurangikhal
28. Nandi Kund
29. Naini Lake (1938m)
30. Naukuchiya Tal (1218m)
31. Nanak Sagar, Nanakmata
32. Nag Kund (4877m)
33. Parvati Lake
34. Painya Tal
35. Roop Kund (4450m)
36. Ruinsara Tal (3350m)
37. Rishi Lake (4880m)
38. Saptrishi Kund, Yamunotri area
39. Seven Lakes (2878m)
40. Sattal

41. Satopanth Lake (4405m)
42. Shasra Tal (4572m)
43. Shyamlal Tal (1600m)
44. Sup Tal
45. TaragTal
46. Thamri Kund
47. Vasuki Tal (4135m)-6 km from Kedamath
48. Vasuki Tal (4880m)-6km from Nandanban

IV. Himalayan Shrines

(a) CHAR DHAM
1. Yamunotri (3185m)
2. Gangotri (3048m)
3. Kedamath (3584m)
4. Badrinath (3096m)

(b) PANCH BADRI
1. Badri Vishal-Sri Badrinath (3096m)
2. Yogdhyan Badri (1920m)
3. Bhavishya Badri (3641m)
4. Vridha Badri (1380m)
5. Adi Badri (1630m)

(c) PANCH KEDAR
1. Sri Kedamath (3584m)
2. Tungnath (3680m)
3. Rudranath (2286m)
4. Kalpeshwar (2134m)
5. Madhyamaheshwar (3490m)

(d) PANCH PRAYAG
1. Deoprayag (813m)
2. Rudraprayag (61 Om)
3. Karanprayag (832m)
4. Nandprayag (914m)
5. Vishnuprayag (1372m)

(e) DEVI DARSHAN
1. Kunjapuri (1665m)
2. Surkanda Devi (3030m)
3. Chandrabadni (2278m)
4. Anusuya Devi (2000m)

(f) GURDWARAS
1. Hemkund Sahib (4150m)—19km trek from Govindghat
2. Nanak Matta Sahib (45 km from Udham Singh Nagar)
3. Reetha Meetha Sahib (900m)–74 km from Champawat.

V. Most Popular Resorts/Hill Stations

1. Almora
2. Auli
3. Binsar
4. Chaukori
5. Dhanouiti
6. Harichvar/Rishikesh
7. Kausani
8. Lohaghat
9. Mukteshwar
10. Munsiyari
11. Mussoorie
12. Nainital
13. Narendra Nagar
14. Ramgarh
15. Ranikhet

Annexure 2

Advantage: Uttaranchal

Utpal Parashar

The Congress government led by Chief Minister N.D. Tiwari has taken Several initiatives towards making Uttaranchal an exemplary state in the country. Thrust areas like power, tourism, industry and information technology have been identified and efforts undertaken to reach specific goals within a set time limit.

The state is lucky to have a dynamic and vastly experienced politician like N.D. Tiwari as its chief minister who has held various important designations at the Centre and been chief minister of Uttar Pradesh four times in a career spanning over five decades.

In an interview with *Hindustan Times*, Tiwari talks about the achievements of his government and mentions about the problems that the State is facing. The Chief Minister also outlines his vision for the State in the next two decades.

"Since ours is a new state, comparisons can't be made with most other states who have been in existence for long. But if one takes into account the two other new states Jharkhand and Chattisgarh that came into being around the same time as us, our achievements have been remarkable in most sectors," he said.

The CM stated that Uttaranchal's biggest resource is its immense potential for power generation. He outlined the steps taken by the government in identifying and exploiting this potential in a planned manner so that the state becomes a 'power house' in the coming years. Several agreements have already been signed with national and international companies for power generation.

Uttaranchal possesses some of the most scenic mountain locales in the world and is also home to several important pilgrimage centres for Hindus, Muslims and Sikhs. "Accepting tourism as a backbone of the state's economy, several steps like the constitution of the Char Dham Tourism Board, a self-employment scheme to improve tourist destinations and master plans with private companies have been initiated.

The state new industrial policy and tax holiday schemes announced by the Centre have been able to lure several leading private companies to set up factories in the state. More than 500 proposals have received till date for the two industrial estates at Pant Nagar and Hardiwar. "The previous regime at the Centre had given tax holiday of 10 years for all new industries setup in Uttaranchal. It was reduced till 2007 in the recent annual budget. We have requested the centre to reconsider the mover. They say that it will be extended after 2007. We are still waiting for a written response, he said.

Tiwari also spoke about the government's resolve to turn Uttaranchal into an IT-hub and the steps taken towards promoting e-governance. Several agreement have been made with software giants like Microsoft towards introducing computer education in school and colleges.

A Developed Uttaranchal by 2020

Chief Minister is confident that the attempts made by the state government for speedy development of Uttaranchal with co-operation from the people would fructify by the year 2020 and the state will become a model state in the country.

He hopes that Uttaranchal would become self-reliant by adopting the long term plans under Vision 2020. It is the highest priority of the government to complete development schemes in a time-bound, qualitative and transparent manner. *"I can visualize that by the year 2020, the foundations that we have laid today would become stronger and Uttaranchal would become a leader in power, industries, IT, agriculture and tourism sectors. The state will make all round progress in other sectors too"*, he said.

He appealed to the state's residents to help the government in its efforts and work towards making Uttaranchal an exemplary state. He hoped that the objectives like economic and social upliftment of the people that had led to the State's creation would be fulfilled within 2020.

Why Is Uttaranchal Tourism most talked about ?

Tourism plans to attract Rs. 2000 crore

Uttaranchal has, these days, become accepted as a synonym for tourism in India. This new hill state has so much to offer—from the most popular pilgrimage destinations like the Char Dham to 21st Century adventure sports— for tourists this part of the Indian Himalayas has become a must destination.

But, even so, in the time to come. Uttaranchal is going to be with the tourist like never before. The reason being simple—better and upgraded facilities for tourists. Besides this, with rejuvenated traditional resorts, as also a kitty of newly developed places, Uttaranchal is all set to steal the hearts of visitors.

The state has announced a forward-looking tourism policy. On this Tourism Secretary N.N. Prasad says, "The Tourism Policy is not merely a policy statement but also an attempt to analyse the tourism potential and strengths of Uttaranchal along with the weakness and challenges that lie ahead."

A series of master plans have been prepared to attract investment of over Rs. 2000 crore and to promote tourism in the many lesser-known destinations.

When you have the right intentions and the planning, the predictable outcome is appreciation and applause. Uttaranchal Tourism has won as many as twelve national awards for providing excellent services to visitors. By winning such laurels in such a short span of time, the new state is naturally the most talked about in the tourism industry.

To provide better facilities to visitors, the State Tourism has set up 13 district level tourist offices and 44 tourism information centres.

Another plan in the pipeline and partially implemented is helicopter services for Badrinath, Kedarnath and Hemkund Sahib.

Considering the fragile eco-system of the Himalayas, promoting eco-tourism remains one of the priorities of Uttaranchal Tourism. An Eco-Tourism Centre has been established in Ramnagar to promote community based tourism.

Another initiative that will involve local people in tourism is the State Goverment's "Veer Chandra Singh Garhwali Swarozgar Yojana". This unique self-employment scheme has changed the fortune of countless number of youths.

Uttaranchal to become the biggest hydropower State in Asia

With a number of ongoing hydropower projects, Uttaranchal is striving to become the biggest hydropower state in Asia in the future. The Uttaranchal Government has signed MoUs for a total of 9 hydel projects, so far, with a capacity of 4000 MW.

To ensure minimal rehabilitation problems, all projects will be run-of-the river. It will be noted, the Uttaranchal Power Corporation Limited (UPCL) is committed to the environment and people-friendly power projects in the new hill state. Last year, UPCL completed electrification of 812 new hamlets. Besides this, under the 'Kutir Jyoti Programme', 37,297 BPL families were benefited.

Commenting on the hydropower projects Principal Secretary Power S. Krishnan told the Hindustan Times, "The State Government has joined hands with the National Thermal Power Corporation for the 600 MW Lohari Nagpala, 360 MW Tapovan Vishnu Gad and 108 MW Lata Tapovan hydro-electric projects, while MoUs have been linked with NHPC for the 1000 MW Kotli Behl and 420 MW Lakhwar/Vyasi Projects". In addition, the Tehri Hydro Development Corporation has inked two Memoranda of Understanding with the State Government for construction of the 340 MW Vishnugad Pipal Koti and the 600 MW Kishau Dam. It will be recalled that the Uttaranchal Jal Vidyut Nigam Limited is carrying out the 416 MW Pala Maneri and the 132 MW Bowala Nandprayag projects. Incidentally, the Asian Development Bank (ADB) has agreed in principle to provide a 300 billion US Dollar loan to Uttaranchal for hydropower projects.

The good news is that the ambitious 1000 MW Tehri Dam will begin generating power from next year.

So, the Uttaranchal Power Corporation Ltd.—with the team of experts and support from the employees—is dedicated to taking electricity to far-flung places in the hill state. With the new hydropower projects, Uttaranchal is all set to attain greater economic prosperity.

500 Industries to set up units in Uttaranchal

With industry friendly policies, no red tape and total transparency, Uttaranchal is fast emerging as the favorite destination among industrialists. Some 500 industries have already signed on to set up their units in two integrated industrial estates in Haridwar and Pantnagar. envisaging an investment of Rs. 4000 crore.

Sanjeev Chopra, Secretary Industries said, "Among major investors that have set up units here are Hindustan Lever Limited with an investment of Rs. 400 crore and Dabur companies setting up units include Sahara Systems, South Africa ; Gujrat Borosil Ltd. Vestel Group of Companies, Globally Managed Serviçe India Maharshi Ayurveda Products Ltd. Woodlands Group, Dalmia Consumer Care, Asahi Float Glass, India; Haldiram, LG India; Videocon, Atlas Cycles, India; Parle, etc.".

"Hindustan Lever Ltd. and Dabur have started their production in IIE Haridwar and Pantnagar", he added.

Land has already been allotted to most units and once these industries start functioning, over 50,000 persons would get employment.

The Union Government has declared an industrial package envisaging special tax concessions for the upcoming industries in the state.

To felicitate investors, the Uttaranchal Government has declared its new industrial Woodlands policy.

Efforts are also underway to develop export zones, food parks, tourism destinations, roads, airports, industrial towns, etc., for the private sector. A single window system is being established to provide all facilities and clearances to investors. It has also set up the 'State Industrial Development Corporation of Uttaranchal Ltd. (SIDCUL) to attract investment.

SIDCUL is the first integrated industrial corporation in India.

"Ten Thousands Crores"—The means of the Memoirs of the Secretary. Industries just published are remarkable inspiring and shows the VISION of CM, CS and Secretary Industries for employment and income generation action programme.

Horticulture, Herbal initiatives to Boost Rural Sector

Export zones have been established in the state for litchi, flowers, herbs and medicinal plants, and basmati rice.

For the first time, three metric tons of Asiatic Lily were exported from the state. As many as 27 orchards are being developed as model orchards.

The Silk Federation has been formed for the marketing of silk. Vibha Puri Das, Principal Secretary Horticulture says, " 'The Uttaranchal' brand of tea is finding wide acceptance. A project has been launched to promote tea cultivation on 717 acres of land. The first tea factory has been launched in the state after many years".

Under the plan for herbs and medicinal plants, against a target sale of Rs. 490 lakh. Rs. 120 lakh have already been earned. MoUs have been signed for the development of aromatic and medicinal plants with various institutions.

Arrangements have been made with Mother Dairy, Delhi for marketing of cash crops and vegetables grown in Uttarkashi. In the current year, 32,939 quintals of tomatoes, 578 quintals of capsicum, 470 quintals of cauliflower, and 3584 boxes of apple have been so marketed.

To make commercial cultivation of herbs and medicinal plants successful, as many as 800 nurseries are being established and 1000 farmers are receiving training.

As many as 20 Mandi Samitis have been set up in the state to provide marketing facilities to farmers.

An aggressive action plan has been launched to transform Uttaranchal into a herbal state and to preserve bio-diversity with the involvement of all departments concerned.

A Nut Fruit Revolution with welnuts, almonds and sweet chestnuts, fruits like Apples, Apricots, kiwi where formers are working with NGO's and Donors for bringing this revolution.

Roads: Avenues of Progress

The Public Works Department is committed to taking development to every village of the state.

Dr. Indira Hridayesh, State PWD Minister, said, "A road masterplan is being prepared in every district to connect the villages with the rest of the country".

These will be prepared with the help of ground mapping, aerial photography and other modern techniques. For better quality and environment protection drainage is being provided along with construction of roads, and trees are being planted alongside.

For the first time, the Department has set up a committee comprising experts from IIT Roorkee and CII Roorkee to identify roads prone to landslides and will act upon their recommendations.

The PWD has 17.074 kilometres of road under its charge. Other departments have to look after 4678 kilometres of roads. The total length of roads in the state presently is 21,752 kilometres.

In one year, under the state and district sectors, 314 kilometres of road have been built, 278 kilometres have been renovated, 15 motor road bridges and 18 foot bridges have been built.

The department has completed 8 major works in the state, including 14.25 kilometre of the Ring Road in Dehradun, renovation of 6.94 kilometres on the Chamoli-Gopeshwar road, while widening of 24.12 kilometres on the Pauri-Srinagar roads is underway.

Under the 'Pradhan Mantri Gram Sadak Yojana', out of the approved 69 roads, in one year, 49 have been completed, totalling 164 kilometres.

Initiatives in Information Technology

Uttaranchal is in the forefront of propagation of Information Technology uses. Many ambitious plans have been launched to generate employment through IT.

'Project Shikhar' has been started with the help of Aptech and ECIL to provide high quality IT education at an affordable price to college students.

Disclosing about the IT initiatives of the State Government Secretary Information Technology, Amarendra Sinha said, "With the assistance of the world's biggest networking company, CISCO, the CISCO Academy has been established in ten colleges and universities campuses".

The most significant task, however, has been that of providing computer education in the state's government run as well as aided schools under 'Project Aarohi'. Students of higher secondary schools have been made computer literate. More than fifty per cent of the state's schools have been covered, so far.

Under 'Project Shiksha', Microsoft has established its first IT Academy in the world in Dehradun. The main objective of setting up this academy is to prepare the quality IT Human Resources within three years and also to promote IT and IT enabled industries for employment generation.

MoUs have also been signed for promotion of IT within the field of IT education with Intel Corporation, CISCO and Aptech.

Departmental information has been made available on the official website www.ua.nic.in . This is among several websites launched by Uttaranchal Government departments and agencies.

Annexure 3

Words of Wisdom from Swami Rama Tirtha and Swami Tapovanji Mahraj

Swami Rama Tirtha (1873-1906)

Swami Rama Tirtha was a great scholar, free thinker, a vedantist, a great patriot and socialist and a man of courage ready to accept challenges. According to Swamiji. "Learning and Wisdom are not identical. They are not always on speaking terms. Learning looks backward to the past. Wisdom looks forward."

Swamiji's message was "know the soul and through it know God." He and his comonks carried the message of Vedanta, i.e. know Brahman through atma throughout the country and outside. Love of solitude for meditation took him to Tehri Garhwal of Uttaranchal Himalayas. He wandered in the mountains with scant clothing and preferred to live in cave for meditation without fear as a lion lived in a nearby cave. He climbed difficult and high mountains. During his journey to Sumeru peak, he reached above (leaving his companions behind) and spread his blanket on a mound of snow and sat down, all above the noise and the turmoil of the world, beyond the fumes and furies of the multitude. "Perfect silence reigned there, unbroken peace, no sound heard expect the 'thunder of bliss" Rama worte

"The veil of cloud became a little less thick—The rays of the sun sifted through the thin cloud, fell on the scene and immediately turned the silver snows into burning gold. Very appropriately has this place been called Sumeru or the "Mountain of Gold". He visited Haridwar, Rishikesh. He found Vashishtha Ashram a very charming breath—taking retreat and in his words.

"This Ashrama is above the snowline. A beautiful stream called the Vashishtha Ganga flows just below Rama's cave. There are five or six waterfalls in the stream. Natural basins are carved out of the hard rocks in the river valley by Shiva's own hands, forming about twenty lovely tanks. The hills are covered with those true, light loving, hardy giants of the forest whose green does not fade even when more than six ft of snow accumulates above them. They are certainly worthy of the great Krishna's kindness and love".

Swami Tapovanji Maharaj (1889-1957)

From his childhood, Swami Tapovanji Maharaj exhibited marked inclination for spiritual life. Puranic stories manifesting the glory of God fascinated him. He wrote several books and here we are giving a few extracts from WANDERINGS IN THE HIMALAYAS (HIMGIRI VIHAR) which consists of poetic description of places of importance in the Himalayas, Sacred in their cultural lore and in traditional faith of the Hindus.

- Hrishikesh, the gateway to Uttarakhand still retains the serenity and remains the resort of saintly men who are skilled not only in the control over external and internal senses, but also in the study of Vedanta.
- God shines everywhere, in stone and earth and water, but men who have not overcome their ego fail to find the Resplendent One anywhere. Conceit of self in ones intelligence, senses and body is egoism.
- Action is the natural order of the world. The life-force continues to stir all living bodies at all times. There is no state of inaction. A desireless, peaceful state of existence where the distinction between the knower and the known disappears is difficult to attain, wherever man may be. That distinction fades away only when man has crossed the stream of action which shows itself in the activities of the physical senses and which produces pleasure and pain. But crossing the stream means the complete conquest of illusion and illusion is certainly difficult to overcome. Even in holy places like Badrikashram it is not easy to reach the stage of Supreme Bliss, where all distinctions disappear, where all actively ceases.
- The Himalayan region is a land of Jnana (true knowledge) the south is the land of Karma (action).
- The snow-clad peaks shining like silver or gold in the sunshine,

and the noise of avalanches that resembles the bursts of cannon convert the region into wonderland, and fill the hearts of theists and antheist alike with astonishment and admiration.

- The Himalayan streams are gratefully singing the praise of the Creator who makes them flow. These fine birds sweeping along the skies are proclaiming the matchless glory of the Lord. Look at these charming flowers, bright with many colours, blooming here on the meadow. They too proclaim nothing else. In this holy land everything seems to join in that universal harmony.
- Sri Gaumukha, the place where the sacred Ganga actually emerges into the world. Of all the places on the earth, it is the holiest. It is celebrated in innumerable songs by the great rishis. It is surrounded by high,snow clad peaks. It stands close to heaven and is occupied by the gods. In that beautiful place, from a huge formation of snow shaped like the mouth of a cow, the Ganga issues forth to purify the world and wash away the sins of the dwellers of the earth.
- It matters little, O Mother Ganga, whether you originate at Vishnu's big toe or Sri Gaumukha, whatever that be the fact remains Ganga is Ganga. O Mother thou art the Supreme Mistress of the world.

Annexure 4

Himcon Mission Statement

We, at *HIMCON MILAN KENDRA, HIMALAYA CONSORTIUM FOR HIMALAYA CONSERVATION,* involved in Conservation, Land and Water Care Movement for Himalayan Mountain System with special reference to the New State of Uttaranchal and Himalayan Communities living therein.

Commit Ourselves towards Achieving

I. The cause of Himalayan Environment, Conservation and Rejuvenation

II. Improvement in Quality of Life of its inhabitants and specially Women, Youth and Children through

- Literacy
- Education
- Health and Sanitation
- Employment Generation
- Income Generation
- Poverty Eradication

III. A Land and Water Care Movement specially in Uttaranchal and other parts of Himalayas and other Mountain System.

Including:

	Bioindustrial Watershed Management:	Highlighting
A.	Awareness and Organisation Building:	Mahila Mangal Dal, Self Help Groups, Seed and Health Banks, Van Panchayats, Grain Banks
B.	Jal Prabandhan/Water Management :	Rainwater Harvesting, Ground Water Recharge, Augmentation Spring,

		Rejuvenation Community Irrigation
C. Silviculture & Agro Horticulture, Pasture Development	:	Greening Movement and Conservation Policy and Strategy
D. Processing Marketing and Quality Control including Value Addition	:	Medicinal and Aromatic Plants, Nuts, Fruits and Vegetables, Milk and Milk Products

IV. School Planting Program, Training Students as Lovers of Himalayas; and Promoting Environmental, Physical, Scientific, Moral and Spiritual Education and Training

V. Renewable Energy
Promoting Solar, Biomass, Biogas, Mini Micro Hydro, Wind and other Renewable Energy

VI. Promote and Run Training Centres

A. HIMCON MILAN KENDRA	:	Training Centre for Environmental and Scientific Training
B. HIMCON DHYAN KENDRA	:	A Spiritual Centre for A Divine Land—HIMCON NIKETAN
C. HIMCON URJA KENDRA	:	A Centre for Promoting Renewable Energy Developing, Demonstration, Extension Training and Optimum Use.
D. HIMCON SHISHU KENDRA	:	A Centre for Promoting Child Development
E. HIMCON VOCATIONAL KENDRA	:	A Centre for Promoting and Training Women and Youth in Vocations—For Environment Generation for Himalayam Communities

Personal Mission Statement of Dr. Madan Dewan (1922)

In my long carreer, I have been Mission Driven and not Ambition-Driven. I have practiced and nursed human values and principles which are changeless with time. They are ***Truth, Nonviolence, Peace, Love*** and ***Right Action.*** I have constantly endeavored to live up to them. I shall share these with you, my personal family our Dewan Family, the Himalayan family and world—human family at large. This sharing has put me in "A Voyage from I to We" My beginning of life in a small town in North West Frontier Province of what was then INDIA and now

PAKISTAN, studying and living with Communities in Pakistan, India, USA, Europe, Bihar, Iran, Italy, Bulgaria and Europe, then in Himalayas, now Uttaranchal, A small village of Ranichauri, and Delhi, Capital city of India are places of my activities.

My Parents, my Grandmother, my Brothers and Sisters are all sources of joy. My own companion, Darshi, whom I saw and sought from NAIROBI, KENYA. Partner Darshi, who is talented, artistic and loving. My two Children, Daugther, Gita, Born in HAZARIBAGH BIHAR (Now Jharkhand) where I worked for DAMODAR VALLEY CORPORATION, a Temple of MODERN INDIA, and Son Vikram Born in Tehran, Iran where we spent almost 13 years of Youthful Life we were working as a part of FAO of UN working as FAO Project Manager, Soil Institute and Pilot Development Project living happily, purposefully, lovingly among people who were friendly, and affectionate like family members. Fourteen years in Rome, Italy as part of FAO (of UN) Headquarters Staff working in Land and Water Development & Program Development in Asia and Pacific amongst friendly Italian People. Two years of work in Bulgaria as Project Manager of Soil and Associated Pilot Development Project in SOFIA, Also as FAO and UN Representatives, an Exciting Period in a Communist Society which enabled both Darshi and myself to travel in all Socialist (communist) countries all except Albania, a year of Sabbatical leave in Maharashtra with MPKV—AN AGRICULTURAL UNIVERSITY—A year which inspired me to bring out a book "AGRICULTURE AND RURAL DEVELOPMENT IN INDIA. A case study on **Dignity of labour".** Help of two friends Dr. M.S. Pawar, Vice Chancellor of MPKV, and Dr. M.S. Swaminathan, Director General, ICAR, GOI was great. My experience as visiting Professor of Cornell University, USA in 1972 for a few months was another great event.

In my pre-retirement period of eight years (1974-82) as FAO Chief of Regional Bureau for Asia and Pacific, I was turned from an Indian Citizen to an Asian Citizen—Nay a World Citizen. I visited almost all parts of the world as an International Civil Servant. The whole mankind is my family-this became and still is part of my mission.

Himalayas—the Divine Land—attracted me from the beginning and specially from 1975 in FAO when I developed a program for *"Himalayan Region Land and Water Resources Conservation, Development and Utilisation"* which decided my Post retirement years and where I am serving now as Servant of the Himalayan Communities, as Chairman of HIMCON, Himalaya Consortium for Himalaya Conservation.

Let me come back to the Personal Mission Statement which I have endeavored to live up to and I share with you all what my close college and life friend late Darbari Seth of TATA based in Mumbai had shared with his friends and others.

1. I have developed a deep sense of partnership with the Divine. I consider myself as an instrument of His Will. I ascribe to Him every success that comes my way. I do not retain any and so nothing goes to my head.
2. To me, my country and my people come first and everything I do is driven by this. I have never done, and I will not do, anything which, according to my own lights, is not in the interest of my country, no matter which other interest it might serve.
3. I am defiantly self-reliant. I am fiercely free and fearless. I have never hankered after any office or reward. I have always worked and lived on my own terms.
4. I always want to be at the giving end, never at the receiving end. I give joyfully and I give, give and give, my effort, experience and funds in Hindi call it humbly and clearly *"Than Man Dhan"*.
5. I love and respect people and try to make champions out of them.
6. I use authority of my influence, and not of power, in dealing with people.
7. I am not deterred by adversity or crisis situations which I look upon as new opportunities for further advancement, new challenges.
8. I trust people, I feel humble. I have no greed and, therefore, no fear. I believe in People's Participation & Partnership in Programmes & Projects.
9. I believe in working with other Social Service Organisation such as Rotary System, other NGO's, Govt and People's Organisations.
10. I am a Soil Scientist, Soil Conservation and Watershed Management Expert, believer in INDIA's greatness and HIMALAYAS INSPIRATION, Must Work Towards Rejuvenation and Greening of Himalayan which is difficult but possible—Work towards plantation brigade—A Land Army—For Tree Planting in Uttaranchal and in all Himalayas and hopefully all India, let us all work together for the noble cause.

Annexure 5

Rejuvenation and Greening of Himalayas

M.L. Dewan and Himconians

Why Himalayas

The Himalaya are not merely a geographical feature, a mere chain of Mountain ranges. They epitomize a people's civilization that goes back to the DAWN OF HISTORY. If these majestic mountains were not there the rain clouds sweeping up from the Indian Ocean would have passed over our subcontinent into Central Asia leaving it a burning desert. The Himalayas have nurtured this land with life sustaining water and enabled a Civilization to Blossom. Archeological evidence reveals that urban civilization emerged in the river valleys coursing down these mountains. When man elsewhere was cautiously emerging from his cave shelters, spectacular cities flourished in the Indus Valley. Vedic hymns, some of the oldest spiritual texts in the world, were composed in the richly wooded valleys of these mountains. The Upanishads were written here more than three thousand years ago. The great poet, Kalidas, in his epic poem "Kumara Sambhava" invested these mountain ranges with Divinity. Divine they indeed are because from times immemorial, the Himalaya have influenced our way of life and thought. The mighty and sacred rivers, on whose banks our ancient civilization took root, survived and flourished have their birth in these snowy vastness.

But today the entire Himalayan range with its rich and biological diversity is facing a deep crisis and is in danger of being destroyed. It is being relentlessly denuded of its forest cover. Man is posing a threat to our ancient civilization by destroying the ecological base that sustains it. The forests are being ruthlessly exploited for their timber without realizing that trees are only secondary producers of timber. Their primary function is to promote rain, absorb moisture, recharge ground water, conserve soil, and produce oxygen, fuel, fodder and fruits. As part of our culture, we worship trees because of this vital nexus between them and life giving soils and waters. Our Vedic verses are centered around the environment. This magnificent vision has been eroded and we seem to have entered into a dark age which is witness to the maligned impact of massive human intervention in the natural processes.

Why Greening

But today the Central Himalayan Range with its rich biological diversity are degrading. These mountains must be protected from further damage from human greed and degradation. They have to be rejuvenated so that their past wounds can be healed. It is a gigantic task. The people who live in the shadow of these mighty mountains need to be involved in this task. People must feel that they are also stakeholders and this resource base belongs to them and not to a distant government.

Trees for Life, HIMCON and many others non profit, voluntary organisation dedicated to helping and encouraging people in rural areas to grow fruit trees in Himalayan Region for the better health of their families as well as to help uplift their socio-economic levels. Each tree protects the environment and provides a low cost, self renewing source of food for large number of people. The trees for life movement empowers people to solve problems for themselves. It is based on philosophy "if you teach him how to fish, he will never be hungry again". By providing people with the motivation and training to plant and care for their own trees, TFL, HIMCON programmes create a sense of dignity, self-sufficiency and pride in themselves. Not only this, they also play an important and integral role in maintaining the ecological balance of their environment. The whole life of trees is to serve. With their leaves, flowers, fruits, branches, roots, shade, fragrance, sap, bark, wood and finally over their ashes and coal, they exist for the purpose of others.

Saving the Sublime—There was a time not very long ago when the hillsides in the birthplace of the Ganga were adorned with thick green foliage. The noble splendour of trees was spellbinding. Colonel Pearson, quoted by Atkinson in his Himalayan Gazetteer, was overwhelmed by the sight and exclaimed:

> "It would be difficult to adequately describe the enormous seas of the Chir forest which lines its (Jumna's) banks. In that the trees must be numbered not by the thousands but by hundreds of thousands, and many of them are of huge size.

Atkinson himself confirmed this and has written:

> " In many parts of the country they (conifers) occur in unbroken masses extending over many miles and present a scene of magnificent grandeur unknown elsewhere. As recently as fifty years back the trees shading the Ganga in its infancy had prompted a Swiss trekker to sigh in ecstacy, 'Never have I seen such variety of trees on this shady side of the Birahi Valley'."

The majestic sight of tall pointed pines from which hung festoons of wild vines and fine specimens of chestnuts, walnuts and oaks as well as bamboo groves were enough to send any visitor into raptures. Holdsworth, who was my Principal of Islamia College Peshawar, NWFP (Present Pakistan) in 1937-39, and was a great Mountaineer who accompanied Smythe on the famous Kamet expedition of 1931 testifies in his journal to "sprawling, aromatic junipers and bigger bush rhododendrons, graceful white birch trees and the dark gothic spires of silver fir and spruce". These were seen with thick stands of deodar and long-leaved pines. Like the lush forests, flowering meadows have been a marvellous feature ornamenting the birth place of Ganga. With good reason these alpine pastures have been named the garden of gods. Not one but many valleys of flowers nestle on the banks of frolicking sisters of the Ganga. The fragrance of exotic blooms often proves intoxicating and the entire stretch of land is identified as the Gandhmadan- mountains of fragrance. It is here that the Brahmkamal (Lily of Heaven) grows in profusion in the shadow of Kedarnath and in the vicinity of Hemkund. Another comparatively rarer flower contributing to the riot of colours is the blue poppy which had bedazzled Frank Smythe. Smythe confessed "In all my mountain wanderings I had not seen a more beautiful flower than this primula. The fine raindrops clung to its soft petals like galaxies of seed pearls and frosted its leaves with silver." All along the water course one can enjoy the splashes of scarlet Buransh (rhododendron) which is an integral part of the Uttarakhand's cultural heritage and is celebrated in many a folk song.

Alas! All this is a thing of the past. Reckless deforestation has denuded the playground of the Ganga and her sisters. Ugly scars threaten to become festering sores and can play havoc with the fragile ecosystem of the entire Himalayan region. It is true that some stretches of woodland have managed to survive and give us some idea 'In the deep cut gorges of Garhwal of 'all the gradual changes which spread from the tropics to the poles' telescoped within a few miles displaying the bounties of nature carelessly spread out up the vertical hillside. However, it is impossible not to notice the destruction of forest cover. Also the ravages of Forest Fires in many areas.

The flowering meadows too with the forest suffered great ravages at the hands of selfish profiteers sometimes ignorant villagers and graziers and careless tourists have imperilled the lovely vast grassland near Rudranath. Nature was inviolate as long as it was sanctified. With encroaching modernisation this does not seem sufficient protection for our valuable heritage in the Himalayas.

All hope is, however, not lost. There is growing awareness of eco developmental issues and the call for conservation is coming from the grass roots. Given a brief respite nature may yet recuperate and nurse the once green hills of the Ganga back to health. At present there is a great deal of concern about pollution control on this great river. We may all pause to ponder whether the river can be kept in good health if its source and environs in the Himalaya are allowed to degenerate.

Quoting Dr. M.S. Swaminathan, "We are fortunate to have abundant sunlight throughout the year. Even in eastern India, in the month of July/ August, the incidence of sunlight seldom goes below 400 calories/cm^2/ day.

To summarise the state of our agricultural and ecological or greening balance sheet, we are endowed with considerable ecological diversity, a large volume of tapped and untapped sources of water, abundant sunlight, and large plant, animal and human populations. Our liabilities, apart from those caused by population growth and aberrant weather, mostly arise from improper use and management of these resources. Attempts to promote synergy, which is the only mechanism which can lead to rapid progress from small resources, have been few and halting. Our urgent needs hence are first, to develop and introduce in each ecological area a production technology which will lead to increased productivity based predominantly on the use of renewable resources. We will have to learn to produce more and more vegetation from less and less land. Secondly, we need to develop and introduce educational tools which will help to impart the relevant technical skills to illiterate peasantry and which will enable educated youth to become catalysts of rural change. Finally, we need to develop and spread management and organisational techniques which will help those living in absolute poverty to overcome their handicaps and obtain their share of the fruits of agricultural and rural advance.

Major Farming and Greening Systems

The following are a few of the major farming systems which need attention particularly in the Indian Himalayas where land is a limiting factor in expanding production:

(a) Multiple Cropping Systems in Irrigated Areas
(b) Rain-Fed farming
(c) Orchards and Garden Land Cropping
(d) Mixed and Inter-cropping
(e) Kitchen Gardening
(f) Agro-forestry
(g) Mixed Farming

Ecological Dharma

In many spiritual traditions, beautiful words have been spoken in promising the glory of Nature. Yet the deep meaning of these words have been forgotten and our consciousness is no longer shaped by the high precepts of the Vedas and other scriptures. Indeed, our consciousness and action have been shaped by the command and imperatives of how to manipulate Nature to our advantage; often with disastrous consequences. Therefore a radical and a spiritual revolution is needed to bring out the seeds of "Ecological Consciousness and Ecological Dharma" to full fruition.

Dharma has many aspects, many layers many depths. In our times, DHARMA must be extended to include our CARE for MOTHER EARTH, OUR LAND & WATER CARE. We have to make the New Millenium one of Sanity, Harmony and Peace. One of the changes we need to make is within ourselves, namely, to realize that many of the old precepts will have to be given a new lease of life. THUS Eco-Dharma is a new awareness of what our present World and Future generations require for a meaningful existence.

ECO-DHARMA is a CALL TO ACTION to protect the beauty and sustainability of the physical world including the SACRED HIMALAYAS which is our cradle, our vessel, the source of our spiritual and physical substance including the source of many of our rivers.

The HIMALAYAN MEDITATIONS AND HYMNS composed by me and my colleague and friend Prof. Henryk Skolimowski, including "Ode to Himalayas". The main aim of Eco-Dharma, applied to the

Himalayan Region, is to make ourselves sacred while taking all creation with us. Thus the Project, the Programme, the Mission, the dream of "*Rejuvenating & Greening Himalayas*" is born as a part of the "LAND AND WATER CARE MOVEMENT", with "the support and blessings of Soil Conservation Society of India with its 2700 Members brought up in the tradition and technology of Soil and Water Conservation, M.S. Swaminathan Research Foundation, also Uttaranchal and Himachal Land and Water Care Movements with the cooperation of the people of the Himalayas and supported by various Regional, National and International organisations. This is also an appeal to all concerned to make it a People's Movement an Ecological Dharma Movement. How to bring this about is spelled out in the following pages.

Task of Greening the Himalayas & their Rejuvenation is formidable but possible and achievable

- As a People's Movement through the land and Water Care Movement.
- As a spiritual and physical action—through tree planting by. Rishi Kumars of Parmarth Niketan, Rishikesh and other Youth, Volunteers and People such as follows.
  * Himalayan Volunteers for Planting Care and Management
    • UN Volunteers
    • International Volunteers
    • NRI Volunteers
    • VOLAGS/NGO Volunteers
    • School Planting Program (Participants, teachers and students jointly with TFL and various participating schools and colleges).
  * Volunteers—Brigades in the name of Dignatories
    • Mahatma Gandhi Tree Planting Brigade (or Himalaya Greening Brigade)
    • Nehru Tree Planting Brigade (or Himalaya Greening Brigade)
    • Pant, Tree Planting Brigade (or Himalaya Greening Brigade)
    • And other Dignitaries—Tree Planting Brigades.
* Tissue Culture Technology for preparation of plantlets.
  • Agrigene International (Dr. Dharam Sharma)
  • Few additional Tissue Culture Labs such as

- SHIMLA, H.P.
- HIMCON, Ranichauri, Garhwal, Uttaranchal
- Sitla, Bhimtal, Kumaon
- Pantnagar Agriculture University, Tissue Culture Lab
- INHERE Proposed Tissue Culture Lab, Masi, Almora Distt.
- On going and active tissue culture lab of Tehri, led by Dr. Dharam

* Poly House Cultures for Maturing Plants
* Let Us Form/Revived Clubs in various parts of the Himalayan Region
  - Millions of Trees Clubs
  - Lakhs of Trees Clubs
  - Thousands of Trees Clubs
  - Association of people for plant, Nurseries in their backyards and marketing analyst users and grades such as of HIMCON and farmers around.
* Aerial Seeding Programme
  - Muniji Task Force (Proposed by Swami Chidanand Saraswati) (Muniji)
  - Dr. Dulcep Matthai Task Force
  - Pilot Commander Parvin Singh Tung Task Force
  - AVM Suresh Sawhney, Task Force
* It is hoped to continue the advise of above for a consolidated Aerial Seding program hopefiilly with the help/advise of Maj. General Vinod Saighal (Retd.) & others in Ministry of Defence, GOI
* Medicinal Plants, Nurseries, Plantation and
  - CARE—Semi Processing Network of NGOs + Processing by Maharshi Ayurved, Dabur Group Enterpreneur in Pant Nagar and around Rishikesh.
  - HIMCON—Swasthya Vatika
  - GANGA KINARE RISHIKESH—PARMARTH NIKETAN
  - CHIRAG
  - INHERE
  - SWATI
  - SHAIKSHNIK GRAMONNATI SAMITI
  - FNN—DehraDun and ONGC
  - Other interested NGOs
* Involvement of Devoted and Retired Foresters
  - Volunteers

- Forestry Centres—Nurseries
- Training Institute—Colleges
- Guidance of Shri C.L Bhatia, Retd. IG Forests, GOI
- Involvement of Prof. Produyt Bhattacharjee, IIFM, Bhopal and Indian Trainees of NTFP—Non Timber Forest Products courses
- Dr. K.D. Singh, FAO Sr. Officer (Forestry Economics Retd.)

* Involvement of Retired Horticulturists
Horticulture Stations, Nurseries, Training Institutes specially
- Dr. Harbans Singh
- Dr. K.L. Chopra
- Other Horticulturists who offer their services

* A Management and Care Task Force—Preferably Girls/Females from Uttaranchal who care for all plants. Leader—HIMCON Trustee Ms. Radha Bhatt, MAHILA SAMAKHYA LEADER Ms. Kusum Rawat.

* Army Eco Task Force—Advice of Lt. Gen.(Retd.) Lalit Kumar Singh

* Eco Monitor Society—Maj. Gen. Vinod Saighal

* Training Programs
- School and College curriculum must have Tree Planting and Caring Schedule
- Prepare a Website—Involve the Media
- Most Wastelands must be planted
  - National Wasteland Development Board
  - Land Resources Dept. of Ministry of Rural Development
  - SPWD—Society for Promotion of Wasteland Development
  - DRDO—District Rural Development Officer of various Himalayan Dist.

* Learn From Canada/USA—Countries of Trees and Forests.
- Canadians—Please Join, Collaborate and support this Greening Movement
- As advised by Dr. M.S. Swaminathan, consult and interact with Dr. Bhujabal Indo-Canadian Environment Facility
- Connection with Canadians with Environment Focus
  - Mr. Ranjit Kumar ED-FIT (Retd.)
  - Betsy McGregor, Deputy Chief
  - Anupam Bagchi, Director IVAN-Indian Volunteer Action Network, Toronto Canada

* Learn from USA specially California, its Plant Nurseries and Universities

* Plants For Greening Himalayas
  - A. High Altitude Plants (+5000' amsl)
    - Deodar
    - Oak—Rhododendron
    - Nut Fruits—specially Walnuts
    - Bhojpatra
    - Special pines
    - Plain trees (Chinar)
    - (varieties from Canada)
    - Selected Medicinal Plants
    - Selected. Temperate Fruits
  - B. Middle Altitude Level Plants (3000'-5000' asml)
    - Nut Fruits (Almonds and other nuts)
    - Temperate Fruits (peaches, pears, apples, kiwi, plums)
    - Fuel, *Fodder*, Multipurpose, specially Mulberry, Trees
    - Bushes through Fodder Trees and other
    - Grasses and Legumes, promote dairy training
    - Medicinal Plants
    - Selected citrus like lemon
  - C. Lower Attitude Plants (Below 3000' × 12 Acre farm such as associated with Parmarth Niketan) Medicinal Plants being planted + other areas offered (H.M. Vyas) and Dehra Dun (ONGC land)—FNN
    - Santji—which has following plants to be promoted
    - Sanjan (Drumstick)
    - Amla
    - Neem
    - Tulsi
    - Jamun
    - Imli
- Sub Tropical Fruits
  - Mango
  - Litchi (Kumkum, Rangard Area+ D
  - Guava
  - Lemon
  - Orange—Tangerine
  - Grape Fruit
  - Mulberry
  - Selected Medicinal Plants
  - Bushes, Grasses, Legumes

* Preparation of Project proposal Hiamalaya Greening Projects (GH 2010) (hopefully funded by ONGC—as a prelude to funding a large Project for Socio-Economic Development.
* Rejuvenating & Greening Himalayas, *PFT*, Project Formulation Team as above.
    - Bio-industrial Watershed I, Garhwal Uttaranchal
      Henval Watershed about 2000 Ha
      Include Medicinal Aromatic Herbal Plant Subproject
      Vegetable, Fruits, Nuts
      Dairy Farming + Processing Project Kumaon Uttaranchal
    - Bio-industrial Watershed II
      Ramgarh Watershed – about 2000 Ha
        - Forestry + NTFP
        - Medicinal Aromatic Herbal Plants
        - Vegetable, Fruit, Nuts
        - Dairy Farming
        - Pre-processing including processing Project involving solar Drying
    - Bio-industrial Watershed III— Himachal
      include III A specially Beas Catchment-III B (ARD Highlands)
    - Renewable Energy Training, Solar Shops (including Aditya Solar Shop)
      Demonstration plus involvement of Students and Youth + Women Involvement in Manufacture and Assembling of Solar Cooker SK 14 and other Models of Equipments as selected by Women and Other Enterpreuner (Guidance of Shri Subodh Kumar & Shri Shanker Banerji).
    - Strengthening Tissue Culture Labs and Ripening Poly House Units
        - Nut Fruits
        - Other Fruits
    - Medicinal, Aromatic, Herbal Plants
        - Bio Fencing Plants
        - Fodder Trees, Bushes, Crops
        - Floriculture
        - Vegetables
    - Training Programme for workers in Nurseries and Students and youth girls and boys including cooperative programmes with International Nurseries such as
        - Richter Herbal Nursery, GoodWood, ONT, Canada

  - California Nurseries such as—Burshell Nursery
  - Medicinal—Aromatic Plant Nurseries in India
  - People's and Association Nurseries in various parts of Himalayas.
- Water Harvesting Programme Including Spring Rejuvenation
  - People is Programme
  - Roof Water Harvesting
  - Fresh Drinking Water Programme
  - Promote "Fresh Water For India's Children and Nature– Learning From Local –Level Approaches –April 1998)+ International Year for Fresh Water 2003.
- Aerial Seeding Programme
  - Jointly with Ministry of Defence
  - Co-ordinator—Dr. Duleep Mathai
  - Associate co-ordinator, Maj. Gen. Vinod Saighal
  - Inaccessible areas in Uttaranchal +
  - Himachal
  - Sikkim
  - West Bengal
  - North East
  - Developing A Technical R & D Team and Servicing Unit for Aerial Seeding
  - Maintenance—Follow up unit for Aerial Seeding
- The Project is going to be called Rejuvenating and Greening Himalayas (GH 2010) A seven year Project—(2003-2010) Goes beyond the Tenth Five Year Plan (Why not?)
  - And request to once management and other donors like Dorabji Tata Transt, Ratan Tata Transt, and others national and international donars.
- Food AID—WFP Programme—As suggested by Dr. M.S. Swaminathan and we need to contact and Prepare Project with Dr. Medrano-WFP National Director in India.

  Building Alliances—Food security and Food aid is an issue that cuts across several Human development needs as well as sectors. It is therefore productive and efficient only when promoted as a sustained collaborative venture. Conscious of the above, World Food Programme (WFP) relies on and values the resources, experience, technical skills, and other strengths that partner agencies and institutions bring to the collaborative process.

WFP—Food Aid is a unique instance of the coming together of the Government, an International agency, and non-governmental organisation to deliberate on a critical challenge before our nation—namely, how to ensure Food for All.

Building on the experience gained in implementing its previous and ongoing interventions. WFP has sharpened the focus of its efforts.

Food for Work
Food for Education
Vulnerable Group Feeding
Disaster Response

Offering food in part or full payment for labour, Food for Work (FFW) contributes through employment generation to poverty alleviation but simultaneously and more importantly to agriculture, tree planting, greening and infrastructure growth as well as disaster mitigation.

- Budgeting unit as part of *PFT–Project Formulation Team of (GH 2010)*
- Mountains India People Forum
  Mobilizing—involving interested People of all parts of the Himalayas
- Fund—Raising Team
  Chairman:
  Advisor: Dr. M.S. Swaminathan, Chairman, Himalaya Task Force 1980 Chairman— M.S. Swaminathan Research Foundation Team: I Senior Officer from Each State involved NGO Forum each state
  NRI Groups from - Indo-American
  - Indo-Canadian
  - Indo-British
  - Indo-European Union
- Requirement of Fund—First Approximation (GH 2010)
  To be prepared by Project Formulation Team
  Operation in the hands of people and NGO's with full cooperation of Govts. concerned and with help of donor agencies.
- GH 2010—Expected Outputs
  More efficient use of solar energy—green cover on wasteland and other lands will reduce/stop soil erosion—benefit in terms

of soil value will need to be evaluated—it will be not less than many tens of crores.

Greening also means increased production, increased employment in Uttaranchal and Himachal additional employment (before and after 2010) in additional thousands. income to farmers/land users in crores.

Water resources—Increased Water in Springs, Streams, Rivulets, Rivers, Lakes Value in terms of tens of crores (Surveys will give exact results)

Additional Production of

- Medicinal and Aromatic Plants
- Forest Products/NTFP
- Fruits and Nuts
- Vegetables
- Flowers.

Annexure 6

Himalaya Task Force-I (1982) Himalayan Expert Group—Executive Summary HTFII (1993) Rejuvenation & Greening of Himalayan (2004) (Details in Annexure 5)

Historical Background

Immediately after independence, the development of Himalayas was taken up on top priority by the first Prime Minister Pt. Nehru. The India Meteorological Department (IMD)brought forward of the idea establishing a High Altitude Research Station for multi-disciplinary research in Himalayas. In 1978, National Committee on Environmental Planning & Coordination from the Department of Science and Technology, under the guidance of Dr. B. P. Pal, sponsored a national seminar on Resources, Development and Environment in the Himalayan Region. The seminar indicated the existence of policy gaps. Most important recommendations made were:

- A high level multidisciplinary group be set up to identify gaps in the ongoing research, design and development pertaining to the Himalayan region and also to identify appropriate financial arrangements for supporting further activities that need to be taken up.
- Initiating a programme on long-term research into functioning and dynamics of the Himalayan Ecosystems.

In 1981 a Task Force for the Study of Eco-Development in the Himalayan Region was formed under the chairmanship of Dr. M. S.

Swaminathan, Member, Planning Commission as urgent need was realized to balance economic development with the imperatives of environmental conservation and to formulate realistic and manageable programmes for tackling the inter-linked problems involved in eco-development of the Himalayan Region. The terms of reference of the Task Force were:

1. To consider the proposal for a centre for Himalayan Regional Studies to be established with the participation of the universities of the region and to make suitable recommendations in this regard.
2. To identify the ecological/environmental problems that require study on a priority basis, recommend the university departments and research institutions for undertaking these studies, and to draw up the guidelines for such studies.
3. To take note of the major environmental activities going on in the States falling in the Himalayan region, to assess the extent of their impact on the hill ecosystem and to suggest suitable modifications.
4. To recommend the national and State level arrangements and interventions necessary in respect of plan formation, funding legislative enforcement and administrative machinery needed to overcome the ecological/environmental problems of the Himalayan region.
5. To identify any inter-State dimensions involved in eco-development and to suggest measures for dealing with such issues. The above task force constituted subgroups on Coordinated Research for Action Oriented Basis. Post Harvest Technology, Transport Planning, and Socio-economic Development for an elaborate exercise involving specialized experiences for issue of proper guidelines

Again in 1992, Planning Commission felt the need to constitute an Expert Group to formulate a National Policy on Himalayas for Integrated Development under the Chairmanship of Dr. S. Z. Qasim, Member (Environment and Science & Technology), Planning Commission. The terms of reference of the Expert Group were as follows:

1. To make recommendations towards development of a national policy on the Himalayas for an integrated mountain development with a view to ensuring that the entire region is used to the best advantage of our country
2. To make an assessment of scientific , environmental and natural resources of the Himalayan region.

3. To identify specific areas of activity which fit into the ecology of the Himalayan region and are consistent with the socio-economic character of the region.
4. To estimate the carrying capacity of environmentally sensitive areas within the Himalayan region
5. To suggest suitable organizational mechanism to implement theproposed policy.

Major recommendations of the Expert Group were:

1. To establish a Himalayan Development Authority (HDA)under the Prime Minister to assure continued high level intervention/or integrated development of Himalayas.
2. To create a National Himalayan Environment Development Fund (NHEDF) to promote the linkage in natural sciences with social sciences and to guide the operation of national policy for integrated development of the region.

During the last two decades the problems related to harmonious socio-economic development of the Himalayas have been engaging the attention of the policy makers, planners and all those interested in the preservation of the environment. There seems to be a general agreement that the ecology of the Himalayas has been endangered, partly because of the innate feeling that the development process in the region has not adequately met the felt needs of the local population. It has been considered, in this light, that there is a need to enunciate clearly a policy for the integrated development of the region, taking a holistic view of all issues, germane to development and environmental conservation. The Planning Commission, therefore, decided to constitute an Expert Group for a comprehensive examination of the issues and suggest a policy with the framework for an integrated development consistent with the conservation of the fragile ecology of these young mountains.

The Expert Group held several meetings, some in the Himalayan states namely Himachal Pradesh, Uttar Pradesh and Meghalaya and carried out extensive discussions with a wide range of people within governmental and non-government agencies as well as with the individuals. The extracts from these discussions as well as with the individuals have been included as annexures to the report The Group also referred to the previous work on this subject, the policies and plans as reflected in the past plan documents.

That the unique ecology of the Himalayas, which has such an extensive and pervasive influence on the life of our people, needs to be preserved, conserved and qualitatively upgraded is accepted by one and all. Equally, the socio-economic life and the living standards must be improved in the region. The Group has urged in the report that for the environmentally compatible development process of this region, it is necessary to ensure the value of the Himalayas as a part of the total socio-economic development of the entire country, avoiding an "Us and They" syndrome. Nevertheless, the unique character'' of the Himalayas calls for a regionally differentiated approach even when we look at similar kinds of problems elsewhere in the country. The report focusses on the rather special resource endowments of the area and suggests that in launching the measures for the utilisation of these resources for furthering the socio-economic conditions of the people inhabiting the area, the ecology of the area is not impaired.

That this process must be supported by effective research and studies is obvious. Several institutions have in their mandate subjects of immediate concern to the region. What appears to be lacking is an effective forum where these institutions can come together and interact to develop appropriate technology which seek to synthesise the solutions to both environmental and development concerns. The need to build into this excess the experience and wisdom of the local people cannot be over-emphasised, as has been brought out in this report. There has to be a wider consultation and the involvement of the local people so that the plans of action and the programmes address themselves to their aspirations and felt needs.

The report stresses that. given the magnitude of the problems and their distinctness, it may be necessary to create an administrative mechanism for achieving a harmonious integration of environmental preservation and development and for its monitoring. The Group has recommended the setting up of a High Power Himalayan Development Authority (HDA) and the creation of a Himalayan Environment & Development Fund (HDF) to support the innovative actions programmes and studies emerging from the recommendations.

The report seeks to provide an insight into the major problems of the Himalayan region as a whole and recognises that sound socio-economic development is only possible through the active participation of the people in the formulation and implementation of the plans. It is only through a process of sustainable development that poverty can be eradicated and prosperity ushered in.

Annexure 7

Proposed Centres of Activities and Action Programmes in Uttaranchal

Human values promotion or in Hindi "Ache Vichar Jeevan Ka Sar" Promotion of all human values such as truth non-violence peace, right action and love.

I. **Uttaranchal Eco-Tourism Promotion Council**—Uttaranchal is both a religious tourism state as well as part of great inspiration in the Himalayan Region . A Eco- Tourism Council is needed and requires coordination of people, NGO's and Govt. of Uttaranchal.

II. **Narindra Rishi Gardens**—A Uttaranchal premier horticultural display Area between Rishikesh and Narinder Nagar can have a premier horticulture garden with hundreds of types of trees, medicinal aromatic & herbal plants as well as flowers of different types. A resort like Ananda Resort can attract lots of visitors. Chairman: Dr. P.L. Gautam, Vice Chancellor GB Pant University of Agriculture & Technology, Pant Nagar.

III. **HIMCON Scholarship Fund**— to brilliant students in Uttaranchal. Test—Every year 4 students 2 Boys 2 Girls

Some funds are available for the purpose. Test for selection includes academic tests, community participation, working as volunteer & entrepreneur potential are needed. A selection committee is needed to interview & examine all the applicants. It is hoped Govt. of Uttaranchal will support this NGO effort & multiply the number of scholarships for brilliant students.

IV. **Northern Uttaranchal Snow and Glaciers**— Chairman: Dr. Jagdish Bahadur Co-Chairman: Lt. Gen. Sushil Kumar/Nominee of Capt. M.S Kohli A book on Himalayan Snow & Glaciers is already printed (author Dr. Jagdish Bahadur) well known Himalayalogist. A recent visit to Gangotri and discussion with Swami Sundaranand & others show large potential for small & medium lakes & development of forestry and hydropower in the area.

V. **HIMCON—Richters Herbs joint cooperative programme**— at Kaantal Herbal Garden & nurseries.

A joint program of MUTUALITY of Benefits has been worked out by Dr. M.L. Dewan on promotion of medicinal and aromatic herbs with Richters Herb — A Canadian organization for promoting nursuries in Uttaranchal.

VI. **Balbir Mathur Centre for Tree Planting**

Balbir Mathur, Founder Chairman of "Trees for Life" - established in Allahabad, UP & Wichita Kansas, USA is requested to promote tree planting, rejuvenation & greening of Himalayas for promotion of fruit trees in Uttaranchal.

VII. **Uttaranchal Yoga and Dhyan Kendra, Ranichauri**— The Kendra is proposed to be established as per the advice of Chairman, Indian Heritage, Research Foundation (IHRF), Swami Chidananda Swaraswati Muniji, and Shri Manoj Pande, Secretary General, Himalaya Seva Sangh, Rajghat.New Delhi & Trustee of HIMCON &HPSS.

VIII. **Promotion of Renewable Energy**— solar energy, briquetting from biomass, solar architecture etc. are required for Uttaranchal. ARSH Electronics, Tata BP Solar & MNES are all interested in promoting renewable energy in Uttaranchal. Already a Centre is established at Ranichauri which needs to be strengthened by NGO's, & Corporate sectors & People's effort for the above.

IX. **Uttaranchal Association of North America** (UANA)— programme with Himcon and other NGO's for environmental improvement

Chairman: Ajay Rawat, President, UANA, Virginia, USA Co-Chairman: Rajiv Rawat , Toronto, Canada A contact has been made with UANA by Chairman, HIMCON and a program for rejuvenation, greening & environmental improvement of Himalayan region specially Uttaranchal is proposed for UANA support.

X. **Uttaranchal Forest And Horticulture Plants**— A Publication— a model book on the lines of "Forest Plants in Northeastern Ontario" is an inspiration for the above publication for

Uttaranchal. A small committee of qualified, experienced & interested persons is proposed. Following have been approached Dr. K.D. Singh, IFS (UP Cadre), Retd. FAO Sr. Forest Officer with over 25 years experience in many part of India & the world and Shri O.P. Srivastava IFS, Retd.

Shri. S. Bartwal, long time employee of BSI (Botanical Survey of India), Dehra Dun Shri.CS. Raghav, NBPGR, IARI, New Delhi. A Representative from FRI & one from Horticulture Department, Govt. of Uttaranchal will be helpful for the above.

XI. **Uttaranchal Thousand Chaals (Mini lakes) Programme**—Suresh Bhai, Chairman of HPSS - Himalayee Paryavaran Shiksha Sanstha, Lamgaon, Uttarkashi has undertaken over last 20 years construction of chaals (mini lakes) in many parts of Uttaranchal.

XII. **Gram Vikas Jyoti—An outstanding bilingual quarterly**—a magazine for Himalayan rural development(editor Dr. Devinder Sharma). July-September, 2004 issue was Uttaranchal special. The journal needs wider circulation in the rural area with the support from the Govt. NGO's and the people.

XIII. **Himalayan Entrepreneur Training Centre**—At Ranichauri through cooperation of Advisors and Consultants like Dr. P.L. Kaul, Dr. N. Rasul Siddique , Ministry of Food Processing Industries and Shri R.P. Agrawal of SPWD and others.

XIV. **Natural Resource Data Management System**—Maps of Uttaranchal are needed with the support from Dept. of Science & Technology, New Delhi & All India Institute of Soil Survey & Land Use Planning, Nagpur, GOI.

Geographical MAP of Uttaranchal- approved by survey of India and Land use Map of Uttaranchal appanded are applied in the folder.

XV. **Herbal Tea Centre**—it is proposed to be established by HIMCON Jointly with Aarogya & hopefully Cheetal Grand Restaurant at Kanatal/Chamba/Nagini.

XVI. **Honeybee Centre for Uttaranchal**—is proposed at Nagini SABLI and Kanatal with advice from Mr. P.L. Kaul & Amit Dhanuka, Chief Executive, Kejriwal Bee Care India (Pvt) Ltd. with funds from Dewan Foundation.

XVII. **Centre for Training in Medicinal, Aromatic and Herbal Culinary Plants**—

Chairman: S.K. Mishra
Co-Chairman: R.P. Agrawal
Source of Funding : National Medicinal Plant Board
Also preparation of Family Ayurvedic Health Kit

XVIII. **Community Plantation for Prosperous Uttaranchal—**
Chairman: Naresh Kumar
Co-Chairman: Ramanand
On the model of Kot, Chamba block
Also plantation of Stevia in village Pali (already started)

XIX. **Vocational Training Centre**—for vocationalization of environmental careers
Chairman: Dr.V.K. Kediyal (Requested)
Co-chairman: Manoj Pande/Shuba Pande
In general approved by sir Dorab Ji TATA Trust for funding at Sabli village

XX. **Nut Fruit Revolution in Uttaranchal—**
Chairman, Gunjan Jain/Vaisakha Jain
Co-Chairman to be decided. Jains are fourth generation Walnut exporters from J & K having outstanding knowledge & work on nut fruits. It is possible to jointly sponsor the program with the Ministry of Horticulture Uttaranchal and Apeda.

XXI. **Harsil—the heart of inspiring and sacred Himalaya**—located at almost 9000 feet amsl near Gangotri needs large scale Planting of Walnuts, Apples, And Deodar Trees.
Promoter Mr. A.S. Rawat, General Manager, APEDA

XXII. **A proposal/blue print for NGO's becoming self reliant**—Efforts are afoot by HIMCON & some other NGOs in the area to work towards self reliance. They are supported by

a) Kedia Group
b) Flex Food
c) Bio-industrial Watershed Management
d) Food Processing Ministry

XXIII. **Bio Industrial Watershed Management For poverty Alleivation in Uttaranchal—**

Chairman- Prof. J.S. Bali
See Note & Reprt on May 15-16-17 "Seminar at Ranichauri, Hill Campus (Being printed separately)

XXIV. **Food & Fruit Processing Industry**—in selected Districts of Uttaranchal to be promoted jointly with peoples organization and the Ministry of Industries of Uttaranchal Govt.

Chairman: P.L. Kaul (Consultant Advisor)

Co-Chairman: Dr. R.N. Rasul Siddique (Retd. Advisor Ministry of Food Processing)

XXV. **"A Health for All"**—Campaign as advised by Dr. Karan Singh in A.P. Dewan Memorial Lecture at Lajpat Bhavan on 19/9/2004 jointly organized by Naturopathy Division of lajpat Bhavan and Dewan Foundation.

XXVI. **The Himalaya Task Force-III,**—Conservation, Rejuvenation and Development of Himalayan Region, proposal by M.S. Swaminathan Research Foundation, Soil and Water Conservation Society of India, National Land Care Movement for Food Water and Livelihood Security and Himalaya Consortium for Himalaya Conservation on behalf of Himalayan NGOs and Himalayan Communities as People's Movement submitted to Planning Commission, Government of India on 31 August, 2004 by Dr. M.S. Swaminathan.

Annexure 8

Improved Water Mills: Answer to Power Generation in Himalayas

Problem/Need Assessment

The Western Himalayas are dotted with rivers, rivulets, streams, lakes etc. Larger rivers are being tamed for electricity generation through huge hydel projects. Micro-hydel projects and small gharats (traditional water mills), which work on run-of-the-stream power, have also been successful. This region is rich in having gharats developed by local inhabitants thousands of years ago using simple techniques and which served them well. In the simplest water mills, energy differentials due to the Himalayan terrain are used to produce shaft power primarily used for grain milling. Later, more complex machines were also used for spinning and carding. The ancient designs did not pose any major problems earlier but now, with the advent of diesel/electric flour mills and also the increased workload of villagers due to various reasons, the low output of the gharats, although at a cheaper rate, has become a major deterrent causing villagers to abandon them. Another factor is the limited function of the gharat, as grain grinders only; for rice husking and oil expelling, the villagers have to resort either to manual labour or use the services of diesel/electric mills. It is estimated that there are over 5,00,000 watermills (Gharats) in the Indian Mountain Regions. These "Gharats" can lead to potential power generation of 2500 MW/hr or 40 million units of electricity and a cash generation of Rs. 1200 million per hour.

Approach/Strategy

Studies conducted by HESCO, Dehradun revealed that the gharats can become functional, using appropriate technology, and can be improved in terms of output/efficiency and also be rendered multifunctional. With little effort, these improved gharats can then be made an important hub of the rural economy.

Technology Package

The following modifications have been made to the traditional water mill:

- High velocity of water makes the surface rough and causes excessive turbulence in water flow at the flume, leading to loss of energy by friction. To avoid such losses, Gl sheet covering the inner surface of the flume was placed.
- The wooden runner has been replaced by a cast steel runner. The diameter of the runner is 500 mm. It has 16 blades. The complete runner is of one piece casting and weighs about 32 kg.
- The flat blades of the water wheel on which the water jet strikes have been provided a curvature, so that maximum pressure energy could be harnessed. This would prevent splashing losses, besides lessening disturbances to the incoming water jet.
- A bearing has been introduced at the bottom of the water wheel allowing more free rotation.

Economics

The additional input involved is Rs. 4500-6000, which improves the efficiency upto 140 per cent. The costs recovered or income from this technology is locally considered m terms of bhagwari i.e. part of the flour is given by the customer to the owner as payment for the service. Such intervention has led to a large number of abandoned water mills being made operational to generate cheap power by harnessing energy from the thousands of tiny streams in the Himalayan region. It has been reported that a water mill, which was used only to grind wheat and maize, can generate up to 5 KW of electricity, more than enough for the small village comprising nine tribal families. Considering an employment opportunity of 3 persons per watermill, it is estimated that about 15 lakh people can be benefited by technological upgradation of the 5 lakh watermills existing in the Himalayan region.

TRADITIONAL WATER MILL AND ITS IMPROVEMENT

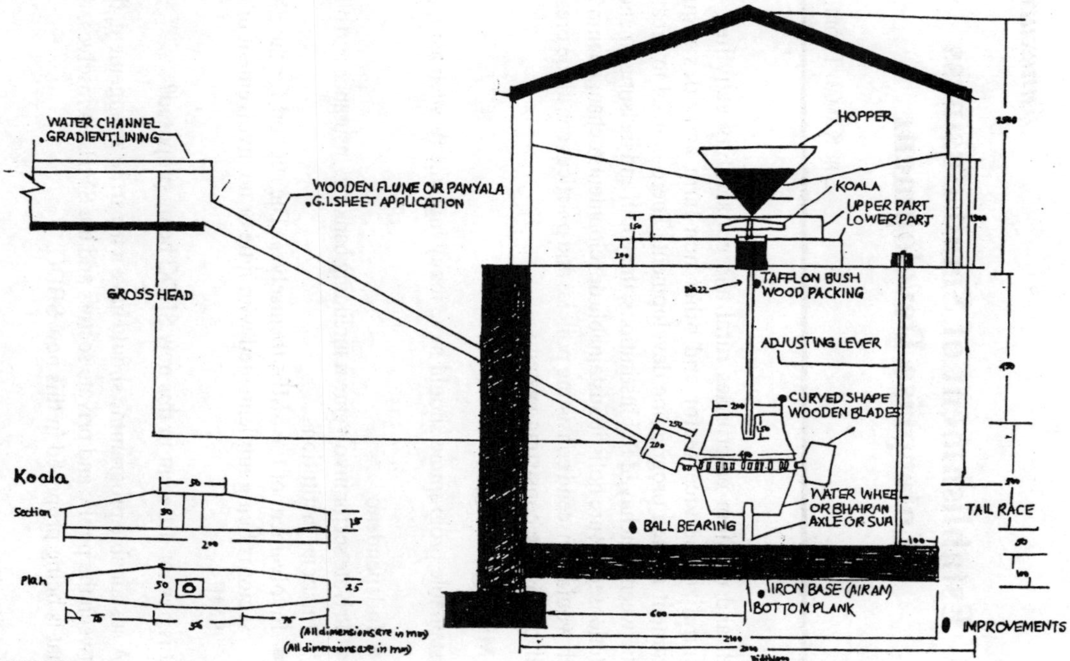

Courtsey: HESCO

Annexure 9

Establishment of Small Business Enterprise Development

DR. KAMAL TAORI *IAS*

Small and medium enterprises rural and cottage tiny activities, the decentralized service sector and other non-farm activities require investment related programme development. There is need to create a link between Panchayad Raj Institutions, the youth and insisting financial institutions to ensure holistic sustainable development A changed mindset which would transcend consisting policies and practices can alone present a collapse o f the consisting systems.

The Missing Linkages

A sustainable programme should have many ingredients such as:

- Independency
- Private sector involvement including banking, insurance and other financial institutions
- Involvement of the SMEs themselves. The support for the SME sector is being implemented with little or no involvement of the SMEs.

What is new or different in this new SBDC being proposed?

A sustainable programme should have a tripartite arrangement, that is between the public and private sectors and the SMEs themselves, this is what is being proposed in this new SBDC.

(a) It tries to examine experiences and lessons of similar other SBDCs.
(b) It looks into those oxygen-like points which will help like new

SBDC to programme holistically, successful establishments keeping in mind the need for self-sustenance, replication and long utility span.

(c) It takes into consideration the diverse conditions of India the venture to start in the first year which will be mutually beneficial in a win-win situation.

(d) Apart from different areas this project constantly looks for challenges and merging investment areas, learned lessons from the past and looks at neglected target groups, neglected areas and total hidden investible potential powers of the area.

(e) It tries to examine holistically lessons and actions for Gross Domestic Product (GDP), Per Capital Income and Human Development Indices (HDI) issues from multidisciplinary angle with viability, shift from charity to creativity, capacity and confidence building.

(f) It believes in rcplicable model development by using existing infrastructure, knowledge and skills of the local area.

Some issues/principles to govern and guide the new SBDC—Oxygen points:

(i) It must have minimum staff, but have more practical consultants.

(ii) It must be governed by market oriented development and provide total consultancy.

(iii) It must work for a total confidence building of the entrepreneur and follow-up.

(iv) It must learn to work with enterpreuners, bankers, insurance company, marketing company, state and local government, community and groups, non residents, private trainers, local and international NGOs, retired experts etc.

(v) Issues in incentive and rewards system, policy options etc. must have an important role to play. This could be developed so that success of business is measurable *not* only in materialistic terms as a holistic business of balancing life.

(vi) Efforts must be to use under-utilized infrstructure, local expertise and local resources so that consultancy is cost effective, relevant easily available.

(vii) Lessons of closures, non-performing assets, redundancy of technology etc. must be used during consultancy.

(viii) Local leaders as low *cost* practical consultants cadre (LCPC) and active involvement of the lowest level of governance will be utilized to make the business of SBDC supportive and based efficient, upon the uniqueness of areas such as Hidden Investible Power Potential Organisation (HIPPO), Known Investible Power Potential Organisation (KIPPO) and Threatening Investible Power Potential Organisation (TIPPO) of the rural people.

(ix) Keep in mind the need of "No Good Pop" or "Need of good developmental policing of policy makers". Issues in policy making to suit areas and people will be kept as priority action.

(x) Emerging investment, employment and immediate concern areas of today and future-areawise, peoplewise, industry service and business (ISB) sectorwise-need constantly revision, upgradation and dissemination.

(x) Oxygen point is to encourage lower to higher *and* small to medium upgradation of enterprise.

(xi) Policy will be to have memorandum of understanding and letters of joint working on win-win basis with various groups including government, nongovernment and semi-governments.

The likely buyers or customers of our SBDC are likely to be in the following categories:

(a) Areawise-local government, community, enterpreuners, other stakeholders, community development leaders and rural and urban planners.

(b) Programmewise-training, marketing, educators, computer users, local skill and potential based users.

(c) Projectwise in the ISB sectors we may have industry business or services or clusters or consultancies for export projects.

(d) Service of retired experts of public administration, finance, taxation, banking, leasing, lawyers, etc. can be utilized efficiently and cost effectively.

(e) Rural non-farm or rural industrialisation or ISB sector has lot of potential in many countries where SBDC has not past base.

(f) Hence there is urgent need to explore and develop systems by Developing organisational structure to meet the challenge of our time; other areas of potential include impact assessment consultancy, organisational networking and marketing of experience and policy for popularizing self-employment, rural development and new business development and preparing standardized training capsules.

Nature of Activity and Target Group

The new SBDC will take on the role of a facilitator instead of a "One Stop" shop.

Services to be provided

The following services would be provided, namely:

- Problem analaysis;
- Exploration of HIPPO-KIPPO-TIPPO;
- Training and development;
- Consultancy;
- Sensitisation programmes;
- Study tours;
- Research and Development and information sharing;
- Information and brochure; and
- Linkage with financial institutions (e.g. banks and insurance companies).

Target Group

The target group for the proposed SBDC is as follows:

1. Self-employed rural consultants and NGOs;
2. SMEs;
3. State and Local Governments;
4. Local Chiefs or herdsmen;
5. The Private Sector; and
6. Training institutions, Bankers, Government, Panchayati Raj Institution

The indicators of holistic development or signs of sustainable development would require very serious examination including policies, lobbying, clarity, brevity and speed. The role of taxation, technology, central support system, rewarding good models, clusters, low cost practical consultancy, marketing issues, financing attitudes and future development models will need cluster approach. His organized sector has many institutions to support it. In the unorganized also there is need to look for common interest, win-win areas, where general interest of not only individuals, communities but the state and centre could be understood in totality. This is a difficult job but needs to be taken up seriously without any waste.

Panchayat Raj Institutions at all levels would benefit immensely if adequate measures for effective servicing and consultancy would be reconsidered. Needless to say all departments of any Government will have to hire the services of this class to make themselves relevant timely and non-partisan. The common points or oxygen points needs to be build up as a part of the exploration for holistic sustainable development.

Annexure 10

The Child Support and Vocational Training Programme

MANOJ PANDE, SURESH BHAI AND M.L. DEWAN

Mission

A programme for the Mountain Youth & Children in the year 2002, which was declared as the year of Mountains has been initiated as a result of sustained dialogue and consultation with the local communities, social action groups and activists while actively working on various community development programmes for almost a decade in the region.

Although there are various programmes and projects run by NGO's and Governmental organisations to uplift and enhance the status of Women, Youth and Children in the Himalayan region, there is a large section of population which is left uncared and unattended by any social support or security mechanism. This section largely comprises of children belonging to the poor and marginalized communities that have been deprived of adequate job or employment opportunities with no or very little cultivable land belonging to them. As a result there is a lot of pressure on all members of the family including children to get involved in so one the other kind of economic activity for their survival. This pressure snatches away the innocent childhood from these children, denies them the basic right to education and forces them into a cruel world of hard labour.

We feel that there is a definite linkage between the social, economic and environmental pressures that the Himalayan communities are going through due to faulty developmental pattern adopted by our market driven consumerist society and the sufferings that the poor and marginalized women and children are going through. We feel it important to sensitize the community and prepare them by making them understand these linkages and organize them to assist this marginalized section of the Himalayan community.

Some Youth & Children are left with no family support system and are forced by circumstances to work under difficult conditions, often exploited by their distant relatives or employer. Their condition is really pitiable and needs some organized external support system to help them come out of this trap. Hence we have initiated a Child Support Programme which is gradually building up its resources and capacities to be able to extend a helping hand to these children in need.

Need

It is strongly being felt that there is an urgent need to sensitize the local communities and draw their support to facilitate Action Programme in the Himalayan region for the deprived Youth & Children. It is important that the Civil Society in the region realizes and acknowledges that these children and youth that are left unattended and exploited is the future generation which can contribute in the development of the region. The intention is to develop this programme as a joint venture with active participation of the local communities, the existing voluntary organisations/NGO's and the Government.

Objectives

The Child Support and Vocational Training programme intends to support the most underprivileged and needy children of our society. Presently we are focusing this programs for children in the Himalayan communities starting from Uttaranchal region in the central Himalayas. The broad objectives of this program are as follows:

- Initiating a campaign to sensitize the Himalayan communities towards the plight of marginalized and needy children.
- To identify needy children with the active support of local community.
- To built a network of Voluntary organisations, NGO's, Activists groups and Village level bodies to develop a Child Support group.
- Providing necessary supports depending upon the individual cases.
- Drawing supports from the local community to assist the child in need.

- Regular visits and follow-up of the Support Groups formed in the different areas.
- Initiating non-conventional education and vocational training programs for these children.
- To create a larger support system through individual child and family sponsorship programmes.

Activities Undertaken

With the support of Voluntary Organisations like Himalaya Seva Sangh (HSS), Himalayee Paryavaran Shiksha Sansthan (HPSS), Himalaya Consortium for Himalayan Conservation (HIMCON) this program has been activated and some supports have been mobilised for running *26 Pre-Primary and Basic schools and Vocational trainings* for Weaving, Sewing, Computer, Typing and Horticulture in the remote villages of Nanital, Udham Singh Nagar, Tehri and Uttarkashi Districts in the newly formed state of Uttaranchal.

Vision for Sustainability of the Programme

We intend to run the *Child Support and Vocational Training Programme* with a cooperation and support of individuals and organisations by developing an extensive network of Sponsors for our programmes and activities. Apart from mobilizing financial support from people across the world, we would also involve the local communities in contributing and successfully executing the programme. The programme is being planned in such a way that marketing of the produce where applicable should earn some income so as to ultimately (in a few years) make this vocational training self-sustaining.

Annexure 11

Clinging to the Earth as an Ecological Prayer

HENRYK SKOLIMOWSKI*

There have been many religions proclaiming the unity between man and God. There have been some proclaiming the unity of all humankind. Yet most past religions are partial. They include only those who believe in their creed, not all humankind. We need a universal religion, which will include all human beings, and perhaps all beings under its wings. Buddhism comes probably closest to this kind of religion, as it proclaims reverence for the blade of grass and reverence for all other beings. Yet the followers of other religions would be taken aback if Buddhism were announced as a universal religion, and not their own. Thus, we need to tread gently when we wish to proclaim a universal religion. Whether a universal religion that encompasses all people will emerge in the future remains to be seen. Perhaps such a religion will not emerge at all. And instead, we shall relish a variety of religions, as we have relished a variety of foods in various parts of the globe. It would be indeed boring to have one kind of food throughout the planet. Perhaps it would be equally undesirable to have one kind of religion.

What is of utmost importance is not whether nominally we have one religion or many, but how existing religions inspire us to goodness, reverence, respect, cooperation, compassion, altruism. The point is not *what* the various religions speak on these matters, but *how* they actually guide, inspire, direct, and sustain us. On the whole, they do not sustain and guide us very well. We need to renew our religious roots in all religious traditions. How we do that is an enormous problem. Going back to the scriptures and then pointing out that all right precepts are there is not the most profitable way. We know what is in the scriptures.

* World Well Known Eco Philospher Based in Warsaw, Poland

We also know that what is there is not sufficient. We need to infuse the scriptures with new light and new energy.

There is a new project that is emerging for all humanity. This project has profound religious consequences. This project could renew our vision and recharge our spiritual energy. This project could be part of the spiritual renewal of all religions—without taking specific characteristics of these religions. What I have in mind is as follows. To worship God in our times truly is to save the planet. If we lose the environment, we lose God. Healing the planet and healing ourselves is spiritual work of the first magnitude in our day and age. Whatever our race and religion, ecology binds us all together. Thus ecology is the religious project of our times. The idea of redemption acquires a new meaning—it means redeeming the world by healing the earth. We need to emphasize: healing the earth is the spiritual work of our time. To understand religious devotion is to recognize that all religions are forms of worship of the beauty and integrity of the planet.

This could be a point of departure and of renewal for many spiritual traditions. This could be the point of our unity. And what could be more worthy of our unitary purpose than working together to save our earth and implicitly ourselves—for without the vibrant earth we shall cease to exist.

Spirituality is also, and has always been, the realisation of our inner potential, the actualisation of the inner god within us. We need to treat each other according to what we can potentially become: divine lights uplifting ourselves and helping others to heal, to integrate, to become more reverential. Working on ourselves to release and articulate our inner divinity and working in the outside world to heal the earth are *complementary* aspects of ecological spirituality. Instead of a quietistic form of spirituality, favored by many religions, we are advocating a *participatory* form of spirituality, a spirituality which resolves itself in the acts of healing in everyday life.

Part of this new spirituality, which I call ecological spirituality, is a new kind of prayer, which I call ecological prayer. Praying to Absolute Deities endowed with divine attributes is well and good. But to save the integrity and beauty of creation, we need to be engaged in *ecological prayer.* Ecological prayer is acting out the ecological dimension of our existence, is bringing all beings into the well of our well-wishing, is the meditative attitude of our daily action which helps to heal on all levels of being; is thus a form of ethics in action, which is based on solidarity and on compassion, and which brings about a larger harmony in the long run.

During my dialogue with Tibetan Buddhists at Dharamsala, some time ago, I chose as my main subject Ecological Dharma. I have proposed that Dharma in our times acquires a distinctly green shade, an ecological dimension. It is not sufficient now-a-days to take care of your spiritual well being, to care about your religious community. You must extend this care to the entire earth. For this is your dwelling, your temple, your Sangha, your vessel in which spiritual attainments can be perfected on your way to Bodhisattva.

I have pointed out during my symposium with the Tibetan Buddhists that we cannot be too detached nowadays. The *principle of* non-attachment is of course beautiful in its ramifications. Yet we need to re-examine its meaning, precisely because of the importance of Ecological Dharma. We cannot be too detached from the Earth, because then we can lose the Earth all together. We need to cling to the Earth. Now the idea of clinging to the Earth and of the questioning the principle of non-attachment alarmed many of the learned monks present at the symposium. The opposition to this idea had become so heated that I was bound to say, "You seem to be very attached to your principle of non-attachment." The monks got my point immediately. Needless to say, we have to tread very carefully when we propose clinging to the earth and when we propose a re-examination of the principle of non-attachment. Yet the main point I wish to make is this: We need to cling to the earth much more passionately than we cling to traditional scriptures. This point applies to all religions. Clinging to the scriptures while the earth is sinking may not be the right way of participating in divinity.

As it is clear, ecological spirituality has a distinctive practical edge. It continually asks the following questions: How do you work on yourself so that you heal within? So that you heal your mind? So that you become a source of health and support for others? How do you help to heal the diseased educational system, the malfunctioning and carcinogenic social and political structures? How do you help to heal the earth in your immediate vicinity? How does your lifestyle help to maintain the equilibrium in distant parts of the world by not contributing to frivolous over-consumption?

All these questions are practical questions and spiritual questions at the same time. They require a new kind of awareness, a new kind of commitment, and a new kind of yoga. What I am describing is a common project for our times. What I am describing is a religious project for our times. What I am proposing is a universal religious project for our times. Let us unite together in the common service to Mother Earth, in one stupendous ecological prayer. Then gods will help us. We need to dance with Shiva a new ecological dance of catharsis, so that Shiva dances with us this ecological dance. We need to engage in Ecological Dharma, so that the Buddhas bless us in this new holy act. We need to help God-of the Hebrews, Christians, and Muslims, so that God helps us to make God's earth green and blessed again.

I do not wish to question strength and the enduring light of past spiritual traditions. Yet these traditions were generated in specific historical circumstances, and in response to problems which are so different from our own. The world was relatively simple in those ancient times, ours is tortuously complex.

The Divine has spoken to human beings in many tongues and its voice included many themes. Now it speaks to us with the voice of ecological awareness as it prompts us to safeguard the integrity of our own lives, which means the integrity of our spiritual lives.

LIFE IS......

- ➢ LIFE IS A CHALLENGE - MEET IT
- ➢ LIFE IS A GIFT - ACCEPT IT
- ➢ LIFE IS A SORROW - OVERCOME IT
- ➢ LIFE IS A DUTY - PERFORM IT
- ➢ LIFE IS A GAME - PLAY IT
- ➢ LIFE IS A SONG - SING IT
- ➢ LIFE IS A PROMISE - FULFILL IT
- ➢ LIFE IS LOVE - ENJOY IT
- ➢ LIFE IS SMILE - GIVE IT TO OTHERS
- ➢ LIFE IS AN EXPERIENCE - SHARE IT WITH OTHERS
- ➢ LIFE IS AN KNOWLEDGE - DISTRIBUTE IT
- ➢ LIFE IS A CHARITY - DONATE IT

Taken from "a Practical Guide to ageless Mind" by Prof. B.B. Puri, 2004

Annexure 12

International Year of Mountains, 2002

(*Resolution adopted by the General Assembly*)

1. *Proclaims* the year 2002 as the International Year of Mountains;
2. *Invites* the Food and Agriculture Organisation of the United Nations to serve as the lead agency for the International Year of Mountains, in collaboration with Governments, the United Nations Environment Programme, the United Nations Development Programme, the United Nations Educational, Scientific and Cultural Organisation and other relevant organisations of the United Nations system and non-governmental organisations;
3. *Calls upon* Governments, national and international organisations, non-governmental organisations and the private sector to make voluntary contributions in accordance with the guidelines of the Economic and Social Council for international years and anniversaries and to lend other forms of support to the International Year of Mountains;
4. *Encourages* all Governments, the United Nations system and all other actors to take advantage of the International Year of Mountains in order to increase awareness of the importance of sustainable mountain development;
5. *Requests* the Secretary-General to submit to the General Assembly at its fifty-fifth session a report on the state of the preparations for the International Year of Mountains.

54th plenary meeting
10 November 1998

Since above 11 December every year is International Mountain Day as declosed by UN.

Annexure 13

The Whole Life of Trees is to Serve

With their leaves, flowers, fruits, branches, roots, shade, fragrance, sap, bark, wood and also their ashes and coal they exists for the purpose of others.

The Value of a Tree

A tree that lives for 50 years generates

- Rs. 5.3 lakhs worth of Oxygen.
- Recycles Rs. 6.4 lakhs worth of retility and soil erosion control
- Creates Rs. 10 lakhs worth of air pollution control
- Rs. 5.3 lakhs worth of shelter for birds and animals
- Besides it provides flowers, fruits and timber.

So when even one tree falls or is felled the community loses something worth "More than Rs. 32 lakhs".

Think before you cut a tree rather plant more trees.

THINK BEFORE YOU CUT A TREE RATHER PLANT MORE TREES

Annexure 14

A.P. Dewan Memorial Lecture by Dr. Karan Singh 'Health for All' on 19.09.2004

A Tribute by a Brother

While giving tribute to a brother an elder brother, whom I have known, loved, admired and partnered longer than anybody else in this hall, anybody living in this world.

Anand Prakash Dewan Born 16.9.1920 in Kohat NWFP, India then, now Pakistan. Left this world on 21.9.2002, was not only a brother always called Bhapaji about 19 months older than me, but he was a friend, a many common interests, both also international Civil Servants, in sister organisations. He was Sr. Officer World Food Programme (1968-82) & myself in FAO—Food & Agriculture Organization (1953-83). Both friends, with lots of love and affection for one another i.e. we both became charter members of Rotary Club of Delhi South Metropolitan (1986 +) at the same time - also member of UN Pensioners Association (since 1983) and of Indian International Centre (1984).

He was member of IAS. Also Development Commissioner Rajasthan and fond of working for a serving people. Same mission that I got as my life mission – to serve people living, in sacred Himalayas and doing conservation and development. Got this from our father who was a social leader and started "Dharampura" in Kohat in early thirteens for all who did not have place to stay and lastly "Dharam Shala" in Haridwar called Dewan Gurditta Mall Soshila Devi Kohati Dharamshala, Railway Road Haridwar started 1950-51. Still welcoming yatris to Haridwar.

A tribute to a brother, to a friend, to a fellow rotarian, to a fellow UN Civil servant is in just a few words "Bhapaji - an affectionate and loving brother - A friend, humanist of first order, a giver of "Tan Man Dhan" for all good causes. Specially " 'Health for All', a great author of 22 Naturopathy Books one with great humour, laughter, bringer of joy to many rather most".

Has left his name alive, his family in all parts doing wonderful jobs and service. I say this also on behalf of his brilliant son Rajan - called Ramesh Dewan who due to his commitment in British Liberal Party in London, could not be present today.

A.P. is living for ever in the minds and heart of all. God will surely. Rest his soul in Peace.

19-9-2004 **Madan Dewan**

Annexure 15

Map of Uttaranchal State
Land Use Map of Uttaranchal

These two maps are provided in the pocket of hardbord binding.

Index